Conspirator

By the same author

Ekaterinburg
No Place for Ladies
Joseph Stalin
Queen Victoria
An Encyclopedia of Women Social Reformers

with William Horwood

Dark Hearts of Chicago

Conspirator

Lenin in Exile

HELEN RAPPAPORT

HUTCHINSON
LONDON

Published by Hutchinson 2009

2 4 6 8 10 9 7 5 3 1

Copyright © Helen Rappaport 2009

First published in Great Britain in 2009 by
Hutchinson
Random House, 20 Vauxhall Bridge Road,
London SW1V 2SA

www.rbooks.co.uk

Addresses for companies within The Random House Group Limited can be found at:
www.randomhouse.co.uk/offices.htm

The Random House Group Limited Reg. No. 954009

A CIP catalogue record for this book
is available from the British Library

ISBN 9780091930936 (Hardback)
ISBN 9780091930943 (Trade paperback)

The Random House Group Limited supports The Forest Stewardship
Council (FSC), the leading international forest certification organisation. All our
titles that are printed on Greenpeace approved FSC certified paper carry the FSC logo. Our
paper procurement policy can be found at www.rbooks.co.uk/environment

Mixed Sources
Product group from well-managed
forests and other controlled sources
www.fsc.org Cert no. TT-COC-2139
© 1996 Forest Stewardship Council
FSC

Typeset by Palimpsest Book Production Limited,
Grangemouth, Stirlingshire

Printed and bound in Great Britain by
CPI Mackays, Chatham, Kent ME5 8TD

For Christina

Polonius: What do you read, my lord?
Hamlet: Words, words, words.

– Shakespeare, *Hamlet*, Act 2, scene 2

Contents

Acknowledgements

Chasing Lenin's footsteps across Europe during a seventeen-year period in which he did a great deal of travelling is a tall order and I was faced with invidious choices during the writing of this book as to which of the many places he lived in that I could afford to get to. In the end I decided on visiting those countries for which I had no knowledge of the language – Finland and Poland – where I had particular need of the help of others in accessing the source material. In September 2008 my dear friend Christina Zaba accompanied me on a trip to Poland, travelling south with me from Kraków to Nowy Targ, Biały Dunajec, Poronin, Zakopane and the Tatra Mountains. By a stroke of good fortune this is an area she knows well, and Christina was a tireless and generous guide and interpreter as well as a good walking companion on a memorable hike up into the mountains. Our wonderful driver, Jerczy, waited patiently on many occasions, as we stopped and looked and took photographs along the way. During that trip I met and talked with many Poles about Lenin's time in the Podhale region. I am particularly indebted to Piotr Bąk, former mayor of Zakopane, and his wife Joanna for entertaining us with wonderful home-made *pierogi* and talking at length, and with considerable insight and humour, about Lenin's legacy in Poland.

In Finland in October 2008, I was given the warmest of welcomes by Leena Kakko, Curator, and Aimo Minkkinen, Director, of the Lenin Museum in Tampere. In this, the last surviving full-time museum dedicated to his life, I was given the free run of their wonderful collection of books on Lenin and provided with photographs for this book, for which I am most grateful. Aimo most generously gave up his time to drive Leena and I all the way down the south-western peninsula of Finland in pursuit of the story of Lenin's escape from Finland at Christmas 1907. Anne Bergström, who runs the small Lenin Museum in the Fredrikssen House, originally located at Norrgården but which has now been moved to Parainen, opened up specially out of season, so that I could see this lovely house and the room in which Lenin stayed. After I had completed my research in Finland, Leena was a good-natured travelling companion on a memorable train journey from Helsinki to St Petersburg's Finland Station and arranged private views at the Museum of Political History and the Lenin rooms at the Smolny. My thanks for their kindness and interest go to Evgeny Artemov and Lora Buday at the former and Ol'ga Evstaf'eva and Natalya Dolgorukova at the latter.

In the UK I was once again assisted in my research by Phil Tomaselli, an expert PRO searcher who hunted out what Lenin material there is, sadly none of it pre-1917. Sir Ian Blair put me in touch with Andrew Brown in the Directorate of Information at the Metropolitan Police, who also confirmed that, much to my historian's regret, no early police files on Lenin's time in London between 1902 and 1911, if they ever existed, have survived. John Callow at the Marx Memorial Library on Clerkenwell Green offered welcome advice and the use of this wonderful repository. Martin Banham and Lorraine Lees at the Islington Local History Centre in the Finsbury Library in London were most helpful in searching for Lenin material and to my delight produced a wonderful box of cuttings from the local press and other material relating to Lenin's time in London. Professor Bill Fishman, an expert in the history of Russian and Jewish East End radicals, offered valuable insights as well as providing me with some of his articles. My friend and fellow Russianist Melanie Ilic, Reader in History at the University of Gloucestershire, was once again supportive and helpful, pointing me to the valuable section on Lenin and Bolshevik Russia at the University of Birmingham's European Resource Centre. Ana Siljak at Queen's University, Kingston, Ontario, offered valuable information on the last days of Vera Zasulich. Bob Henderson provided copies of his articles on Lenin's time at the British Library Reading Room.

Thanks to the wonders of the internet I was able to track down information on the European railway system in the 1900s, with the expert knowledge of Richard Putley, Janusz Lukasiak and Peter Northover. In Oxford, Reija Fanous very kindly translated material for me from Finnish and Dag Martinsen did likewise from Swedish. I am also particularly indebted, here in Oxford, to my friend Linora Lawrence, for putting me in touch with Professor Ronald Chaplain who offered not only a fascinating and extraordinary personal story behind the Iron Curtain but valuable evidence on both Lenin's final illness and Nadezhda

Krupskaya's physical condition. Professor John Wass offered additional information on thyroidism. During my research I drew on the opinions of Professor R. Carter Elwood and Michael Pearson who have both written books on Inessa Armand. In a late breakthrough on Lenin's time in Paris, Ross King passed on information on the bohemian life of the city in the 1900s. Richard Davies at the Leeds Russian Archive kindly checked through my bibliography and Professor Harry Shukman at St Antony's College, Oxford, once again offered advice and moral support in the writing of this book.

An especial word of thanks must go to the generosity of Stephanie Weiner in California, whom I found, in a moment of researcher's serendipity, on the net, and who provided me with information from an unpublished family memoir as well as a wonderful photograph of Mendel Singer, the Jewish storekeeper in Poronin, and his family; I am indebted to her for permission to reproduce it in this book. Hayley Millar kindly allowed me to use her photograph in the Epilogue. I could not end these acknowledgements without commending the work of the Marxist Internet Archive, which is making available online the entire forty-three-volume English-language edition of Lenin's *Collected Works*, an invaluable aid in the writing of this book. See www.marxists.org/archive/lenin/

I set out in *Conspirator* to provide an alternative view of Lenin the man during his long years in exile in Europe, a part of his life that in standard biographies often gets neglected in favour of the years in power. It was something of a challenge to approach my subject, as a woman, a feminist and a non-academic, against the grain of traditional biographies of major male political figures. During my research I made a point of seeking out lost, forgotten or undiscovered accounts of Lenin in exile during 1900–17, many of them in foreign languages. There is still more material out there waiting to be discovered, I am sure of that. For this reason, I would greatly welcome any new information readers might like to share, as well as comments and suggestions, to the contact page at my website, www.helenrappaport.com/

Throughout this project, my brothers Peter and Christopher were once again an enormous support to me, as, too, my agent and friend, Charlie Viney, who continues to guide and encourage me in everything I do. Fellow writer Susan Hill has been a wise and valued mentor, as too has been my commissioning editor at Hutchinson, Caroline Gascoigne, whose tireless enthusiasm and support for my work is greatly appreciated. Caroline's assistant, Tess Callaway, provided invaluable assistance in locating images for the book and in seeing it safely through the production process. I would also like to thank publicity director, Emma Mitchell, and Cecilia Durães for their ongoing work in publicising my books.

I should, in closing, point out that the Russian transliteration system used in this book is that by Oxford Slavonic Papers. Finally, for the sanity of the reader and to avoid confusion, because Lenin spent most of the years 1900–17 in Europe – outside the events going on in Russia – all dates given are according to the European Gregorian calendar and not the Russian Orthodox Julian one.

Helen Rappaport
June 2009, Oxford

List of Illustrations

Unless otherwise indicated, all images are from the author's own collection.

Photographs at the beginning of each chapter are from the author's own
collection except for the following: Chapter 3, St Petersburg in the 1900s
(Courtesy of Neil Harvey/www.nevsky-prospekt.com); Chapter 5,
Holford Square, London (Photo by Hans Wild/Time & Life
Pictures/Getty Images); Chapter 8, The Winter Palace, St Petersburg
(Courtesy of Neil Harvey/www.nevsky-prospekt.com); Chapter 9, The
Villa Wasa, Kuokkala (Courtesy of The Lenin Museum, Tampere);
Chapter 10, The Brotherhood Church, London (Courtesy of The Lenin
Museum, Tampere); Chapter 13, The Café du Dome, Montparnasse
(Hulton Archive/Getty Images); Epilogue, bust of Lenin (Courtesy of
Hayley Millar/http://coffee-helps.com)

Map on pp xviii and xix by Martin Lubikowski at ML Design

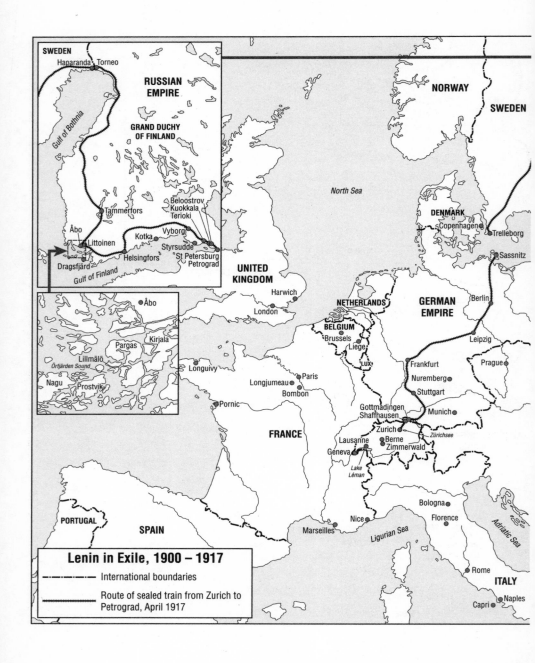

SWEDEN
Haparanda Torneo

RUSSIAN EMPIRE

GRAND DUCHY OF FINLAND

Gulf of Bothnia

Beloostrov
Kuokkala
Terioki

Tammerfors

Åbo
Littoinen
Kotka
Vyborg
Styrsudde
Dragsfjärd
Helsingfors
St Petersburg
Petrograd
Gulf of Finland

Åbo

Pargas
Kirjala
Lillmälö
Örtjärden Sound
Nagu
Prostvik
Longuivy

North Sea

NORWAY

SWEDEN

DENMARK
Copenhagen
Trelleborg
Sassnitz

UNITED KINGDOM

Harwich

London

NETHERLANDS

BELGIUM
Brussels
Liège

LUX.

GERMAN EMPIRE

Berlin

Leipzig

Prague

Frankfurt
Nuremberg
Stuttgart

Longjumeau
Paris
Bombon

Pornic

Gottmadingen
Shaffhausen
Zurich
Zürichsee
Munich

FRANCE

Lausanne
Berne
Zimmerwald
Geneva
Lake Léman

Bologna
Florence

Adriatic Sea

PORTUGAL

SPAIN

Marseilles
Nice
Ligurian Sea

Rome

ITALY

Naples
Capri

Lenin in Exile, 1900 – 1917

— ·— ·— International boundaries

——— Route of sealed train from Zurich to
Petrograd, April 1917

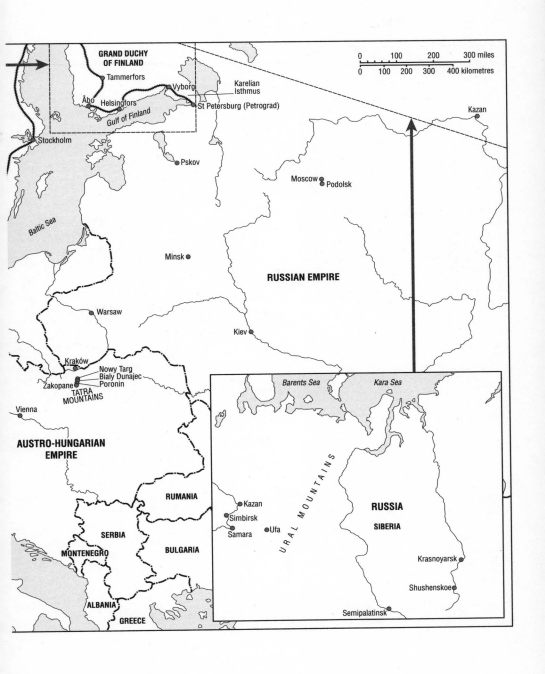

GRAND DUCHY
OF FINLAND

Tammerfors

Åbo Helsingfors
Gulf of Finland

Vyborg
Karelian
Isthmus
St Petersburg (Petrograd)

Stockholm

Pskov

Moscow Podolsk

Kazan

Baltic Sea

Minsk

RUSSIAN EMPIRE

Warsaw

Kiev

Kraków
Nowy Targ
Bialy Dunajec
Zakopane Poronin
TATRA
MOUNTAINS

Vienna

AUSTRO-HUNGARIAN
EMPIRE

RUMANIA

SERBIA

MONTENEGRO

BULGARIA

ALBANIA

GREECE

0   100   200   300 miles
0   100   200   300   400 kilometres

Barents Sea   Kara Sea

U R A L   M O U N T A I N S

Kazan
Simbirsk
Samara Ufa

RUSSIA

SIBERIA

Krasnoyarsk

Shushenskoe

Semipalatinsk

INTRODUCTION

Shlisselburg Fortress, 1887

Shlisselburg Fortress, Lake Ladoga

There were five of them to be taken to Shlisselburg that night, 5 May 1887; the five leading conspirators in the latest foiled assassination attempt against a Russian Tsar. This time, only six years after revolutionaries had successfully blown up Alexander II, his son Alexander III had been the target. They called themselves the 'Terrorist Section' of The People's Will (Narodnaya Volya), an organisation that in 1881 had been driven out of existence by widespread government repression, but whose flame they had nevertheless dedicated themselves to carrying forward. They had no experience of terrorism, yet alone of making bombs. As conspirators they were inept, to say the least. It was only their youth – the youngest was only twenty – and their bungling incompetence that had saved St Petersburg's Nevsky Prospekt from yet another outrage. A spot check on two of the conspirators by suspicious police agents had uncovered the crude bomb filled with bullets dipped in strychnine that was being carried by one of them inside a copy of Grinberg's *Dictionary of Medical Terminology*.

It might sound like the stuff of tragicomedy, but the plot's perpetrators were in deadly earnest, even if their bombs were later shown to be defective. But what had driven them to such violent action? Russia had ever been a country of extremes; a place where the opulence and extravagance of the Imperial Court underlined an endemic indifference to the privation suffered by Russia's silent and unseen masses. By European standards, nineteenth-century Russia was a backward country, its population largely illiterate and rural, its infrastructure – roads, railways and industry – lagging far behind that of the West. The vast majority of its multinational population of 180 million (by World War I), in an empire covering one-fifth of the world's surface, had been enslaved by serfdom until 1861. But emancipation had done little to liberate the peasantry from illiteracy, poverty and land hunger, or to assuage the social conscience of a growing intelligentsia that passionately sought to redress the imbalances of the old order. Official corruption and repression in Russia drove such young people to seek political answers to the questions that so tormented them about Russia's position in the world. They wanted to work towards a better political and economic future, in which the peasantry and the urban proletariat would play key roles. For a while, hopes were pinned on the model of the existing village communes providing a shortcut to socialism and the institution of a democratic system. But the populist 'To the People' movement of 1873–5 – an ill-judged propaganda drive by the intelligentsia among the peasants of rural Russia – had collapsed amidst widespread peasant mistrust of these newcomers and had ended in thousands of arrests, and exile for many to Siberia.

The response to official repression was the establishment in 1876 of Land and Freedom (Zemlya i Volya), the first political party to openly advocate political change in Russia. But before long the party became divided between those who embraced the peaceful path of agrarian reform and took up work in the rural areas for local government, while in 1879 a more extreme group formed The People's Will faction, embracing terrorism as a political weapon. But such extreme methods were short-lived; by the time the would-be assassins were arrested in 1887, The People's Will was a spent force. Arrested in March, the five men were held for two months in solitary confinement in the grim Trubetskoy Bastion of the Peter and Paul Fortress in St Petersburg. At their five-day trial in April, they were condemned to death.

The other prisoners on the isolation wing of the Trubetskoy Bastion heard the cell doors being unlocked the night the men were taken away to their place of execution; even thick stone walls could not muffle the resonant tread of footsteps matched by the ominous clank of the chains which bound the men hand and foot. The five men's shadows flickered and fell as they passed along the dark prison walls by the light of dingy kerosene lamps and were led out across the cobbled courtyard to the iron gate. Here the police vans – little more than cages on wheels –

waited for them. They knew this would be the last time they would see the city. Just out of sight, the River Neva lapped softly along its long, flat embankment, where, on the dark and deserted quayside, a steamship waited, its tiny cabin windows curtaining the outside world from view.

The men were now on their way to Shlisselburg, a forbidding medieval fortress built on a small island looking out over Lake Ladoga, thirty-five miles from St Petersburg along the Neva. Every Russian revolutionary knew the name of Shlisselburg; it was the Russian Bastille and very few survived incarceration there. Built in the fourteenth century by the people of Novgorod, it was later captured by the Swedes and then recaptured by Peter the Great. It had gained notoriety when Ivan VI was held and murdered there in 1764. In the 1820s it became a staging post for conspirators in the Decembrist uprising on their way to exile in Siberia. But since 1884 it had served a much more specific purpose, when a special isolation prison was built within its ancient walls for the incarceration of forty of the country's highest security political prisoners. Shlisselburg was a place, it was said, from which people were only carried out; they very rarely walked. If they took you there it was either to hang you or because your death sentence had been commuted to life imprisonment. And life meant life. One way or another, you'd die at Shlisselburg.

After five hours on the steamship the green, iridescent waters of the River Neva suddenly broadened out as it flowed into the lagoons of Lake Ladoga. Here, Shlisselburg, with its white walls and towers of limestone, loomed into view in the early dawn. At the top of a tall spire shone a gilded key – the key that had given the fortress its German name from the word *Schlussel*. As the five men passed through the high white walls of the main entrance, the huge, two-headed Imperial eagle above it looked down on them as though ready to swoop. Inside everything seemed white and quiet and orderly – like a tiny village with its own small white church at one end. But beyond this seemingly peaceful setting there stood a two-storey redbrick building with dirty windows and two tall chimneys – the special wing for political prisoners. Inside, the poorly lit first and second floors were divided by a net to prevent suicide attempts from the top floor; connecting the two levels from one side to the other, there was a narrow walkway – a Russian Bridge of Sighs.[1]

Ranged round the circumference were forty black iron doors leading into forty isolation cells – set like a row of coffins standing on end, for incarceration here was a living death – with only the fuzzy outline of the far horizon beyond each cell's opaque windowpane. Inside there was nothing but the overpowering stillness of solitary confinement – where the real becomes unreal and the imaginary can become so vivid that it takes on a life that confuses the senses and drives men mad. The only sounds breaking the silence were the hissing of water in pipes somewhere far below, or, in the distance, the faint tubercular cough of another prisoner. Sometimes there came the soft tap-tap of prisoners communicating with each other by their own improvised Morse code. And, sooner or later, the rattle at the door, as its peephole was slid back by the gendarme on duty.

Three days later, on 8 May, having been lulled into a false sense of security that their sentences were to be commuted, the men were woken at 3.30 a.m. and informed that they were to be executed in half an hour's time. The prison officials had been so secretive in the construction of the gallows during those intervening three days that none of the prisoners in the isolation block had known. But they only had room for three gallows, which had been made up in sections, outside the prison, and silently assembled near the main entrance, without so much as a single blow of an axe being heard.

As the rest of the prisoners slept the heavy sleep of those with an eternity on their hands, the commandant, priest and guards accompanied the five prisoners in single file to the place of execution. The condemned men were offered the consolation of a priest but all refused. There being only three gallows, they had to hang them in two batches: Vasily Generalov, Pakhomiy Andreyushkin and Vasily Osipanov embraced each other and cried out 'Long Live The People's Will' before the sack was thrown over their heads and the stools kicked from under them. The condemned in Russia were not yet accorded the merciful death of the trapdoor, but a slower one, by strangulation.

After their corpses had been taken down, the other two men were brought forward. Petr Shevyrov, the ringleader of the conspiracy, pushed away the cross as the priest offered it to him, but the last man, with absolute composure, stopped and kissed it before they hanged him, too.

His name was Aleksandr Ulyanov.

Nine hundred and thirty-five miles away, in provincial Simbirsk, Ulyanov's younger brother was studying hard that day for his final, rigorous school examinations, unaware of what had taken place. That sixteen-year-old boy was the man who became Vladimir Ilyich Lenin.

*   *   *

Aleksandr Ulyanov's corpse had already been hastily consigned to a common grave with his fellow conspirators in the grounds of Shlisselburg before his mother Mariya, who had been lobbying the authorities for weeks to commute his sentence, learned that her son had been executed – in an announcement in a broadsheet handed out on the streets of St Petersburg. Her emotional control and fortitude, at a time when one of her daughters, Anna, was also in police custody in the city, implicated in the same plot, was extraordinary. It was a characteristic inherited by her younger son Vladimir.

Aleksandr could have appealed to the Tsar for mercy, but he refused. All he asked for in his final days was a volume of verse by his favourite poet, Heinrich Heine. He was in fact not one of those designated to throw the bomb (although, as a student of natural science, he had manufactured the nitroglycerine needed) and would have been reprieved had he petitioned for clemency. But he would not compromise his beliefs. He wanted to take on himself the burden of responsibility for the conspiracy, to be a martyr and to die an exemplary death. Tsar Alexander found his frankness 'touching' but he did not commute the death sentence. Shortly after the executions, students at Aleksandr's university had rushed to bring out their own statement on the heroism of the five hanged men who had died for the 'common cause'. They had fulfilled their duty with absolute integrity and had 'firmly upheld the banner of struggle for freedom and justice'.[2]

Aleksandr Ulyanov was one of the last of a generation of romantic idealists devoted to the cause of the downtrodden masses, who had espoused the Russian populist movement and in so doing been drawn ultimately into a desperate act of terrorism. But despite achieving some spectacular murders of senior officials and the Tsar himself in 1881, The People's Will had ultimately been ineffectual in forcing constitutional change in Russia through the use of terrorism. In later years, Lenin, in an extremely rare public allusion to his brother's death, would state that such an act of martyrdom as Aleksandr's had not and never could achieve the conspirators' immediate and passionate aim – 'that of awakening a popular revolution'. A year before his death, Aleksandr had won a gold medal for his dissertation on 'The Segmentation and Sexual Organs of Freshwater Annula'. The young Vladimir had watched him at home, huddled over his microscope from the early hours of the morning examining slides. 'No, my brother won't make a revolutionary, I thought then,' he later told his wife Nadezhda. 'A revolutionary cannot devote so much time to the study of worms.'[3]

In the unequal struggle between a repressive autocracy, which banned political opposition, and small groups of disaffected and disorganised intellectuals who shared no common doctrine, sporadic acts of self-immolation made little difference. Even the five corpses on the gallows at Shlisselburg, and before them the six People's Will leaders hanged in front of 100,000 people in St Petersburg's Semenovsky Square in April 1881 had succeeded only in provoking an entrenchment of official reaction. True, such events drew attention to the importance of the democratic process of the law and the responsibility of judges and lawyers. But the proliferation of committees, clubs and secret and mutual aid societies, as well as the torrent of resolutions and exhortations to protest that accompanied their inception did not dent the oppressive machinery of the state.

For Vladimir Ilyich Ulyanov there would have to be another way. Like many of his peers he saw the answer in Marxism, as pioneered and interpreted by its Russian 'father', Georgy Plekhanov. Marxism provided a sound and scientific rationale for political change, as opposed to the emotional, anarchistic idealism of the populists. It defined history as one of class struggles: capitalism had replaced the old feudal system and, with time, would be the means of its own destruction, leading to the ideal, classless society. The working classes would be capitalism's nemesis. Plekhanov's interpretation of Marx within the Russian context offered young radicals an objective philosophy based on economic thinking and the belief that, sooner or later, a major clash between the capitalist bourgeoisie and the proletariat would bring about political change. But to arrive at this objective democratically – at a point when the masses were sufficiently enlightened to accept that change and willingly take part in it – knowledge, patience and careful preparation would be needed. The key to Plekhanov's Marxist vision – and it was one which inspired so many young Russians from the 1880s onwards – was the need for tactics based not on sentiment but on scientific training and a widespread programme of political education among the Russian population at large.

In the coming revolutionary struggle, therefore, heroism, self-sacrifice, the unshakeable power of belief – none of these would ever be sufficient to effect real change. As Plekhanov's brilliant pupil Vladimir Ilyich Ulyanov would soon so forcefully demonstrate, what was required was a unique kind of iron-clad, pitiless will.[4]

CHAPTER ONE

Leaving Shushenskoe

Siberia: January 1900

The village of Shushenskoe, Minusinsk province, Siberia

The sky is big at Shushenskoe. Nowhere in the world is so far from the sea as this remote region in south-central Siberia. Beyond the broad expanses of the great Yenisey river, on whose right bank this forgotten village of exile once sprawled in a huddle of low, wooden houses, loom the dazzling, snow-capped Sayan Mountains. The wastes of Outer Mongolia lie unseen on the other side. In the old days Shusha, as the local peasants called it, seemed so remote that those great shimmering mountains seemed to them 'the very edge of the world' itself.[1]

For many centuries it was a remote region, unmapped by geographers, settled only by fur traders and Cossacks. But during the nineteenth century the tsarist authorities found a use for Shushenskoe – as a suitably remote place of exile, closed to the outside world, hundreds of miles from the railroad and accessible only to the intrepid few. But Siberian exile for political prisoners then was not necessarily an ominous word. The Stalin years turned the prospect of Siberia and the Gulag into a death sentence for many, but for those lucky enough to be sent to Shushenskoe under the tsars, life was not always arduous. The climate here was kinder than in the primeval, frozen east of Siberia where prisoners endured appalling, punitive conditions. Shushenskoe was, in comparison to the repressive prison system the Soviets would later institute, a virtual holiday camp. No wonder they called that part of the Minusinsk district where the village lay the 'Siberian Italy'.[2]

On 31 January 1900 the Russian revolutionary Vladimir Ilyich Ulyanov was preparing to leave Shushenskoe after spending three years there as a political exile. It was a timely moment in the new century, and in the life of an extraordinary man whose political thinking would come to dominate most of it under the pseudonym of Lenin. In many ways Vladimir was sorry to leave. After ten years as an activist in the Russian revolutionary underground and all the uncertainties that such a life had brought with it, he had found a degree of peace here – and, paradoxically – freedom. Police surveillance had been lax and, despite money being short, restrictions on movement had been few. He had achieved much in Siberia: recovered his often febrile health, grown fit and well and enjoyed the vigorous outdoor pursuits of hunting, shooting and ice skating. He had even been able to swim in the nearby River Shush during the short-lived Siberian summers. And he had benefited, too, from the comfort and companionship of his wife and political comrade, Nadezhda Krupskaya, herself an exile.

*   *   *

The path to Shushenskoe was a long one; the man who became Lenin did not turn revolutionary overnight, after the execution of his brother in 1887. On the day his brother died he finished his maths exam early and was the first to leave the examination hall.[3] At school he remained an exemplary pupil; at home he was always the first to finish his homework. In June, only a month after his brother's death, he was awarded the gold medal for academic excellence. Headmaster Fedor Kerensky noted in the citation that Vladimir was 'diligent, prompt and reliable' and that there was 'no single instance on record either inside school or outside of it' of his behaviour inviting any adverse criticism. Perceptively, Kerensky noted that 'rational discipline' seemed to be this young man's guiding light; as too was a marked preference for solitude and 'a certain unsociability'.[4]

There was no reason for the robust and boisterous Volodya, as he was known in the family, to be other than ordinary, for he came from a loving and stable home that valued learning and respected intellectual enlightenment. His early life, as one of six children – Anna, Aleksandr, Vladimir, Olga, Dmitri and Mariya (two others had died young) – had been far from rebellious or controversial. However, after the Revolution, and particularly after his death in 1924, Soviet hagiography succeeded in manipulating an archetypal, red-blooded proletarian background for its great leader by suppressing the true details of his less than working-class ancestry. Vladimir Ulyanov was not a full-blooded Russian: the narrow, Asiatic-looking eyes always gave him away. The man who became Lenin turned out to be what a great many other Russians were – a mongrel – a Russian whose blood was diluted with Jewish, German, Swedish, Slav and Kalmyk genes. On his father Ilya's side, Vladimir's grandfather, Nikolay Vasil'evich Ulyanov, was possibly of Tatar or Kalmyk descent. The son of a former serf, he had worked as a tailor in Astrakhan and married a Kalmyk woman. Vladimir's mother, whom Ilya had married in 1863, had more upwardly mobile antecedents. She was born Mariya Aleksandrovna Blank, to a family of good Lutheran merchants from Germany and Sweden on one side and middle-class Jewish converts on the other. Vladimir's Jewish grandfather, Aleksandr Blank, was a medical man with progressive if somewhat eccentric views on hydropathy who imposed his water cures on his children. Strict, authoritarian and frugal, he bought an estate at Kokushkino, near Kazan, complete with serfs.[5] With its beds of flowers, fruit bushes and graceful linden trees, it would become a happy holiday home for the Ulyanov children as they grew up, a place where the young Volodya revelled in the bucolic pleasures of the Russian country estate, as epitomised in the novels of his favourite writer, Ivan Turgenev.

Ilya Nikolaevich Ulyanov had attained minor nobility status, as did many others in Russia in the nineteenth century, not by birth but by dutiful service to the state. He was in many ways that archetypal Chekhovian figure, a loyal *chinovnik*, one of a breed of tsarist bureaucrats who ran the vast, antiquated machinery of state. He had started out as a teacher of maths and physics after studying at the University of Kazan. Promotion through the fourteen ranks of the Russian Civil Service to number 4, and the honorific of Actual State Councillor (the civilian equivalent of a major general), followed in later years for his diligence, first as a primary school inspector and from 1874 as Director of Public

Schools for Simbirsk province. With it came the right to be addressed as 'Your Excellency'. One of the perks of the system was that the father's entitlements extended to his sons – thus ensuring that Vladimir could later claim noble status to lessen the harshness of his exile in Siberia.

From photographs of his father sitting in his high-buttoned uniform, it is clear that Vladimir inherited his high cheekbones, domed, Socratic forehead and patrician look, as well as a strong work ethic, and with it the stern mentality of the pedagogue and the moral puritan. Both parents were well educated, politically enlightened and supporters of the liberal reforms of Alexander II, who had emancipated the peasants in 1861. Ilya Nikolaevich was a devout member of the Russian Orthodox Church, a staunch patriot, loyal to his Tsar and a conscientious public servant. Mariya Ulyanova was less religiously observant but thrifty and long-suffering. As a family the Ulyanovs believed in self-education and the liberating power of scientific progress and encouraged all their children to have a curiosity about the world.

From both parents Vladimir learned to be frugal and unostentatious, to work hard and persevere, despite a propensity to be loud, clumsy and in the habit of breaking things. His cultured mother taught him to appreciate music. She taught him languages – French, German and English; his sisters Anna, Mariya and Olga played the piano and sang. There was much joy and laughter and shared amusement in their young lives. But Ilya Ulyanov's professional status was hard-won. A humane and conscientious man with a mission to modernise the tsarist school system, he drove himself relentlessly, at the expense of his health. His work involved long periods away from home. Yet the reward for his diligence in trying to raise education standards throughout Simbirsk province was to be forced into early retirement in 1885, as a result of the political retreat in the wake of the murder of Alexander II. Ilya Ulyanov's dedicated, progressive work was suddenly cut short. His premature death in 1886 spared him the agony and humiliation of his son Aleksandr's involvement in a plot against the Tsar, for years of overwork and stress carried him off with a cerebral haemorrhage at the age of only fifty-three.

Vladimir Ulyanov's early life in Simbirsk, a regional trading port of 30,000 inhabitants stretched out along the slopes of the River Volga, was uneventful. Life in the Russian provinces in the nineteenth century was legendary for its hidebound tradition and lethargy. But being stuck in a provincial backwater did not seem to worry Vladimir, nor did the fact that his family were not rich enough to live on the leafier, more salubrious side of town where nightingales sang in the apple and cherry orchards. His attachment to the broad, flowing waters of the Volga dominated his early years and would stay with him throughout his life, as too would a love of the outdoors; being out in the natural world became for the adult Lenin an essential release from stress and anxiety, as well as the setting for vigorous and regular exercise. But such moments became increasingly few and far between as he grew older; his mind, his time and his prodigious energies were, from young adulthood, focused entirely on his work and the ardours of an exacting Classical curriculum. Quiet, studious and solitary, he absorbed himself in his books and had few friends. He gave up his favourite subject, Latin, because it got in the way of his more important studies; as too did his love of skating, which was abandoned until he rediscovered it in Siberia. Such things were 'dangerous addictions'[6] – his great passion as he grew older would be for statistics. At school he garnered the respect of his peers and teachers for his diligence, but Vladimir Ulyanov was not particularly popular. Aleksandr's hanging, the death of his father and the tragic death in 1888 of his favourite and extremely gifted sister Olga from typhoid crushed his natural joviality and drew down the shutters on all discussions of the personal life, creating a reticence in him for ever after. He became, as his younger brother Dmitri later observed, 'grimly restrained, strict, closed up in himself, highly focussed'.[7] He was crippled by remorse about his strained relationship with his elder brother, whom he had tried hard to emulate. The truth was that Vladimir and the dreamy, ascetic Aleksandr had not got along; there had been a certain amount of rivalry between them. Aleksandr was revered in the family for his quiet intelligence, his modesty and moral integrity and he had found his younger brother too disruptive. He had taken great exception also to Volodya's arrogance and his rudeness to their mother.

Despite this, Vladimir took his brother's death in pursuit of political change very hard and was bitter at the subsequent ostracising of his loyal mother and siblings in their community in Simbirsk. It prompted the family to move to the Blank estate at Kokushkino, near the city of Kazan. Here Vladimir enjoyed the rural pleasures of hunting, swimming, sailing and walking, combined, as always, with a wide range of reading, shut away in his sparsely furnished room. In August 1887 he moved into Kazan to study law. Four months later his involvement in relatively low-key student demonstrations against a university inspector ensured his prompt expulsion from the university and banishment by the Ministry of Internal Affairs back to Kokushkino, where his elder sister Anna had already been confined for her own political activities. As the brother of a would-be regicide, Vladimir had been and would remain under close police surveillance.

Moving into Kazan in September 1888, Vladimir associated with a clandestine political discussion group led by Nikolay Fedoseev, which finally prompted his first study of Karl Marx's *Das Kapital* in his search for the answers to the pressing social and political questions facing Russia. For a pragmatist like Vladimir, Marx's book had enormous appeal on rational, scientific grounds. But his guiding light in this early period was undoubtedly the 'plodding genius'[8] of a home-grown Russian social thinker – Nikolay Chernyshevsky. Chernyshevsky's didactic novel *What Is To Be Done?*, written in prison during 1862–3, presented a vision of a socialist utopia based around communes of politically like-minded young people living and working together for the common good. The novel's revolutionary heroes, the feminist Vera Pavlovna, doyenne of a cooperative of seamstresses, and the dark and driven activist Rakhmetov, had become icons to a whole generation of idealistic Russian revolutionaries, including Aleksandr Ulyanov. In Rakhmetov, known to his revolutionary comrades as 'the rigourist', Chernyshevsky presented a man with all the austerity of a religious fanatic, who lived life pared to the bone: 'No luxury, no caprices; nothing but the necessary', as he put it. His Spartan, uncorrupted existence was dominated by the strict use of his time. There was no room in his highly disciplined schedule for 'minor affairs' or personal matters; his only indulgence was time set aside for physical exercise to maintain his strength and energy for the revolutionary struggle to come.[9] In the rationalistic, enigmatic Rakhmetov the young Vladimir saw a man of ruthless dedication on the road to self-perfection and revolution. He read the novel five times, convinced that 'every right-thinking and really honest man must be a revolutionary'; and, in order to emulate him, adopted similar self-denying precepts ever after in his own life.[10] The book was, so Lenin later claimed, 'a work which gives one a charge for a whole life'.[11]

Worried about the dangerous political influences to which her son was succumbing in Kazan, and in dread that he should follow the same path as his brother, Mariya Ulyanova sold the family home in Simbirsk and her share in Kokushkino in 1889 and with this money and some other family legacies bought an estate at Alakaevka, 150 miles south of Kazan. Here she tried to divert Vladimir's interests into farm management. He did not take to it or to the local uncooperative peasants. Worrying about a neighbour's cattle trampling the Ulyanovs' crops was no substitute for the political literature he was now devouring at a prodigious rate. Thanks to his mother's petitioning of the authorities – she would spend a lifetime doing so on behalf of all her politically active children – Vladimir, after kicking his heels as an idle country squire, was finally allowed to return to St Petersburg in March 1891 to complete his law studies. With his characteristic ferocious intellectual energy he crammed three years' worth of study into a year and, despite his mother's perennial anxieties that he was over-exerting his brain, just as his poor father had done, he emerged with top marks as a qualified lawyer in January 1892. But the pursuit of a career in the legal profession in the provinces spent largely defending peasants and artisans accused of petty offences was not much of a challenge for a man of his exceptional intellectual abilities.

By now Vladimir's mind was well and truly elsewhere – caught up in the serious study of Karl Marx and in the preparation of a riposte to traditional Russian populist thinking. There was enough money in the 'family fund' to subsidise his continuing political work and he soon abandoned the legal appointment he took up in September 1893 in St Petersburg. He now concentrated his energies on turning out political pamphlets expounding a Marxist view of Russian economic development and agriculture and engaging in regular debate at illegal political meetings. His life as an active revolutionary had begun and would be subsidised thereafter by his mother's income, party funds and handouts from sympathisers.

In 1894 in St Petersburg, one of many political activists to be impressed by the intellectual ascendancy of this 'certain learned Marxist who had arrived from the Volga' was twenty-five-year-old Nadezhda Konstantinovna Krupskaya. A teacher and activist among workers in the Nevsky factory district, she was impressed by Ulyanov's lively, 'concrete manner' and the skill with which he set out political theory and with it a wealth of statistical evidence to back it up. Such was his maturity of thought that he had the knack of making complex political ideas simple, of describing the objectives of the revolutionary struggle with such clarity and sobriety.[12] Their paths crossed at various workers' study circles, with Vladimir at that time propagandising among workers at the British-owned Thornton textile mill and local shoe factories. Through their shared political views, Vladimir and Nadya developed a mutual respect

and sense of comradeship and, crucially, for a man of Vladimir's pathologically suspicious nature, enduring trust.

By now Vladimir had already grown used to a life constantly on the
move. In barely two years – from 1893 to 1895 – with the Russian secret
police always on his tail, he changed his address eight times. The secret
police, or Department for the Protection of Order and Public Security,
was better known by its acronym, the Okhrana. It operated from its base
at 16 Ulitsa Fontanka in St Petersburg, ably assisted by a semi-military,
uniformed police known as the Special Corps of Gendarmes who
specialised in the surveillance of politicals in provincial towns. Ulyanov
revelled in the daily game of cat and mouse with the Okhrana and was
already familiar with the maze of back alleys and courtyards where you
could give them the slip. Evasion and subterfuge and, with it, the use
of codes and false names and passports would become, for the mature
Lenin, the 'revolutionary art' par excellence.[13] Within St Petersburg revolutionary circles he disseminated his conspiratorial skills, learned from a
close study of the methods of Narodnaya Volya. He was rapidly making
his mark as the *starik* – the 'old man'; it was as though his youth had
long since been sucked out of him. Ulyanov was only young according
to his identity papers, as his political associate Aleksandr Potresov
observed.[14] He had gone bald in his early twenties, another colleague,
Ivan Babushkin, remembering, 'We used to say among ourselves that he
had such big brains that they pushed his hair out'.[15] Potresov also noted
Vladimir's ordinariness. He could have been 'a typical merchant from
any north Russian province – there was nothing of the "radical" intellectual about him.'[16] With his neat, reddish beard and his drab clothes
he looked like a man who could blend into the background. But the eyes
always gave him away: they were quick and shrewd, and betrayed his
speed of thought. They also projected a certain craftiness of manner,
and, as time went on, a cruel glint. Coupled with an unnerving, laconic
laugh, those mocking eyes would come to unsettle many of his political
associates in later years.

In May 1895, Vladimir Ulyanov made his first trip abroad, ostensibly
for educational reasons, in reality to broaden his knowledge and understanding of socialist thinking in Europe. The Okhrana were not fooled
and details of his departure were duly passed on to Petr Rachkovsky,
head of the organisation's Paris Department, charged with the surveillance of Russian political exiles in Europe:

According to information available to the Police Department, the above-mentioned Ulyanov occupies himself with Social Democratic propaganda among Petersburg workers. The objective of his trip is to find ways of bringing into the empire revolutionary literature as well as to establish contact between revolutionary circles and emigrants living abroad.[17]

In Switzerland, Vladimir's primary objective was to visit the father of Russian Marxism, the émigré socialist Georgy Plekhanov, who had founded the Emancipation of Labour group there in 1883 to propound his own interpretation of Marxist industrial socialism. Unfortunately, his hero was not at home when Vladimir arrived but on holiday in the mountains at Les Diablerets above the Rhône Valley. Even now the necessity for subterfuge was paramount in his mind; Vladimir made his way to Les Diablerets on foot, by a roundabout route across the Col des Mosses, in order to avoid any police who might be tailing him.[18] His travelling companion and political colleague on that trip was Aleksandr Potresov who noted Vladimir's awe for his political master. The sardonic and urbane Plekhanov, despite his sense of moral superiority, was duly taken with Vladimir as 'one of the best of our Russian friends'.[19] His colleague and fellow exile, Pavel Axelrod, was happy to talk politics with Vladimir too, at his Alpine retreat at Adoltern, and was impressed with the eager, unpretentious young political thinker from Kazan. Vladimir might have seemed somewhat unprepossessing in appearance but there was no doubt in Axelrod's mind of the power of his logic; his writing, he wrote to Plekhanov afterwards, 'had the temperament of a fighting flame'.[20]

During this trip, Vladimir's health broke down – the first of numerous physical collapses provoked by the relentless pace of his work, his failure to eat properly and a propensity for bouts of stress-induced insomnia and depression. He suffered from a chronic but ill-defined 'nervous stomach' – probably an ulcer – and sought a rest cure for it at a spa in Switzerland, to fund which his mother, who was already subsidising his trip out of her private income, obligingly sent more money from Russia. In Berlin, where Plekhanov had directed him to visit the German Social Democrat Karl Liebknecht, Vladimir found time for therapeutic bathing in the River Spree. He enjoyed the pleasures of the Tiergarten and went to the theatre, while applying himself to political study at the city's Royal Library. In Paris he made a special point of meeting Karl Marx's son-in-law, the socialist journalist Paul Lafargue.

During five months' continuous travel, from Switzerland to France and Germany, Vladimir, like other seasoned activists going in and out of Russia, filled the false bottom of his specially made suitcase with illicit political literature, which he took back with him. Within weeks of his return, fired with enthusiasm by his European trip, he met up with another young socialist new to the city, Yuli Martov, and together they formed the League of Struggle for the Emancipation of the Working Class, for which he began writing illegal propagandist literature.

But on 9 December Vladimir's luck ran out. The Okhrana, whose agents had been tailing him for months, finally pounced and arrested him. A short time later, Yuli Martov and other members of the League were also seized. Vladimir took the inevitability of his arrest and imprisonment with calm and equanimity. They were an important rite of passage for any political activist, and in his case lent essential credibility to his meteoric rise through the revolutionary ranks. He quickly adapted to incarceration and kept his sanity by sticking to a strict routine. Soon he was having messages smuggled out of the House of Detention on Shpalernaya Street, using milk as invisible ink kept in inkwells made of bread that could be hastily consumed if the warders came too close (on one day alone he had been obliged to eat six ink pots[21]). Fourteen months of solitary confinement might have been arduous for the average prisoner but they did not dent Vladimir's sense of purpose or his now convinced political objectives. If anything, prison allowed him precious time to consolidate his ideas. Life in cell no. 193 was almost congenial. He was allowed to receive the books he needed, delivered on Wednesdays and Saturdays. Such was the volume of material arriving that the familiar scraping sound of warders dragging heavy cases along the corridors meant one thing to the other prisoners: yet more books being delivered to prisoner Ulyanov.[22] Many arrived with secret encryptions – minute dots placed inside letters on the page, creating a coded message, or inscriptions in milk which were readable once exposed to a candle flame or dipped in hot tea. Vladimir also learned the valuable prison codes of tapping on walls, by means of which he could play games of chess with near neighbours in their cells.

More importantly, he now had time on his hands to make considerable headway with what would be his first, significant political work – *The Development of Capitalism in Russia* – while turning out articles for the Marxist journal *Novoe Slovo* (New Word), and drafting the programme of what would eventually become the Russian Social Democratic Labour Party (RSDLP). He read and wrote feverishly to make full use of his time in jail, barely noticing the prison walls that surrounded him. Throughout his life, so long as he had books, quiet and a table to work at he could function anywhere. His family ensured the provision of additional food parcels and mineral water for his delicate stomach and even the luxury of pillowslips and towels. A political associate, Petr Struve, whom he had met in St Petersburg in 1893 and who was a leading editor of Marxist journals, sent in books and magazines and procured writing commissions for him. But he also made sure he took time out from them to maintain his own health and fitness, doing exercises every day to prevent his joints from stiffening. His advice was passed on to fellow politicals: they should be sure to perform fifty 'prostrations' a day (touching toes), non-stop in their cells. Daily gymnastics and a vigorous rub down with a wet towel (as advocated by his Jewish grandfather) kept his mind and body sharp. When his cell was icy cold in winter, he moved about vigorously to warm his body so that he could sleep. But even in his sleep the words crowded in on him and he told his sister Anna that he dreamed whole chapters of the book in progress.[23]

After two months in the House of Detention, in February 1897 Vladimir Ulyanov was informed that he was being summarily exiled by Administrative Order from St Petersburg, without any formal trial. But there would be no long forced march to Siberia in chains, the fate of many political exiles before him. Because he was the son of a civil servant promoted to the nobility, he was allowed to arrange his own passage into exile, at his own expense. He was even given the luxury of time to arrange what he needed to take with him and to say goodbye to family and friends. He would not be penniless either; the government provided eight rubles a month to political prisoners towards their board and lodging. To get to his place of exile he had to take the Trans-Siberian Railway at an interminable crawl – the further west it went the slower it got. The thought of exile *per se* did not trouble him, but he was a man constantly in a hurry and the 'devilish slowness' of the journey irritated him, as too did the 'monotonous, bare and desolate steppe'[24] that passed by his window. Day after day of snow and sky – nothing more. The whole journey proved more uncomfortable and expensive than he had bargained for.

Once arrived at the provincial capital of Krasnoyarsk on the River Yenisey, he was forced to spend several weeks waiting for the spring weather to melt the ice on the river so that he could carry on by paddle steamer downriver to his place of exile. But although the temperature was 20 degrees below, Vladimir knew that the air at Krasnoyarsk was 'softer' than in other parts of Siberia. When he was initially ordered to the harsher climate of Irkutsk, he had put in an application to be allowed to remain. His mother petitioned on his behalf too, stating that her son's weak health would not endure the harsher conditions further east. The request was granted but it was not till 24 April that Vladimir learned that home for the next three years was to be the village of Shushenskoe.

Until he was able to leave, Vladimir made good use of the time in Krasnoyarsk, as he would do in whatever town, city or village he might find himself over the next twenty years. He had been lucky to obtain comfortable lodgings where he was well fed and from where he could fill his days with vigorous walks, reading and study. He knew that on the outskirts of Krasnoyarsk a merchant and bibliophile, Gennady Yudin, had amassed an extraordinary library of some 80,000 books and periodicals. Armed with a letter of referral, Vladimir had found a 'hearty welcome' from Yudin, who allowed him free range of his collection in which he could access the economic data and statistics he needed for his work on *The Development of Capitalism in Russia*.[25] But one library was never enough to satisfy his insatiable appetite for material; back in St Petersburg his sister Anna was enlisted to seek out further books at the Rumyantsev Library and to send them to him on long loan. He became miserable when letters from home failed to arrive and urged his family not to wait for replies from him before writing again. His life took on a monotonous turn of familiarity: 'There is nothing new I can write about myself; my life goes on as usual. I stroll to the library outside town, I stroll in the neighbourhood, I stroll round to my acquaintances and sleep enough for two – in short, everything is as it should be.'[26] The town library provided access to newspapers and journals, too, but it frustrated Vladimir that these took eleven days to arrive. Always anxious to be on top of the current political situation, he couldn't get used to such old 'news'.[27]

Leaving Krasnoyarsk at the end of April, he took his time travelling the 280 miles south by horse and cart and then paddle steamer down the Yenisey. Beyond Minusinsk the water was too low and the final thirty-six miles to Shushenskoe had to be travelled, once again, by horse and cart. He enjoyed the scenery along the way, particularly the spectacular vistas (some of which reminded him of the view of Mont Blanc from Geneva, in Switzerland, which he had seen in 1895), sleeping soundly and breathing the good, clear air. When he finally arrived he was not disappointed; he knew he was a lot better off than the rest of his arrested comrades:

> Shu-shu-shu is not a bad village. It is true it is in a rather bare locality, but not far away (one and a half to two versts) there is a forest, although much of it has been felled. There is no road to the Yenisey but the River Shush flows right past the village and there is a fairly big tributary of the Yenisey not far away (one or one and a half versts), where you can bathe. The Sayan Mountains or spurs from them are visible on the horizon; some of them are quite white, the snow on them probably never melts.[28]

With the rigour that would characterise his entire career, Vladimir ensured that he did not succumb to the melancholy and lethargy that consumed so many exiles. He planned each day down to the last minute, as he had done in prison, allotting set amounts of time for work, rest and recreation. At this remote spot, populated by a few hardy peasants and a gaggle of geese, ducks and pigs rooting in muddy puddles, he hunkered down through the howling winds of autumn and the freezing sub-zero days of winter, grateful for his father's heavy bearskin coat that he had brought with him. He remained mentally vigorous, engaging non-stop in a voluminous correspondence with activists in St Petersburg, Moscow and various underground cells across Russia. His network of contacts stretched from Astrakhan to Yakutsk and beyond Russia itself to the major Russian colonies of exiles abroad – in Switzerland. But he also drove himself to distraction over the slowness with which news filtered through, as he wondered where associates were, why they had not been in touch and what they were getting up to. When letters did arrive en masse 'from every corner of Russia and Siberia' it left Vladimir in a 'holiday mood' all day.[29] He was also allowed access to newspapers and journals, which he read voraciously when they arrived in batches, ensuring before he started that they were systematically arranged in date order.[30] Such were the huge amounts of mail reaching him in this remote outpost that he gave the local postman power of attorney to collect his mail in the regional centre at Minusinsk.

Vladimir also wrote frequent letters home to his mother and sisters requesting a succession of creature comforts: warm socks, and a mackintosh cape for when he went out hunting, for example. He needed his kid gloves too and his favourite straw hat – essential protection from mosquitoes during the brief but insect-ridden summer in this boggy region (though a fellow exile told him that the Siberian mosquito would even bite through gloves). He made a point of requesting a certain kind of Harmuth pencil and squared paper, sealing wax, scissors (he had been struggling to make do with the landlord's sheep shears); a pen wiper too was needed – he had got into the bad habit of wiping his pen on his jacket lapel.[31]

Continuing his work and study at a distance from libraries and borrowing books on a six-week turnaround – thanks to the good offices of Anna and Mariya – constantly frustrated Vladimir. It took up to thirty-five days for a letter to reach Moscow or St Petersburg and a reply to be sent. The delays over receipt of books were an endless source of frustration and he was particularly irritated when volumes eventually arrived that proved useless. But he never let up on his demands: books on politics, economics, industrial history, agriculture, statistics, public commissions and government reports, book catalogues and 'literary manifestations' of every kind were his lifeblood, ensuring that he could keep in touch with all the new writing at home and abroad.[32] Such was his hunger that he told his sister Anna to accept them in exchange for payment for his journal articles and translation work. Otherwise he asked for nothing and only solicited money when his meagre income from writing and translating ran out, in order to keep body and soul alive. His letters reveal little about himself or his inner feelings – except to reiterate that life was monotonous and uneventful: 'inwardly day differs from day only because today you are reading one book, tomorrow you will read another; today you take a walk to the right of the village, tomorrow to the left; today you write one article, tomorrow another'.[33]

There were, however, opportunities to associate with a dozen or so fellow exiles scattered across a fifty-five-mile radius. He was able to stay in touch with fellow activists from the League of Struggle for the Liberation of the Working Class – Gleb Krzhizhanovsky, Vasily Starkov and Panteleimon Lepeshinsky – who had also been rounded up and sent into exile at Minusinsk. Krzhizhanovsky clearly was suffering from bouts of melancholy, but Vladimir was worried too about the far more arduous conditions being endured by their other colleague, Yuli Martov, now suffering from tuberculosis in Turukhansk, nine hundred miles to the far north.

When Vladimir did manage to tear himself away from his books there were many bucolic pleasures at Shushenskoe: time in the forest, on the river and in the fields. By the end of September 1897 everybody was telling him how well he looked, how much weight he had put on. His healthy suntan made him look 'like a real Siberian'.[34] 'That is what shooting and village life do for you! All the Petersburg ailments have been shaken off!' he told his mother. As a believer in the need for a well-honed physique he took to skating again that winter with great aplomb. Gleb Krzhizhanovsky showed him a number of tricks and Vladimir practised them 'with such industry that once I hurt my hand and could not write for two days'. He was glad that his 'old skill has not been forgotten'. He found skating far better than shooting, 'when you flounder up to your knees in snow, spoil your gun and rarely see any game!'[35] But he had been keen enough to write asking his brother Dmitri to acquire a gun for him and had no difficulty gaining permits to go on expeditions with other exiles and local peasants to shoot duck and great snipe. Wild goats, sable, bear, deer and squirrels abounded in the taiga and the mountains around. Hunting was a practical as well as a recreational choice: 'Shooting is the only form of amusement here, and some sort of "loosening up exercise" is necessary because of my sedentary life', as he told his mother,[36] who worried about her son's skill with a gun. Vladimir was never much of a huntsman; his best potshot was hares but in the autumn there were so many of them around the little islands on the Yenisey that even he got sick of them. Black grouse, partridge and grey hen were more of a challenge, but for that you needed a good dog. He borrowed his landlord's while trying to train up a local mongrel puppy as a gun dog. But it let him down badly and eventually he was able to get a Gordon setter, Zhenka, sent out to him.

When that first winter in Siberia came, Vladimir sealed up the windows, stoked up the stove and hunkered down with his books, pleased that he had enough to keep him going as he sat at his high desk through the long dark days. 'I am in no hurry for books,' he told his mother at Christmas. 'I now have so many that I cannot manage them all, let alone more.'[37] Vladimir knew that, without work, a man could 'go under' in exile. Troubling stories filtered through to him of quarrelling and back-biting among comrades elsewhere in the region. The stresses of exile provoked despair, poor health, madness and even suicide (including that of his close friend Fedoseev in the following year, 1898). On Sundays he offered free legal advice to local peasants. But the bulk of his time was still devoted to completion of *The Development of Capitalism in Russia*. This forty-page economic treatise would be the first pioneering work on Marxism that preached a socialist revolution to come in Russia, preceded by a capitalist stage of development. It was published in an initial print run of 1,200 copies in April 1899, thanks to the good offices of Petr Struve back in St Petersburg, under the pseudonym 'Vladimir Ilyin'. But Vladimir was never satisfied and always worried that control over the final publication was out of his hands: he was obsessive about misprints and the quality of the proof reading of his work and whether the final article would measure up to his own meticulous standards. Distortions of his very specific meaning and trifling issues over semantics troubled him greatly, as did endless problems over late payments.

★   ★   ★

The cold, westerly wind that howled across from the Yenisey, so strong that it blew down pine and birch trees, persisted well into May 1898, as did the heavy spring rains. The last vestiges of the cold had only finally begun their slow and reluctant retreat when Nadezhda Krupskaya arrived in Shushenskoe by steamer from Sorokino, the boat making very slow headway against the high floodwaters of spring. She had come to share Vladimir's exile but was sick and ailing, loaded down like a packhorse with all the books he had instructed her to bring. And she had brought her mother, too. But when they knocked on the door of the house where Vladimir lodged, Nadya discovered that he was out hunting.

Nadya had been arrested in August 1896. When Vladimir had requested that she be allowed to join him at Shushenskoe from her place of exile at Ufa, the Russian authorities had agreed only on condition the couple marry immediately; otherwise she would be sent back. Vladimir had petitioned the district police superintendent for the requisite documents, but the wheels of the tsarist bureaucracy ground slow in Siberia and it was not until 10 July that the couple were married in Shusha's tiny Orthodox church, making do with two rings fashioned from a five-kopek coin by a fellow exile. Neither partner ever alluded to this being a love match; it was, rather, a collaboration between politically like-minded comrades that grew into love, respect and mutual dependency as time went on.

The threesome of Volodya, Nadya and Elizaveta Vasil'evna Krupskaya got on well enough in their accommodation, where Nadya struggled with her limited cooking and domestic skills. She grew vegetables in the kitchen garden that were bottled and pickled for the long winter months and dragged Volodya out mushroom picking. They were joined by a scraggy little servant girl, Pasha, whom Nadya taught to read and write, and then by a kitten. Despite annoying Volodya with her imperious manner and arguing with him about religion, Elizaveta rapidly proved her usefulness as cook, bottle-washer and copyist, and would become an almost permanent fixture during the couple's exile in Europe.

Nadya's first task as wife and helpmate was to assist her husband in preparing the final text of his *Development of Capitalism in Russia*, as well as a Russian translation of Beatrice and Sidney Webb's substantial tome *The Theory and Practice of Trade Unionism*. They struggled with the English geographical and proper names, with which they had no familiarity, and resorted to the German version (a language they knew better and which Ulyanov worked at during his exile) as invaluable back-up. It was an arduous task, requiring them to copy out one thousand pages of translation between them before it could be sent off to the printers. As literary amanuensis, Nadya was following in the tradition of other literary wives, such as Tolstoy's, who also made a lifetime's work of copying out her husband's manuscripts.

Volodya was extremely glad of the companionship of Nadya, and even of his mother-in-law, and glad to be well away from the 'exile scandals' of other colonies in Siberia. But money was always short; when they weren't having to borrow it from either of their mothers, the couple were constantly obliged to beg loans and advances on their publishing work. When books arrived, Vladimir and Nadya consumed them eagerly; one such in September 1899 was the latest thinking of the German economist and writer Eduard Bernstein – who had recently attempted to revise Marxism in a revisionist tome entitled *Die Voraussetzungen des Sozialismus und die Aufgaben der Sozialdemokratie* – hardly the stuff of normal recreational reading, but the Ulyanovs weren't like ordinary people. After careful scrutiny, Bernstein's book was dismissed by them as 'unbelievably weak' and 'opportunistic'.[38]

★   ★   ★

As Volodya's term of exile progressed, the festive seasons of Christmas 1898 and Easter 1899 were spent happily and noisily among comrades, skating, playing chess, singing (which he enjoyed with great gusto, drumming out the rhythm with his foot), arguing, drinking mulled wine by the stove. When his exile was up, he left Shushenskoe with few possessions, having accumulated none bar a gun for shooting, some ice skates and a very heavy load of books. Five hundred pounds of them were despatched home from Siberia. As the horses carrying himself, Nadya and Elizaveta Vasil'evna made their way along the frozen Yenisey north towards Krasnoyarsk, Vladimir Ilyich Ulyanov breathed in the invigorating Siberian winter air for the last time. Three years of enforced isolation at Shushenskoe had produced thirty works of political theory and had clarified and consolidated his political thinking. As he boarded the train at Krasnoyarsk, he was not to know that, unlike many of his less fortunate associates in the Russian revolutionary movement, he would not be returning to Siberia.

He had by now a head full of very clear ideas and political ambitions and was intent on one consuming objective: the establishment of an underground newspaper as a rallying point for the disparate and currently poorly organised elements of the revolutionary movement in Russia. It would also set out to combat all forms of political 'deviation' and set a clear party line on tactics and objectives – namely, his own.

CHAPTER TWO

Igniting the Spark

Munich, 1900–1901

The Englischer Garten, Munich

On 18 February 1900, Volodya and Nadya, with her mother in tow, arrived in the town of Ufa in Western Siberia, still hundreds of miles from Moscow and St Petersburg. It was as far as Nadya was allowed to travel under the terms of her exile, which still had a year to run; for Volodya, however, Ufa was much too far from the centre of things. He was too restless to sit out the months with her here, even though her health was poor and she could have done with his moral support. She might be his wife but, as political comrade first and foremost, she nursed no personal precedence over and above her husband's bigger mission. Volodya had important things to do.

He had the full support for his newspaper of his fellow exiles Yuli Martov and Aleksandr Potresov, now also on their way out of Siberia, as well as the important financial backing of the influential Petr Struve who had been an important contact while in exile, in return for which he had guaranteed him a voice in the paper. But how could he launch a major newspaper when the terms of his release banned him from

Moscow, St Petersburg and all major Russian cities? St Petersburg had long been the mecca for revolutionaries, 'the laboratory of ideas, the centre of life, movement, and activity', as the revolutionary Vera Zasulich described it.[1] And so, like other committed revolutionaries, he ignored the ban and made his way illegally to Moscow at the end of February. He took time to visit his mother and sister Anna, before travelling to St Petersburg to meet Vera Zasulich – herself an illegal in the city, who had come from Switzerland (where she had fled in 1878) specially to meet with him. Together they discussed plans for the newspaper, particularly the urgent need for substantial funding. Soon afterwards, Volodya was obliged to leave or risk arrest.

He settled in Pskov, 170 miles to the north-west near the border with modern-day Estonia. From here he appealed to the authorities for Nadya to be allowed to join him to complete her term of exile but was refused. Languishing alone in lodgings on Arkhangelskaya Ulitsa, he went out for long walks, eked out fifty kopeks a time for essential German lessons and headed for the nearest library. But he couldn't concentrate on work and did little but sit and read the newspapers and send his mother postcards reassuring her that he was in good health. In fact, he was plagued by catarrh and insomnia and losing weight; but Nadya was the sick one – suffering some kind of gynaecological problem.[2] Volodya was worried about her, even more so when in May the authorities refused permission for him to visit her in Ufa. She urgently needed money for medical treatment and he sent what little he could until finally given permission to visit for six weeks at the end of June. He took advantage of the trip, sharing it with his mother and Anna, and enjoyed a memorable cruise down his beloved Volga.

Once again, the Okhrana were watching Ulyanov's every step but the underground was now his natural habitat and he was hungry for real revolutionary experience again. His friend from exile, Panteleimon Lepeshinsky, remembered him during those days in Pskov as being perpetually driven, racing to 'gather together the bricks for the great edifice' that he was in the process of constructing.[3] The Okhrana did not deter him from ducking and diving their surveillance to secure secret meetings with Martov and Potresov in April about the essential fundraising for the costs of printing their newspaper. An estimated 30,000 rubles were needed to get the paper under way. Struve came to Pskov too to consult with Ulyanov and provided some funding, but the bulk of it came from a rich philanthropist and bookseller, Aleksandra

Kalmykova, code-named 'auntie' among revolutionists. Kalmykova's grand apartment on St Petersburg's Liteinaya Ulitsa had become a safe haven for their meetings. After discussion, Ulyanov drafted a 'declaration' of the paper's putative editorial board before he and Martov risked another trip to St Petersburg in early June with a suitcase full of illegal literature. They had no sooner offloaded it than they were picked up by the police, interrogated and imprisoned for ten days. They were released thanks to the intercession by Ulyanov's mother, once more falling on her knees to the authorities on behalf of her troublesome children. It's likely, however, that the police let them go knowing the two men were more valuable to them free where their links to other revolutionaries could be watched and tracked. Ulyanov and Martov got out of jail with the 2,000 rubles they had been carrying still in their possession (a recent donation from Kalmykova towards printing costs, which Ulyanov managed to persuade the police was 'payment' for his publishing work) and a secret list of European contacts and addresses in invisible ink undetected. But his arrest once again underlined the impossibility of running an underground newspaper in Russia. It would put far too many people at risk of discovery and arrest. Police surveillance of himself, Martov and Potresov was just too close and sooner or later they would all end up back in Siberia.

After further talks with Marxist circles in Samara and Smolensk, Ulyanov resolved that his newspaper would have to be established abroad. He sent Potresov on ahead to Switzerland for talks with Plekhanov and Axelrod, who, as the founding fathers of Russian Marxism – albeit exiles – had long been revered from afar and would play an important role in the paper. After seeing his mother and Anna for one last time in late July, he boarded a train at Smolensk that would take him out of Russia. Surprisingly, the authorities responded positively to his request to leave the country on the pretext of 'medical treatment' for his stomach problems and to further his studies. He was granted a six-month passport on 18 May with no questions asked. But, simultaneously, his Okhrana surveillance, and that of Martov, too, was stepped up, though the police had not yet discovered anything about the planned launch of the journal.[4] Nevertheless, Ulyanov's trail across the revolutionary enclaves of Europe was clearly worth more to them than keeping him penned up in a provincial town. He would not see his homeland again for five years.

The village heartland of the Pale of Settlement – the western borderlands of the Russian Empire to which Russia's Jewish population were confined – passed by his third-class carriage window as he endured the hard, wooden seats all the way past Minsk and Warsaw to Vienna, capital of Austria-Hungary, from where he took a connecting train to Geneva. By paying a supplement Ulyanov could travel on the 'express' train but even that attained a speed of only 35–40 mph. This exhausting, thousand-mile trip was the first of a succession of long rail journeys crisscrossing Europe that he would make over the next seventeen years. No sooner had he arrived in August 1900 than he had to face a summit meeting with Plekhanov at Bellerive, outside Geneva. He needed the support of Plekhanov and Axelrod and their Emancipation of Labour group, but there were clear divergences in objectives and tactics. The two older men, along with Vera Zasulich, saw the newspaper primarily as a political discussion work for the promotion of Plekhanov's theoretical views on Marxism, while Ulyanov, Martov and Potresov saw its role as being far more radical – nothing less than an instrument of revolution.

The gathering may have agreed amicably on a name for their newspaper – *Iskra* (The Spark) – but for the rest the meeting was a stormy one. It was characterised by suspicion and distrust, temper tantrums and Plekhanov's implacable opposition to any conciliatory moves towards factional groups within the movement. Intractable and arrogant, he condemned Ulyanov's draft declaration and what he saw as its plodding and unimaginative style. He also resisted the suggestion that *Iskra* be produced three hundred miles away in Munich, with Ulyanov and Potresov as chief editors. With his inflated sense of superiority, Plekhanov would have none of it. He had, after twenty years in exile, as Nadezhda Krupskaya later averred, 'already lost all capacity for directly sensing Russia'.[5] He did not want the life of a conspirator in Munich; his residence in Switzerland was legal, and reasonably comfortable. He insisted on keeping control of the operation in Geneva, and became increasingly dictatorial, throwing up objections to the involvement of Petr Struve's group of 'legal Marxists' (so-called because they published only in legal, as opposed to underground, publications) or any freedom of expression being given in the paper to detractors of his own 'orthodox Marxist' message. He also demanded a larger say in things over fellow editors Axelrod, Zasulich, Ulyanov, Potresov and Martov.

Eventually, Plekhanov resigned in a fit of pique; his resignation was then followed by those of Ulyanov and Potresov in retaliation, until the ever pragmatic Ulyanov realised that, despite the humiliation, capitulation to Plekhanov's vanity by giving him two votes on the editorial board was the only viable tactic. For the time being, Plekhanov had won the argument, remaining the figurehead of the new publication, but Ulyanov was determined he wasn't going to win the war. After he and Potresov had taken the steamer back down Lake Geneva to their lodgings at Vésenaz, their 'pent-up feelings' got the better of them. 'The charged atmosphere burst into a storm. Up and down our little village we paced far into the night; it was quite dark, there was a rumbling of thunder, and constant flashes of lightning rent the air. We walked along, bursting with indignation,' Ulyanov wrote.[6]

As for his admiration of his erstwhile political hero: 'Never, never in my life, had I regarded any other man with such sincere respect and veneration, never had I stood before any man so "humbly" and never before had I been so brutally "kicked".' As a result, Lenin's 'infatuation' with Plekhanov disappeared 'as if by magic'. A week later he unleashed his rage in a scribbled account of the dispute entitled 'How the "Spark" Was Nearly Extinguished'. It remains one of the most emotionally revealing and fluent of his voluminous and often ponderous writings.[7] Historically, it is hugely ironic; for in his railing at being swept aside unceremoniously by Plekhanov as a 'careerist', and his condemnation of him trampling his fellow comrades underfoot, utilising 'chess moves' to outmanoeuvre them, Ulyanov derided precisely the kind of ruthless tactics that would soon become the hallmark of his own growing dominion in the party.[8] But Ulyanov had learned an important lesson from his misguided hero worship of Plekhanov. From here on he would exorcise all personal feeling in his political dealings and trust nobody. One had, as he put it, to 'keep a stone in one's sling'.[9]

Meanwhile, Ulyanov was fighting other pressing theoretical battles with a new faction – the so-called 'Economists' led by Eduard Bernstein whose ideas were echoed in Russia by Ekaterina Kuskova in her *Credo*. Bernstein disagreed with Marx's basic tenet that the collapse of capitalism was inevitable and argued that evolutionary reform, not revolution, was the only way forward. Peaceful political change in Russia could come through parliamentary politics and unionisation of the workers in a campaign for social reform, economic freedom, better pay and conditions. Such thinking – suggesting conciliation with capitalism and the monarchy – enraged Ulyanov, as too did Kuskova's call for vigorous pursuit of the economic struggle through strikes against starvation wages rather than insurrection. These arguments were, in his eyes, 'reactionary'; they subverted his insistence on relentless class war leading to the violent overthrow of the tsarist order. From exile in Siberia he had already issued a written salvo against the Economists, fearful that their 'revisionism' would split the Russian Social Democratic movement. Political heresy such as this sent his stress levels rocketing and provoked a recurrence of his stomach problem.[10] In a long letter to Nadya in August he vented his spleen on the Economists at length, without a single word of enquiry about her health, her life in Ufa or any regret for his own solitary life without her. Politics unfailingly took precedence over intimacy.

After a lonely few weeks in and around Geneva, Ulyanov finally left Switzerland with Potresov, telling his mother in code (in case the police intercepted his letter) that he was going for a 'trip down the Rhine'.[11] In fact, he was heading for Nuremberg, in Germany, and discussion with a leading German Social Democrat and newspaperman, Adolf Braun, on the technicalities of typesetting and printing *Iskra*. Then, on 6 September, he boarded the train again, this time for Munich (heading for 'Paris', as his mother was told, on instructions to send letters via a contact in Prague) in search of an editorial base and a sympathetic printer for his newspaper.

During the years of reaction after the assassination of Tsar Alexander II in 1881, many revolutionaries not arrested and sent into exile had decided to carry on their activities from outside Russia; twenty or so European cities, including Zurich, Geneva, London, Paris and Berlin, now formed the Russian revolutionary diaspora. None of this deterred the Okhrana, who matched this emigration of politicals out of Russia by setting up its own foreign agency with offices in Paris, the Balkans and a newly opened one in Berlin approved by the German government, where detectives were hired locally to keep the Russians under close surveillance.[12] The police in Munich were waiting for Ulyanov when he arrived. A circular, no. 2104, had already been issued by the Okhrana to them and its foreign bureaus in Paris and Berlin to keep a lookout for 'a man of medium height, reddish hair, eyebrows and beard, roundish head, high forehead, normal nose, round face, medium-sized mouth'. He was, they alleged, a 'serious and energetic person' intent on subversive activities.[13]

Since the eighteenth century, the university cities of those seats of the European Enlightenment had been refuges for Russian political and religious dissidents; by 1900 there were 47,000 Russians living in Germany.

The writings of the great German thinkers such as Kant, Fichte, Schelling and Hegel, and more recently Marx, had long influenced the development of radical thought in Russia. It was the present rise – in turn-of-the-century Germany – of an extremely active and vocal movement for social democracy that encouraged Ulyanov and his associates to choose Germany as the location for their first venture.[14] Munich was well placed on the European rail network for easy access to Zurich, Vienna, Paris, Berlin and, across the Channel, London. Many Russian students had enrolled in Munich's university and polytechnic seeking the freer educational facilities there and openly associating with German social democrats. Ulyanov's German colleagues could offer the facilities of their illegal printing presses, reading rooms and meeting halls, as well as advice on the smuggling of literature across European borders and into Russia.[15]

Upon arrival, Ulyanov took lodgings at the house of a social democratic sympathiser and beer seller, Georg Rittmeyer, on the corner of Romerstrasse and Kaiserstrasse, in the city's bohemian quarter of Schwabing. It was hardly an oasis of calm, filled as it was with an assortment of tenants from carpenter to bricklayer and their children, but here at least he was truly among the workers. At that time Schwabing was a picturesque suburb of Munich located north of the old medieval centre of the city on either side of the grand, poplar-lined boulevards Ludwigstrasse and Leopoldstrasse. It lay at the heart of Munich's social and political life and by the 1900s had assumed a character akin to that of Paris's Latin Quarter or New York's Greenwich Village. In Schwabing Ulyanov was in the heart of Mitteleuropa, surrounded by a community of leading German and European intellectuals, writers and artists, many of them gravitating to the area's celebrated café culture at the Café Luitpold or the Café Simplicissimus – the latter home to a leading satirical journal by the same name. The *Jugendstil* art movement (a German form of Art Nouveau) was founded here; in time, Schwabing increasingly offered sanctuary 'for the dispossessed and the culturally restless, providing a forgiving and inexpensive environment for radical experiments in art, politics and sexual protocols'. The writer Thomas Mann, the playwright Frank Wedekind and poet Rainer Maria Rilke, the Swiss abstract painter Paul Klee and his Russian counterpart, Wassily Kandinsky, were all embraced in the community. 'Anyone who painted behind the thousand atelier windows in Schwabing, who kneaded clay, wrote poetry in the garrets, sang or wrote music, amassed debts at little inns, and proclaimed Nihilism or Aestheticism in the cafés' was welcomed. 'The only prerequisite was that the artist had to appear un-bourgeois in both clothing and behaviour', as the writer Dirk Heisserer observed.[16]

Vera Zasulich had arrived in Munich, from Geneva, around the same time as Ulyanov. In 1878, after a sensational trial in which she was acquitted of the assassination of General Fedor Trepov, the savage governor of St Petersburg, she had fled to Switzerland. Here she had endured many hard, lonely years of exile, during which she had become greatly attached to Georgy Plekhanov. Like him, she had never stopped yearning for Russia. Under the code name 'Elder Sister', she now willingly transferred to Munich to help run *Iskra* in a triumvirate with Ulyanov and Martov, but she worried terribly about the growing rift between Ulyanov and Plekhanov. She took an apartment on Schraudolfstrasse, which she shared with Potresov and later Martov, and which was used as *Iskra*'s base. Editorial meetings were sometimes held in the Café Norris on Leopoldstrasse, especially when Axelrod and Plekhanov visited from Switzerland.

Although her revolutionary fame went before her as a political assassin of the legendary Narodnaya Volya school, Zasulich shunned public attention. Her private life was shambolic. She had no family and she lived for her revolutionary ideals, her large grey eyes expressive of her undying hopes for the yet-to-come Socialist Apocalypse. She cared nothing for herself and her appearance and dressed shabbily, like an old-style nihilist; she chain smoked and didn't eat properly. By 1900, she was fifty-three, increasingly overweight and dishevelled.[17] Extremely reserved and cautious, she lived much of her life in intense introspection; she suffered the effects of depression, often locking herself away for days on end to work and existing only on cups of black coffee. But Ulyanov held her in great affection despite her idiosyncrasies, a comrade whom he respected as being 'true to the core'.[18]

Meetings in Munich were also held at the apartment of a local Russian émigré and radical journalist, Aleksandr Helphand (who wrote under the pseudonym 'Parvus'), on Ungererstrasse. Helphand ran an illegal printing press in his flat. Esteemed by Russian and Polish students in the city, he was also an important intermediary for Ulyanov with the wider German movement for social democracy beyond the Russian colony. With Helphand's assistance the first issue of *Iskra* and a subsidiary bimonthly journal *Zarya* (The Dawn) were prepared for publication with advice on the logistics of printing and storage from local German Social Democrats.[19] Security was always uppermost in Ulyanov's mind. *Iskra*'s very survival depended on the postal service, on communicating on editorial matters with Plekhanov in Geneva and Axelrod in Zurich and getting information and material for its editorials from Russia. To avoid interception, letters to and from Ulyanov in Munich had to go via a series of complex staging posts. Letters out went to safe addresses in Berlin, Hamburg, Königsberg and Stuttgart and were often diverted yet again via Paris and Prague before reaching Russia. Letters in – from revolutionary circles in key cities such as Kiev, Petersburg, Moscow, Poltava, Samara and Tula – were directed to a friend of Helphand's, a physician, Dr Carl Lehmann, who ran his medical practice at 46 Gabelsbergerstrasse in Munich.

In the first half of December, Ulyanov went to Stuttgart to prepare *Zarya* then travelled 270 miles north to Leipzig, where the first issue of *Iskra*, most of it written by him, was typeset on 11 December and printed on Christmas Eve by a Polish typographer, Joseph Blumenfeld. In it, Ulyanov wasted no time in giving pole position to his own article 'The Urgent Tasks of Our Movement' which, in a swipe at the Economists, argued that the economic struggle in Russia was inseparable from the wider political one. Several thousand copies of *Iskra*, printed in a close typeface on four pages of onion-skin paper, were sent out to addresses in Switzerland and Belgium. Echoing the sentiments of the poet Pushkin in response to the failed Decembrist uprising of 1825, the paper's title predicted hopefully the creation of a new party. As the precious copies were being sent to Russia, the year 1901 began in fervent hopes that the flame of change would spring from this small political spark, bringing with it revolution in Russia.

Christmas 1900 had been a lonely and 'purposeless' one for Ulyanov. He was, he told his mother (pretending to be writing from Prague), 'wandering aimlessly in a strange land and still only "hoping" to put an end to the fuss and bother and settle down to work'.[20] In the reality of a dreary, rain-drenched Munich he missed the great snowy wastes of Siberia. The cold here was different:

> Actually there is no winter at all, it is like a rotten autumn; everything wet and dripping. It is a good thing it is not cold and I can manage quite well without a winter overcoat, but somehow it's not very nice without snow. I am fed up with the slush and recall with pleasure the real Russian winter, the sleigh rides and the clean frosty air.[21]

Nor could he enjoy ice skating, in the way he had done on the frozen Yenisey: here the ice rink was artificial. Back in Russia his mother worried whether her Volodya needed any extra winter woollies sending out to him. No, he reassured her, the winters here were positively mild in comparison to Russia. The Germans complained of the terrible cold if it was minus 10 or 15, and had no comprehension of how Russians 'manage to stay alive' at minus 20 and 30.[22]

Back in Ufa, where she had endured yet another sub-zero winter of the kind that Volodya now missed, Nadya had completed her term of exile. She and Volodya had remained in contact via coded messages sent inside books that were circulated to activists in Ufa. She had made the most of her time, translating and writing articles to support herself and maintaining important contacts with exiles passing through on their way back from Siberia. Volodya in the meantime had travelled to Vienna in March to arrange her passport with the Russian Consul there, finding time to enjoy a city he found beautiful and lively, visit the Museum of Fine Arts and see a Viennese operetta (he 'did not like it very much', he told his mother).[23]

Leaving her mother behind in Moscow, Nadya made her way across the frontier by train 'looking purposely like an innocent provincial going abroad for the first time' in order not to attract police attention.[24] She had, however, misguidedly set off for Prague on the assumption that the Herr Franz Modraczek she had been writing to at an address there was Volodya under a false name. But things turned ominous when he did not meet her at the station. Alone and friendless, she took a cab to the tenement building in the working-class district from where Volodya's letters had been forwarded to her at Ufa, only to encounter the *real* Herr Modraczek. 'Oh no,' she was told, 'you want Herr Rittmeyer and he lives in Munich'. So, after sharing some Czech rissoles with Herr Modraczek and his sympathetic wife, Nadya wearily resorted to the invaluable *Henschel's Telegraph* of European train times that Volodya had recommended and boarded yet another train, this time for Munich, weighed down with baskets and her heavy Russian fur coat.

Once she had arrived, she left her luggage behind at the station and got on the tram to Kaiserstrasse to seek out 'Herr Rittmeyer'. The address turned out to be a beer cellar and when she confronted Rittmeyer, he was not her Volodya but a burly German publican. 'Ah, you want Herr *Meyer*', the publican's wife told Nadya and escorted her across a yard to a small room at the back containing only a minimum of furniture. It was only then that Nadya discovered that her husband had been going to the station several times a day in hopes she would be on a train; the book he had sent her in which his real, Munich, address had been concealed, had never been redirected on to her.

Having overcome her extreme annoyance at being sent on a wild goose chase, Nadya unpacked the particular kind of English pen nibs she had been instructed to bring Volodya from Russia (the German ones were useless, he said) and took over the important day-to-day correspondence of the underground organisation on his behalf, especially the key work of sending and receiving information in code. When her mother joined them a month later, she was able to devote more time to her role as secretary to the board of *Iskra*, a post engineered for her by Volodya to ensure his close control over things.

It was now essential that their work be protected from Okhrana infiltration and to ensure this Zasulich, Martov, Potresov and the reunited Ulyanovs were all living illegally in Munich on fake Bulgarian passports, as well as under fake names. To their landlords, Volodya and Nadya were Dr and Mrs Meyer, but they also went under a Bulgarian passport in the name of Jordan K. Jordanov, a doctor of law, supposedly from Sofia (the real owner of the passport had died in Varna in 1890), and his wife Maritza.[25]

Although Volodya was, after years of revolutionary training, highly self-sufficient – he was naturally tidy, kept his clothes neat and could sew on a button – there is no doubt that Nadya's presence was enormously calming and reassuring for him. Till then he had been living on cups of tea from a tin mug and his landlady's stodgy food. He never did any cooking, though he knew where to find things in the larder when he was hungry. Nor did Nadya have very much inclination towards cooking and housekeeping. Her expertise was limited to a variety of concoctions with eggs and she often burned things. Yet even she blanched at the slovenly habits of Vera Zasulich, whom she once observed cooking herself some meat and then 'clipping off pieces to eat with a pair of scissors'.[26] Volodya endured Nadya's attempts at home cooking with surprisingly good grace, having very simple needs. Certain foods aggravated his stomach problem anyway, and he had always been one of those people who ate to live rather than lived to eat. Even much later in the Kremlin, he would often be happy with a late-night snack of herring and black bread. When work overtook him he sometimes forgot to eat at all. During their exile, when money allowed, Nadya sometimes offloaded some of

her domestic duties and paid her landladies to change the beds and wash
their dishes. On other occasions, such as in Siberia and later in Finland
and Galicia, she hired young local girls to come in and cook for them.
On the rare occasions when they had money to spare, the couple treated
themselves to meals in cheap local eating houses.[27] Volodya enjoyed a
glass of German beer but took no part in the *Bierkeller* culture of the
city and never gave himself long to sit and relax and enjoy it. Under pressure from colleagues, he did occasionally frequent some of Munich's
cafés such as the Café Altschwabing on Schellingstrasse and the Osteria
Italiana nearby.

For a month after Nadya's arrival the couple lived in lodgings further
west, on Schleissheimerstrasse (where a couple of doors down in 1911 a
certain Adolf Hitler came to live). Here they made do with a single room
in a small apartment occupied by the Kaisers, a working-class family
with six children, who crammed into the other room and the kitchen.
Such close proximity didn't seem to bother Volodya; he liked 'mingling'
with poor workers more than he did with other revolutionaries, as Nadya
later observed. The weather that April and May was very cold and Hans
Kaiser noticed that his Russian tenants kept to their room. It turned out
that they were too poor to buy a stove. Taking pity on them, Kaiser
rigged up a special tube to circulate warm air from his own apartment
below. He liked the Meyers, as he knew them; they were serious-minded,
genuine people, forever huddled at their work tables. They were sociable
too and clearly loved small children, taking an interest in the landlord's
own. Only occasionally, however, did they venture out – to the Zur
Frankenburg snack bar across the road.[28]

But Volodya was sick with influenza and catarrh and their accommodation was dreadfully small. Nadya would creep around trying not to
clatter the dishes as she prepared meals, while her husband paced back
and forth on tiptoe muttering as he gathered his thoughts. When asked
in later life why Volodya walked in this way, Nadya asserted that this was
in order that his footsteps should not disturb his train of thought.[29] After
a month they decided to move and rented a small house on Siegfried-
strasse in the heart of Schwabing, furnishing it with the basic necessities
bought second-hand. Quiet, modest and homely, Nadya made no
emotional demands. She never complained about her enormous work-
load and put up with long and interminable late-night discussions round
her kitchen table when Volodya had editorial meetings with Zasulich and
Martov. In March 1901 the team was joined by Martov's sister Lidiya and

her husband Fedor Dan. Martov, the dreamy intellectual with the mournful face and the pince-nez, was Volodya's physical and polar opposite. An archetypal bohemian revolutionary, he was unmarried and was 'by predilection a haunter of cafés, indifferent to comfort, perpetually arguing'.[30] He was an eccentric émigré *intelligent* of the restless, distracted kind later epitomised in Joseph Conrad's *Under Western Eyes* and *The Secret Agent*. Despite his ineptness he joined in the communal spirit of life in Munich and took his turn at the washing up, as did Volodya, longing, however, for the day when someone would design crockery that needed no washing and which could be thrown away after use.[31] Martov loved to stay up all night talking with fellow émigrés. On occasion, when even Volodya threw in the towel after five or six hours of Martov's exhausting company and went to bed, the insomniac would take Zasulich off to continue their dialogue as they sat rolling their own cigarettes, in all-night cafés. Volodya disapproved; it broke the strict rules of conspiracy to sit talking in places like the Café Luitpold, where they might be overheard.[32]

After the 'immobility' of Shushenskoe and much travelling back and forth across Europe, Ulyanov was eager to get down to his writing again and he did so now with alacrity, between May 1901 and February 1902 working hard on a major new essay, 'What Is To Be Done?'. He hated delegating – he wanted to see *everything* himself and to be the first to do so, but that was clearly impractical. So Lidiya Dan helped Nadya with the daily task of sorting the mail once it had been picked up from Dr Lehmann's flat. Nadya would iron letters written in invisible ink to reveal the words, which Lidiya then decoded. Ulyanov got very annoyed if the decoding was unclear, although the original writing was often obscure and difficult to read. But worse – and this was something Ulyanov considered virtually 'a crime against revolutionary ethics' – was when letter writers were slow to respond to instructions or enquiries from the *Iskra* board. He was soon insisting that each letter sent out should say on it in invisible ink 'Please reply on day of receipt'. And he was infuriated by the way Martov would snatch up the latest copies of newspapers just arrived from Russia; he already spent every evening sitting in the Café Luitpold reading them; wasn't that enough?[33]

There would always be conflicts among a group where one was as disciplined as Ulyanov, and the other as undisciplined and slovenly as Martov, and also where one of the triumvirate – Zasulich – was still deeply devoted to Plekhanov. 'She would have jumped off a cliff for him,' observed Lidiya Dan. While Ulyanov was at times a control freak and a martinet, Lidiya found Nadya easy to get on with. She was not an intellectual and nor was she beautiful, but her plainness was illuminated by her charm. She was warm and kind – 'a very honest, good person'. Ulyanov clearly held her in high regard but 'she was entirely under his spell'; privately Ulyanov's mother-in-law, Elizaveta, complained to Lidiya about how stern and bad-tempered he could be.[34] With time, Lidiya came to the conclusion that Nadya only ever saw things Volodya's way, and slavishly deferred to him as always being right.

Throughout his life in exile, Ulyanov opted to live in cities where foreigners were more easily assimilated, while eschewing the disorderly and noisy lives of Russian exiles, fuelled by idleness and little to eat. He and Nadya did not engage with local life either or make any non-Russian friends. They relied on letters from home to dispel their loneliness. Work was their life and they stuck to the small extended family of illegals gathered round them in Munich – Zasulich (to whom Nadya became particularly attached), Martov, Potresov and the Dans. As a group, they had a sense of mutual responsibility and their closeness would prove to be a golden time before major rifts in the party in 1903 destroyed that sense of unity for ever.[35] With Nadya around, life quickly settled back into a familiar, reassuring pattern. She had the gift of being a good listener, of being unobtrusive and silent when needed. If late nights and his workload wore Volodya out, and she saw him heading for physical crisis, she took him out of himself, for long walks in Munich's famous Englischer Garten (English Park) off Leopoldstrasse or along the more remote stretches of the River Isar; in summer they went swimming in the Ungererbad, the municipal pool. Just before Nadya's arrival, Volodya had enjoyed watching the carnival procession in Munich; he had indulged his long-standing love of opera by going alone to the Bavarian Royal Opera to see a French opera, *Daughter of the Cardinal*, by J. F. Galevy. After Nadya arrived they enjoyed the occasional trip to a concert or the *Volkstheater* when money allowed, but their lives remained pretty isolated, with few visitors. Nadya's mother, who had been sick on and off all summer, was bored and talking of returning to St Petersburg; and what was this, they asked in a letter, about a new play from Anton Chekhov – *Three Sisters*? They had heard such wonderful reports of it at the Art Theatre in Moscow. Yes, life in exile was so alien; it was hard being so cut off from Mother Russia. 'To get the most out of a foreign country,' Nadya wrote, 'you have to go there when you are young and are interested in every little thing.'[36]

By now Ulyanov's sense of frustration and isolation was matched by increasing disenchantment with Plekhanov and alienation from his former colleague Petr Struve, who visited him in Munich and whose liberal sentiments and advocacy of constitutional reform were now clearly out of tune with his own brand of radical Marxism. Ulyanov refused to see him on his second visit, abandoning him to Vera and Nadya. Struve was deeply wounded. The atmosphere, Nadya recalled, 'was as tense as a scene from Dostoievsky'.[37] Struve came away convinced of his and Ulyanov's irreconcilability – morally, politically and socially. Both Ulyanov and Plekhanov had been brusque, to the point of mockery, in their rejection of him, but he found something unnerving and 'repulsively cold' in Ulyanov's behaviour. Such coldness was 'organic', a characteristic of Ulyanov's love of power and his dealing so contemptuously with people once he had fallen out with them.[38] In Ulyanov's view, Struve had betrayed orthodox Marxism with the 'bourgeois apologetics' of his conciliatory, legal Marxism. He was nothing but 'a politico, an artful dodger, a huckster, and an impudent boor' and had tried to best him.[39] Such crudely worded and violent character assassination was now a hallmark of Ulyanov's writings as he struggled to impose his vision on a still-fractured movement. Soon after, Struve set up his own, rival journal, *Osvobozhdenie* (Liberation) and moved increasingly away from Marxism, towards constitutional liberalism.

Life in Munich was stagnating and money was very tight until a cheque arrived from Ulyanov's publisher in Russia. *Iskra* was now being distributed on a regular basis, but the burden of masterminding it all was taking its toll on his health, as too was the constant need to protect it from seizure by the German police. In collaboration with Social Democrats in Berlin, copies of *Iskra* were being sent to the warehouse of their own newspaper, before being taken in double-sided and double-bottomed trunks, or even in smaller quantities in specially lined jackets, by legal 'Sunday Travellers' into Russia, via East Prussia, Upper Silesia and Austrian Galicia. Once delivered to an agent on the Russian side, such as the Ulyanovs' good friends from Siberian exile, Panteleimon Lepeshinsky and his wife Ol'ga in Pskov, or Martov's brother, Sergey Tsederbaum, a first-rate organiser in Poltava, they were collected by others for distribution locally in the various cities. Issue no. 2 had already been printed at Helphand's flat in Schwabing before Ulyanov heard the bad news: three thousand copies of the first issue that had been smuggled across the Russian frontier at Memel in East Prussia in January had all been seized at

Polangen.[40] Another thousand copies did, however, find their way into safe hands in false-bottomed trunks.

Once the second issue, printed in Munich, had evaded the Prussian police and arrived safely, the groundswell of demand for more copies on a more regular basis rapidly grew inside Russia. Starved of political literature and a vehicle for expressing their discontent, people – particularly out in the Urals at Ekaterinburg and Perm – were writing to the *Iskra* office begging for more. *Iskra* had indeed ignited the voice of political protest in Russia. But in 1901–2 there was enormous police surveillance and repression inside Russia in the·wake of a new tide of opposition to the tsarist state, with student and worker demonstrations in major cities, nationalist discontent in Poland and Finland, and professionals in local government protesting proposed restrictions in their reforming powers. Such events exhilarated Ulyanov with their promise of change but he could not bear the lack of detailed information. 'The devil knows what is happening in Russia,' he wrote to Axelrod on 20 March 1901, 'demonstrations in St Petersburg, Moscow, Kharkov, Kazan; martial law in Moscow (by the way, they arrested my youngest sister there and even my brother-in-law, who had never taken part in anything!); bloody battles; prisons crammed full, and so on.'[41]

With Mariya arrested and in solitary confinement and Anna's husband Mark Elizarov also in jail, Anna was forced to flee to Europe, settling in Berlin, where she was now organising the despatch of *Iskra* into Russia. Ulyanov wrote with a rising sense of frustration: they had to do something to improve *transportirovka* – the despatch of copies into Russia – which was too irregular and random. The constant uncertainty of copies not getting through and, when they did, of whether they achieved results, was very stressful. Ulyanov bombarded his agents in Russia with complaints:

> Things with us are going none too well. We are badly off financially, Russia gives almost nothing. Shipping is still unorganised and haphazard ... Our daily bread, by which we barely manage to keep alive, consists as before solely of suitcases. For a couple of them we pay about a hundred rubles, and the chance nature of the persons sent entails a vast amount of delay, carelessness, loss, etc. [42]

Running costs were now up to 1,599 German marks per month for every issue of eight thousand copies.[43] It was essential that a much more disciplined and covert distribution network of *Iskrovitsy* (Iskra-ites) be created closer to the frontier, to raise money for the paper, obtain false passports and provide safe houses for conspiratorial meetings and decoy addresses for correspondence.

CHAPTER THREE

Konspiratsiya

Russia: 1901–1902

St Petersburg in the 1900s

While Vladimir Ulyanov and Nadezhda Krupskaya were busy issuing meticulous instructions on organisation, codes and tactics from their bolt hole in Munich, a mass of *praktiki* – party agents – inside and outside Russia were living with the real and present dangers of work in the revolutionary underground. Those who had committed themselves to spreading the word of *Iskra* as well as printing and disseminating other illegal literature on crudely made presses hidden in safe houses were taking enormous risks. They lived on false papers, with no fixed place of abode and often in extreme penury; the spectre of arrest, imprisonment and Siberian exile loomed perpetually over their lives. It would come at least once for many of them.

Political and industrial unrest, as well as a new wave of student activism, was now reinforcing the revolutionary will in Russia. Students had recently been incensed by new legislation under which any of them caught taking part in strikes or demonstrations could be summarily despatched into the army; in the winter of 1901, 183 students from Kiev University were punished in this way for their acts of protest. More students suffered arrest and were killed in a demonstration in Kazan two months later in support of the Kiev students.

The radical tradition now rising once more from the ashes of the 1881 repressions in fact dated back to the 1820s, when intellectual discussion groups and secret societies had first sprung up in Russia. Such societies had thrived in an atmosphere of secret debate which by the 1860s had mutated into organised conspiracy against the tsars, much of it fired from a distance by the propagandising in his London exile of Alexander Herzen through his socialist journal *Kolokol* (The Bell) and assisted by fellow exiles Nikolay Ogarev and Mikhail Bakunin. Leadership of the movement for democratic change in Russia came from a distance for much of the nineteenth century, with many of the leading lights of Russian radical thought forced into exile abroad, chiefly in Switzerland. By the 1900s, such were the levels of state censorship in Russia that a huge range of activities had to be authorised by the police – from setting up a Sunday School or medical practice, to simply selling books and newspapers. A great list of political and social issues – some 1,896 of them – was expressly forbidden from public discussion.[1] Even the most innocuous seeming literary and discussion groups for workers were subject to raids by the police; and rightly so, for they were the recruiting grounds for revolutionists and now *Iskra* agents; even chess clubs were used as covers for seditious activities.

The objectives of the dedicated revolutionary had first and most emphatically been laid down in a pamphlet written in 1869 by the nihilist Sergey Nechaev in collaboration with Bakunin. 'The Revolutionary's Catechism' asserted that conspirators should operate in small, self-sufficient cells of no more than six people (in order to prevent infiltration by spies and, in so doing, betrayal of the wider network). Like Rakhmetov in the Chernyshevsky novel so admired by Ulyanov, the ideal revolutionist described by Nechaev must submit himself to the collective will. He should have no personal life, feelings or attachments – 'not even a name'. He should shut out all self-indulgent thoughts of kindness, love, sentiment or romance and have only one single-minded passion – revolution. His overriding intellectual commitment should be to the 'science of destruction'.[2] And all this, paradoxically, in the pursuit of the 'complete liberation and happiness' of the people.

By 1901 Ulyanov was having serious doubts about the effectiveness of the still embryonic *Iskra* network in effecting change. It was too diverse, too lacking in unifying objectives and overall control. The Marxism of its participants was too vague and elusive, the party as a whole fragmented, harassed by police and demoralised by *provocateurs*. The stress and worry of seeing his carefully laid instructions go awry, of disorganisation and inefficiency, gave him many sleepless nights. He worried constantly that *Iskra*'s work would be undermined by splinter groups and rival factions in the Russian regions, working without authorisation from the centre and thus outside his control. He was paranoid that his agents would desert to other, rival political organs. There was too much laxity: ciphered letters often proved unreadable because keys had not been properly used, the paper was too poor quality, or the handwriting illegible. Important agents failed to carry out directives correctly or to meet their deadlines in communicating; others proved downright inadequate. And worse, the methods of importing *Iskra* into Russia were too small-scale; huge numbers of copies languished for lack of an effective system of distribution.[3] In Ulyanov's view, the revolutionary movement was at a crossroads, faced with a tough battle against a powerful, modern state that was 'straining every nerve in order to crush socialism and democracy'. It now needed an injection of power and, more importantly, legitimacy. Back in 1897 he had written, 'To be able to conduct a systematic battle against the government, we must raise the revolutionary organization, discipline and conspiratorial technique to the highest level of perfection.'[4] But he and those around him in Munich knew that the party in Russia had a membership that varied greatly in its abilities and calibre and it needed urgently to be channelled and directed. For although the *Iskra* network was a good vehicle for organising activists, it also opened the party up to the constant risk of infiltration by double agents and informers.

The success of the whole operation in Russia now rested upon what, to Ulyanov, was the most crucial element: *konspiratsiya*. The word in Russian did not mean 'conspiracy' or plotting as we know it, but, rather, the utmost *secrecy* or stealth in the avoidance of detection. The principles of *konspiratsiya* had been tested during the years of Narodnaya Volya's guerrilla activities and their violent campaign of political assassination up to 1881 and had since become Ulyanov's guiding principle: a necessary foundation to all other revolutionary work.[5] In maintaining high levels of secrecy, economy, brevity and punctuality were the watchwords as far as Ulyanov was concerned: economy of words and actions in public so as not to give oneself away, brevity in verbal communication and the prompt fulfilment of assignments. His instructions were clear: 'When you are taken up with secret, conspiratorial matters, you must not speak with those whom you normally converse, nor about the things you usually talk about, but only with those you need to talk to and only about things you need to talk about.'[6]

There were now hundreds of activists working covertly in Russia's big cities, who had given up the personal life and gone underground. Although they worked as full-time, professional revolutionaries they received no 'wages' as such. The movement relied on funds raised from sympathetic and wealthy donors to help support them, but the bulk of this money went on costly printing equipment, paper and ink. The agents themselves lived from hand to mouth, mainly on the goodwill and kindness of others. In the city they operated as 'illegals' – living in safe houses without work permits on false identity papers and using a string of code names: Ulyanov's friend and leader of the Pskov group, Panteleimon Lepeshinsky, went by the names of Lapot', Bychkov and a numerical alias – 2a3b. Leonid Krasin, an engineer and explosives expert and a key agent in charge of a printing press in Baku, was known as Vinter, Zimin, Johanson and simply 'the horse'.[7] Another major contact in Moscow, Bauman, was known as 'Victor', 'the Tree' and 'The Rook'. Sometimes the introductory codes between agents were risible, such as that used by Cecilia Bobrovskaya – 'We are the swallows of the coming spring'; or another devised to greet a Norwegian contact who knew no Russian – 'Ich bin der Freund von Herrn Anders', positively the stuff of schoolboy comic-book spies.[8]

Nevertheless, all the codes, secret knocks and passwords employed by illegals, however inept, were essential in the attempt to preserve the operation's secrecy. Underground activists lived very insular lives, rarely communicating beyond their own close-knit world and very often knowing little of the identity and location of others beyond their own groups. Agents on their way to meetings or delivery points were forbidden from carrying anything in their hands: they could only be hidden in their clothes. In order to print leaflets on crude hectograph machines they had to make their own mixture of gelatine and glycerine, but the latter could only be bought in small quantities and so dozens of agents would be needed to buy supplies across a wide area. Paper too had to be bought in small quantities from many outlets in order to avoid arousing suspicion. If safe places could not be found in which to meet, agents would go out into the woods to hold meetings under the guise of picnics or mushroom-picking expeditions or 'boat trips' downriver. One group in Kiev met in a laundry; another in Chernigov was offered the waiting room of a sympathetic doctor.[9] The eminent Russian painter Ilya Repin, a family friend of agent Elena Stasova, allowed the use of his studio at the Academy of Arts.[10] Meetings could always be held at legal workers' clubs or the offices of trade unions, but with the police for ever on the lookout for seditious activity, these were held at greater risk of discovery.

The clandestine cells ensured that at all times they were prepared for the inevitability of police raids. They circulated a pamphlet, 'How to Conduct Oneself under Interrogation' in the eventuality of arrest;[11] in such situations the utmost loyalty towards colleagues was demanded. Anyone who did not master conspiratorial techniques was considered a *kustar'* – an amateur; amateurism was anathema to Ulyanov and he was obsessive in eradicating it. But as the movement grew, it urgently needed fresh converts from the working classes in Russia's growing urban centres. Circulating *Iskra* – known as the process of 'sowing' – and other propaganda among them was the quickest means of recruitment. Although the paper was aimed at converted Marxists with a degree of political acumen and literacy, such was the hunger for freely produced, radical literature inside Russia that everybody wanted to read it. There were never enough copies to go round. *Iskra* was read avidly by workers to other, illiterate, co-workers and then passed on from one group to the next until the well-worn copies literally fell apart. Other propaganda leaflets produced by the *Iskra* board were disseminated by agents who took enormous risks going into theatres in Moscow and St Petersburg and showering audiences with leaflets. They also strewed them on factory courtyards near the water pumps where people congregated, at army barracks, and along the city streets. Sometimes the leaflets would be surreptitiously pasted on walls but with so many police on the streets this was highly dangerous.[12]

But such dangers were welcomed by the eager young *Iskra* agents who had committed themselves to the challenge. Underground work, and with it the threat of arrest, gave them a sense of comradeship and purpose. It also offered a unique environment where women took equal risks with the men.[13] Like Nadezhda Krupskaya, they were often self-effacing and took little credit for the work they did, performing an important but subordinate function as couriers, helping produce and distribute propaganda leaflets and providing valuable financial and physical back up. They learned how to make bombs and shoot guns but they did not appear in the ranks of the party's theoreticians.[14] The Russian revolutionary movement did not encourage women to promote themselves, a fact to which the increasingly slovenly Vera Zasulich was living testimony. But it valued their 'plodding, tireless work,' as Nadya described it and nominally treated them as equals.[15] There was no traditional division of labour between male and female within cells; a good female activist learned to go without sleep and without food, just like the men, and no concessions were made to her sex. And she never complained. Ulyanov's devoted sisters Anna and Mariya understood this and were part of the valuable and stable network of female activists who kept him going through the long years of exile. Anna had already suffered arrest and confinement to the family estate at Kokushkino in the 1880s, only to go straight back into the underground on her release, fundraising and helping to circulate illegal literature, as well as arranging secret meetings and passing on news and instructions from Ulyanov in Europe.[16] In 1899 Mariya had been arrested in Moscow and, after enduring seven months in solitary confinement, spent the next three years in exile in Samara, but this did not prevent her from continuing her revolutionary work. Meanwhile, in Berlin Anna was now playing an important role in copying and coding letters to and from the *Iskra* board and its agents in Russia.

By the time Lidiya Dan arrived in Moscow in January 1901 on an undercover mission for Ulyanov to consolidate *Iskra*'s position after a series of police raids and arrests, she found that the enclave in Munich had seriously underestimated the growth of the socialist movement back home and its now explosive tenor. It was a 'seething cauldron', she reported. The students in the city were beginning to stir and Moscow was becoming 'a hotbed of provocation'.[17] She had arrived one evening unannounced, on a passport generously given to her by a Jewish student in the Russian colony in Berne. Her only place of refuge in the city was her sister-in-law's apartment, but she would not take the risk of putting Lidiya up. Lidiya's only option, as night drew in, was to get on a train going somewhere, anywhere, so long as she was not walking the streets. There were gendarmes watching the stations for precisely this ploy – some illegals lived for weeks riding the trains back and forth across Russia and sleeping in railway station toilets. But it was a risk Lidiya had to take. She lived like this, endlessly and aimlessly criss-crossing on trains for about a month, occasionally being offered a room for the night in the apartments of sympathetic strangers (never her own relatives), making sure she did not arrive back late, but around the time people usually returned from the theatre – when she would not appear conspicuous to the concierges on duty by her arrival. She could never risk staying late at workers' meetings – an illegal was not safe out on the streets after 11.00 p.m. Occasionally she would be allowed back to her sister-in law's for a change of clothes; at other times she went to the public baths, where you could hire a room for a ruble and wash, rest and change. During this time Lidiya managed to hold meetings with activists at safe 'bourgeois' apartments or doctor's surgeries. Here anyone who needed to talk could come so long as they knew the password. But, overall, she soon realised that the level of personnel and organisation in Moscow was extremely poor and people were demoralised by the high numbers of police raids and arrests.[18] There were few facilities for organising and printing leaflets and it took an inordinate amount of effort and risk for Lidiya to obtain just 250 copies of one.

One night, Lidiya was caught out late at a meeting and could not get back to her safe house in time. Her only option was to go out on to the Tsvetnoy Boulevard and bribe a prostitute to take her back to her place for the night, assuring her she was not a lesbian but on the run from an abusive husband. The prostitute offered to share her bed with her but Lidiya balked at the suggestion and spent an uncomfortable night in an armchair. She left first thing the next morning, being sure to leave a five ruble note on the table. Her socialist conscience would not allow her to leave the woman's loss of earnings unrewarded.[19] But in May 1902 Lidiya was arrested on the street as she met another activist. She was sent to Butyrki prison prior to being exiled to Olekminsk on the River Lena in Siberia. She was to be out of circulation for three years before managing to escape to Geneva.

Another devoted female activist, and one on whom Ulyanov in later years greatly relied, was Elena Stasova. In St Petersburg she became legendary as a master of *tekhnika* – the essential business of running an organisation – information gathering, distributing illegal literature, arranging safe houses for meetings and hiding revolutionaries on the run and liaising with other groups across Russia and in Europe. Stasova shared with Ulyanov the classic conspiratorial qualities of self-discipline, energy and austerity as well as a photographic memory for names, aliases and addresses.[20] She had chosen the alias of 'Absolute', Ulyanov thinking it most appropriate since Stasova's unquestioning loyalty could always be counted on. She came from a comfortable, privileged background (as did several other women activists) and received financial support in her underground work from her family, making use of its country estate as a safe house for meetings and a hiding place for illegal literature. Stasova's parents also allowed the use of their spacious St Petersburg apartment for evening lectures – ostensibly on uncontroversial subjects – where considerable covert fundraising went on for *Iskra*. Her parents stood bail for her when she was arrested and sent money to exiles in financial need. For Stasova, as for many other young women at this time, the party became her 'family' and she bonded strongly with her fellow activists. Some of these women married, but of those who formed relationships most lived together, always opting for the cause over and above personal and emotional concerns. There was never any question in Stasova's mind of where her primary loyalties lay, no matter how great the parental pressure to give up: 'my life is in this, in this and only in this', she was to write from prison when later arrested. 'No other work can give me the strength to live . . . without this work of mine I cannot live. This is the flesh of my flesh.'[21] Stasova's dedication brought spectacular results: by 1902 the St Petersburg group under her direction was printing and distributing political broadsides weekly, often in print runs of 10,000 copies, as well as smuggling in large supplies of books and newspapers from abroad.[22]

One of Stasova's close associates in the illegal transportation of *Iskra* and other Marxist literature from Europe was Nikolay Burenin. He remembered how copies of *Iskra* were sent into Russia pasted together to create the boards of children's books, using a special glue invented by a Swiss bookbinder. On receipt, the covers had to be soaked in warm water to disengage the material, which then had to be painstakingly peeled, page from page, and dried. The method also worked successfully for cartons and the backing to pictures and even ornaments. One *Iskra* agent fashioned cheap plaster figurines for smuggling literature, which were then sold in markets after they had served their purpose.

One of the most dramatic close shaves experienced by a courier was that of Lidiya Gobi. Gobi was the daughter of an eminent botanist and professor at Petersburg University, one of the devoted female agents of the 'repentant privileged classes' who dedicated themselves to 'righting the emotional wrongs of Russia'.[23] Her svelte appearance belied her passionate revolutionary fervour. She was every inch the elegant lady:

tall, beautifully dressed and aristocratic. When carrying illegal literature she passed the police by unnoticed on the street. Indeed, so good was her classy cover that she became one of the group's best agents in St Petersburg and her family dacha at Piki-Ruki on the Vyborg side of St Petersburg was also used by them as a safe house. So safe, indeed, that Ulyanov stayed here during one of his illegal visits to the city. On one occasion Lidiya was sent south to Kiev with a set of orders for local activists from the Petersburg committee. She got off the train, convinced that no one was following her, and headed straight for her secret assignation. Having handed over her documents she received others to take back to St Petersburg. But outside on the street she suddenly noticed she was being followed. Pretending that she had come out for a stroll, she made her way to the nearby public park, but soon noticed that the *shpik* (spook – an Okhrana agent) who was following her had been joined by another. Not only that, they were tailing her without any attempt to disguise the fact. Lidiya resolved to destroy everything she was carrying the minute she got back to the train. But now, as she left the park, there were three men on her tail. If she went to the station she'd be caught like a mouse in a trap. As she walked through the old Podil district of Kiev her brain was racing. The three men were closing in when she noticed in front of her an old house with a garden leading down to the edge of the cliff above the Dnipro river, and headed towards it. It was a long way down and all she could see below was dense undergrowth. She was wearing a large fur cloak that day – perfect for hiding the illegal literature she had brought. Unflinching, she sat on the edge of the cliff, pulled her cloak tight around her and let herself fall. Much to her amazement, Lidiya landed safely at the feet of startled onlookers below. Such was her self-possession that she picked herself up, apologised for landing so unexpectedly in their midst and refused all offers of medical help – her expensive and bulky fur cloak having saved her from injury. After tidying herself up in a nearby house, she was on the next train out of Kiev.[24]

★   ★   ★

By the end of 1901 *Iskra* was getting into Russia by several routes: via the border areas of Poland and Lithuania, especially the town of Vilna (these areas then part of the Austro-Hungarian and Russian empires), thanks in no small way to the assistance of members of the Bund – a Jewish socialist organisation, founded in Vilna in 1897 that was active within the Pale of Settlement in promoting Jewish nationhood and culture. Other copies came by the most roundabout, but safest, route, through Persia via Tavriz and Alexandria. French, and sometimes Russian, steamers brought copies from Marseilles to the Black Sea ports of Batumi and Baku, or Odessa in the Crimea; from there, wrapped in water-proofing, they were dumped overboard where they were picked up and taken across the Caucasus and on into Russia. By far the most dependable route was that via Romania and the border town of Teofipol.[25] For a short while political literature was also smuggled from Vardo, in Finn-marken in the extreme north of Norway, wrapped in greaseproof paper inside boxes of salted fish. These transports, arranged by the Norwegian social democrat Adam Egede-Nissen, arrived at the Russian seaport of Archangel. But when this method was discovered Nissen began sending literature in with sympathetic Russian sailors arriving at Vardo and returning to Russia via the White Sea.

The northern route into Russia via Sweden and Finland proved extremely efficient. It was the brainchild of the Russian activist Vladimir Smirnov, who was married to Karin Strindberg, daughter of the famous Swedish playwright. With a Finnish mother and fluency in Swedish and Russian, Smirnov had many socialist contacts in Finland. As ardent patriots the Finns were opposed to the Russianisation of their home country and played important roles not just in the distribution of *Iskra* but the Russian revolutionary movement as a whole, particularly in the border towns of Terijoki and Kuokkala, located on the railway line into St Petersburg. Initially, illegal literature arriving from Berlin and Geneva at Stockholm was packaged up and sent hidden in loads of coal on steamships plying the service between Sweden and the south-west archipelago of Finland near Åbo (now Turku). But from the autumn of 1902 Smirnov's important middleman was the Finnish journalist and socialist Konni Zilliacus, who organised a network of smugglers (many of them women) to take copies of *Iskra* from Sweden into Finland by train and by steamship, hidden in their clothes and luggage. Zilliacus also used his own yacht for smuggling copies. The Okhrana soon became aware of his activities, but such were the navigational difficulties posed by the six thousand tiny skerries and islands around Åbo to anyone who did not know the area inside out that Zilliacus constantly slipped the net.[26]

As well as assisting in organising the sea routes for *Iskra* smuggling, Vladimir Smirnov also carried out able work on the ground, via his home in Helsingfors (now Helsinki). He was assisted in this by his old mother

Virginiya, who often travelled into St Petersburg on the train, her basket full of illegal literature and lists of coded addresses hidden under her knitting. But what policeman would think to stop and question such a kindly old lady who looked like any other Petersburg children's nurse?[27] And who would suspect the notable Finnish opera star Aino Akte, another sympathiser and Finnish patriot, of smuggling copies of *Iskra* into Finland in her elegant luggage after a tour to Paris?[28]

With so much material coming in via Finland, Smirnov and his fellow *Iskra* agents grew to rely heavily on Finnish workers on the railway line into St Petersburg from the northern suburbs of Vyborg to ensure the safe transfer of illegal literature hidden in boxes of apples and potatoes. Other items were secreted in the deep skirt pockets or corsets of women agents, or special undervests worn by men, who crossed into Vyborg to collect the literature from the homes of railway workers. Later they used the country estate of Nikolay Burenin, at Kiriasali, on the Finnish border, as a way station for illegal literature travelling in both direc-tions.[29] Transports would arrive at the little local railway station of Raivola and Burenin and his colleagues would dress up as though going out into the woods hunting and travel by horse and cart to pick them up, hiding the copies of *Iskra* under straw in the back of the carts. Back in Petersburg, at his family's fashionable apartment on Ruzovskaya Ulitsa, Burenin used his profession as a pianist as a front for illegal trans-ports, forever treading a delicate line of subterfuge in order that his mother should not know what he was up to. Their apartment was a regular venue for musical gatherings and rehearsals. The toing and froing of 'musicians' with instrument cases duped the vigilant porter (who, like many others in St Petersburg at the time, was under instructions from the secret police to keep an eye open for gatherings of illegals). On such occasions, as a recital went on in the drawing room overseen by Burenin's mother, small groups of activists would slip away and congregate in Burenin's room nearby to smoke and plot revolution. But he was always on his guard and kept the packets of illegal literature in a pile ready to be doused in kerosene and burned in the stove should the police knock at the door.[30]

The most dangerous work, however, was that carried out by those who ran the illegal printing presses. Most of these were hidden on the premises of legitimate shops and businesses and the people who oper-ated them lived the life of troglodytes, working away in the dark. The locations of the presses were known to only a tight-knit circle of people and the texts to be printed were passed from agent to agent at public places full of people – such as art exhibitions – where agents rendezvoused in front of pre-arranged paintings to surreptitiously pass on material. The most successful printing press was located far from Russia – at Baku in Georgia. Here illegal literature had first been reproduced from crude cardboard stencils smuggled from Europe and Russia inside scientific and technical books, from which metal stereotype blocks were cast. By September 1901 a local Georgian activist, Lado Ketskhoveli, had obtained a far more efficient rotary stereotype press and set it up in Tiflis's Muslim quarter. But it constantly had to be moved in order to keep it safe from the Tiflis branch of the Okhrana, which tried hard to locate it. In the end they caught up with Ketskhoveli, who refused under torture to reveal the press's location and was shot in his cell. Leonid Krasin took over the running of the press and vastly improved its techniques. For the next four years, 'Nina' – as the press was code-named throughout the Russian underground – proved invaluable to the *Iskra* organisation.[31]

* * *

With the revolutionary movement across Russia entering a dramatic upswing, so too were the activities of the Okhrana, now engaged in a massive recruitment drive for spies and double agents. Across Russia Okhrana 'spooks' were deployed as porters, newspaper sellers and cabbies, watching railway stations and hotels for strangers and any sign of illegal activities.[32] With the extremism of the Narodnaya Volya years having largely been repressed by the Okhrana in a wave of arrests and executions in the 1880s, it now was increasingly turning its attention to the interception of letters and telegrams (a practice known as *perlyustratsiya*, 'perlustration') to and from the *Iskra* board. Through the offices of its Department of Posts and Telegraphs, popularly known as the *Chernyi Kabinet* (Black Cabinet), surveillance of mail coming in and out of the main post offices of Moscow, St Petersburg, Warsaw, Odessa, Kiev, Kharkov and Tiflis enabled the interception and copying of thousands of letters a year.

Despite the assiduous use of carefully laid down procedures among *Iskra* agents, there was still a degree of naivety and carelessness in many of the codes, which proved far too easy for the Black Cabinet's expert cryptographers to crack.[33] Many codes had been adapted from tapping codes devised, with considerable perseverance and ingenuity, by activists during prison sentences. The number of taps used referred to a simple checkerboard (or 'Polybius square') of 5 x 5 rows of letters of the old Russian alphabet. Prisoners memorised this universal system in order to 'talk' to each other wherever they found themselves in jail – achieving speeds of ten to fifteen words a minute. The tapping had then been adapted to a series of dots and dashes, used to conceal messages inside individual letters on particular pages of innocuous looking books or letters. The key to these codes was to be found by reference to a specific page, line and pair of numbers indicating a particular letter of the alphabet on a previously agreed book, such as the journal *Family Pictures*, a biography of Spinoza and a volume of poetry by Nekrasov, all used by Ulyanov and Nadya to send message to *Iskra* members at this time. In their correspondence with Elena Stasova in St Petersburg, they used one of Ivan Krylov's animal fables – Stasova became so adept at the code that she was often coding and sending hundreds of letters a month by it.[34] Other messages could be conveyed in the use of Aesopian language and allusion in what seemed on the surface legitimate, published literature or innocent sounding letters. Thus, references to 'illness' meant arrest and 'hospital' meant prison; any enquiry about someone's health was about their imprisonment. If an 'epidemic' broke out in a particular town, this was a warning that there had been a series of police raids and arrests and agents should steer clear.[35]

Once coded letters were intercepted and decoded, often thanks to the help of double agents and infiltrators, all names were extracted from these letters and recorded in a vast Okhrana card index. It was claimed that the Okhrana specialists were able to identify suspicious letters merely by the handwriting on the envelopes; once opened and read, such letters had a discreet black mark known as a 'fly' (*mukha*) put on them, in order to avoid their being opened more than once.[36] Throughout the period up to the Revolution the Okhrana maintained a high success rate in its perlustration activities thanks to the *Iskra* movement's continuing underestimation of the skills they were up against and the lack of sophistication of their own codes. Nadezhda Krupskaya, herself at the heart of the operation and responsible often for as many as three hundred coded letters a week, was the first to admit the amateurishness of those early days:

All those letters about handkerchiefs (passports), brewing beer [propaganda shipments via Sweden and Finland], warm fur (illegal literature), all those code names for towns beginning with the same letters as the name of the town (Ossip for Odessa, Terenty for Tver, Petya for Poltava, Pasha – Pskov) – substitution of woman's names for men's and vice versa – all this was transparent in the extreme.[37]

One such inexperienced agent was Osip Pyatnitsky, who was arrested not long after joining the *Iskra* network. Taken to the Lukyanovka Prison in Kiev, he discovered that it was a holding centre for other *Iskra* agents – a dozen or more had been arrested in a roundup in February 1902 – where they could be systematically interrogated by the notorious General Vasily Novitsky, head of the Kiev gendarmerie, who was already planning a great state trial for them. The arrests were a serious blow to *Iskra* and Ulyanov was greatly disturbed when he received the news. But from inside their prison the *Iskra* agents were quick to apply the methods of their mentor. They made the most of their time in prison, exploiting its lax regime to their advantage and turning their cells into classrooms, reading all the political literature they could lay hands on, teaching themselves languages and debating among themselves. Prison for many new recruits such as Pyatnitsky became a university and a Marxist training ground. But for the revolutionaries confined with him in Kiev that summer, imprisonment was also a torment, keeping them from taking part in the wave of demonstrations and strikes going on across Russia's cities.[38] When they heard it would be months before their trials would come to court, eleven of them resolved on an escape plan. Security was so poor that they were able to have smuggled in everything they needed: false passports, 100 rubles each in money, as well as vodka and sleeping powders to dope the guards. An iron grapple, to help the escapees get over the twenty-five-foot prison wall (using rope ladders made from bed sheets), arrived hidden inside a basket of flowers for one of the prisoners' birthdays. The group of prisoners boldly practised making human pyramids during their exercise period in the yard in order to gauge the height of the walls over which they would have to shin and plotted the route they would take across neighbouring fields, to a series of safe houses set up for them. They practised the best techniques for tying up the guards and in a softening up campaign began inviting them to share drinks with them. On 18 August 1902 they effected their escape as planned.

Despite the Okhrana sending out urgent alerts to all border posts and 295 Russian cities, Pyatnitsky and all but one of the ten others managed to get across the Russian frontier and rendezvous with the other *Iskra* escapees at a restaurant in Berlin. Here, from the cold, damp cellar of

the German Social Democratic journal *Vorvärts* Pyatnitsky worked for
Iskra under the code name 'Freitag', investing considerable energy and
commitment to his key role and earning the respect of his German coun-
terparts. The Germans, by comparison, complained that their Social
Democrat ranks contained 'too many bureaucrats and not enough revolutionaries'.[39] The building was under constant surveillance by both the
Russian secret police and the Germans, yet despite this Pyatnitsky engaged
in regular contraband trips back and forth across the border, before
making his way to London in 1903.

CHAPTER FOUR

Becoming Lenin

Munich: 1902

Что дѣлать?

Наболѣвшіе вопросы нашего движенія

Н. ЛЕНИНА.

.... „Партійная борьба придаетъ партіи
силу и жизненность, величайшимъ доказа
тельствомъ слабости партіи является ея
расплывчатость и притупленіе рѣзко обозна
ченныхъ границъ, партія укрѣпляется тѣмъ,
что очищаетъ себя"... (Изъ письма Лассаля
къ Марксу отъ 24 іюня 1852 г.).

Цѣна 1 руб.
Preis 2 Mark = 2.50 Francs.

STUTTGART
Verlag von J. H. W. Dietz Nachf. (G. m. b. H.)
1902

The title page of Lenin's 'What Is To Be Done?', 1902

In the autumn of 1902, when a delighted *Iskra* board published details of the mass breakout of activists from Kiev prison, it pointed out that the mission to free them had cost the party 1,795 rubles. Shortly afterwards, the letters of support and donations rolled in from all over Russia and Europe, including £11 from the British-based Friends of Russian Freedom.[1] But Vladimir Ulyanov was never content with such small successes. In September he and Nadya travelled to Zurich to attend a conference of the League of Russian Social Democrats Abroad that had recently been set up on Ulyanov's initiative in hopes of unifying the various revolutionary cells in Russia. He made the most of the opportunity by speaking to a group of Russian émigré students at the university library there, in order to recruit more *Iskra* agents for the cause. There was a desperate lack of revolutionary cadres back in Russia, he told the students, urging them to consider throwing up their studies and return home to take up the struggle. Many of those present that day were infected by the irresistible power of Ulyanov's argument, his charisma and sense of purpose. Such was their romantic idealism about initiating change in Russia that they sat late into the night discussing Ulyanov's message. *Iskra* offered new hope; its message was the gospel truth and Ulyanov the revolutionary movement's prophet. Soon after, some of the students in Zurich who heard Ulyanov that night decided that they would do exactly as he had suggested – give up their studies and go home.[2]

Such willingness to sacrifice personal ambition to the cause of Russian freedom was impressive but Ulyanov was still fuelled by rage against amateurism and the threat of heresy in the *Iskra* movement. His invective was as colourful as it was crude: 'To hell with all conciliators, people of "elusive views" and shilly-shallyers! Better a small fish than a big beetle. Better two or three energetic and wholly devoted people than a dozen dawdlers,' he raged.[3] He was now looking to print every third or fourth copy of *Iskra* in Russia itself, so that a much larger print run could be undertaken, its objective to achieve widespread circulation of its message across the whole of the country. Recently, there had been 'arrests galore' in Voronezh and Ufa and Ulyanov's sense of urgency was escalating. It was of paramount importance to get the *Iskra* group's 'own *reliable* people' into the largest possible number of revolutionary committees. [4]

Since the previous autumn he had, uncharacteristically, been labouring long and hard on a new work – 'What Is To Be Done?'. Censorship prevented its publication in Russia so it was printed in Stuttgart in March 1902, its title a deliberate allusion to Chernyshevsky's novel of the same name that Ulyanov so admired and a clear statement of intent that was unequivocal in its militancy. It had no literary pretensions but rather, in its torrent of vigorous political argument, carried with it the characteristic energy and sense of urgency of its author. At times violently hectoring and witheringly dismissive of political opponents, it veered from the kind of crude invective that Ulyanov was now making his own, to rousing political tub-thumping, to moments of messianic prophecy. On the surface it was written with a clear distinction between 'us' and 'them'. Ulyanov and his shock troops were relentlessly moving forward into history, leaving the rest of the world behind. There was no room for talk of compromise with the enemies Ulyanov saw as threatening his own brand of Marxism and with it party unity. Groups such as Bernstein's Economists, Struve's liberals and the newly established Socialist Revolutionaries (who advocated a return to old-style terrorism in support of their own brand of agrarian socialism) all came under savage attack. While aimed at bringing such heretics into line, Ulyanov's essay also laid out, in suitably conspiratorial language, what the work's subtitle suggested were 'The Burning Questions of Our Movement'. These, in essence, were the need to move away from flabby thinking and with it the lethargy and carelessness of loosely knit political groups, to a highly disciplined and centralised party with a clearly defined programme.

'What Is To Be Done?' would henceforth be taken as Ulyanov's defining interpretation of Russian Marxism, based on the conditions then prevailing in Russia, no matter that there were many hundreds of thousands of words yet to pour from his pen over the next twenty-two years. In Ulyanov's view, Russia was a profoundly backward country where there was as yet no mass movement towards spontaneous revolution; the socialist conscience of the Russian proletariat had still to be properly awoken and marshalled. Even among politicised, urban workers the mentality was still very much that of the 'trade union' and would remain so without proper leadership. Ulyanov had no faith in the mass movement of the proletariat per se as a force for change: if left to its own devices, it would inevitably disintegrate and become petty and preoccupied with everyday bourgeois issues.

Education – or, more correctly, indoctrination – was the key. The masses must be educated into class consciousness and a proper awareness of the battle ahead. But even with this level of political awareness they could achieve nothing in the wider arena without the leadership of an elite, scientifically informed, Marxist intelligentsia, whose role was to organise in the vanguard, in the utmost secrecy. Ulyanov was convinced that true political struggle had to be orchestrated by such a group of hardened, experienced professionals; they would do the thinking for the masses. The proletariat would remain, for him, merely an amorphous mass, the collective instrument of the party's elitist will. Having been indoctrinated by the party into a new, revolutionary class consciousness, the masses would eventually bring into being the great socialist vision:

the dictatorship of the proletariat. This would be the culminating triumph of his all-consuming socialist experiment; but it was political thinking in a test tube and would be achieved without his ever knowing the Russian masses, from whom his long years in exile detached him.

In order for revolutionary change to be carried out effectively no factionalism or in fighting could be countenanced; Ulyanov demanded a slavish uniformity of thought and objectives from all his associates, his uncompromising demands sowing the seeds of considerable dissent and political rivalry later. On this he was adamant and immovable: iron discipline was necessary, he argued, in the defence of Marxist orthodoxy and the Revolution to come. The movement had to operate as a conspiratorial one, in the Jacobin tradition of the French Revolution and its Russian successor, The People's Will, whose inner core would initiate the revolution from above. The vast majority of working-class supporters would, in the end, find their place – just as Nadya had accepted her own role – as willing but anonymous 'cog[s] in the revolutionary machine'.[5] The imposition of a rational and calculated 'Germanic method', inspired in no small part by the Social Democratic movement he had observed in Germany, was a logical extension of Ulyanov's highly pragmatic approach: it was needed to knock the amateurism and indiscipline of the traditional Russian revolutionary spirit out of romantic idealism and into militant line.[6] Ulyanov was there to lead the way, and 'What Is To Be Done?' announced the fact loud and clear. [7]

If the first chaotic two years of the distribution of *Iskra* had proved one thing, it was that training, discipline and tactics were paramount in the underground network in order to sustain the levels of *konspiratsiya* and in this respect 'What Is To Be Done?' provided the blueprint for future activism. A broad, grassroots movement of uncoordinated and undisciplined groups in Russia would remain prey to endless police infiltration and, with it, arrests. Such 'broad democracy', argued Ulyanov, 'amidst the gloom of the autocracy and the domination of the gendarmerie, is nothing more than a *useless and harmful toy*'.[8] His demand for an elitist, professional leadership was highly logical at the time, given the political conditions prevailing in Russia and the high incidence of arrests and imprisonment of activists. There would be no shortage of enthusiastic volunteers for the task ahead, but, as history was to show after 1917, once the edifice of a revolutionary elite was firmly in place, the leap from centralised control to ultimate dictatorship was a very small one.

On paper *Iskra* continued as a collaborative effort, but the publication of 'What Is To Be Done?', even though in it Ulyanov continued to pay lip service to Plekhanov as figurehead of the movement, sounded the death knell of his turbulent partnership with the Marxist old guard. He now began distancing himself from Plekhanov, Axelrod, Martov and Zasulich. It was time to move on, not just theoretically but physically, too. When they had first arrived in Munich the *Iskra* board had deliberately kept a low profile and had stayed away from the Russian émigré colony, hoping they would not attract attention. But their presence in the city had quickly become common knowledge to émigré Russian students, many of whom had become radicalised in Germany. They sought out their revolutionary heroes, following them around and trying to engage in conversation with them in cafés. This in turn attracted the Bavarian police and Ulyanov's German socialist colleagues began worrying that it would, in turn, cause problems for them. A recent agreement between the Russian and Bavarian police on the exchange of political prisoners now put the whole *Iskra* operation in Munich in jeopardy. The Okhrana had tracked down the whereabouts of the *Iskra* board in Schwabing with the help of the German police and *Iskra*'s German printer no longer wanted to take the risk of printing the paper. Ulyanov sensed that arrest was imminent. The group must move to a larger city where they could live in greater anonymity. Plekhanov and Axelrod once more argued vigorously for Switzerland, but, determined to maintain a considerable distance from Plekhanov's interference, Ulyanov insisted on moving the operation to London.

He and Nadya packed up what few possessions they had that were worth taking with them. They sent their books on ahead, care of a Russian colleague, Nikolay Alekseev, who lived near King's Cross, and sold off their few sticks of furniture for a paltry twelve marks. From Munich station they took the train to Stuttgart, and then Frankfurt. They stopped off to admire Cologne's historic medieval cathedral before entraining for Belgium and, from there, the Channel crossing from Ostend to Dover. Before leaving mainland Europe they spent a couple of days in Liège and Brussels, where an old friend of Nadya's, Nikolay Meshcheryakov, showed them round the city. Having eagerly anticipated meeting his political hero, Meshcheryakov was disappointed that Ulyanov did not cut a more romantic figure. He had 'the most ordinary, Russian, rather Asiatic face', he recalled. 'There was only one striking thing about it – the eyes. There was no evading their gaze. They were extraordinarily penetrating.'[9] Ulyanov's interest had been quickly aroused when, in Liège, he heard about a recent clash between police and striking workers and, eager to know more about the ongoing tensions in the workers' district where it had occurred, he went to visit the scene of the confrontation. He loved being in the thick of such things. When Plekhanov passed through some months later, ever the aesthete all he wanted to do, noted Meshcheryakov, was to see the art galleries.

There was now very little time for culture in Ulyanov's scheme of things. As a political leader he had passed a point of transition; having created through his political writings a rationale for the emergent Russian Social Democratic Labour Party, that had been founded in 1898 during his Siberian exile, he now needed to assert his dominion over it. With the battle for ideological leadership in the party escalating, he took issue with Plekhanov's constant critiques of his editorials in *Iskra*, tartly accusing him of making their 'common work impossible';[10] the discord between them was briefly patched up but resurfaced again later in 1902 as their personal relationship degenerated.

The time had come for Vladimir Ulyanov to clearly set out his stall independently of Plekhanov and the old guard; and to do so he needed to adopt a consistent and unmistakable identity of his own. For years, like all political dissidents, in the tradition of *konspiratsiya* he had used a confusing succession of pseudonyms in his work (he employed more than 150 during the years to 1917).[11] These ranged from mere initials (including variant groups of his own such as V., V.I., V.U., V. UL., V. Il.) to names that he particularly favoured, such as Tulin, William Frey (interchangeable with a Germanised form as Wilhelm Frei), Meyer, Richter, Karpov and Petrov. V. Ilyn or Ilin (from his patronymic Ilyich) was a favoured one; he even signed some letters by his nickname *starik* (the old man). But by early 1901, Ulyanov had taken up a new pseudonym that had gained favour within *Iskra* as the year progressed: Lenin.

It had been January that year when he had first written to Plekhanov in Zurich signing himself 'Lenin' and in December he published the first four chapters of a pamphlet on the agrarian question in *Zarya* under the same name. He favoured the name again in March 1902, when 'What Is To Be Done?' appeared under the same pseudonym – 'N. Lenin', – the 'N.' signifying literally 'nothing' but widely misread in the West as representing the name Nikolay. However, even Nadezhda Krupskaya was unable, after her husband's death, to explain where he got the name from. It certainly bore echoes of other similar two-syllable pseudonyms that became fashionable in the party – beginning with Plekhanov's early use of 'Volgin' (from the River Volga – a fact which to many suggested Lenin's was taken from the River Lena in Siberia, as a reverential nod to his then mentor) and ending with Josef Dzhugashvili's adoption of Stalin in 1913. Whatever the origins, there was, one might say, a pleasing congruence about all of them.[12]

To his wife, Vladimir Ilyich Ulyanov would affectionately remain Volodya in private, as he would to his family; publicly, Nadya would increasingly refer to him as Vladimir Ilyich or just plain Ilyich, the use of the patronymic being at a remove from the familiarity of his first name yet still retaining a degree of respect. And, indeed, although the official name of Lenin rapidly gained currency at home and abroad, Lenin's close comrades among the Bolsheviks would likewise address him as Ilyich. As the years went on, particularly after he came to power, Lenin would also become – for the many millions who adored their 'great leader and teacher' but never met him – simply Ilyich.

By 1902, history for Lenin, as for his predecessor the Nihilist Andrey Zhelyabov, was moving too slowly. It was time for him to give it 'a push'. 'Give us an organization of revolutionaries,' he exhorted in 'What Is To Be Done?', 'and we shall overturn the whole of Russia.'[13] This clarion call certainly struck a nerve with activists back home such as Lenin's fellow Siberian exile Gleb Krzhizhanovsky, who greeted his messianic vision for the revolutionary movement with huge enthusiasm. 'What Is To Be Done?' undoubtedly came at an opportune moment, tapping into the current thirst among the intelligentsia for active work in Russia after years of repression. Its treatise on organisation offered the movement a much-needed programme for practical supremacy over its ill-equipped opponents. But while devotees rapidly inculcated its principles and its unmistakable Leninist political jargon, others were more sceptical about the less than democratic arguments it contained for a revolutionary elite.[14] Nevertheless, committees in the major cities such as St Petersburg and Moscow, Nizhniy Novgorod, Saratov and Kharkov began officially acknowledging *Iskra* as the 'leading organ of the party',[15] publishing declarations of loyalty not just to Lenin's theoretical hegemony but also his leadership of the *Iskra* organisation. Lenin had shown he was a man of serious intent and action, not just an empty theorist of revolution. 'What Is To Be Done?' was his preparation for the revolution that he was convinced was to come. And now he was about to carry the movement towards revolution a stage further, in a new venue: London, the very 'stronghold of capitalism'.[16]

As Lenin and Nadya made their way across Europe on a succession of trains to their next, transitory home, in St Petersburg the Okhrana opened a new file – no. 872 – on the subject of one N. Lenin, having noted the publication of his pamphlet abroad and the 'great sensation' that 'What Is To Be Done?' had aroused. In brackets below this comment a dutiful officer had added, 'This, undoubtedly, is the pseudonym of Ulyanov'. But Lenin was now the man to watch.[7]

CHAPTER FIVE

Dr and Mrs Richter

London: 1902–1903

Holford Square, Lenin's London home 1902–3

On a dismal, foggy morning in April 1902 a shabby looking and undistinguished couple emerged from London's Charing Cross Station into the hectic thoroughfare of the Strand. Dr and Mrs Jacob Richter, fresh from the leafier environs of the Bavarian city of Munich, arriving, as ever, on false passports, found their senses immediately assaulted by the hubbub of the great British metropolis and the stink of a highly industrialised city. Outside, the air was thick with the smoke of thousands of chimneys as the busy thoroughfares lay before them suspended in the soupy gloom of an English fog. London, the great Leviathan, had a population of around 6.6 million at the time, double that of Paris. It was a shock to the system for Lenin and Nadya after the solitude of Shushenskoe and the relatively bucolic delights of Schwabing.

At Charing Cross they were extremely glad to see the familiar face of

Nikolay Alekseev, a colleague from Russia, who had fled Siberian exile in December 1899 and was living in Frederick Street, off Gray's Inn Road. Alekseev escorted the couple to the busy Pentonville Road, near King's Cross Station. This noisy and overcrowded part of north London, with its crush of horse-drawn omnibuses and trams and the nearby rackety open cutting of the King's Cross to Farringdon Circle Line, was to be their home for the next year.

England – and notably London – had a long tradition of offering refuge and freedom of speech to the politically oppressed. Russian and German political exiles such as Marx, Engels and Herzen had taken refuge here in the 1840s–50s, as too had the revolutionists Louis Blanc from France, Lajos Kossuth from Hungary and Giuseppe Mazzini from Italy later in the century. Such was London's reputation for political and racial tolerance that the Italian anarchists who arrived towards the end of the nineteenth century called it 'the most comfortable place in the world'.[1] Much of the British sympathy for the Russians stemmed from a respect for their culture and literature and a contempt for the repressive nature of tsarism. The welcome was extended even to perceived extremists such as Prince Peter Kropotkin, the father of Russian anarchism, who turned out to be a kindly and genial old man who lived amidst piles of books in a tiny house in Highgate.[2] Political assassins such as Sergey Kravchinsky (also known as Stepniak), who in 1878 had murdered the much-hated head of the Russian Corps of Gendarmes in St Petersburg, had also been given refuge, seen as a romantic figure fighting a cruel and despotic system. He and Russian émigrés like him were taken under the wing of The Society of Friends of Russian Freedom – established by British socialists and sympathisers in 1890 – which campaigned tirelessly for an end to political repression in Russia. The society did much to expose flogging in the Siberian prison camps, fundraised for Russian famine victims and strikers and protested the persecution of Russian Jews, and in 1892 even the construction of Russian prison ships at British yards on the Clyde. It frequently challenged apologists for the tsarist regime in the British press and did its best to ensure that the public were well informed about the political situation inside Russia. It all belied the claim of the tsarist apologist Olga Novikoff that 'as a rule the only thing known in England about Russians is that they take lemon with their tea'.[3]

The British police, and in particular Special Branch, created in 1887 to monitor Irish Fenian terrorist activity, took a jaundiced but tolerant view of 'all the foreign scallywags in the world' that seemed to be congregating in London in the 1900s. Half-hearted attempts by the government to control the entry of aliens in 1892 and 1894 had not been successful. And although the British police had been engaged in 'shadowing' or 'housing' the activities of foreigners in their refugee clubs and cafés across the city from the 1880s, so long as they didn't cause trouble British officialdom remained indifferent and they were left alone.[4] The Okhrana tried hard to solicit the help of Special Branch in flushing out Russian political émigrés – frequently advising them that some undesirable or other was on his way to England. But often, as Detective Inspector Brust of Scotland Yard later recalled, 'a wholly false and perfectly dreadful catalogue of crimes would be tacked on to a man's record with a view to earning his disfavour with the British police', a tactic that proved self-defeating, for the British 'attached not the slightest importance to what they said'.[5]

By the 1900s London had a thriving Russo-Jewish community in the poor East End communities of Stepney, Whitechapel and Hackney, many immigrants having arrived in the 1880s in the wake of the wave of pogroms provoked by the assassination of Alexander II. Here, among the immigrant slipper makers and tailors, cabinetmakers, seamstresses, skin dressers and boot makers, bow makers and milliners who crammed into the dilapidated tenements of Whitechapel, there lurked an inner circle of highly politicised Jewish revolutionaries. Yet, despite a period of serious and violent anarchist activity in the 1890s emanating from the East End, Britain continued to hold to its traditional, liberal reputation of offering safe refuge to the politically oppressed. It was noted with almost respectful amusement that the new Russian émigrés, 'even of the higher order', were fundamentally 'socialists at heart' and had a propensity to 'preach the "Religion of the Future" with the fervour of the Apostles'.[6] The British could not help but admire the passion of their commitment and the Russian ability to endure suffering. The educated Russian exile was seen as 'poor, and noble and proud', having little 'but his books and few enjoyments'.

The sober looking Lenin and Nadya, when they arrived, therefore must have seemed the archetypal new immigrant, modest in manner and frugal in their ways, yet passionately Russian in their socialist beliefs. Although they now found themselves in the far freer environs of London, old habits died hard and in their correspondence Lenin and Nadya continued to refer to their location as 'Munich' or 'Prague' in a rather tepid attempt to confuse the Russian secret police. Soon they realised that, with none of the usual demands for identity papers made wherever they went, work for the party in London could not have been better 'from the conspiratorial point of view'.[7]

The couple's first lodgings – a pokey bed-sitting room in a row of terraced houses off Gray's Inn Road, at 20 Sidmouth Street, were abandoned within a week for something slightly better. There was one thing Lenin firmly rejected at the outset and that was any talk of living in a revolutionary commune with his comrades Martov and Zasulich, who were soon to arrive from Germany. He could not work with the noise and distraction of other people around him other than his self-effacing wife (and mother-in-law when she later joined them).[8] The British weather, with its indeterminate drizzling rain and endless fogs, had a profoundly depressing effect on him at first. Lenin disliked the place: 'at first glance, it makes a foul impression', he told Plekhanov in Geneva.[9]

But the situation improved within days, when another Russian couple, Konstantin Takhtarev and his wife Apollinariya, who had fled to London in 1898, helped Lenin and Nadya find their way around and were instrumental, around 23 April, in persuading the landlady of no. 30 Holford Square into taking them as tenants. The new lodgings seemed the perfect solution. They were only a few minutes' walk from Alekseev in Frederick Street and, although it might still be a poor, overcrowded area within sight and smell of the choking smoke and din of King's Cross and Pentonville Road, it was decidedly more welcoming. The house, one in a row of brick-built Victorian terraced houses fronted by iron railings, faced a communal garden square. The slums of King's Cross might be a couple of minutes walk away but the denizens of Holford Square considered themselves decent, respectable people.

Lenin and Nadya's new landlady was forty-eight-year-old Mrs Emma Louise Yeo, a dressmaker, who had been widowed only a few weeks earlier. Living at home with her were a daughter and four sons – three of whom worked as printer compositors.[10] With the loss of her husband's wages she had decided to take in lodgers, but after her first talk with the strange Dr Richter about rooms, Mrs Yeo, so one of her sons later recalled, was so worried by his 'foreignness' and broken English that she fainted.[11]

In return for twenty shillings a week rent Lenin and Nadya had the use of two small rooms on the first floor, one facing the street, the other the back yard. The back room served as both kitchen and dining room and was also where Nadya's mother Elisaveta Vasil'evna slept when she joined them later in the year. The other was where Lenin worked and he and Nadya slept, crammed in with their books and writing materials. They had very little luggage and as the rooms were unfurnished had to go out and buy the minimum of cheap furniture on the Tottenham Court Road: two deal tables, a couple of chairs, a pair of iron bedsteads and a few pieces of cutlery and crockery. They also bought linoleum to cover the floors but there were no pictures or decorations.[12] Lenin and Nadya were now paid workers for the party and living on very slender means – they had only ten shillings to live on after they had paid their rent.[13] Everything struck them as being very expensive in London. There were no concessions to comfort of any kind: they had to bring their coal and water up from the basement and carry their dirty washing-up water back downstairs to dispose of in the yard outside. The family laughed at Dr Richter's inability to master the art of lighting a coal fire in an iron grate (a quite different procedure from a Russian wood-burning stove) and Mrs Yeo had to show him how to do it.

Once settled at Holford Square, Nadya was anxious to cook their own food in order to save money. The kind of food on the menu in local working-class restaurants where they had been obliged to eat during their first few days – oxtail stew, skate fried in lard and indigestible cakes – turned their Russian stomachs, used as they were to very plain fare. Soon Nadya was cooking as best she could on the open fire in their rooms or a tiny primus stove. When she encountered domestic difficulties she asked 'Muzza' – as she called the motherly Mrs Yeo – for help in her few words of English, but in the main Lenin was the mediator with their landlady, gratefully receiving instruction in the ways of English shopping. He never took umbrage and was always willing to learn.[14]

He needed to be, for Mrs Yeo was a paragon of bourgeois respectability. She might have been alarmed at the strange habits of her 'German' tenants, as she thought them to be, but she was not reticent when it came to laying down the law about acceptable standards of behaviour: Where was Mrs Richter's wedding ring? she asked. It was not the done thing to be without one. Takhtarev assured her that the couple were indeed married according to Russian law. But whatever was Dr Richter doing hanging curtains – at her insistence – on their bare windows, on a Sunday of all days? Mrs Yeo did not approve, any more than she did when she saw Dr Richter walking across Holford Square on a Sunday morning with an unwrapped loaf of French bread under his arm. She wasted no time in telling him such things were not done in England. In every other respect, however, as Leonard Yeo later insisted, the Richters kept themselves to themselves and were 'good, quiet tenants', although 'completely unused to English ways'.[15] They were always respectful to his mother and always paid their rent on time. 'Mrs Richter' was a sweet, kind lady who became very fond of their tabby cat, talked to it often in Russian and taught it to shake hands and miaow good morning to her. As for the studious Dr Richter, Leonard could not fail to notice his highly educated manner and quickness of thought and action – 'his face was alive with great intelligence', though in every other respect he seemed a 'most ordinary little man'.[16]

As time went on Mrs Yeo became increasingly alarmed at the procession of foreigners with peculiar black beards coming 'in heavy top coats' for meetings at the Richters' rooms in the evening – so many that there weren't enough chairs. To her horror, they sat on the floor. Even more perplexing was the fact that they were all too poor to eat or drink and did nothing but sit and talk late into the night. Words, indulged in in the free environment of London, were, it seemed, sufficient food for them.[17] But such visitations caused trouble for Mrs Yeo with her neighbours. They didn't like all the comings and goings of these suspicious foreigners in their respectable neighbourhood. And the visits had markedly increased with the arrival of Martov and Zasulich a couple of weeks later. Alekseev rented five small rooms on two floors of a house at no. 14 Sidmouth Street for all of them, to serve as a base for *Iskra* agents visiting from Europe, a clearing house for illegal propaganda and an editorial office. Here they also produced crudely faked passports for comrades from Russia. The rooms quickly became untidy and shambolic, the smell of boiling soup pervading the air. Lenin visited every day for editorial meetings but was quick to retreat to the Spartan and orderly conditions back at Holford Square. When Ivan Babushkin, who had just escaped from Ekaterinoslav prison by sawing through the bars of his cell, joined the commune in September he did his best to clean and tidy the rooms, but grumbled that 'The Russian intellectual is always dirty. He needs a servant as he is himself incapable of tidying up.'[18] Babushkin's tidy up did not help and the other working-class tenants in the house remained hostile to the presence of the Russians. A couple of months later, the landlord at Sidmouth Street gave notice to the commune, having become irritated with all the scruffy foreigners – who bedded down on the landings and floors and filled the place with the stink of their cigarettes. The commune moved a few streets away, to 23 Percy Circus, very close to Lenin's lodgings on Holford Square.[19]

The strongest argument for bringing the *Iskra* operation to London had been the presence in Clerkenwell, a short walk from Lenin's lodgings, of the socialist-run Twentieth Century Press, which was sympathetic to the Russian cause and willing to print their journal. The press operated from a cramped and run down eighteenth-century building at 37 Clerkenwell Green that had been a centre of socialist activism since the days of the Chartists in the 1840s, when working men's clubs had met here. Political demonstrations and trade union rallies had been held on the green outside. From the 1850s the press had been a supporter of the work of Karl Marx when he settled in London and the first Marxist group in the country, the British Social Democratic Federation, was established there in 1881, one of its early members being the socialist writer and painter William Morris. The Twentieth Century Press had printed some of the first translations of Marxist theory, as well as a range of speeches and socialist pamphlets by leading continental socialists. In 1884 it established its own weekly journal, *Justice*, edited from the 1890s by the able and likeable Harry Quelch.[20] After being approached by Alekseev, as well as the German émigré Max Beer, to whom Lenin had brought a letter of introduction, Quelch had no hesitation in offering Lenin the use of their facilities. Upstairs, a corner of the printing room was partitioned off to create a tiny editorial office where Lenin could read and correct proofs. But, as he later recalled, there was only just enough room for himself, a desk and a chair.[21] Here the 'small, stocky, ginger-haired young man' was often observed hard at work by Quelch's son, Tom.[22]

Once the editorial work was complete, the paper itself had to be sent to an East End printer for the Cyrillic letters to be typeset by *Iskra*'s own compositor, Blumenfeld (one of the escapees from the Kiev prison). It was then returned to Clerkenwell Green for running off on the Twentieth Century Press's flatbed machine. But the whole operation of the press in such premises seemed a very modest affair to Osip Pyatnitsky, given that Britain was a free country. Here was a British socialist organisation producing a journal – *Justice* – not much bigger than their own, illegal one.[23]

On arrival in London, Lenin wasted no time in accessing the facilities of 'the richest library in the world' – the central, domed Reading Room at the British Museum in Bloomsbury.[24] Before leaving Munich, he had, with his usual punctiliousness, carefully checked the maps of London to work out the quickest route on foot to the library from the Pentonville area where he knew he would be living. This was as much out of financial necessity

– to save money on buses – as it was for personal fitness. Through his British socialist contacts, he was given a letter of recommendation by Isaac Mitchell, secretary of the General Federation of Trade Unions, and made his application in late April, explaining on the form that he had come from Russia to 'study the land question'. A British Museum reader's card no. A 72453 was duly issued to Dr Jacob Richter, LL.D, on 29 April. The library was Lenin's lifeline during his time in London. His daily visits gave both shape and routine to his life; without them he could not function and became highly stressed and irritable. He retreated to the sanity and peace of the library whenever he wished to escape the endless stream of 'comrades from Russia' and elsewhere who regularly beat a path to his door and who would 'pester him in the Russian fashion' for hours at a time. 'What do they think we're here for – a holiday!' he would say in annoyance.[25] Such encounters always deteriorated into interminable debates and the 'émigré gossip and empty chatter' that he so despised. All he wanted to do was lock himself away and get on with his own serious theoretical studies, leaving the bulk of the day-to-day editorial work on *Iskra* to Martov.[26] By September 1902, Lenin was complaining of a 'crowd of people here and altogether too much commotion', with yet more arriving in the next few days, a reference to the escapees from Kiev prison who were now on their way to England to seek him out.[27] But in the British Museum, in the comfort of a solid leather chair and with a desk complete with ink and blotting paper and reading lamp, he could set to work uninterrupted.

Marx, Blanc and Mazzini had all made use of this oasis of peace and scholarship during their time in London and officials at the British Museum would come to remember the modest Russian well. Fellow Russian émigré Theodore Rothstein often encountered Lenin at the library and was impressed by his 'amazing capacity for work'; the attendants too remembered how Mr Richter 'simply swallows books'.[28] No one, they asserted, asked for such vast quantities. At lunchtime, Lenin would stop for a brief meal at a nearby café in Great Russell Street before walking back for his regular 1.30 meeting with Martov and Zasulich at Sidmouth Street; then home and many more hours of reading and writing.

There was, however, one problem that had immediately made itself felt on arrival in London and that was the standard of Lenin and Nadya's English. It was one thing translating Sidney and Beatrice Webb on the page with the help of dictionaries, as they had done in Shushenskoe, but quite another attuning the ear to the peculiar cadences of English, especially as spoken by the working classes. 'We found we could not understand a thing, nor could anybody understand us,' remembered Nadya.[29] Vera Zasulich never even bothered to try to learn English, shut away as she was with other transient Russians in Sidmouth Street. But Lenin, determined as always to do things properly, resolved to improve his. He placed a small ad in the *Athenaeum* magazine: 'A Russian LL.D (and his wife) would like to exchange Russian lessons for English with an English Gentleman (or Lady).'[30] A clerk called Williams and a workman, Mr Young, responded, as did the venerable looking Mr Henry Rayment (whom Alekseev thought not unlike Charles Darwin in appearance), who worked for the publishers George Bell & Sons. Lenin appears to have developed a particular friendship with Rayment, whose aptitude for several foreign languages, including Russian, proved invaluable.[31]

Meanwhile, the quickest way of learning the language was to go out and about and hear it as it was spoken. Speakers' Corner at Hyde Park on a Sunday morning was particularly popular with Lenin and Nadya. They were sometimes accompanied by the British socialist Zelda Kahan, who noticed how intently Lenin listened to the speakers at the Atheist and Socialist platforms, as well as the Christian Evidence and Salvation Army ones, in order to access British socialist thinking of the day.[32] One particular speaker with an Irish accent was easier for him to understand than the others; it may well have been the young George Bernard Shaw, who often spoke in Hyde Park at that time in defence of civil liberties. But often, as Kahan observed, Lenin took far more note of the behaviour and reactions of the crowd listening than the speakers themselves.[33]

Having already read much on the economic history of Britain and the work of Marx and Engels on the subject, Lenin arrived well informed, eager to study London and its life with the forensic attention of a scientist. Living London and its working people were of far more interest to him than the dead history of its museums and galleries, which he found tedious. Wherever he went Lenin was eager to get to the heart of the working classes and their language and culture – in pubs, in clubs and churches and at socialist meetings. Once he had learned to accept the vagaries of the English weather, he was excited and impressed by the immensity of London and loved riding the open-topped omnibuses. It was not the city's tourist sights that attracted him but, rather, the sharp contrasts the city provided for study of Britain's 'two nations' – the rich and poor.[34] But he and Nadya knew that not everything could be seen from the top of a bus. Before long, having studied the maps in great detail, they were out exploring the working-class areas of the city on foot. They often went walking down the filthy, winding backstreets with washing strung up across them, where pale, sickly children played in the gutter and drunken workmen consorted with prostitutes outside cheap public houses. They visited the reading rooms for poor immigrants (such as the Free Russian Library in Church Lane, off the Commercial Road, which stayed open until ten at night). When they got hungry and could afford it they, and the commune at Sidmouth Street, ate in cheap restaurants for workers. They came to like the staple of fish and chips, bought at the Little Inn Restaurant, or Adams Chop House on Gray's Inn Road.[35] Indeed, it turned out that Lenin knew the backstreets of London better even than his English tutor, Mr Rayment. He took him out to Whitechapel, a part of London that Rayment had never ventured to, to see at first hand how the immigrant Russo-Jewish poor lived. He also walked the streets at night with Takhtarev, observing the throng of traders with their market stalls lit up by naphtha tubes; the traffic was extraordinary, the energy and vitality of London life – albeit capitalistic – was thrilling. For here, all around him, Lenin could grasp at the raw material of socialist argument and mould it to his own purpose.[36]

Although Lenin was not a drinker he realised that the public house culture of London and its music halls was an important facet of working-class life. Not far from Holford Square, the Pindar of Wakefield on Gray's Inn Road, with its 'Aba Daba Music Hall' in a room at the back was conveniently placed for the occasional meeting with Russian colleagues visiting Sidmouth Street. The Crown and Woolpack and Old Red Lion on nearby St John Street also became regular venues for the Russians. Sometimes Lenin bought himself lunch at the Crown on Clerkenwell Green opposite his *Iskra* offices and looked in at its music hall. The culture of popular musical theatre intrigued him – not just in London, but also in Munich, Paris, Zurich and many of the other cities he visited. There was something about the subversiveness of British music hall that particularly appealed, though when it came to translating his response into words Lenin was hamstrung by the clumsy, dead hand of jargon that infected all his work: 'In the London music halls there is a certain satirical or skeptical attitude towards the conventional,' he wrote rather starchily, that 'attempts to turn conventions inside out, to distrust it somewhat, to point up the illogicality of the everyday.'[37]

Throughout their long exile getting out into the countryside was the most important aspect of Lenin and Nadya's life – the countryside was free and whenever the weather was fine and they had the time they grasped the opportunity of fresh air and exercise at their favourite haunt of Primrose Hill. It was only sixpence on the bus from King's Cross and they could visit Karl Marx's grave in nearby Highgate Cemetery before standing on the hilltop to view the whole of the 'smoke wreathed city' stretched out below them.[38] But this wasn't sufficient for the energetic Lenin and often they took their sandwiches and went beyond the suburbs in search of field paths into the real English countryside. All that good clean air went to Lenin's head and, as he told his mother, he had to lie down and recover. He was perpetually disappointed that his lethargic fellow exiles did not follow their example: 'we are the only ones of the comrades here who are studying the country round London'.[39]

Another essential component of Lenin's life in London was seeking out political debate. There was no shortage of clubs and discussion groups for foreign immigrants in the East End; nearer to Lenin at Holford Square there was the Working Men's Institute and Club – better known as the Communist Club – at 49 Tottenham Street, off Tottenham Court Road. It had been established back in 1840 as the 'Educational Society for German Working Men' offering a main room for conferences as well as smaller meeting rooms, a library, billiard room, card rooms and a cheap restaurant that sold good German beer. Always full and buzzing with debate, it was increasingly frequented by Russian émigrés from all over London by the time Lenin arrived.[40]

Another venue for political debate to which Lenin was attracted was Toynbee Hall in Whitechapel. Established as a settlement house in 1884, where volunteers offered advice and practical help to the area's largely immigrant Irish and Jewish population, it had become an important rallying point for social reform in Britain. Its 'Thursday Smoking Conferences' attracted political refugees who worked in the East End or the local docks, whose consuming passion was 'Marxist Revolutionary Socialism'.[41] One particular evening in November 1902, the subject of 'Our Foreign Policy' was to be debated by journalist and politician John Morley. As the members gathered in the thick fug of cigarette smoke, a shabby looking stranger with a short reddish beard, who was 'Oriental in appearance', took his place among them. One of the settlement workers, William Bowman, thought the man looked 'sick and impoverished' and took no further notice of him until, after Morley had spoken, the man, announcing himself as Richter, got up to speak in broken

English. 'What is the use of you coming to the East End and talking about your foreign policy?' he challenged Morley. 'Go down to Limehouse or Shadwell and see how the people live. Their slums, bad food, low wages, impoverishment, degradation and prostitution – that's where your foreign policy should lie. They are the victims of your capitalist organisation.' By the time Lenin had finished delivering a catalogue of similar criticism of the English social system everyone had taken notice of him and a heated but friendly debate ensued.

Some days later Dean Robinson, head of Balliol House, where some of the Toynbee Hall volunteers lived, announced that he had 'invited that Russian fellow, Richter' to tea on the coming Saturday and asked Bowman to join them. Lenin turned up, looking as shabby as ever. He tucked into the plate of toasted buttered muffins offered him with such enthusiasm that it was clear to everyone that he was very hungry. He said he found English food unpleasant, but he liked the muffins. Despite wrinkling his nose if anyone smoked at 30 Holford Square – though he had to tolerate his mother-in-law's occasional cigarette – he happily accepted a pipe as the three men drew their chairs round the fire to smoke and talk. Once more, and despite his broken English, the ever confident 'Richter', self-appointed champion of the British dispossessed, launched into a highly articulate attack on British imperialism, insisting that it would inevitably 'dissolve'. And when that happened he warned, 'you will have to live on your own industry or else starve'. As for organised religion, that, in his view, was 'an opiate used by the capitalist classes to dope the people'. The Bible was 'just a lot of old Jewish fairy-tales . . . of no value to anyone'. As Christian pacifists, the mild-mannered Dean Robinson and Bowman were rather disconcerted by Richter's arrogant, if platitudinous, statement. There was no mistaking his insistence that *his* point of view was the right one. Nor did he make any attempt to conceal his distaste for their own brand of socialist evangelism. As he rose to leave in order, so he said, to visit his 'friends down in Limehouse', Richter reiterated his conviction that no great change in society would ever be brought about 'without the shedding of blood and revolution'; soon it would be the turn of Russia – and Britain too – he was convinced of that.[42]

Wherever else he went around London, Lenin was equally scathing about the speakers he heard, many of whom, in his opinion, 'talked rot'. To his mind, a large part of educated British socialists were in fact supporters of the liberal bourgeoisie, isolated from the mass of the proletariat. (Strangely, he does not seem to have noted his own isolation from the Russian masses at this time.) He dismissed trade unionism in Britain as parochial and petty, but he was impressed by the class instincts of the British workers who attended some of the meetings he went to. Socialism, he asserted, was 'simply oozing from them' and in their responses they laid bare 'the essence of Capitalist Society'.[43] Nevertheless, Lenin did have some contact with members of the British Social Democratic Federation apart from Harry Quelch at Clerkenwell Green – he often visited Theodore Rothstein at his home at 6 Clapton Square in Hackney. Zelda Kahan (as well as being Rothstein's sister-in-law and a leading light in the Whitechapel branch of the British Social Democratic Federation) also lived there and remembered Lenin's visits with affection. She recalled his fondness for Theodore and her sister Anne's children and the unself-consciousness with which he played with them. On one occasion she found him 'playing at bears' with them, 'covered with a fur coat beneath the table'.[44] Although the Rothsteins and Kahans become good friends, Lenin made no attempt to integrate with other British socialists while in London. And so British Socialists in 1902–3 remained largely oblivious to his presence in London: Richter aka Lenin was just one of many shadowy Russians who came and went at that time.

Meanwhile, the ardours of Lenin and Nadya's life at the centre of *Iskra* and the emergent party took their toll. By the summer the draft programme of the RSDLP was finally published in *Iskra* but by now Lenin was suffering from extreme exhaustion. His nerves, he said, were 'worn to shreds'.[45] So, in the second half of June, he took a month's holiday at Loguivy, in Brittany, on the northern coast of France, where he met up with his mother from Russia and his sister Anna from Berlin. He enjoyed his stay, paid for by his mother and sister, but was still under par when he returned to London at the end of July. The stress of keeping contact with the network of *Iskra* agents was unending. He admitted to feeling 'all done up' and in a letter to a colleague in Zurich, on 4 August, poured out his frustrations about the network. He was being driven to distraction by criticism of the poor quality of some of his agents. It was nothing less than a tragedy that the movement, for lack of numbers, had 'recruited too "lightly"'. He was frustrated that he had not been able to exert personal control over the calibre, selection and training of every last recruit: the '"creaking" of the machinery', he declared was causing him enormous stress. But there was nothing for it: agents volunteering to go into Russia undercover had to be taken on trust:

More often than not we can't even get letters, and *in nine cases out of ten* (I speak from experience) all our plans in regard to the future activity of the 'agent' end in smoke *as soon as the frontier is crossed*, and the agent muddles along just anyhow. Believe me, I am literally losing all faith in routes, plans, etc., made here, because I know beforehand that nothing will come of it all. We 'have to' make frantic efforts *doing (for lack of suitable people)* other people's jobs. In order to appoint agents, to look after them, to *answer* for them, to unite and guide them *in practice* – it is necessary to be everywhere, to rush about, to see all of them on the job, at work.[46]

The realities of the organisation's failings seemed only to underline even more the arguments of 'What Is To Be Done?' for a dedicated team of 'practical organisers and leaders' to take over all but the most basic initiatives.

★   ★   ★

All was quiet in Holford Square one early morning in October 1902 when a hansom cab drew up outside no. 30. A young man with a mass of thick curly hair, wrapped in a cloak and wearing pince-nez approached the front door and knocked, very loudly and purposefully, at it. Alert to the coded knocks employed in the Russian underground, Nadezhda Krupskaya leapt out of bed and opened the door. There before her, all the way from Verkholensk in far Siberia, from which he had escaped several months before, stood one of the party's brightest and most ambitious new activists. She knew him by his code name 'Pero' – the pen; his real name was Lev Bronstein but he became better known to history as Leon Trotsky. A few months before he had made his getaway from his place of exile hidden under a load of hay in a peasant cart, leaving behind a dummy in his bed. With a change of clothes and false passport provided by friends in the underground at Irkutsk, he had made his way to the Trans-Siberian Railway and travelled to *Iskra* regional headquarters in Samara, from where Gleb Krzhizhanovsky had sent him on to Vienna, Zurich and finally London.

Trotsky had no compunction about disturbing the household early in the morning; he'd already woken Axelrod up in the middle of the night in Zurich. He was twenty-two and bursting with self-confidence and had come a long way to meet Lenin, having being sent on Krzhizhanovsky's recommendation. Axelrod had given him enough money to get to London via Paris, but he was now penniless. Nadya went down to settle up with the cabbie as Lenin emerged, half asleep, from his bed. Soon he was engrossed in the arrival's news from Russia as they sat over tea and a frugal breakfast. Lenin interrogated Trotsky on the strengths and weaknesses of the Russian underground as he had observed it in Kiev, Kharkov and Poltava (where Krzhizhanovsky had sent him prior to his departure). He was, as ever, particularly anxious to hear of the effects on the party of the conflict created by the heretical Bernstein's Economists as well as the activities of the newly emergent Socialist Revolutionaries, who were threatening a renewed terror campaign. Trotsky told how he and his colleagues in prison and exile had studied Lenin's every written word, especially his *Development of Capitalism in Russia,* and were impressed by the skill with which he marshalled a wealth of statistical evidence.[47]

Trotsky returned the next day, having spent the night at the commune in Sidmouth Street, to be taken by his mentor on a walking tour of the capitalist sights of London – the Tower of London and Westminster Abbey, heartland of 'the enemy' – which epitomised the aristocracy and old order that Lenin so despised. Lenin was intent on sounding out Trotsky's political and intellectual acumen and his clever young protégé was quick to respond. Later Lenin took him for a subject lesson in that strange brand of British conservatism – prevalent even among the working classes – that allowed socialist sympathies to coexist alongside religious belief. In a Socialist Church at Seven Sisters in Tottenham, north London, they observed how exhortations to God for an end to the gulf between rich and poor came hot on the heels of political speeches on social revolution, as though the congregation were hedging their bets by keeping a foot in both the temporal and the spiritual camps.[48]

Although he spent most of his time in the company of Lenin, Trotsky did not fail to notice the self-effacing role of Nadya, forever hunched over her desk organising contacts, issuing instructions, coding and decoding letters to and from the *Iskra* board. He remembered how there was always a particular 'faint smell of paper warmed up over a flame' in her room. The 'state of rank disorder' at Sidmouth Street in which Martov and Zasulich lived was a very marked contrast. He could not help but be charmed by the endearing idiosyncrasies of Zasulich, whom he found an 'exceptional person', although her and Martov's slovenly habits around food left much to be desired. Puzzlingly, Vera appeared to live on only two things: tobacco and thin slices of ham spread with copious amounts of mustard.[49] Poor Vera, observed Trotsky: she found writing such a torment, and public speaking was hard for her too. Her 'diffuse radicalism, her subjectivity and her turbulence' were all irritants to the punctilious Lenin. She paced about in threadbare slippers and shapeless, crudely made clothing, forever rolling cigarettes (as too did Martov), showering herself and visitors with ash and discarding her cigarette ends wherever the whim took her, while Martov absent-mindedly dropped tobacco in the sugar bowl. Both were romantic, old-school bohemians who were rapidly becoming redundant in the new, hard-edged party envisaged by Lenin.[50]

While Trotsky was in London, Lenin encouraged him to give a public lecture at Whitechapel where he debated politics in Russian with other exiles. Lenin himself took part in a workers' study circle for Russian immigrants set up by Alekseev, in which he carefully took them through the recently finalised programme of the Russian Social Democratic Labour Party.[51] In November he gave another lecture at a Whitechapel workers' club in which he attacked the programme and tactics of the Socialist Revolutionaries. The following 21 March, 1903, he took great pleasure in addressing a meeting at the New Alexandra Hall in Whitechapel on the anniversary of the Paris Commune, which he so greatly admired.[52] And then there was a May Day rally in 1903 at the Alexandra Palace, at which Lenin was one of the speakers who addressed the crowd in their own languages of Russian, German, Italian, Polish, French and Spanish.

Despite Trotsky's youth and inexperience, Lenin was extremely impressed by his energy and his abilities. More importantly, he sensed that this forceful young man had grasped the essential, conspiratorial nature of the party. His approval was echoed by Martov and Zasulich. By March 1903 he suggested Trotsky be co-opted on to the board of Iskra. Seven would simplify the voting and ensure stability – avoiding hung votes, as often happened, with Axelrod and Zasulich invariably siding with Plekhanov. But the haughty Plekhanov objected, disliking Trotsky's flowery style of writing. He was antagonised by the possibility of this brash arriviste gaining a foothold on the board. With Plekhanov vetoing Trotsky, Lenin sent his protégé to Paris on a lecture tour on behalf of Iskra. But confrontation with Plekhanov was brewing once again.

Meanwhile, Lenin couldn't get used to the mild, damp winter weather – which gave them all colds. Nor was he enjoying the hiatus of Christmas. It would be a dull time and he could not bear the waste: 'few meetings, the Reading Room will be closed and it will not be easy to get into the theatres, because everything is crowded out'.[53] By the spring of 1903 things were no different. He and Nadya were 'jogging along as usual'. Eliza-veta Vasil'evna was frequently sick, but they had at least managed to go to their first concert that winter, at Queen's Hall, where they had heard Tchaikovsky's 'latest symphony' – the *Pathétique* – followed shortly after by a visit to the German theatre.[54]

That same month Lenin was back on the road again – in Paris this time, to deliver a lecture at the Russian Social Sciences Higher School, followed by four more on 'Marxist Views on the Agrarian Problem in Europe and in Russia', one to the Paris *Iskra* group. By the time he returned to London in early March, change was in the air. Plekhanov was once more lobbying to move *Iskra* out of London and to Geneva. Lenin was deeply opposed to the move; it would mean a dramatic loss of his political independence from the rest of the board, which he had so fiercely defended. The stress and worry brought on terrible insomnia and made him very ill.

But in any event his health was already worn down by overwork and there was no denying that the running of the paper was suffering from a lack of efficient personnel. Zasulich, who took little part in the mechanics of producing *Iskra*, remained hopelessly disorganised. Potresov had by now fallen ill with tuberculosis and was in a sanatorium on the Continent and the restless Martov, who hated London, had decamped for the cafés of Paris. He was delighted when the relocation of *Iskra* was confirmed; he could return to his old haunts in Geneva. It meant too that Lenin's increasing stranglehold over the editorial board could be loosened.[55] More and more of the burden had devolved to Lenin and Nadya, while he was also increasingly preoccupied with complex prepara-tory work for the 2nd Party Congress to be held that year.

When the vote went against him over the relocation to Geneva, Lenin was extremely reluctant to leave Holford Square. He and Nadya were happy and settled, 'like cats which get used to a particular spot', as Nadya told Lenin's mother back in Russia.[56] But in April 1903 they departed, leaving behind them a pile of incomprehensible papers in Russian. Sensibly, the Yeo family took them out to the backyard and burned them. But Lenin did not forget his English landlady. After he and Nadya arrived in Switzerland he sent a book of views of Geneva, dedicated 'to the good kind lady, Mrs Emma Yeo'. She treasured it, remembering Mr Richter as a lodger who had been 'far better to deal with than many an Englishman'.[57] But she and her children never did work out what those long visits from groups of strange foreigners amounted to, nor did they ever suspect their highly seditious objectives. Nadya herself had remarked on the 'naive perplexity' with which the British in general had regarded the oddities of their émigré way of life and their incredulity of the fact that she, a woman, had even gone to jail for her political beliefs. Years later, Leonard Yeo still found it hard to believe that 'such a quietly good-natured little man' who looked like a student should have gone on to become 'such a world shaker'.[58]

But there was one thing the Yeos did remember, for many years after, and that was the distinctive and emphatic three Russian knocks at their front door.[59]

CHAPTER SIX

'The Dirty Squabble Abroad'

Geneva–Brussels–London–Geneva: April–December 1903

Cheapside, London

Lenin arrived in Geneva a sick man. The stress of his escalating work-load in London had led to the outbreak of an extremely painful red rash on his back and chest. Consulting a medical dictionary, he and Nadya diagnosed it as a viral infection of the nerve endings commonly known as 'holy fire'. Not having the guinea needed to consult an English doctor before leaving, Nadya's amateurish attempt at curing the condition by dabbing the inflamed areas with iodine had caused her husband excruciating pain. For the first two weeks in Geneva he was, to his intense frustration, confined to bed at the Pension Morhard on avenue de Mail.[1] He was thin and pale but it didn't stop him working. The pension was a regular haunt of visiting Russian revolutionaries and allowed a stream of colleagues in to Lenin's bedside. It wasn't just the regular consultations he needed to maintain; no matter how unwell he felt, Lenin insisted that anyone arriving from Russia should come and tell him all the news in the minutest detail.[2]

As soon as he recovered, he was out looking for somewhere to live. An activist named Kulyabko, who was visiting from Russia, bumped into him out flat hunting one day. Was Lenin happy to be back in Switzerland? he asked, his first, brief visit having been in 1895. 'No, not much' was the response. He liked the scenery and it was a good country for walking. The mountains, of course, were wonderful, and reminded him of Russia, but Geneva itself had nothing attractive about it. Kulyabko was surprised that someone as busy as Lenin was doing the legwork of looking for a place to live. Surely there were others who could do that for him? 'Oh no', responded Lenin, he had made sure to factor in time out of his busy schedule expressly for the purpose.[3]

Lenin's 'schedule' was, as always, crammed with activity. So much so that when Kulyabko arrived one day to collect a couple of articles from him for the printers he was told: 'I'll have one for you today, it's already in my inkwell but I don't even have the other one in my head as yet.'[4] Such had been their joint workload that when Lenin and Nadya had moved to a small two-storey house on Chemin privé du Foyer in the northern, working-class suburb of Sécheron, all they bothered to unpack were their piles of manuscripts, books and newspaper cuttings. They didn't have much but didn't seem to mind using packing cases as improvised furniture; at least there were no landladies laying down the law. The day Kulyabko turned up, all he saw in Lenin's bleak little room was a mattress and pillow on the floor, a rickety stool with a candle in a bottle – and one solitary, large glass inkwell. Downstairs, Elizaveta Vasil'evna was squeezed into a tiny room off the kitchen, where she had taken command of the domestic chores, complaining that all Vladimir Ilyich and her daughter did was 'pore over their books and notebooks'. Her son-in-law was worrying himself to death over his work, she was convinced of it, and Nadya was worn out. Unsurprisingly, the three of them lived in a state of transit until July.[5]

Downstairs on the kitchen range, the large enamel kettle was, however, always boiling. Tea and conversation were for ever on offer to visitors; but not much more as Lenin and Nadya were now extremely short of money. Ever a creature of habit, Lenin went daily to his editorial office located at a workers' printshop on rue de la Coulouvrenière but most of his time was taken up with preparations for the coming Party Congress: drafting rules and procedures and preparing a report on the *Iskra* operation. Lenin was determined to rally as many supporters to his camp beforehand as he could, which is why, uncharacteristically, he welcomed so many visitors to his home at this time. Nadya, meanwhile, was working long hours corresponding with the *Iskra* network. There were endless editorial meetings with Martov and Potresov, and Trotsky had now arrived from Paris. As delegates for the congress began gathering in Geneva from Russia and making their way to Lenin's house, the talk in the small, stuffy kitchen at Sécheron became noisy and heated. It often had to be continued out in the more calming atmosphere of Mon-Repos Park, on the edge of Lake Geneva, with its spectacular views of the snowy peaks of Mont Blanc in the distance.

Within three months Lenin and Nadya were on the move again, to Brussels, where it had now been decided to hold the Party Congress and where they lodged with a Belgian working woman. Delegates arriving from Russia and elsewhere were told to congregate at comrade Koltsov's flat in the city to register for the congress. But the procession of suspicious looking Eastern Europeans soon provoked the same response from Koltsov's landlady as those in Britain. She objected to all these strange men banging at the door. Koltsov and his wife were told to find some other rendezvous and the congregating delegates decamped to a hotel called the Coq d'Or. Here the exuberant Russians, intoxicated by the freedom of Belgium, often indulged in rowdy singsongs after their evening meal, drawing attention to their presence in the city. No doubt such exuberance was partly a reaction to the stress of getting to Brussels illegally from Russia and now finding themselves in the free world. Back home, scores of Social Democrats had been arrested, including two or three of Lenin's delegates, almost wrecking his plans. Elena Stasova in St Petersburg had worked very hard to reorganise and appoint new agents in their places. Among them was Aleksandr Shotman, one of only three workers to attend the congress among a majority who were Marxist intellectuals and professional revolutionaries.

On 30 July 1903, fifty-seven delegates representing a cross-section of twenty-six Russian, Jewish and other organisations – forty-three delegates with voting rights and fourteen with a consultative voice only – assembled for the 2nd Congress of the Russian Social Democratic Labour Party. They did so in hopeful secrecy in a large warehouse attached to the Maison du Peuple, a cooperative society in Brussels.[6] It had been selected by Koltsov

with the help of Belgian socialists, in hopes that this run-down venue
might not attract police attention. The congress had been long awaited
and everyone anticipated that it would be one where a common language
could be found and with it common objectives for the huge task in hand
in Russia.

Inside the warehouse, Koltsov had improvised a dais with a table and
a couple of chairs; the rest of the delegates had to cram up on crudely
knocked together planks of rough wood. The main window was draped
with red cloth to keep out prying eyes but it meant the place was ill lit
during the day, and it felt like being in a dark garret. By night, at least,
the lamplight gave the whispering group the appearance of conspirators.[7] But no sooner had the congress started than a strange fidgeting
began among the delegates. One by one they leapt to their feet and
started wrestling with their clothing. To compound their discomfort,
they discovered that they were having to share the premises not just with
rats but with a plague of fleas that had grown fat and comfortable on
the bales of wool previously stored there.[8]

The congress carried on disjointedly for a few days afterwards,
constantly changing venues and sitting twice a day, from nine to one and
from three to seven. Each speaker was allowed half an hour, with ten
minutes allotted to each respondent from the floor; no one could speak
on any one topic more than three times.[9] Even though it was taken for
granted that Lenin's *Iskra* group were the unspoken leaders of the party,
Lenin was frantic to assert his dominion over every session. He beat
down the factions threatening party unity, in particular the independently minded Jewish Bund – the General Jewish Labour Union – with
five delegates, and the Economists, with seven. Another four delegates
remained uncommitted.

In deference to Plekhanov's perceived seniority as author of the Party
Programme and Grand Old Man of Russian social democracy, Lenin
invited him to give the opening address. He fitted the part, impeccable
as ever in his neat frock coat. It was an auspicious moment in the history
of the Russian Social Democratic Labour Party – whose first 'congress'
in 1898 had amounted to a meeting of eight members in a back room
in Minsk to decide on a name and manifesto for their party. As Plekhanov
rose to take the rostrum, the long years of emigration seemed at last to
be fading into the past as the gathering he had dreamed of for twenty
years began.[10] It was clear that he intended to assert his leadership over
the party but Lenin, shortly afterwards elected deputy chairman of the

presidium to Plekhanov, was in a highly combative mood. Debate raged for the first two days over the membership of the Party's Organisational Committee. The Jewish Bund, with its powerful breadth of support in the Pale of Settlement, immediately threw up objections about its lack of sufficient representation at the congress and it demanded autonomy as a separate group. Ironically, it was Jewish delegates such as Martov and Trotsky who repudiated their demands, arguing that to give special preference to one group would destroy party unity and set in train demands for similar status from every other national group. The Bundists lost the vote 46:5. Although he took a back seat during this clash, Lenin watched approvingly, having already made it clear to his colleague Krzhizhanovsky in April that if necessary they must 'make war against the Bund' in order to achieve peace with it – 'War at the Congress, war even to the extent of a split – whatever the cost. Only then will the Bund be sure to surrender.'[11] In the event the split Lenin predicted would be far more profound than a quarrel with the Bund.

During the congress Lenin's unorthodox thesis on the party programme as outlined in 'What Is To Be Done?' became the subject of intense controversy when the Economists raised objections to Lenin's plans for a centralised organisation, and Trotsky defended Lenin's position, affirming the need for vigilant control.[12]

Unfortunately, the congress had by now attracted the unwanted attention of the Belgian police, who had been surprised to see so many Russians arriving in Brussels. They followed delegates to their lodgings, to evening meals at the Coq d'Or, on walks in the park, and searched the baggage in their rooms in their absence.[13] The Okhrana had been happy to fill the Belgian police in on the details of several wanted men and soon four delegates were stopped and summarily ordered to leave Brussels within twenty-four hours. Surveillance of the remainder was cranked up. The Russians could not but be amused by the Belgian police's heavy-handed tactics; they were used to giving the law the slip in Russia and took great pleasure in occasionally grabbing the only hansom cab in the street, leaving the 'spooks' to run down the road after them.[14] One day when the police stopped Shotman and some friends, demanding to know their identity, one of them answered in somewhat basic Swedish that they were Swedish students. Since the Swedes were the least likely nation to be plotting revolution, the gullible police, whose Swedish was equally poor, went away satisfied.[15]

But clearly there was no hope of continuing the congress under threat of arrest and extradition back to Russia for many of the delegates. With voices already raised in argument the Leninist principles of *konspiratsiya* disintegrated; the naturally passionate, if not violent opinions of so many Russian radicals gathered together in a confined space were rapidly undermining the security of the congress. It would have to decamp and London seemed the best option. After the thirteenth session on 6 August the group made its way by train to Ostend and the boat to Dover. The crossing was a stormy one. Nadya and the others took to their beds, groaning with terrible sea sickness. But not Lenin. Reinvigorated by the prospect of a move to the familiar territory of London, he pulled his cap down tight over his head and paced the deck, watching the storm.[16]

On arrival in a drizzly and misty London, the delegates were directed to Nikolay Alekseev's flat in a 'small square' near King's Cross (possibly Holford Square, to where he appears to have moved late in 1902) and told to make the prerequisite three hard knocks at the door.[17] Martyn Lyadov, a delegate from Saratov, whose first trip to London this was, found the whole experience bewildering, even more so because of the squalor in which Alekseev lived. Resident in London for some time, he still lived 'like a student', the furniture in his small third-floor room consisting of a 'broken bed, two chairs barely standing on their legs, and a rickety table', and the only other furnishings being piles of Russian and English newspapers. Aleksandr Shotman was similarly appalled; it looked as though Alekseev lived only on tinned food, the empty evidence of which lay scattered in every corner of the room. Soon Nadya arrived with Lenin and got the kettle on the boil and plied the delegates with tea as Lenin rushed round organising cheap places for them to stay and, meticulous as ever, provided them all with maps for finding their way to wherever the congress was meeting. He also made a point of visiting the delegates in their lodgings in the days that followed to ensure that all was well with them and that their landladies were not giving them any trouble.[18]

On 11 August the congress reconvened with its fourteenth session. This took place at 'The English Club' – probably another name for the Communist Club that had recently moved from Tottenham Street to a house at 107 Charlotte Street.[19] Konstantin Takhtarev, who was also still living in London, had found an assortment of venues for the congress, another being an anglers' club somewhere in the same area, having informed the landlord that its use was for a 'meeting of Belgian trade unionists'.[20] This time, at least, the principles of *konspiratsiya* prevailed;

indeed, so much so that the details of the precise locations used for the 1903 congress – possibly trade union halls and cafés or restaurants with small conference rooms attached – are still not known. One day, however, when members were leaving a session, local street kids – who had been unsettled by the sight of groups of foreigners arguing and gesticulating as they came out – threw rotten potatoes and rubbish at them. At the request of the congress, a policeman was put on duty outside the door the following day, but this appears to be the extent of the British police presence at the time.[21]

Despite the change of location to London, the atmosphere of the remainder of the congress was extremely tense. There was a constant furore, one minute of hissing, the next of applause, with everyone clamouring to speak at the same time; in the midst of it all Lenin became increasingly frenzied in his attempts to shout down the opposition. Crisis point was reached on 15 August over what on the surface seemed a minor point of interpretation in the very first paragraph of the statute, with regard to membership of the RSDLP. Martov stood up and argued for a broad-based party allowing secondary members and sympathisers who supported the party programme and underground activities to be allowed to participate – either personally or materially. Lenin, still wedded to the old Jacobin traditions of secrecy, hated the diffuseness of Martov's suggestion and took a much more authoritarian line: the party should remain narrow – for professionals only, with all members fulfilling the precondition of 'personal work in one of the Party organisations'.[22] It all seemed perfectly logical and above board to Lenin; he had already made clear his views on the subject in 'What Is To Be Done?'. There had to be a firm leadership – 'either the "organised utopia" of Lenin or 99/100 outside the party'; the notes scribbled on his copy of the agenda testify to the extent of his ambition.[23]

But many delegates gathered in London during those August days viewed Lenin's demands as undemocratic and un-Marxist, sensing with alarm the inherent slide to dictatorship that such a closed party might bring. The levels of mutual mistrust and recrimination escalated. The hopeful atmosphere of unity and compromise in which the congress had opened in Brussels at the end of July evaporated into one of suspicion, if not outright enmity. The breakdown in Lenin's relationship with Martov, which had been brewing for months, was rapid, as Martov's perceived 'softness' bore the brunt of Lenin's mauling. Lenin was, as Zasulich had remarked, a bulldog, with a 'deadly grip' when it came to fighting his corner.[24] Aleksandr Shotman pitied the dishevelled and shambolic Martov with his pale face and his sunken cheeks and his pince-nez perpetually sliding down his nose. The pockets of his shapeless baggy suit were stuffed full of papers. He seemed cowed, yet when he spoke his analytical strength and the passion of his intellect still shone through.[25]

Despite having Plekhanov's support on the need for discipline in the party, Lenin was nevertheless defeated by 22 votes to Martov's 28. There were plenty of people at the congress who agreed with the broad outlines of Lenin's plan for a tighter and more centralised party; the problem was the unbridled jockeying for control of it that Lenin was engaged in. It smacked of Bonapartism and it was mirrored in a toughening up of attitude among his own supporters who began to manifest their 'hardness' in contrast to the 'softs' of Martov and his supporters.[26] Antagonised by Lenin's attempts to dominate, the Bundists and Economists had sided with Martov. Lenin, as he himself later admitted, fought like 'a madman' to impose his view.[27] Worse, he unexpectedly found himself opposed by his newest and brightest acolyte – Trotsky – who also took Martov's side. All Lenin's subsequent attempts behind the scenes to talk Trotsky round failed.[28] The split between the hard and soft camps continued for the rest of the congress. But then, on 18 August, during the twenty-seventh session, the Bundists – having failed to win support for their independence within the party from either Martov or Lenin – walked out, followed soon after by the Economists. Martov lost his slim majority and the tables were turned.

A meeting on the evening of the 18th saw the final break between the two camps when Lenin revealed his plans for the reorganisation of the *Iskra* editorial board. Nadezhda Krupskaya later claimed that he had been so stressed by the prospect of breaking with his former friends Zasulich, Axelrod and Potresov that he had sat up all night shivering. But the fact was, they were inefficient and had so far contributed little editorially or in organisational terms. To Lenin's mind the cosy 'family character' of the original board of six had been impeding efficiency for three years now. From the moment that '*Iskra* became the Party and the Party became *Iskra*', Lenin had known such a break was inevitable; it was the best solution to three years of endless wrangling on the board.[29] And so, with utter ruthlessness he now forced out the three 'softs' – Zasulich, Axelrod and Potresov. Trotsky thought his treatment of the venerable pair of Zasulich and Axelrod callous in the extreme. It might be politically right, he conceded, but it was morally wrong. Nevertheless, Lenin (thanks to the exit of the Bundists and Economists, both of which groups would have opposed him in this) narrowly won the vote to change the board to the three most 'politically decisive' operators – Plekhanov, Martov and Lenin himself.

Vera Zasulich accepted her ejection with a strange passivity considering that work on the *Iskra* board was the main focus of her lonely life in exile. Even Nadezhda Krupskaya noted that to be removed would for her 'have meant cutting herself off from Russia again, sinking back into the slough of emigrant life abroad'. Her work for *Iskra* was 'not a question of ambition, but a matter of life and death'. Yet she was reticent about protesting, perhaps out of concern that in so doing she would create further friction. The unity of the party must come first even at the expense of her own lifetime's dedication.[30]

Elections followed for the Central Committee and the Council of the Party. Lenin's men, Gleb Krzhizhanovsky, Fridrikh Lengnik and Vladimir Noskov, gained the crucial places on the Central Committee. Lenin, Plekhanov and Martov were elected to the new three-man editorial board of *Iskra* based abroad, while a three-man Central Committee would operate inside Russia in consultation with an elected-member Party Council. But Martov, out of loyalty to his rejected colleagues, refused to continue working with Lenin and Plekhanov on *Iskra* and resigned, although he accepted election to the Party Council. The party was heading for a fatal split with Lenin's 'majoritarians', or *bolsheviki*, thereafter lined up in opposition to Martov's 'minoritarians', or *mensheviki*.[31]

Having been the only delegate to attend every single session during the twenty-four days – during which he had spoken on more than one hundred separate occasions – Lenin was, by dint of his extraordinary energy and will, now effective leader of the party. During the congress he had never let up in his constant verbal assault – cajoling, arguing, hectoring delegates at every opportunity on party issues and making careful notes on where their loyalties lay and carefully filing it all away in the card index of his rigorous political mind. 'I realise that I often behaved and acted in a state of frightful irritation', he later told Krzhizhanovsky. His manner had, he admitted, been frenzied. 'I am quite willing to admit *this fault of mine to anyone*, if that can be called a fault.' But as far as he was concerned, his behaviour had been 'a natural product of the atmosphere, the reactions, the interjections, the struggle'.[32]

Before the delegates who had taken his side left for home, Lenin spent several days in their company. On 24 August he took them to Karl Marx's grave in Highgate Cemetery, having already introduced them to Speakers' Corner at Hyde Park and the British Museum.[33] Now more than ever Lenin attached great importance to keeping them on side and impressing upon them the need to go back to Russia and recruit more workers for the party – and his own faction within it. Pulling the strings of the Russian revolutionary movement from the distance of Europe meant that he rarely had the opportunity to meet agents in person; but Lenin now took full advantage of having his disciples sitting at his knee. Running the revolutionary underground was, as he later wrote, like conducting an orchestra. One had to know 'precisely who is playing which fiddle, and where, and how he does it'. Should any member of that orchestra strike a false note, it had to be understood where and why, 'who ought to be shifted, and how and whither'. With the mind of an impartial clinician Lenin argued that every and any 'discordant tone' had to be removed.[34]

As far as he was concerned his split with Martov had in essence been a fairly superfluous one in the greater scheme of things; the sacrifice of Zasulich, Axelrod and even Martov himself, as it now turned out, had been necessary, in the best interests of the revolution. But he had made enemies by the manner in which he had shown so little respect for the old guard and Plekhanov, caught between a rock and a hard place, soon came to regret having supported Lenin over the *Iskra* issue. Delegates could not understand how Lenin had had the nerve to behave so dishonourably towards his former colleagues. Where did he get the 'supreme self-confidence' that allowed him to ride roughshod over people?[35]

Lenin's intransigence and ruthlessness – though he would call it revolutionary purity – had won the day, but such now was the personal animosity between him and his former *Iskra* colleagues that the breach was irreparable, with accusations of chicanery, intrigue, 'opportunism' and unscrupulousness being hurled back and forth on both sides. As far as Trotsky was concerned, Lenin, with his ominous Jacobin tactics of extreme centralism, was now imposing 'a state of siege' on the party with his 'iron fist'.[36] But there was no denying his gift for leadership. He was, as Trotsky perceptively noted that August, 'a man with every fibre of his being bent on one particular end. Lenin alone, and with finality, envisaged "tomorrow", with all its stern tasks, its cruel conflicts and countless victims.'[37]

In Geneva, Lenin's former friend and colleague Aleksandr Potresov took a particularly cynical view of the events of the summer of 1903, at the end of a seven-year friendship with Lenin. As in everything, Lenin had made it impossible to find a middle ground – both in the running of *Iskra* and, more ominously, in the future direction of the party as a whole. Everything with Lenin boiled down to extremes – of being either for him or against. There was something destructive in his 'monolithic, one-note nature', wrote Potresov later, and in particular the way he 'over-simplified' the complexities of the human condition, reducing everything to narrow-minded sectarianism.[38]

As Martov and his supporters left London, Lenin and his faction set off for Geneva. Once again, three weeks of enervating debate and factional infighting had left him prostrate with exhaustion and unable to sleep. But the 'battle of recriminations' had only just begun.[39] And worse, those in the party at large siding with the Martovites were now transferring their crucial financial and practical support to that faction. Lenin's renewed state of physical and mental collapse continued into the autumn and no doubt directly contributed to a serious accident he had in October. Out cycling one day on his new bicycle (purchased with money sent by his mother and siblings – there was one for Nadya too),[40] his wheels got caught in some tram rails and he went headlong into the back of a tram. As he fell, Lenin gashed his head on a stone, just missing his eye and badly bruising his arm and side. Undaunted, after obtaining rudimentary medical help, he went straight on to his next appointment – the Conference of the League of Russian Social Democrats Abroad – a frightening sight as he entered the room set aside for the purpose in the Café Landolt, on the corner of the rue de Candolle, his head swathed in bandages.[41]

The League had played an important part in liaising between the different Russian émigré communities in Switzerland, Paris and London since 1894. But the personal animosities of the London RSDLP Congress were still rankling and inevitably infected it. Martov, now losing all sense of tactics and moderation, immediately went on the attack, screaming first at Lenin and then at Plekhanov. For the best part of five days pandemonium reigned at the Café Landolt, with Martovites jumping up from their seats shouting and gesticulating, pushing and shoving and threatening with their fists.[42] In the midst of it all Lenin stood calmly adjusting the bandage over his eye, his self-possession as all around him degenerated into chaos serving only to enrage the Martovites further.

Next, Plekhanov back-tracked on his support for Lenin in London; in an attempt to conciliate, he persuaded the old editorial board to return to the *Iskra* fold. This was the last straw for Lenin; on 1 November he resigned from the board in protest, saying it was impossible for him to work with the Martovites. Having overseen forty-five issues of his brain-child *Iskra*, he had now, so it seemed, wilfully cut himself off from his own political mouthpiece. The unthinkable was about to happen: *Iskra* would revert to the control of the 'softs' of Martov, Zasulich, Axelrod and Potresov, all now reconciled with the traitorous Plekhanov. It was the lowest moment in Lenin's revolutionary career so far. For him, there could be 'no worse a blind alley than to leave work' and for the last three years *Iskra* had been his life.[43]

To enter such a blind alley, as well as having to face up to the loss of one of his closest friends and political allies, Julius Martov, was a bitter pill to swallow. Martov had been one of the very few male associates whom Lenin had ever allowed close. But pragmatics, as ever, took prece-dence over sentiment: Lenin was forced to admit to an unbridgeable gulf between his friend's tragic lack of political will and his own iron deter-mination.[44] In a letter to one of his remaining political allies, Gleb Krzhizhanovsky, he wrote: 'There is no longer any hope, absolutely no hope of peace. You can't imagine even a tenth of the outrages to which the Martovites have sunk here, poisoning the whole atmosphere abroad with their spiteful gossip, encroaching on our contacts, *money*, literary material, etc.' For Lenin it was a terrible moment: 'War has been declared', he continued, and he and his supporters must now 'get ready for the most legal but desperate struggle.'[45]

The loss of *Iskra* now left Lenin politically isolated and without his all-important platform, despite the arrival of letters of solidarity from local committees in Russia. He would not only have to remake his career as a journalist and a professional political analyst but he would also have to build new personal and political alliances. In the meantime, he was determined to tell his side of the story and keep the network of *Iskra* agents in Russia on his side. In a pamphlet published in December 1903 he explained 'Why I resigned from the Iskra Editorial Board'; he elabo-rated on this at even greater, self-justifying length in another pamphlet attacking Martov and his 'hysterical scandalmongers' in 'One Step Forward, Two Steps Back', published the following year.[46]

Lenin's manoeuvring for position thereafter was relentless. He simply would not let go of his vision for the party and the future – not ever. Later, in November, he contrived to have himself co-opted on to the Central Committee, thanks to the influence of his friend and committee member Krzhizhanovsky.[47] It was an undemocratic and underhand act, but such things did not concern Lenin in the cause of reasserting his position. 'We must by all means fill the places on *all* committees without exception with our own people.'[48] Krzhizhanovsky regretted being browbeaten into this act, feeling, as many did, that the 'old man' should end his quarrel with Martov for the sake of the party. When he continued to try to conciliate with the Martovites his relationship with Lenin became the inevitable casualty.

Such personal conflicts with colleagues and friends took its inevitable toll in the pattern of Lenin's physical health, which throughout his life veered from extremes of high energy to lows of absolute exhaustion. The clashes of the 2nd Party Congress and its aftermath left him distressed, depressed and unable to eat or work. He became thin and sickly, plagued by a recurrence of his old stomach problem, as well as insomnia and migraines. He sought medical advice but nothing short of total withdrawal from political life would have put an end to his many physical ills. The specialist Lenin consulted advised that he was suffering from the then fashionable condition of 'neurasthenia' – a catch-all for stress. Yet, as Nadya knew only too well, not being able to work was far worse for her husband than any illness. Not even a severe health warning would derail him now from his chosen path towards revolution in Russia.[49]

Political life in Geneva seemed unutterably gloomy for the remainder of that year until, on 12 December, the whole of this rather sedate city came alive for four days when workers' communities took to the streets for the annual celebrations of *L'Escalade* – 'the scaling of the walls'. The festival commemorated the day in 1602 when the citizens of Geneva, who had been independent from the French state of Savoy since 1536, had heroically repulsed an attack by the Duke of Savoy, when he attempted to regain control. Genevans took enormous pride in the event and the streets were humming with carousels, a circus and fairground stalls. At night the streets were ablaze with fireworks and a torchlit carnival with masked revellers.

In the midst of it all the Russians sat indoors, gloomy and discouraged, poring over their political tracts and documents, far too preoccupied and too depressed to join the celebrations. But then, as one of them later recalled, came a knock at the door. It was Lenin, demanding to know why they were not out on the streets soaking up the atmosphere. 'Let's go,' he shouted. 'You can leave all your important questions till the morning.' It was a warm evening despite the lateness of the year; the streets were full of flickering lights, the River Arve nearby rushing noisily along its course, as the group of comrades, laughing and singing snaked their way down the streets serpent-style, no one's laughter more hearty than Lenin's.[50] Eventually they wound their way to the Café Landolt, which served the best sausages and sauerkraut, and where, amidst its plain wooden tables and chairs, Lenin had his own table – number 40, near the window.[51] It had for some time been the focus for Russian political émigrés who occasionally held conferences and meetings here in a small room at the back, with its own discreet emergency exit out into a narrow lane.[52]

That evening, it was as though the experience of being out among the masses on the streets had entirely reinvigorated Lenin. He had come this far, but only at the loss of his stalwart friends from the early days of his revolutionary career – Martov and Potresov. Together with Plekhanov, Zasulich and Axelrod, they with Lenin had formed the heart of the Russian émigré community. But now the party was fractured and in confusion. Supporters of the two camps back in Russia thought their leaders had gone mad to allow such a schism to occur over technical points of organisation. Seeking to conciliate and save the party from further disruption, many regional committee members left their leaders to carry on quarrelling in exile while they continued the practical work of the underground as best they could.[53] For Lenin, there was a hard road yet to travel, but his determination persisted on New Year's Eve 1904, when he and a group of friends met again at the Café Landolt and raised their glasses to the growing success of the Russian revolutionary movement back home.

CHAPTER SEVEN

'Strong Talk and Weak Tea'

Geneva: January–December 1904

The Café Landolt, Geneva

On 31 December 1903, weakened by eleven days on hunger strike, party activist Nikolay Valentinov emerged blinking from his dark prison cell on to the streets of Kiev. Expecting to be reunited with family and friends he was warned that if he did not leave the city immediately he risked being rearrested and sent to another prison where this time his death from a hunger strike would be allowed to go unnoticed. Instead, on the orders of local RSDLP leader Gleb Krzhizhanovsky, he was to take the train to Geneva with an important letter for Lenin. There he could rest up, get the inside story on the recent party split, take instruction and return to Russia 'as a professional revolutionary'. The temperature was 16 degrees below zero the night Valentinov managed to cross the frozen River Dnestr into Galicia in Austria-Hungary by smuggler's sledge, after hiding overnight in a snowdrift. From here he picked up the railway line to Vienna and travelled on to Geneva, arriving with nothing to his name but 'a toothbrush, a piece of soap, a towel' and Krzhizhanovsky's secret letter in invisible ink sewn into the lining of his coat.[1]

Cold and hungry, he shuffled his way to Lenin's apartment, where Nadya promptly ripped open his coat to get at the letter while Lenin assaulted him with 'an avalanche of questions', eager to find out how the party split was being viewed in Russia. Hours later he allowed his exhausted messenger to take to his bed in the cheap hotel on the Plaine de Plainpalais were many of his supporters regularly stayed. For a while Valentinov (nicknamed Samsonov by Lenin, for surviving the sapping of his strength under hunger strike) found himself welcomed into Lenin's inner circle and regular visits to his home. Lenin had heard about his activism in Kiev, how he had taken part in demonstrations during which he had been beaten with police truncheons and knocked unconscious, and wanted to know more about the tactics of violence: 'The autocracy will not collapse at the sound of the trumpets of Jericho,' he assured Valentinov. 'One must start destroying it physically by means of mass blows . . . we must learn to smash mugs in the proletarian way!'[2] It seemed to Valentinov then, that when the day came Lenin would be the first to mount the barricades.

For Lidiya Fotieva, who also made her way to the city that spring after release from prison in Perm, it had cost fifteen rubles to bribe the commander of the frontier post to allow her to get out of Russia; the soldier on duty at the border who turned a blind eye as she passed was cheaper at only twenty kopeks for a bottle of vodka.[3] Soon after, another eager acolyte, Ceciliya Bobrovskaya, had arrived from Tver in northern Russia, having been smuggled across the Prussian border by a succession of Jewish, Polish and German villagers with whom she had shared their filthy hovels, at a bribe of even less – ten rubles. Ceciliya was eager to meet Lenin, who had exerted a powerful ideological influence over her party work in Tver. She had heard of the 'scandalous' split in the party in London and sided very strongly with the Leninists. Once arrived in Geneva, this estranged her from her former friend and mentor Axelrod, who had sided with the Mensheviks in opposition to Lenin and his 'rams'. Having met Lenin, Ceciliya, like Valentinov, created a good impression with her detailed report on party work in Tver and was invited to visit him and Nadya at their home.

Valentinov, Fotieva and Bobrovskaya were just three young revolution-aries who passed through Geneva that year. Located in the south-west tip of Switzerland on the border with France, Geneva had long been the classic heartland of Russian exile and the unacknowledged capital of the Russian revolutionary movement abroad. It had, like London, begun welcoming refugees since European Protestants had fled there during the Reformation in the sixteenth century. Throughout the nineteenth century Switzerland had become a centre for Russian intellectual emigration, especially from the 1860s, although wealthy Russians had also chosen to live there for access to its spas and the clean air of its mountains. In so doing they had created an émigré community known as 'La Petite Russie' with its own Eglise Russe funded by Grand Duchess Anna Fedorovna.[4] But the city and Switzerland's links with exiles were largely political thereafter. The first three congresses of Marx's First International had been held here in the 1860s and after 1871 many French Communards fleeing the barricades of Paris arrived. Finally, in 1883, the Emancipation of Labour group had been founded in Geneva, after which the city for the exiled Russian became 'a sort of revolutionary Olympus' lorded over by the cultured Plekhanov, as the acknowledged father of Russian Marxism.[5]

During those years, Geneva witnessed the largest diversity anywhere in the West of Russian political exiles – from the first Populists, to Narodnaya Volya extremists, to nihilists to anarchists and finally to Bolsheviks and Mensheviks, with Lenin's group gravitating to Geneva and Martov's, later, to Zurich.[6] No sooner had they arrived than these factions set up their own printing presses, lending libraries, reading rooms and bookshops, which became a focus for the dissemination of radical literature. They shared a propensity to physical austerity and an intense preoccupation with science and politics over and above concerns about personal comfort. For many political exiles, to dress, eat and live better than the working classes back home in Russia whom they championed was positively criminal. A young Italian émigré, Benito Mussolini, who was studying in Geneva in the early 1900s, observed with curiosity and often admiration this 'strange, dissolute, eccentric, fantastic group' of nihilists and bohemians, who seemed to him 'the last word in fervid, feverish modernity'. Nor could he fail to notice the 'orgies of strong talk and weak tea' that punctuated the daily round of the Russians' lives and how they would sit up all night talking and arguing, 'following along the track of an idea like so many bloodhounds'.[7] Whenever Russians came together to talk they shared a very particular commonality of feeling. They were, as the novelist Joseph Conrad observed, haunted always by a spectre:

'the shadow of autocracy', which forever coloured 'their thoughts, their views, their most intimate feelings, their private life, their public utterances – haunting the secret of their silences'.[8] They might be in the free environment of Switzerland, but spiritually and intellectually they were still in Russia.

Sober and orderly Calvinist Geneva might therefore have seemed the least compatible environment for the turbulent Russians. For the Pole Joseph Conrad, it seemed passionless and indifferent to the world outside. But by the 1900s it had a burgeoning new Russian heartland in the streets around the southern end of the rue de Carouge, a newly built workers' district on the outskirts of the city. This broad thoroughfare of four- and five-storey stone houses with trees planted down one side was not far from the Arve, a fast-flowing, murky tributary of the Rhône which flooded regularly in the spring. Here the new Russian enclave of political émigrés, who congregated around the rue de Carouge and the nearby boulevard des Philosophes, gave the area its nickname – *karuzhka*. Amidst the city's neatly manicured parks such as the Jardin Anglais, with their graceful promenades of plane trees and poplars, their bandstands and cafés, the overwhelming air of gentility belied the often desperate political machinations of its Russian community. Beyond the steamboat piers on Lake Geneva and the rows of shiny hansom cabs lined up along the public gardens and the efficiency of the new electric trams, the only thing dispelling what Lenin and Conrad both saw as the banality of the city was the power and majesty of the Jura Mountains beyond.[9]

The local response to the Russians was no different here than in London and Brussels. The Russian students in particular were noisy and disruptive, with their 'yells of savages fit to wake up the whole city', when they came home late from their long debates and meetings. Their rowdy singsongs in bars and cafés became notorious.[10] During Russia's war with Japan in 1904, they held victory parades along the rue de Carouge every time Nicholas II's army suffered a defeat.[11] The majority of the Russian community lived a miserable, impoverished existence, doing translation work, giving lessons, waiting on tables, or even taking whatever manual labour they could get, forced to live in dark, cold attics on the outskirts. With only their own close community to fall back on for support it was inevitable, as Herzen had earlier observed of his own Russian community in England, that these narrow circles increasingly consisted of 'inert memories and hopes' that were cut off from home and their source of inspiration and thus 'could never be realised'.[12]

Homesickness was compounded during this time of uncertainty by much coming and going in the wake of the party split, as the now fractured RSDLP began to realign itself into two opposing groups. So frequent had the visits to Lenin become that out of a conscientious respect for his greater work, the comrades agreed to call only once a week. So, on Tuesdays or Thursdays, Lenin and Nadya held open house around the kitchen stove out at Sécheron. It wasn't just about socialising: it was also a necessary act of consolidation. Valentinov was somewhat disturbed by the air of almost religious worship around 'Ilych'. This unexceptional looking man, as he saw him, was clearly possessed of a 'hypnotic influence' that was lacking in his rivals Plekhanov and Martov and it had a very clear effect on many idealistic young revolutionaries such as Ceciliya Bobrovskaya.[13] She was desperate to 'go to Ilyich for a chat' as often as possible. Nevertheless, she worried about taking up the leader's precious time and was dismayed by the lack of creature comforts enjoyed by her hero.[14]

But there was no denying the warm welcome offered to all-comers by Nadya and her mother, who always had plenty of soup on the boil. During such convivial gatherings Lenin delighted in good company and would laugh heartily. He always enjoyed being around new arrivals who 'breathed of Russia', joining with them in singing revolutionary anthems and Siberian folk songs. The Internationale was obligatory, as too the Marseillaise and a very popular Russian revolutionary song, 'You Have Fallen in the Struggle'. Mariya Essen (code-named zver, 'wild animal'), one of Lenin and Nadya's most valued supporters from the Central Committee in St Petersburg, was also a regular visitor. A distant relative on Lenin's mother's Swedish side, she was a seasoned survivor of arrest and imprisonment and had recently escaped from exile in Yakutiya, Siberia. At Sécheron she noticed how Lenin seemed always to particularly enjoy Petr Krasikov's rendition of Tchaikovsky's Barcarolle on the violin.[15] (Krasikov had narrowly escaped arrest in Moscow to get to Geneva, clutching one small suitcase and his violin – art for some revolutionists, was never, ever dispensable). When the comrades performed there were occasional, all too fleeting moments when Lenin revealed a different, private side. He became particularly engrossed whenever Sergey Gusev sang in his deep baritone; for a moment he would let go, 'leaning back on the sofa, his arms around his lifted knees' as though lost in memories – of home and his mother, of what he had left behind in Russia. Perhaps these melodies reminded him of the spiritual life that he had so ruthlessly sacrificed in favour of the relentless world of politics. But if anyone took notice, Lenin soon shut off his emotions from view; 'Lenin's corner,' as Valentinov later wrote, 'was a very extensive one, and he did not permit anyone to penetrate it.'[16]

In fact, such moments of tranquil introspection belied the thoughts now seething inside Lenin's head. The party had been torn apart by the split with the Martovites and, with it, Lenin's own support in Geneva – both physical and financial – had now been reduced to a handful of loyal followers. The atmosphere that year was very strained with endless wrangles and squabbles punctuating the life of the revolutionary exile community. Lenin's response as always was highly combative, as he filled his often long and dictatorial letters to party workers in Russia with endless instructions, for ever demanding details of underground activities in Russia, emphasising one thing – the need for organisation, and yet more organisation. There were constant calls too for money; Lenin and his faction were now virtually without funds.

By March 1904 Lenin had once again worn himself to a shadow, this time writing 'One Step Forward, Two Steps Back – The Crisis in Our Party', his analysis of the 2nd Party Congress based on his careful examination of the minutes. In violent and ever more vitriolic tones, the pages of this pamphlet reflected his mental turmoil as he now openly attacked the Mensheviks, branding them as 'traitors'. Their refusal to accept the essential disciplines of a tightly controlled party had invited nothing but anarchy and 'opportunism' – one of Lenin's favourite catch-alls for anyone who opposed him. Martov responded in vitriolic kind, proclaiming Lenin 'a political corpse' on the pages of *Iskra* in an article entitled 'In Lieu of a Funeral Oration'. Panteleimon Lepeshinsky, a talented artist, in response produced a series of cartoons, 'How the Mice Buried the Cat', depicting Lenin – 'the big tomcat', as Vera Zasulich had nicknamed him – hanging precariously from a beam while being baited by a group of visibly recognisable Menshevik mice, including Martov, Zasulich and Trotsky. Later in the sequence the tomcat, having fallen to the floor, rises up to tear the mice to pieces. Soon the cartoons were being circulated all over Geneva, enraging the Mensheviks.[17]

The community in which the warring Russian exiles now uneasily coexisted was a small one – the size of an average London borough. Relations between the two political camps led by Lenin and Martov became so strained that they were now reduced to crossing the road to avoid each other within Geneva's tight-knit Russian community and of meeting in separate back rooms at the Café Landolt. By the spring of 1904 it was clear that the ongoing stress of the rift with Plekhanov and Martov had deeply undermined Lenin's health and, for once, his self-belief – Lepeshinsky had never seen him 'in such a depressed state'.[18] By April he was on the verge of total breakdown. He was so exhausted that he didn't even have the energy to play chess – his one enduring passion. Valentinov, who spent a great deal of time in his company, was convinced that Lenin had arrived at a turning point in his political life, where he knew he had to choose between committing entirely to his ruthless Bolshevik line or conceding to the Mensheviks for the sake of party unity. Fundamentally, there were no real and telling differences of principle between Lenin and Martov – it all boiled down to the issue of leadership and discipline, of whether or not Lenin should be allowed to wield 'the conductor's baton'.[19] He truly believed that he was the man for the job: Plekhanov was undeniably a great scholar but no good at organisation, any more than Axelrod, Zasulich and Potresov were. As for Martov, he was an 'excellent journalist' but a 'hysterical intellectual', too soft to be entrusted with the leadership of the party. The conclusion was not one of self-aggrandisement on Lenin's part, but one of sheer logic and practicality. It was a mark of his unshakeable faith in his own qualities as leader and his inbred sense of destiny.

Valentinov could see that this faith would never be shaken. During the days when Lenin was working on 'One Step Forward, Two Steps Back', Valentinov often joined him for his strictly regulated walk, at 4.00 p.m. precisely along the Quai du Mont Blanc by the lakeside. As they walked, it would not be long before Lenin would launch into one of his contemptuous attacks against all the 'riff-raff' that in his view diluted the effectiveness of the party, before proceeding to demolish the Martovite objections to his extreme form of centralism.[20] Sometimes his levels of nervous energy and rage against the Martovites grew so intense that his face flushed and his eyes became bloodshot as he stopped from time to time, stuck his thumbs in the armholes of his waistcoat and stamped his foot. Throughout he barely took note of Valentinov – he was, in reality, talking to himself. Valentinov listened patiently as Lenin railed at his rivals' wishy-washy 'bourgeois spirit' and their hatred of 'proletarian discipline', warning that sooner or later they would break with orthodox Marxism altogether. And that to Lenin was anathema. The fight for a dictatorship of the proletariat was 'absolutely meaningless' without a 'Jacobin mentality in the people who set it up'. So let Plekhanov and

Martov accuse him of being a Robespierre in the style of the French Revolution. A true Social Democrat had to act in that way in order to achieve his ends.[21] It was time for an end to 'shilly-shallying' – it was time for the formation of an 'unswervingly revolutionary Marxist party'.

Lenin was now very sick, his eyes 'heavy and dead-looking' and his eyelids swollen from lack of sleep. By the time 'One Step Forward' was published he had once again shifted his political position, back-pedalling on his call for an irrevocable split as Valentinov had heard only a few weeks earlier. This late and limited attempt to compromise was an indication that his energy levels had collapsed, giving way to doubt and taking a toll on his deeply inflexible and intolerant nature. Nadya, who spent her life perpetually worrying about her husband's wellbeing and monitoring his rage levels, knew she must get him away. She had also become jealous of Lenin's regular walks with Valentinov; having always considered herself to be Lenin's first and most important political sounding board, she now felt marginalised.

Besides, Nadya too needed a break, not just from her burden of party work but also from the 'constant turmoil' of housekeeping for the stream of visitors at Sécheron.[22] So in early July, with her mother away visiting friends in St Petersburg, she and Lenin gave up their rented house and, leaving Martyn Lyadov in charge of things, set off on a walking tour with their copy of Baedeker's *Switzerland* and not much more. By mutual agreement there was to be no talk of work or politics, or 'business' of any kind. 'Work,' Volodya assured Nadya, 'is not a bear and will not escape to the woods.' Five days later they sent Lenin's mother a postcard from the mountains with 'greetings from the tramps'.[23] They took a few books with them but sent most of them back unread to Geneva when they arrived in Lausanne.[24] They had very little money and subsisted on eggs, cheese and other staples.

The Ulyanovs did not, however, travel alone: they were accompanied on their trip by Mariya Essen. During the first week the threesome headed on foot along the northern side of Lake Geneva for Lausanne and some mountain walks, then they took the steamer further east along the lake to Montreux. Lenin was 'indefatigable on outings' and a prodigious walker, according to Mariya. At Montreux they visited the sombre, turreted Château de Chillon perched on the lakeside, and the tiny cell where the Swiss patriot François Bonnivard had been held in chains during the sixteenth century, the inspiration for Lord Byron's 1816 poem *The Prisoner of Chillon*. As a reaction to this oppressive interior, and no doubt with it unpleasant reminders of their own incarceration under the tsars, the group decided to climb a nearby snowy peak, the Rochers de Naye. It was too much for Nadya with her weak constitution and she returned to the hotel, leaving Lenin and Mariya to continue without her.[25]

The climb was very hard but Vladimir Ilyich, as Mariya recalled, 'strode briskly and confidently', chuckling as she struggled to keep up with him. The terrain was so perpendicular that eventually she was reduced to crawling on all fours. But it was worth the effort to take in the view from the top. Below, in all their marvellous variety, ranged first the brilliant whiteness of the snow, then great ranks of dark green pine trees, and far in the distance the luxuriant Alpine pastures. It was a magical moment; Mariya was moved to recite poetry: something suitably uplifting from Shakespeare or Byron. Lenin too seemed deep in thought. But no flight of poetic fancy fuelled his contemplation of so much beauty; the monomania, as usual, was bubbling only just below the surface. 'Hm,' he muttered after a pregnant pause, 'the Mensheviks are making a fine mess of things.'[26]

On the way down Mariya and Lenin agreed not to talk politics 'so as not to spoil the landscape'. She was touched and surprised, when, on entering a field full of wild flowers, Lenin stopped to gather a bunch to take back to Nadya. From here the party headed south along the Rhône through Bex-les-Bains, turning north again up the valley to Leuk, then entered the Bernese Oberland via the Gemmi Pass. At some point during this section of the hike, Mariya Essen left them to return to Russia, where she was arrested again at the end of the year.[27] Thereafter Lenin and Nadya walked a deliberately lonely trail down the Kandertal to Frutigen and skirted the shores of the Thuner See and Brienzer See, before arriving in Iseltwald, happy but exhausted. En route they stayed in local farmhouses and inns and ate cheaply with the workers rather than the tourists, collapsing into bed at the end of each day and sleeping for ten hours at a time. But it was impossible for Lenin to cut off from party matters altogether; he kept in touch by letter and had newspapers forwarded to him. From Iseltwald they crossed the mountains again in sight of the magnificent Jungfrau and down through the Bernese Oberland to Meiringen.[28]

Holiday or no holiday, Lenin was becoming increasingly worried that, with the Mensheviks now running *Iskra*, the absence of a rival Bolshevik newspaper was giving Martov too much of an advantage. Lenin had for months now been sending out appeals for supporters in Russia to submit material for a new newspaper in anticipation that sufficient funds could be raised. In July a series of arrests of party members in Russia had led to the co-opting of new members on to the Central Committee and its insistence on a reconciliation between Bolsheviks and Mensheviks (his old friend and committee member Gleb Krzhizhanovsky was among the conciliators, now of the opinion that Lenin had lost touch with reality and was an obstacle to party unity). One thing was clear: so much protracted and enervating conflict was dissipating the party's strength. And so, in August, while staying at a pension at the Lac du Bré, Lenin called an urgent, secret conference of his closest associates.

The subsequent 'Meeting of the Twenty-Two' – for such was the limited extent at that time of Lenin's Bolshevik support in Geneva – took place in the back room of a small hotel across the River Arve from the city in a working-class district well away from the Menshevik and other Russian enclaves.[29] One of Lenin's circle, Vladimir Bonch-Bruevich, had hired the venue, supposedly for a meeting of Russians intent on founding a hiking club for walking the Swiss mountains. The Swiss *patron* was flattered by the Russians' interest in alpinism and urged them to link up with the local Swiss society. After the delegates arrived under strict rules of *konspiratsiya* – instructed not to talk to anyone en route or ask directions to the hotel – they quickly agreed to launch an appeal 'To the Party' written by Lenin. This document outlined the current crisis and urged that the only hope of overcoming current political differences was immediately to summon a 3rd Party Congress. At the meeting, two new and significant political allies for Lenin first made their mark. Aleksandr Bogdanov, a gifted Marxist theoretician, writer and philosopher, would, despite having strong revisionist leanings, become a Bolshevik stalwart for the next six years and an important fundraiser. The second newcomer, and Bogdanov's brother-in-law, was Anatoly Lunacharsky. Primarily a poet and philosopher, he also seemed an unlikely recruit with his interests in the wider, human aspirations of revolution; such political romanticism did not square with Lenin's narrow, authoritarian political approach. But just now Lenin needed all the support he could get.

Lenin and Nadya ended their holiday at the Lac du Bré in mid-September, having walked over 250 miles, by which time the conscientious Nadya was feeling extremely guilty about having taken such a long holiday. The effect on Lenin, however, had been transformative: 'It was just as though the mountain streams washed away all the cobwebs of petty intrigue.'[30] He returned in peak physical condition. The holiday had performed an essential function; to Lenin's logical mind it was his duty, as a revolutionary, always to be physically ready for the fight to come.

On their return the couple decided to find somewhere new and more central in Geneva to live. They rented a small apartment at no. 91 rue de Carouge, but soon after transferred to 3 rue David Dufour so that the apartment on rue de Carouge could be used as an office, party archive and library for the Bolshevik faction of the RSDLP. At rue David Dufour, they squeezed into two small rooms: Nadya and her mother in one, Lenin in the other. There were, as usual, only the bare necessities – iron bedsteads with bast mattresses, a few chairs and a plain table. They shared a modest meal at four in the afternoon in the tiny kitchen; Lenin, as Lidiya Fotieva noted on sharing meals with them there, was a hearty eater but it 'did not make much difference to him what he ate'.[31] After his return, as in London he kept himself apart from the rowdy lifestyle of the other Russian émigrés, eschewing the cafés of Geneva, unless, like the Café Landolt, they served as a necessary venue for meetings. His living accommodation being so cramped, he daily decamped to the calm of the city's libraries. The imposing surroundings of the Bibliothèque Publique et Universitaire, located in a grand nineteenth-century building on promenade des Bastions, might have seemed the obvious choice but Lenin preferred the smaller and more intimate Société de Lecture, a private library in the heart of the city at Grand Rue 11, where he regis-tered on his return from holiday as 'W. Oulianoff, gentilhomme russe'. He went here day after day to work on the bulk of his political articles. The library was quiet and under-used, largely the preserve of elderly professors who rarely came, so Lenin had the full range of the reading room to pace up and down as he composed.[32] Soon he became a familiar figure to the librarian there in his shabby trousers 'with the bottoms turned up against the mud in Swiss style' and which he often forgot to turn down. Every day he would arrive, 'take out the books unfinished the day before . . . about barricade-fighting or the technique of offen-sives, go over to his usual place by the window, smooth down the thin hair on his bald head with a customary gesture, and bury his nose deep in the books'.[33]

He also liked to spend his evenings in the modest, twenty-five-seat RSDLP library that he had established with Vladimir Bonch-Bruevich at 91 rue de Carouge. Soon it was carrying a valuable selection of important socialist writings as well as newly published legal and illegal literature from Russia, Paris and London and a selection of periodicals in sixteen languages. It relied heavily on donations to keep it going and both readers and staff helped out on a largely voluntary basis. The prime instigator in the setting up of this library, which now became known as the Central Russian Library, had been Bonch-Bruevich, who donated to it many of his own books, as did Lenin. A Tolstoy scholar and writer on religious sects, Bonch-Bruevich seemed an unlikely Leninist. Quiet and intellectual, he had settled in Geneva in 1901. After the party split he and Lenin set up a publishing outlet for the printing and distribution of party literature, coming to an agreement with a group of Russian émigrés who ran a printshop. The newly established publishing house produced its first pamphlet 'Down with Bonapartism', by Mikhail Olminsky, that September; further pamphlets followed, all demanding the convocation of a 3rd Party Congress, notable among them Lenin's 'Letter to a Comrade on Our Organisational Tasks'. With party committees also lobbying in Russia for another congress, it was now essential that the Bolsheviks produce a newspaper of their own. The party was extremely short of the money needed to fund the paper and its typesetting. Lenin was rigorous: 'To spend money on anything else now is the height of folly.'[34]

That autumn, with her husband once more obsessively writing and studying, Nadya threw herself back into her party work. It was terribly burdensome. Martyn Lyadov had given her a couple of months' help initially and when she arrived from Russia, Lidiya Fotieva took over, working daily with Nadya on the voluminous party correspondence. Lyadov and Fotieva both noted how many party workers in Russia were inexpert in coding letters and how it often took Comrade Krupskaya hours of patient, tortuous persistence to decipher them – and there were hundreds passing through her hands every month. They could only marvel at her fantastic recall of the names of committee members, and their aliases, from all over Russia. When problems occurred, having no news-paper of their own the Bolsheviks resorted to the personal columns of the newspapers. Here cryptic messages, intelligible only to the recipients, were placed and 'gave directions and suggestions, requested information, acknowledged the receipt of letters or queried answers long overdue', as well as often announcing the failure to decode a particular letter.[35]

Much to Nadya's joy an old friend from teaching days in St Peters-burg, Ariadna Tyrkova, arrived in Geneva that year for treatment for a medical condition. But she was shocked to see how straitened Nadya and her mother's living circumstances were. Even in St Petersburg they had had domestic help. There was still much empathy between the two women despite Ariadna now having thrown in her political lot with Petr Struve's liberals. It was the first time she had met Lenin and she could not help noticing how Nadya was totally in thrall to her rather small, undistinguished husband with the deep set 'Mongolian' eyes. Lenin was very much the master, sitting behind closed doors through which one could just discern the scribbling of his pen and shuffling of his papers. When he emerged to join in their meal, Nadya's plain little face lit up, her large blue eyes shining with a kind of girlish love and admiration. She was entirely absorbed in him and his work, even though she had her own very strong personality, quite different from his. She was still the same warm, loving Nadya and Ariadna could not but admire the depths of her devotion to a man who at that time was, to all intents and purposes, just another Russian émigré political journalist and pamphleteer. Nikolay Valentinov had also noticed Nadya's complete sublimation in Lenin and his work: her speech was littered with her husband's revolutionary truisms. There was 'nothing of her own' in anything she said; in his view, 'she borrowed everything, from A to Z, from Lenin'.[36]

After supper on their last evening together, Nadya asked Lenin to accompany Ariadna to the tram stop as she didn't know her way round Geneva. En route, Lenin berated her for her liberalism and for being a 'bourgeois'. Ariadna gave as good she got, attacking the Marxists for their lack of understanding of human nature and their desire to drive people like a military machine. Lenin lashed her with his sharp tongue, his words deeply sarcastic and his eyes glittering in a way that Ariadna found disturbing. Then, as the tram came into view, he turned and looked her straight in the eye: 'Just you wait,' he said with a smile as she boarded the tram. 'Soon we will be hanging people like you from the lampposts.'[37]

Much of the life of the Russian political community in Geneva, and especially that around Lenin, centred at that time on the Russian canteen opened by Panteleimon and Ol'ga Lepeshinsky at no. 93 rue de Carouge on the corner of Quai de l'Arve, next door to the RSDLP library. Panteleimon Lepeshinsky had arrived in December 1903 as an illegal ahead of his wife, who had come on legitimate papers to study medicine at the university. They had decided to borrow money to set up a canteen to offer food and shelter to impoverished Russian exiles, as well as making a small profit for the party. The canteen opened in September

1904 and quickly became the Bolsheviks' unofficial club and meeting place, the venue for lectures and classes, as well as endless games of chess. The canteen itself had once been a shop and had a main entrance and two large windows overlooking the street. Inside were ranged six long wooden benches, fifty or so chairs and, in a corner, a piano (made use of in the evenings by the resident musicians Gusev and Krasikov for impromptu recitals, accompanied by Lidiya Fotieva). Through an archway beyond the dining area, there was a kitchen and one small room that served as living quarters for the Lepeshinskys and their five-year-old daughter. The canteen's success became, however, a poisoned chalice for the couple; every day seventy to eighty people crowded in for a 'democratic lunch' costing about forty centimes and again for supper and invariably overstayed their welcome. Soon Panteleimon and Ol'ga found themselves unable to extricate their private life from their business one. There were constant interruptions and knocks at the door at all times of the day and night; and in between it all, Ol'ga was still attempting to cycle down to the university every day to continue her medical studies.[38] But the canteen's uses as, effectively, a 'party school', were essential to Lenin, for here he held regular meetings and political classes with party activists leaving to take up underground work in Russia. In time the canteen's popularity spread to the international émigré community in Geneva and it became a regular haunt also of Polish, Bulgarian and Czech political exiles.

At the beginning of November, Lenin wrote to Aleksandr Bogdanov describing the desperate need for funds to alleviate 'the intolerable, depressing vegetable existence we are leading here'. Things were reaching a critical point: 'We must get that money if it kills us.'[39] Only a few days later his rising anxieties abated a little when Vladimir Bonch-Bruevich secured a deal with a French firm to supply the paper for their newspaper and do the printing on credit. A meeting of the Bolshevik group was held in early December at which the name *Vpered* (Forward) was decided on. The editorial board consisted of Lenin, Anatoly Lunacharsky, Vatslav Vorovsky and Mikhail Olminsky, with Nadya as secretary. Lenin was elated, hoping that his new mouthpiece, the first issue of which appeared on 4 January 1905, would revitalise his leadership of the party and bring to it many new recruits in Russia. The simple fact was that, at the end of 1904, his hold on the embryonic Bolshevik faction was tenuous. Some have gone so far as to say that Bolshevism at this time was little more than 'a library, a restaurant and a small publishing house' in Geneva.[40] Support – both moral and financial – had fallen away since the summer of 1903 and Lenin was faced with the prospect of rebuilding his element of the party into a new organisation while the title *Bolshevik* (from the adjective for 'majority') itself remained an absurd misnomer. At this point in time, Martov's 'minority' were in fact comfortably in the majority.

Anxious, beleaguered and broke, in Geneva that winter Lenin drew in on himself and his reserves. After a brief speaking tour in early December to Paris and Zurich to rally support for his faction, he retreated to the company of the loyal supporters who venerated him: Bonch-Brue-vich and his wife Vera, the Lepshinskys, Martyn Lyadov, and new arrivals Bogdanov and Lunacharsky, as well as his sister Mariya, recently released from several months in jail in Russia, who had arrived in Geneva urgently to recruit more activists to go back into Russia.

But by the end of the year Lenin had already fallen out with one of his newest and most promising political apprentices: Nikolay Valentinov. During his time in Geneva, Valentinov had become increasingly uneasy at the feuding within the RSDLP and Lenin's inflexible political line. When he had ventured an interest in the scientific philosophy of the Austrian Ernst Mach and his pupil, the German-Swiss Richard Avenarius, he was shocked by Lenin's venomous response. Any straying from the orthodox materialist thinking of Marxism was 'primitive and vulgar' in Lenin's view. As far as he was concerned, Marxism, like the Bible for Puritans, answered all questions and there was no need for philosophy. Anything that attempted to go beyond his own brand of orthodoxy was sham and reactionary, 'meaningless verbiage', 'ignorant chatter', 'clap-trap'.[41] Lenin's shrill and narrow-minded vocabulary revealed the intensely defensive position he always took on even the most tepid challenge to Marxist orthodoxy, surrounding himself with a picket fence of jargon and theory and lashing out at anything that tried, however tenuously, to breach it. After encountering the full brunt of Lenin's savage intolerance of his own broader, humanist views Valentinov realised that he had been marked by Lenin with the 'convict's badge' of theoretical heresy and party disloyalty. At a last meeting with Lenin on the Quai du Mont-Blanc he was informed he was now Lenin's enemy; he would no longer shake his hand or sit down at table with him. Nor would Lenin give him any help in getting back to Russia.

As 1904 came to an end in Geneva, in Russia rumblings of discontent had been building since summer and were now reaching a crescendo.

The costly imperialist war with Japan had brought only a series of crushing defeats, culminating in the besieging of the Russian navy at Port Arthur. This exacerbated the economic crisis in Russia that had been gathering since 1900. With prices rising in the shops, calls were mounting to improve factory conditions and wages and regulate the long working day. Students were turning out regularly for mass rallies in protest at the abuses of the tsarist government. In the south a general strike had broken out and spread to Transcaucasia. With troops being called in by provincial governments in Russia to control unrest, and clashes between police and workers in the major cities of Petersburg, Odessa and Moscow, the Okhrana had reported that 'universal attention was utterly transfixed by the unusual growth of the anti-governmental, oppositionist and social-revolutionary movement'.[42] The reactionary Minister of the Interior and Chief of Gendarmes, Vyacheslav von Plehve, had been assassinated on 28 July 1904, a warning of things to come. On the streets of St Petersburg, with increasingly vocal calls for civil liberties and constitutional reform mounting, there was the whiff of revolution.

Even the reticent Nicholas II had noticed the dramatic air of change: 'It is as if the dam has been broken: in the space of two or three months Russia has been seized with a thirst for change . . . Revolution is banging on the door.'[43]

In Geneva, too, Lenin sensed an approaching storm. But, with the RSDLP hamstrung by dissent, what would he, or the party, have to offer when the moment came?

CHAPTER EIGHT

'On the Eve of Barricades'

St Petersburg and Geneva: January–November 1905

The Winter Palace, St Petersburg

It was a quiet Sunday morning in St Petersburg, the air crisp with the kind of frosty winter cold – just 6 degrees below – that invigorated worshippers on their way to the city's great churches and cathedrals for the morning liturgy. However, that morning, 22 January 1905,[1] the vast majority of people on the streets of the city were not, for once, on their way to religious worship within the great porticos of St Isaac's Cathedral on Nevsky Prospekt or the other nearby churches whose golden cupolas glinted in the brilliant morning sunshine. They were heading instead towards St Petersburg's great focal point, Palace Square, at the far, northern, end of the Prospekt in front of the Winter Palace.[2]

St Petersburg had been rife with expectation for days. A major strike in the Putilov Iron Foundry in the south-west of the city, organised by the Assembly of St Petersburg Factory and Mill Workers, had spread, crippling industry. One by one, the factories, mills and workshops of the city had ground to a halt and the smoke from their chimneys ceased belching forth. By now 125,000 workers were on strike across 625 factories.[3]

The strike had rapidly become the rallying point for a major appeal to the Tsar for factory reform, a statutory working day and a range of long-overdue civil liberties. One hundred thousand people from working-class districts all over St Petersburg signed a heartfelt statement of their grievances addressed to the *tsar-batyushka* – their little father – begging for his intercession. That Sunday, it was their intention to march peacefully to the Winter Palace and present to Nicholas their humble petition:

> Sire! We workers and people of St Petersburg . . . our wives, our children and aged and helpless parents, are come to Thee . . . to seek for truth and protection. We are become beggars, bowing under oppression and burdened by toil beyond our powers, scorned, no longer regarded as human beings, treated as slaves who must suffer their bitter lot in silence. And having suffered, we are driven deeper and deeper into the abyss of poverty, lawlessness, and ignorance. We have been strangled by despotism and arbitrary rule, and we have lost our breath. We have no more strength, Sire. The limit of our patience has been reached. There has come for us the grave moment when death is preferable to a continuation of our intolerable torture.[4]

The faithful making their way in the naive hope of seeing the Tsar that morning had about them an air of almost religious fervour. But they did not know that Nicholas had already decamped to the safety of his palace at Tsarskoe Selo outside the city, having been assured that the situation was well under control. Intent on preventing a breakdown in public order, the authorities had approved the deployment of 12,000 troops and police to intercept the marchers before they even reached the palace.

Early that morning, at six assembly points across St Petersburg around 200,000 men, women and children, many of them in their Sunday best, had gathered round braziers by lantern light to warm themselves before heading off along the major thoroughfares of the city. It was still pitch dark as the first columns moved off, some of them having as far as ten miles to cover before reaching their destination. But in those early hours, their charismatic leader, Father Georgy Gapon, a self-styled worker-priest, had heard a sinister sound out in the streets – the dull thud of soldiers marching and the metallic clang of horseshoes of the Tsar's elite mounted regiments along the cobbled streets. Father Gapon's contingent had assembled not far from the Putilov Works at the historic Narva Gate, a massive triumphal arch built to honour Tsar Alexander I after his heroic victory over Napoleon in 1812. Twenty thousand or so of them headed off at midday. Gapon, carrying a large cross, took the lead with the workers following with all the solemnity of a religious procession, their icons, banners and a large framed portrait of the Tsar held high at the front of the column. They sang hymns too; it was all part of a deliberate statement of their peaceful intentions, as was the presence of so many women and children. They wanted to appeal to the Tsar as a family man. Though some, it is said, already had a profound sense of martyrdom to come.

A mile and a half north of the Narva Gate, Gapon's contingent found their way barred by troops ranged across the road, and in front of them mounted Cossack cavalry with drawn swords. Without warning, the cavalry charged the marchers, cutting them down. Gapon saw his followers 'dropping to the earth like logs of wood'. But that was not the end of it. The Cossacks then turned and cut their way back through the crowd, slashing at them with their sabres like madmen. This attack was followed by several volleys from the troops, the first two over the marchers' heads.[5] A similar pattern followed elsewhere – in the St Petersburg Quarter, the Alexander Park, on Vasilevsky Island, at Kolpino – as the other columns of marchers found their way barred by armed troops; in some cases a warning volley was fired over their heads first, in others not. In many cases the marchers by now were so intent on reaching their destination that they recklessly defied the orders to halt and turn back and rushed straight into direct gunfire. Some even stopped to tear open their coats, baring their chests to the soldiers as proof that they were unarmed. As the soldiers fired and the marching columns broke up and regrouped, many still tried to press on towards Palace Square, now finding themselves joined by a mixture of students, members of the public and innocent bystanders, all caught up in the terrifying momentum of events. But when they got there, the whole of Palace Square was cordoned off by 2,300 mounted troops and infantry and once again the now enormous crowd of about 60,000 was fired on without provocation, this time by the elite Preobrazhensky Guards. It was at this point that 'the passion of the mob broke loose like a bursting dam' when they saw the dead, wounded and dying lying in dark pools of blood-soaked snow. The corre-spondent of *The Times* wrote that what had started as a peaceful protest now became 'no longer a workman's question', as members of the public pressed forward in horror and indignation at what they had seen.[6] In side streets, students led groups of people in tearing down telegraph poles and dragging up benches to make barricades; here and there red flags appeared as the crowds surged forward inexorably, attempting to mass on the square in the midst of chaotic firing from the troops.

No one has ever been able to calculate accurately how many were killed and wounded that day. The official dead numbered fewer than fifty but those were only the bodies taken to public mortuaries. Many more of the dead and injured were carried home by their friends and families and it is thought that there were around one thousand casualties, with as many as five hundred killed.[7] By three o'clock that afternoon a heavy fall of snow had deadened the noise on the streets as darkness suddenly fell and the traumatised survivors struggled to make their way home. Troops were bivouacking round campfires at the corners of every city street, at the Narva Gate and outside all the factories, wrapped in their heavy greatcoats. Looters came out on the streets of St Petersburg that night, wrecking shops and stealing from wine stores; the sound of windows being smashed pervaded the city.

For Gapon and his followers the massacre of Bloody Sunday was a defining moment. 'There is no God anymore, there is no tsar,' they shouted bitterly.[8] Later that evening, Gapon, now a wanted man, appeared at a meeting of the Free Economic Society – his hair cut and his beard shaved off. He was visibly shaken and exhausted as he cursed the soldiers who had fired on his fellow workers and the 'traitor Czar who had ordered the shedding of innocent blood'. He fled Russia for Geneva and a meeting with Lenin in order to organise the smuggling in of guns for the workers back home.

★ ★ ★

News of the events of Bloody Sunday reached Geneva the following day. That morning, Lenin and Nadya had set off for a day's reading at the Société de Lecture when they saw Lunacharsky and his wife coming towards them down the street, Anna frantically waving her muff at them. Throughout the day the sedate streets of Geneva resounded with the shouts of newspaper boys – *'Révolution en Russie!'* – as the daily *Tribune de Genève* ran through five editions. The Russian community hurried out to buy as many papers as they could, constantly checking for new editions and incoming telegraph messages from Russia at newspaper offices. Everywhere, there were demonstrations of unbridled joy as exiles kissed and hugged each other and joined in singing the revolutionary funeral march 'You Have Fallen in the Struggle' in honour of the dead of Bloody Sunday. Political exiles of all nationalities and persuasions gathered in Geneva's Eglise Russe to give thanks, a pattern repeated in exile communities in Zurich, Berne, Paris, Munich and Berlin.

In Geneva, there was one place all the Russians were instinctively drawn to: the Lepeshinskys' canteen on rue de Carouge. It was hard to find the words to express their shock and excitement. Over at the *Vpered* printshop, Lenin managed to hold the front page of the new issue long enough to insert in bold type a banner headline: 'Long Live the Revolution!' Late into the night the exhilarated Russians were still out walking the streets, singing Russian revolutionary songs on the Plaine de Plainpalais until they were reprimanded for disturbing the peace.[9] All over Geneva the same words were being spoken over and over again: *'Nado ekhat' v Rossiyu'* – we *must* go back to Russia.

The pull of Russia, that peculiarly Russian *toska* – the longing for home – was incredibly powerful. The next day, as Lenin's followers congregated punctually at Lepshinsky's canteen for a briefing and were brusquely reprimanded if they were so much as seconds late, others went out collecting funds for the families of the dead and wounded in Russia. Many of the Geneva émigrés were already packing and heading for home, no matter what they might have to face when they got there. Each needed to be supplied with a passport and money for their journey, which stretched what little party funds remained. They all took advantage of their return by carrying illegal literature in double-bottomed suitcases and 'breast plates' inside their clothing.

But Lenin and Nadya did not start packing. The revolutionary leader was not yet ready to risk his personal safety; he believed, at this stage, that he was of more value to the movement as its leader, in the free West.

*   *   *

Bloody Sunday changed Russia irrevocably. The massacre finally shifted public opinion against Nicholas and his government across all sections of society, providing the long-awaited catalyst for upheaval. Students went out on strike; the government, anticipating further unrest, closed down all institutes of learning for the rest of the academic year. In

1905, the confused and often inarticulate response of the masses never-theless brought the Russian socialist movement finally into the open. On this, 'the eve of barricades',[10] as Lenin described it, a rash of serious industrial strikes broke out in the major cities, but none of the socialist parties held sufficient sway to marshal this outpouring of public anger and turn it to political advantage. In January the Japanese had taken the strategically crucial Russian naval base of Port Arthur. On 17 February the Tsar's uncle and brother-in-law, the reactionary Grand Duke Sergey, was assassinated by a Socialist Revolutionary bomber (the same group that had assassinated the despised Minister of the Interior, Vyacheslav von Plehve, the previous year). Any lingering confidence in the government was swept away by the almost total annihilation of the Russian navy at the Battle of Tsushima at the end of May. A humil-iated Tsar was forced to sue for peace soon after; his heroic imperial war had failed to bring a quick victory and turn the tide of public opinion in his favour. Rather the reverse; a month later the crew of the battleship *Potemkin* mutinied in port at Odessa, a city already crip-pled by civil unrest. Where were the local Bolsheviks when the moment came? The truth was that their power base in Odessa, as elsewhere, was almost non-existent.

As the tumultuous year wore on, it was marked increasingly by a descent into criminal violence in the cities and especially in the coun-tryside, where peasant rent strikes escalated into anarchic bouts of looting and vandalism of country estates. Strikes and marches spread to the borderlands of Latvia and Poland and the key industrial cities of Łódź and Warsaw. Even the professional middle classes, such as professors and industrialists, were joining the revolutionary protest. In an article in *Vpered* soon after Bloody Sunday, Lenin wrote that a civil war for freedom was now blazing across Russia. But he made no move to return to his native land to lead it. In Geneva his major preoccupation was still doctrinal rather than practical: the party split gnawed away at him and with such a volatile situation in Russia he was anxious to reconstruct the RSDLP and consolidate his own position. He did, however, express his regret at the 'accursed distance, the disgusting "beyond-the-frontier" existence of the émigré', which kept him from Russia.[11]

The catastrophe of Bloody Sunday and the popular response to it had not, of course, played to any of the preordained scenarios argued by the political theorists of the Russian diaspora, and none of them were suffi-ciently prepared to seize the moment when it came. In the big cities the

Bolsheviks did not have the depth of worker support sufficient to galvanise revolution under their leadership. They were weak and disorganised, still being largely made up of members of the intelligentsia and students; if anything, the Mensheviks had a broader base of support in Russia at the time and, crucially, more money.[12] Russia had seen moments of spontaneous civil unrest and protest before and they had always rapidly withered away. Lenin, like many others, simply did not believe that the insurgency would last. The chances of the RSDLP holding sway had been further undermined by the factional infighting that had been going on since the split at the 2nd Party Congress. Activists in Russia had become demoralised and Bolshevik support among the workers had fallen away. No one was even reading the few illegal leaflets they were able to produce. Crucially, the Bolsheviks were also too poorly armed. An up-and-coming underground worker, Maxim Litvinov, had written to Lenin from St Petersburg the previous December: 'The mass of party workers up to now continue to regard us as a handful of disorganisers with no strength of our own . . . our situation is impossibly rickety and precarious.'[13] In the Nevsky district populated by 30,000 industrial workers only six or seven Bolshevik underground circles remained – with barely six workers in each. Overall working-class support for both Bolshevik and Menshevik factions in St Petersburg that January was as little as a thousand. Support had evaporated, while the charismatic Gapon had garnered a massive popular following.

Why had Lenin not seized the moment in person, and headed for the barricades, as Nikolay Valentinov had anticipated when he met him the previous year in Geneva? When it came down to it he made no move to travel to St Petersburg, any more than did Plekhanov, Martov and Axelrod. Trotsky, however, although only just arrived in Geneva, immediately headed back to Russia under a false passport as 'Petr Petrovich'. But none of the long-term Marxist theorists of revolution in Russia, who had by now spent as many as twenty years in exile propagating millions of words on the subject, thought the moment would last. They had become too parochial, too preoccupied with their own endless theoretical squabbles, which had dangerously retarded the movement: the internal conflicts over revolutionary technique had become more important than the end of revolution. Ironically, Lenin, a man who loved the outdoors and who had committed his brain and his body obsessively to this one objective, was no Man of Action. The years of exile had turned him into a dedicated career politician and theorist, leaving him irredeemably wedded to books. All he could do was spin out his days at the Société de Lecture, reading French and German tomes on military science about barricades and street fighting during the 1848 Revolution or the Paris Commune of 1870–71, turning out yet more pamphlets and articles about the *practice* of revolution, without showing any desire to experience the reality.

And so, as he sat dreaming in Geneva of the proletariat smashing tsarism and setting in train the revolutionary conflagration across Europe that he so longed for, Lenin did not see how rapidly events in Russia were actually moving that year. His ultimate preoccupation, even now, as Valentinov had concluded, was to preserve his own position, and with it the leadership of the party, for when he deemed to be the right moment: 'He was the chief of the general staff and he never forgot that in times of emergency he had to safeguard the supreme command.'[14] This did not, however, stop Lenin from sending out repeated exhortations from rue David Dufour to his supporters in Russia to form fighting units and use whatever weapons they could lay hands on against the state. But for himself, his preferred plan of action was to set about urgent preparations for a 3rd Party Congress, at which he could galvanise his own Bolshevik power base, establish personal contact with delegates from Russia and send them back, re-energised, to recruit more workers in Russia for an organised, armed insurrection to follow later. At all costs he wanted to nip in the bud the mounting calls within his own ranks for reconciliation with the Mensheviks. The congress, he declared, 'must be simple – like a war council'.[15] Soon Lenin's real intentions became clear; it might have been formally announced as an RSDLP event but it was in reality a rump Bolshevik congress. The Mensheviks very rightly refused to take part (although a handful of delegates did in the end turn up). Mistrustful of Lenin, they saw another congress as providing no more than a forum for more Lenin-led divisions and held their own separate congress in Geneva, with Plekhanov declaring Lenin's congress unlawful.

London again seemed the safest venue for their deliberations and, although it was spring, the city as usual was hidden in a pall of rain, fog and the stench of coal fires when Lenin and Nadya arrived. From 25 April to 10 May, thirty-eight delegates from twenty regional Bolshevik committees congregated there. Lenin and Nadya stayed in lodgings at 16 Percy Circus, just around the corner from their old home at Holford Square. The leafy environs of Percy Circus became something of a Little

Russia for the next two weeks, with several delegates taking lodgings there and in houses at numbers 9 and 23 that had been specially rented by Alekseev for the purpose. He and Lenin, much as in 1903, did their best to help the newcomers find their way around London and obtain lodgings in Whitechapel for those not accommodated at Percy Circus. Quite a few, however, ended up dossing down in the pigsty that was Alekseev's tiny two-roomed flat, sitting and sleeping on piles of English and Russian newspapers.[16] In between sessions there was time for a cheap lunch at a café on Gray's Inn Road or a drink at a German club on Pentonville Road,[17] but for the rest of the time the delegates kept a very low profile. As in 1903, the levels of *konspiratsiya* were considerable, with the venues for the congress being two or three rented rooms in clubs or the back rooms of pubs around King's Cross and Gray's Inn Road, not far from Percy Circus.[18]

But one thing had changed; by 1905 the Special Political Branch, a division of the Metropolitan Police, had woken up to the activities of this new breed of Russian political exile and, despite the best efforts of the Russians to conceal their activities, they were being watched. One of the venues hired for the 1905 Congress was an upstairs room of the Crown and Woolpack pub on St John Street, under the laughable guise, as in 1903, of a supposed meeting of the 'Foreign Barbers of London'. At Scotland Yard one morning that April newly recruited Detective-Constable Herbert Fitch was instructed to investigate a meeting of this group about which Special Branch had had a tipoff from the pub landlord, Mr Moore. Fitch was fluent in German, Russian and French but knew that because the meeting would be relatively small there was no way he could infiltrate it in disguise.[19] The only solution would be to squeeze himself into a narrow, airless cupboard built into the wall of the upstairs room booked for the meeting, from which he would, he hoped, be able to overhear the proceedings. From his hideout, Fitch heard the password 'Liberty' given in Russian as, one by one, the delegates entered. As he crouched in agony, feeling increasingly dizzy, inside his cupboard Fitch heard 'Oulyanoff' take the floor and demand 'bloodshed on a colossal scale', without mercy, 'in Russia first, and then from one side of Europe to the other'.[20] The speech was greeted by fierce cheering. Although he could not see Lenin's face, Fitch later wrote that such was the 'passionate magnetism' of his voice 'that it would have incited a multitude to madness'.[21]

At this congress, as at the 2nd, Lenin interrogated delegates in detail about the state of the party in Russia. What was morale like? How many worker members did they have? From the first of twenty-eight sessions to the last, he threw all his energies into dominating proceedings, taking the floor more than a hundred times and frequently intervening during the speeches of others. Prior to the congress he had spent considerable time drafting resolutions and listing the major subjects for discussion, which would revolve around three major issues: the crisis in the party; organisation, in particular the setting up of fighting units in Russia; and insurgency tactics.[22] Even his most loyal followers were shocked by the aggression with which he attempted to impose his views, the first being to throw out Martov's loose definition of party membership – the cause of the 1903 split, over which he had lost the vote. They might now agree to drop this resolution, but many still called for reconciliation with the Martovites, particularly at this critical time in Russia.

On 1 May – International Workers Day – the Russians were disappointed not to see any British workers out parading along the streets of London or clashing with police and troops, as was now the case in Russia. Instead, all they saw were demure young women with flowers and collecting boxes, out raising money for the fight against tuberculosis. In Russia the day was marked somewhat differently – a new wave of industrial strikes once more gripped the country, while Lenin and his cohorts gathered in another back room of a pub off King's Cross. Herbert Fitch was still on the case, but there was nowhere this time for him to hide so he had to resort to shaving off his moustache and disguising himself as a waiter. When he carried a tray of drinks into the room where the meeting was being held, he recognised Lenin immediately because of the 'devilish sureness in every line of his powerful magnetic face'. Nevertheless, by sleight of hand Fitch managed to catch Lenin out by knocking a pile of agenda papers next to him on to the floor as he served the drinks, hiding one under his linen napkin as he retrieved them. As the meeting progressed Fitch stood on a chair by the door outside, his ear to the fanlight, taking further notes on Lenin's 'cut-throat ideas of revolt'.[23]

In the end the congress did little more than rubber stamp the position of Lenin as leader of the Bolshevik faction, endorsing his calls for the recruitment of more workers to party committees (eight to every two intellectuals was his suggestion), supporting the appeal for an armed uprising in Russia and the urgent acquisition of arms. Lenin was elected to the Central Committee and also voted editor of a new party newspaper, *Proletarii* (Proletarian) which was to replace *Vpered*, aimed at popularising recent party decisions at the congress. But from now on the work of the Central Committee and the party newspaper was to be led not from Geneva but St Petersburg. Among the delegates there were many who thought the time had come for Lenin to return.

Before leaving London, Lenin took his colleagues to see the British Museum Reading room where Marx and Engels had worked; there were visits too to the Natural History Museum and the Zoo in Regent's Park. A final, obligatory, pilgrimage was made to Marx's grave, during which he warned delegates to be on the lookout for British police and Okhrana spooks, who might try and photograph them. In Paris, the group stopped off to see the Eiffel Tower, and the Louvre. Now, of all times, it seemed most appropriate to complete their political education by Lenin with a visit to the Wall of the Communards in Père Lachaise Cemetery where, on 28 May 1871, troops had executed 147 Paris workers involved in the uprising. There was even time for a visit to the Grand Opera and an evening's laughter at the *Folies Bergère*. Meanwhile, Russia for Lenin remained an abstraction, still a long way away.

By the time Lenin returned to Geneva in May 1905, the euphoria of the January days had long since dissipated. Despondency ruled, with many exiles unable to go back home and frustrated by lack of up-to-date news. Lenin wrote to Anatoly Lunacharsky, now in Italy, that his people in Geneva were 'down in the dumps', berating them for being 'awkward, inactive, clumsy, timid . . . They're good fellows, but no damn'd good whatever as politicians. They lack tenacity, fighting spirit, nimbleness and speed.' The 'colonial conditions' of life abroad bred the worst habits in political exiles, who were prone to contracting 'the disease of squabbling, gossip and tittle-tattle'.[24] The party was short of everything right now: money, weapons and even good speakers. It was down to him single-handedly to lift them all 'above the Geneva marsh into the sphere of more serious interests and problems'. Lenin was certainly doing as much in his urgent missives to party activists in Russia, which were becoming increasingly shrill and impatient: 'We have been talking about bombs for more than six months,' he railed, 'and not a single one has been made.'[25] He went on to list the use of every available weapon – bombs, revolvers, grenades – even knives and knuckledusters and crudely made firebombs of rags in bottles – whatever the Russian underground could lay their hands on. 'Form fighting squads at once everywhere!' he commanded – despite having no practical experience of what effect such ad-hoc and ill-equipped fighting units might have against the power of the Tsar's crack troops.

By Lenin's estimates two or three hundred such brigades (of five or six insurgents each) were needed in Petersburg alone to seize the revolutionary opportunity. They should be out on the streets attacking police stations, assassinating spies, robbing banks and expropriating funds for the revolution. If all else failed they could beat up policemen. It was, of course, all too easy for Lenin to fire off such extraordinarily naive directives from the safety of Geneva. And his clarion calls did indeed find their recruits: a wide range of striking workers, deserters from the army and navy and other denizens of the under classes, often on the run from the police, joined the fighting groups.[26] But what was needed were people with real frontline experience to lead it all, Communard-style, from the barricades.

A hard core of dedicated activists in St Petersburg was, however, willing to attempt the kind of crazy heroics demanded by Lenin. In January, Nikolay Burenin, who had originally been recruited by St Petersburg party chair Elena Stasova to disseminate illegal literature, had been given responsibility for setting up a Fighting Technical Group to smuggle in arms from Finland and set about bomb-making. Burenin was already experienced at organising safe houses for the storage of literature and illegal printing presses and now these storehouses made way for weapons, ammunition, dynamite and other bomb-making materials. He knew something of working with explosives for he had already had experience developing special belts and corsets for carrying fuses and dynamite and jackets for concealing revolvers. There had been considerable difficulties with the carrying of dynamite: it had a pungent smell and when it came into contact with the inevitable nervous sweat of the person carrying it, it smelled even worse. Women turned out to be the best couriers, dousing themselves in sickly perfume to conceal the smell, and when forced to travel on trains standing on the open platform of the end carriage, even in the coldest weather, in order not to draw attention to themselves. Even rifles were carried into Russia piecemeal by female couriers. They would be broken down into barrels and stocks and suspended from pieces of cord around the courier's neck under her clothes. Some female students became so skilled at this that they were able to smuggle up to eight rifles at a time, though it was impossible for them to bend or sit down.[27] One pretty and particularly fearless female member of Nikolay Burenin's Fighting Technical

Group, Feodosiya Drabkina, went on missions back and forth across the city in the cold and snow that winter, taking her three-year old daughter Lizka with her as cover. The daughter later remembered how puzzled she had been at how her mother would constantly change shape and size from fat to thin as she delivered the smuggled arms she carried under her clothes.[28]

For the bomb-making programme, Burenin recruited the scientific expertise of a professor at the Kiev Polytechnic, Mikhail Tikhvinsky, code-named 'Ellipsis', and two St Petersburg-based chemists, 'Alpha' and 'Omega' (there were only two of them originally in this secret cell, hence the choice of names).[29] Alpha was a young female chemistry student, Lyubov' Peskova; Omega – Mikhail Skosarevsky, a part-time teacher and scientific laboratory worker, both of whom secretly manufactured the components for bombs in their official place of work. Finding the right explosives and suitable containers for the bombs under the strict practices of *konspiratsiya* was another matter. One day, Burenin arrived at Alpha's lab with a highly amateurish and volatile bomb manufactured from a large sardine tin hidden under his father's raccoon coat. It was one of a consignment sent by activists in Riga, Latvia, and he wanted her opinion on the workmanship. Picking it up from the lab table, Burenin shook it, at which Alpha heard the rattling of pieces of glass which had been packed inside. It was a cack-handed effort, too small to be effective, but nevertheless dangerous enough to cause injury at close hand. Alpha took one horrified look at the object and advised Burenin to take his bombs – he had left two more behind at home – and get rid of them as quickly as he could. Later that evening, having donned his frock coat and patent leather shoes for a concert at which he was to perform, Burenin headed out to the Obvodny Canal with one of the bombs under his raccoon coat. It was a filthy night and the banks of the canal were slippery and thick with mud, as he struggled to reach the water and dispose of his bomb, almost falling in in the process. He had to take shelter at a friend's flat to clean himself up before continuing his journey, arriving late for his performance. He was later reprimanded for breaking all the rules of *konspiratsiya* in such a foolhardy and bungling way.[30]

The bomb makers soon realised they needed a better template to work from and sought guidance from Macedonian partisans – the Chetniks – who for years had been waging guerrilla war against their Turkish oppressors in Bulgaria. Skosarevsky was first sent to Lenin in Geneva in March for a secret briefing on contacts and addresses in Bulgaria before departing on a secret mission to liaise with these activists on bomb making. He later reported back to Lenin on progress, which was greatly hampered by the difficulty in obtaining good enough quality fuses. Soon after, Burenin was sent back to Bulgaria to buy large quantities of British Bickford safety fuses from the Chetniks.

Meanwhile, in St Petersburg, all sorts of vessels were being tested as containers for improvised bombs and hand grenades – and rejected: tins for sardines, fruit drops or preserves, pieces of gas piping. In the end some iron casings were obtained from a factory on the Liteiny in St Petersburg and taken to an innocent looking factory out of town that made lead soldiers and toy metal trains and cars for children, where they were remodelled into bombs. The moment there was a suggestion of police curiosity about the toy factory the bomb-making operation was transferred to a workshop ostensibly for the repair of samovars and other domestic goods.[31] With the technical advice of Tikhvinsky, who had headed a very successful bomb-making operation in Kiev, Burenin organised the production of dynamite, pyroxilin and fulminate of mercury in a workshop that supposedly made cameras. Those who worked on the production of bombs did so in the strictest isolation, giving up all contact with the outside world. They were not allowed out to meetings or to take part in demonstrations and did not even know the identities of those who came and went with materials, all in order to maintain the absolute secrecy of the operation. Husbands and wives lived apart – as did Feodosiya Drabkina and her husband, who was also a member of the group – and hardly ever saw each other.

When the time came to test their newly made bombs Alpha and Omega took the risk of travelling by train to a remote country estate at Akhi-Yarvi in the Karelian Isthmus of Finland, north of St Petersburg. In order to prevent them from being discovered by highly vigilant customs officers, they strapped their 'bombs' to their legs and hid them under their clothes, making it extremely awkward to walk normally.[32] The estate at Akhi-Yarvi, owned by the family of one of the Technical Group, Aleksandr Ignatiev, was already a secret laboratory for the production of picric acid which was a key component in the explosive agent melinite. The highly toxic yellow crystals of the picric acid stained everything that came into contact with them – even the eye whites of those who spent their time making it turned yellow. On one occasion during that winter the agents took a consignment to the station at Raivola, but discovered to their horror that the melinite had leaked, leaving a bright yellow trail in the snow – all the way back to Akhi-Yarvi. They set to work trying to disperse the traces but it was only a heavy fall of snow soon after that saved them from detection.

⋆　⋆　⋆

By October, despite his many and repeated exhortations to organise in Russia, Lenin had reached the conclusion that the best time for insurrection would be the following spring after a defeated and demoralised army returned from the Far East. He wrote of this to Mariya Essen, now back in St Petersburg working for the party, the assumption being that the unpredictable, inchoate train of events unfolding in Russia could be clinically controlled in the same efficient way he timetabled his own life: 'The time of the uprising, I repeat, I would *willingly postpone* until the spring,' he wrote, admitting, however, that 'it is difficult, of course, for me to judge from a distance.'[33] For all his undoubted polemical and political gifts Lenin never seemed to appreciate the one essential: that history never runs to any preordained schedules; time and again he would find himself having to improvise and amend his tactics to fit the changing political situation. Earlier, in August, he had published another densely written treatise, 'Two Tactics of Social Democracy', in which he outlined the reasons why he felt Russia was not yet ready for a fully socialist revolution. The first and necessary step was the establishment of a bourgeois-liberal regime that could then be overthrown by the urban workforce allied with the peasantry. Only then, according to Lenin, could the great vision of the 'democratic dictatorship of the proletariat and peasantry', led by the intellectual leadership of the RSDLP, come into being. Yet in the middle of October events once again exploded in Russia. A General Strike broke out when the shipbuilding, steel and rail industries downed tools and paralysed the infrastructure and industry. The lights went out all over cities; shops, schools and theatres closed. Water supply was affected; bread and food stocks began to run out. Even wealthy industrialists and professionals – ballet dancers, doctors, lawyers, stockbrokers – came out in support of the strike, which within days had spread to every major city.[34] Workers took to the streets with banners and marching songs. When the electricity supplies in St Petersburg stalled, all the authorities could do to monitor unrest was to sweep the Nevsky Prospekt by searchlight mounted on the Admiralty building. Where were the bombs and fighting brigades, railed Lenin in a torrent of demands by letter from Geneva, as he realised he and the party had again failed to catch the *Zeitgeist* in his home country.

It was not Lenin's cadres of professional revolutionaries but the workers themselves who this time took events into their own hands. And now they were learning how to organise. On 26 October striking workers, with help from the Mensheviks (Lenin's Bolsheviks misguidedly having chosen not to be involved), set up an elected committee known as the St Petersburg Soviet of Workers' Deputies. The dynamic twenty-six-year-old Trotsky, now returned from hiding in Finland, where he had been forced to flee that summer, was nominated as vice-chair. Declaring freedom of the press, the Soviet began publishing its own newspaper, *Izvestiya*. It organised trade unions and distributed welfare to strikers and soon its example was emulated by fifty more Soviets, set up in major industrial cities across Russia, including Moscow. The workers were at last organising themselves without recourse to the out-of-touch theorists of Geneva and the Russian diaspora. It was a heroic venture, and one in which Trotsky, with his outstanding oratorical skills in front of a crowd, unexpectedly took centre stage. It only lasted fifty days but the Soviet undoubtedly sowed the seeds for 1917 as a potent opposition force.

The advent of the Soviets was the final push needed to force political change on a stubborn and dogmatic Tsar. On 30 October, Nicholas II, still vainly clinging to the principles of absolute monarchy instilled in him by his father Alexander III, was finally forced to agree to political concessions or face a bloodbath in putting down the disorder. Even his arch-reactionary cousin, Kaiser Wilhelm, had advised constitutional reform. Nicholas's October Manifesto thus reluctantly created an elected state Duma promising freedom of conscience, speech and assembly and abolishing censorship, with Count Sergey Witte as head of the Council of Ministers. Strikes and civil unrest abated as law and order was gradually restored, but in the provinces a right-wing backlash against the revolutionaries prompted savage pogroms against the Jews, who were blamed as being the instigators of unrest.

There was yet to be one last gasp of rebellion when the Moscow Soviet, dominated by the city's textile workers who till now had seemed less militant than the industrial workers of St Petersburg, called another general strike in November. Meanwhile, on 3 December, Trotsky was arrested along with most of the St Petersburg Soviet's executive committee. (In November 1906 he and fourteen others, after languishing in the Peter and Paul Fortress, were condemned to exile in Siberia – for life.) The strike spread from Moscow to St Petersburg and other cities. But the main focus of the rebellion was in Moscow. Here, on 10 December, the workers in the Presnya District mounted an armed insurrection, manning the barricades with all the fervour and heroism of the Paris Commune of 1871. For a while the infectious atmosphere spread. Students and members of the public rolled up their sleeves and helped to raise barricades on one of the city's main streets, the Tverskaya.

At this time Feodosiya Drabkina was sent to Moscow with a travelling bag full of Chetnik bombs for the insurgents. Before she left, she was sent out with party funds to buy herself a smart outfit and bag on the fashionable Nevsky Prospekt. She travelled by train with her daughter. The child was perfect cover for such a dangerous assignment: little sweet-faced Lizka, nicknamed the party's 'conspiracy device' by Nadezhda Krupskaya, held suspicion at bay en route, on a train filled with troops.[35] Their destination was the apartment of the popular and fashionably 'proletarian' writer Maxim Gorky who had become an important party fundraiser and figurehead, having been jailed earlier that year for protesting against Bloody Sunday (his release secured by an unprecedented worldwide protest). When Feodosiya and Lizka arrived at Moscow's Nikolaevsky Station it was ringed by troops with fixed bayonets, and as they crossed the deserted streets they could hear regular volleys of gunfire. Gorky's apartment was a hive of activity when they got there, having become a nerve centre for the insurrection, as well as a bomb-making factory. The dining table was laid out with food and the samovar was bubbling as people came and went from all over Moscow with news of the latest situation and took instructions. In a small room off Gorky's study set aside for his aviary (he was a passionate bird-keeper) activists were taking instruction in how to prime the bombs.[36]

For days the whole of Moscow resounded to the sound of gunfire, but the insurgents were poorly armed and by the 15th the street fighting had been put down by the crack Semenovsky Guards, brought in from St Petersburg (the authorities fearing the Moscow garrison would mutiny in sympathy if used) and backed up by heavy artillery bombardment. In the heavy shelling and conflagration that followed, much of the Presnya district was laid waste and as many as a thousand civilians killed.[37]

With new civil rights promised by the Tsar, including enfranchise-
ment of Russia's urban workforce and a full political amnesty, the strikes
across the country were called off as industries were at last allowed to
set up their own trade unions. Political parties were emerging into the
open, with Lenin's erstwhile colleague Petr Struve founding his own
party, the Constitutional Democrats (known as the Kadets). What Lenin
later called the 'Dress Rehearsal' for revolution was over but some important lessons in militancy and street fighting had been learned from the
debacles of Bloody Sunday and the Moscow insurrection. Lenin now
recognised the logic in unity and damage limitation within the party,
offering the olive branch to Plekhanov and the Mensheviks in a last-
ditch attempt to end the factional infighting. He had been coming under
increasing criticism by European socialists in the Second International,
particularly the German Social Democrats, to put an end to the discord
in the RSDLP and he needed to retain their support. He therefore drew
on all his skills in political improvisation in order to lay the ground for
his hoped-for insurrection the following year and wrote an unchrac-
teristically flattering letter to Plekhanov at the end of October. In it he
stressed the 'need for Social-Democratic unity' and his appreciation of
the 'entire movement's *extreme need* of your guiding, close and immediate participation' and asked for a meeting with him.[38] The ulterior
motive was to gain Plekhanov's' respected voice on the editorial board
of a new Russian-based newspaper, *Novaya Zhizn'* (New Life). But Lenin's
letter was ignored; it was too late now, in Plekhanov's mind, for the
wolf to lie down with the lamb.

By November 1905, with the political amnesty now in operation, it
seemed safe at last for political exiles to return to Russia. In any case,
Lenin finally had to concede that he could not mastermind armed insurrection from a distance, based on erratic and incomplete reports in
Western newspapers, with intelligence gathering from his own activists
in Russia subject to constant police surveillance and interception. In mid-
November he left Geneva, but not before meticulously sorting through
all his papers with Nadya, packing them into a trunk and leaving them
in safe keeping with a Bolshevik comrade. En route back into Russia via
Stockholm, he met up with a Finnish agent, Ula Kastren, sent by Burenin
in St Petersburg, who provided him with a false passport to enter Russia.
Lenin needed to get back quickly; the rail route would take too long –
forty-eight hours – and involve risky police checks at the border at Torneo,
so on 17 November he and Kastren travelled to Åbo in south-western

Finland on the steamship *Bore II* and the following day took a train to Helsingfors.[39] After an overnight stay in a safe house owned by Kastren's brother, Lenin took the train into St Petersburg's Finland Station, where Nikolay Burenin was waiting for him. From there he headed straight for a meeting of his local Bolshevik committee. He had been away from Russia for five years.

CHAPTER NINE

Stolypin's Neckties

Russia and Finland: December 1905–April 1907

The Villa Wasa, Kuokkala, Lenin's Finnish hideout

For once, Lenin had arrived in Russia on legal papers – in the English name of William Frey – now assuming he would be able to move around unimpeded by the police, to whom he was obliged to report daily. Nadya joined him ten days later, but she had been closely followed on the train from Finland by a police spy. For a while the couple tried to live legally in a flat on the Grechesky Prospekt with friends of Lenin's sister Mariya. But very quickly they noticed that the flat had been staked out by Okhrana spooks, whose presence so alarmed their host that he prowled up and down the flat at night with a pistol in his pocket, terrified of a police raid.[1] So, after a succession of short-term stopovers in safe houses, often living apart, on 17 December the couple were forced to go underground again.

Once more they found themselves living under the constraints of *konspiratsiya* at its most difficult and dangerous level, something they had not experienced in the relative tranquillity of Geneva for the last two years. Lenin was terrified of being arrested and rarely emerged into public view. Nadya, who was able to move around more freely, became her husband's 'zealous reporter', finding out about events in the city from servant girls and her activist friends in Sunday School circles.[2] A bewildered Elizaveta Vasil'evna, who had been alarmed by the suddenness of their departure from Geneva and had dutifully followed them back to Russia, complained that she hardly saw either of them: 'they passed like comets'.[3] But Lenin played little or no active role in events, apart from appearing at secret Bolshevik meetings or sneaking out for the occasional meeting with Nadya at the Vienna restaurant on Gogol'skaya. In later years, in an attempt to defuse the obvious questions about his low profile at the time, it would be claimed that the party had expressly forbidden Lenin from taking any personal risks.[4] It was true that he lived an extremely watchful existence, forever looking behind him, coming and going from different entrances in the buildings he took refuge in, constantly moving from one Bolshevik safe house to another and changing false passports every couple of weeks. For the rest, his time was consumed by writing for *Novaya Zhizn'*, the first legal Bolshevik newspaper to enjoy the new freedom of the press. Its leading light was Maxim Gorky, who was not just the darling of the Russian literary world but was well connected and had the ear of powerful, liberally minded industrialists willing to put money into the journal and the Bolshevik faction. A donation of 15,000 rubles from a wealthy benefactor had set the journal up, with Gorky's common-law wife, a well-known actress called Mariya Andreeva, as its nominal publisher. The original non-Bolshevik literary contributors, all friends of Andreeva's and Gorky's, were soon ousted when Lenin arrived and was co-opted as editor, bringing in his own politicised people. The *Novaya Zhizn'* editorial offices thereafter became the centre of Bolshevik underground activity, as a safe house for visiting activists, for the distribution of false passports and illegal literature and the issuing of directives, with Nadya at the administrative helm in her role as coordinator and secretary to the Central Committee. The paper's success was meteoric, building to a circulation of 80,000. Lenin was once more in his element at the centre of party propaganda, just like in the old *Iskra* days, and would sit late into the night, obsessively checking the page proofs of his articles.

One evening in a Tatar restaurant in the Nevsky quarter not long after his arrival, Lenin had been introduced by a *Novaya Zhizn'* colleague, Petr Rumyantsev, with whom he had been staying on Rozhdestvenskaya, to a cultured and attractive party member, Elizaveta de K. A week later he met her again at the offices of *Novaya Zhizn'* and at Rumyantsev's suggestion Elizaveta, who was separated from her husband and came from a comfortable background, offered Lenin the use of her apartment for secret party meetings. Located in a fashionable part of town, the premises offered a good front and were used by Lenin on a dozen or so occasions. One of the first things Elizaveta noticed was how pathologically obsessive he was about security. Arriving 'as discreetly as a detective' ahead of his fellow conspirators, he would stand by the window for some time viewing the street below and examining the faces of the people he saw there. He would carefully drill her on the passwords of the day and instruct her to let in only those who gave them correctly. After meetings he would always be the last to leave. Elizaveta would watch as he stepped cautiously into the street 'as though about to plunge into cold water', casting anxious looks this way and that.[5] Sometimes, Lenin stayed late. She cooked him simple food, which he seemed to greatly appreciate. He often helped with the washing up and lighting the samovar and he seemed to be very domesticated. Occasionally she played the piano for him – Beethoven's *Sonata Pathétique* was a favourite. Whenever she came to the third section she noticed that there was something in the music that Lenin was incapable of resisting emotionally. The perpetual, ironic smile, a form of self-protection that always played across his lip, would occasionally slip and a world weariness would descend over him. At times Lenin appeared deeply exhausted and depressed – Elizaveta could tell he drove himself very hard and there was something in the music that lifted him from the otherwise arid, conspiratorial life he was living. But how mortified Lenin was when he realised he had let his emotional guard slip.[6] On such occasions, Elizaveta had visions of him returning to his secret lodgings to read Marx with that furious, self-flagellating energy of his, in order to drive away his emotional demons.[7]

During those first weeks in St Petersburg, Lenin found living in other people's homes extremely inhibiting for his work. Words and argument were his familiars and his weapons and it was only once more in the world of political debate that he found his metier. At the end of December 1905, he left Russia for the 1st All-Russian Bolshevik Conference. As the insurrection in Moscow was being brought to a brutal close he arrived in Tammerfors in southern Finland. Now called Tampere, and Finland's third largest city, it was then still known by its old Swedish name – war between Sweden and Russia in 1808–9 had resulted in Finland, then under Swedish dominion, being ceded to the Russian Empire. It was granted the status of an autonomous Grand Duchy by Tsar Alexander I, but in reality, throughout the nineteenth century, it had been subject to much of the same censorship and political oppression as prevailed in Russia. The Finns had responded with a campaign of passive resistance to tsarist rule. Patriotic feeling ran high and resisted a concerted programme of Russianisation late in the century, in preparation for Finland's full absorption into the Empire. It therefore quickly ignited in the wake of events in 1905, when Finnish Social Democrats offered their solidarity with the striking workers of Russia and showed themselves eager to join in the action.

In the autumn of 1905, activists in Finland, led by the journalist Konni Zilliacus, who now edited the leading underground newspaper *Fria Ord* (Free Words) had been indispensable in organising gun-running to St Petersburg from Europe. The old *Iskra* smuggling routes developed by Zilliacus in 1901–3 were again used, but much larger quantities of weapons and explosives were now needed and only small amounts could be smuggled into Russia by individual couriers. A massive arms-gathering campaign was therefore initiated by Zilliacus, who began by obtaining Mausers and Brownings from a firm in Hamburg and Wetterli rifles from Switzerland. Other revolvers as well as explosives were bought in England. Eventually, a cache of 15,500 rifles, a quarter of a million cartridges, 2,500 revolvers and three tons of explosives were ready for transportation into Russia.[8] In collusion with Motojirio Akashi, the Japanese Military Attaché in Stockholm charged with masterminding subversive action against Russia, Zilliacus organised the purchase in England of a small steamship, the *John Grafton*, and two yachts to run the guns, along with machine guns acquired by Akashi, into the Baltic with a crew of British, Norwegian and Latvian seamen. But disaster struck when the *John Grafton* proved unseaworthy and ran aground on 7 September off the coast of Finland. Some of the arms were evacuated but the ship had to be blown up in order to prevent it falling into the hands of Russian customs. Most of the unloaded rifles were seized and the bulk of the arms scattered in and around the wreck were salvaged by a Russian naval diving unit. But some Wetterli rifles got through and were put to good use during the general strike in Moscow.

In Finland that autumn activists had followed the Russian example of the Moscow rebellion and taken control of Tammerfors's town hall on Keskustori, the city's central square. From its masthead they raised the red flag and set up their own strike committee, seeing off the few Russian gendarmes and police based there with no difficulty. Soon after, they issued their own 'Red Manifesto' echoing the political demands of those made in Russia. Now, in December 1905, The People's House, a workers' meeting place and library a short distance away on Halli-tuskatu, welcomed Lenin and his delegates on a bitterly cold 23 December. The conference was a modest affair. Those delegates who could get there despite the railroad strike sat on plain wooden benches ranged around long tables, during which the major topics for discussion were reunification with the Mensheviks, calls for an armed uprising in Russia, to which Lenin still held firm, and a boycott of the 1st Duma. With events in Russia still unravelling there was an air of excitement throughout the proceedings and practical skills were foregrounded; in between sessions, delegates went out into the woods for target practice with an assortment of Mausers, Brownings and Winchesters. In grati-tude for their solidarity Lenin promised the Finnish Social Democrats that, when the revolution finally came in Russia, Finland would be granted its independence.[9]

At Tammerfors, a promising, newly elected party delegate had arrived from the Caucasus. Code-named 'Ivanovich', like Lenin he operated under a wealth of pseudonyms; in the Georgian underground he was known as Koba or Soso, but his real name was Josef Dzhugashvili (the name Stalin was not adopted till later). Stalin had been greatly impressed by Lenin's 'Letter to a Comrade on Our Organisational Tasks' at the time of the party split in 1903, the boldness of his polemic convincing him that 'the Party had a mountain eagle' at its helm.[10] On arrival in Tammerfors, his first trip out of Russia to a party conference, Stalin stood around for a while with the other delegates, waiting for the great leader to make his entrance. It was some time before he realised that the stocky little balding man talking animatedly to colleagues nearby was Lenin himself. Stalin's disappointment at first sight of the party's leader mirrored that of many others in the pre-revolutionary years. At a distance, Lenin seemed 'the most ordinary man', but when he spoke it was quite a different matter; Stalin could not but be impressed by Lenin's charisma as a speaker and his extraordinary strength of will.[11]

Lenin and Nadya's return to Russia early in 1906 after the Tammerfors conference was a discouraging one. The inevitable official reaction to the events of December was rapidly setting in. The Moscow insurrection had been poorly organised and armed, with little or no coordination with the party in St Petersburg. Lenin knew that the time had come to face reality: 'We are now confronted with the new work of assimilating and refashioning the experience of the latest forms of struggle', he wrote. 'We must definitely, practically get down to the tremendous tasks of a new active movement, preparing for it more tenaciously, more systemically, more persistently.'[12] The lessons of 1905 had to be learned. The party must adapt and regroup – and to do this effectively it had no option but to go underground again.

Lenin now channelled his irrepressible nervous energy into his political writing and work on *Novaya Zhizn'* at its offices on Nevsky Prospekt and for the next year spent most of his time attending conferences and congresses abroad as well as secret Bolshevik meetings in St Petersburg and Finland. He wrote obsessively, pouring out more than one hundred newspaper articles on party policy, the peasants and the land question, organisation and tactics, for *Novaya Zhizn'* and a succession of short-lived underground newspapers. Many of the articles, such as 'Lessons of the Moscow Uprising', analysed the events of 1905. He made only a couple of public speeches at this time, the most notable being on 22 May when, under the pseudonym Karpov, he slipped into a political meeting being held at the palace of Countess Sofya Panina, addressed by a member of the Kadet party. When given the floor, Lenin publicly denounced the Kadets for negotiating with the Duma, which he declared a fraud, the tsar having thrown out most of its proposed programme of trade union and land reform. There were three thousand people present and Nadya recalled how pale and nervous Lenin had seemed until he began to speak – rightly so, for it was the first large gathering of its kind he had ever addressed. When word got round the audience that Karpov was in fact Lenin, he was given an ovation, but the breach of his anonymity unnerved him. Although he spoke again in June to an All-Russian Congress of School Teachers he was again greatly discomfited by venturing forth into public. Lenin had every reason to be nervous: on the rare occasions he did go out he was often followed. On one such occasion in March 1906, instead of going back to the flat where he had been briefly living with Nadya, he immediately slipped his tail and took the train out of the city to a safe house in Finland. A bewildered Nadya was left to wait and wonder where her husband was until finally informed

– but by now she had become used to the perpetual insecurities of their life together.

Lenin's Finnish refuge was the Villa Wasa, a large, attractive wooden dacha with a covered verandah conveniently located not far from the station at Kuokkala, forty miles from St Petersburg. Surrounded by a high fence and set in a clearing in dense woodland, it was the perfect conspiratorial location. It had been rented from a sympathetic Finn for party use and Lenin stayed here working undisturbed on resolutions for the next Party Congress to be held in Stockholm at the end of April. On paper, it was intended to be a 'Reunification Congress' where Bolsheviks and Mensheviks had pledged to bury their differences but the element of 'reconciliation' was entirely cosmetic, with even Nadya later admitting that the proceedings had been 'decidedly factional'.[13] The presence of the congress in Sweden remained a well-kept secret with Lenin registering in a nearby hotel under the name of Weber; Nadya was given status as a consultative delegate representing Kazan. At the congress, the Mensheviks were in the majority, with sixty-two mandates to the Bolsheviks' forty-six. Since the debacle of 1905 the Bolsheviks had lost the working-class centre of St Petersburg to the Mensheviks. Although Lenin was elected to the presidium of the congress he was not voted on to the board of the Central Committee, the balance of which remained seven Mensheviks to three Bolsheviks. Being in the minority did not discourage Lenin; adversity never did. He rose to the challenge and with his usual verbal dexterity dominated proceedings, the main topic of which was agrarian policy. Lenin's proposal that a future Social Democratic government would nationalise the land did not go down well with delegates. Even his own Bolshevik colleagues objected: nationalisation, they argued, would incense the peasantry with their age-old assumption that the land was theirs. Eventually Lenin was forced to shift position and concede that the land should be the property not of the state but of *all* the people. At the congress he did not capture the majority he had hoped for – the Poles, Latvians and Bundists increasingly holding the balance and forcing him, on the surface, to compromise. But having lived by the principles of *konspiratsiya* for so long he was not willing to abandon them now. For all the superficial air of unity, he had every intention of keeping his own Bolshevik faction alive.[14] 'We won't permit the idea of unity to tie a noose around our necks', he confided to Lunacharsky, 'we shall under no circumstances permit the Mensheviks to lead us by the rope.'[15] Soon after the congress was over, he was back on the offensive, trying to whip up animosity towards the Menshevik-led Central Committee. As far as Lenin was concerned, in politics all things were permissible. His objective remained the same: to destroy his opponent, 'wipe his organization off the face of the earth'.[16]

At the end of May 1906 Lenin returned to Russia via Finland and immediately went into hiding with Nadya, under the name Chkeidze, her alias being Praskoviya Onegina. On 10 May the 1st Duma was convened at the Tauride Palace, with the Kadets commanding a majority, the Mensheviks appealing for reconciliation and Lenin and his Bolsheviks stubbornly boycotting the whole process. The Kadets, for Lenin, were nothing less than 'the worms in the grave of the revolution' and he would have no truck with them.[17] As the Duma took its first tentative steps, troops were out on all the streets in anticipation of trouble. Cossack units were being sent out into the countryside to quell peasant unrest, burning villages as they did so. An orgy of firing squads, courts martial, mass floggings and arrests exploded as the Russian government systematically stamped out protest across Russia while in St Petersburg offering the supposed olive branch of democracy.

The architect of this new wave of repression, appointed in April 1906 and from July promoted to Prime Minister, was Petr Stolypin, a staunch patriot loyal to the Tsar and committed to crushing revolt. Suppression first and then reform was Stolypin's motto as he offered land reforms in the countryside with one hand to conciliate the still volatile peasantry and with the other brought in emergency decrees against insurgency. The most draconian of these was the introduction in August of field courts martial for political crimes and an increase in the penalties for producing revolutionary propaganda. Stolypin also engaged in a concerted shutdown of radical newspapers and the abolition of many trade unions. Acts of official revenge against the insurgents in the Russian territories in Poland and Latvia were particularly savage. Courts martial – previously only employed for naval and military mutinies – were ordered to effect the trial and execution of a verdict within seventy-two hours and were savagely imposed to quell remaining peasant unrest in the countryside. Under this new provision, 883 executions were carried out between August 1906 and May 1907 alone. Between January 1905 and January 1909 the Police Department would record 3,319 condemnations to death with 1,435 executions, bringing into usage the grim epithet 'Stolypin's necktie' to allude to the hangman's noose.[18] The executions were accompanied by a concerted roundup of political activists: by 1909

the number of political prisoners in Russia – many of them sent on the
long rail journey to Siberia in 'Stolypin's carriages' – had risen from
86,000 in 1905 to 170,000.[19]

Such measures did nothing but engender further acts of revenge as
levels of Socialist Revolutionary-led terrorist attacks increased, culminating in an attempt on Stolypin's life at his villa in August 1906 when
an explosion killed thirty-eight people. Public officials and government
ministers were now prime targets, while other indiscriminate violence
was rapidly becoming part of a desperate new campaign to wrest funds
for revolutionary groups by bank robberies and other forms of banditry,
euphemistically referred to as 'expropriations'. Lenin had no problem in
countenancing the 'exes' or any other violent means employed in raising
much-needed funds to buy arms for attacks on the police and government. These activities were overseen by one of his most trusted associates, his former *Iskra* agent in Baku, Leonid Krasin, now in overall charge
of the Fighting Technical Groups. Together with gun-runner Maxim
Litvinov and expropriators in Georgia led by Stalin, Krasin was responsible for bringing in thousands of much-needed rubles to run the party
machinery and buy weapons.

That summer the token constitutional experiment of the 1st Duma
stuttered and stalled after Nicholas II rejected most of its called-for
reforms; he dissolved it on 21 July 1906 after only forty-two days. A brief
flurry of protest, including mutinies at the military bases at Kronstadt
and Sveaborg, followed and were harshly dealt with. Lenin did not,
however, abandon his calls for mass terror, having demanded a general
strike in response to the mutinies, but people did not have the energy
or will for another insurrection so soon after the events of 1905. With
continuing political repressions and the difficulty of life underground,
Lenin knew that the writing was on the wall: in order to secure the
future of the party and his own leadership of it, he would have to transfer
the Bolshevik Centre out of Russia. Southern Finland seemed the best
option – not quite in Russia but not quite abroad either. On 2 September
he moved back to the Villa Wasa, where he established open house for
his Bolshevik inner circle and in particular his two closest co-conspirators, Leonid Krasin and the rising star of the Bolshevik faction, Aleksandr Bogdanov, whose organisational and prolific writing skills were
being put to good use. The three Bolshevik leaders became popularly
known as the 'Small Trinity' or the 'Board of Three'. Lenin and Nadya
occupied the ground floor of Villa Wasa, she sharing with her mother

when she later joined them. Bogdanov and his wife were installed in an adjacent stone building used as the party library.

There were none of the constraints and anxieties of Russia at the Villa Wasa, though Nadya repeatedly ran the gauntlet of travelling into St Petersburg daily to continue her important party work, often returning late at night. She made a point before retiring to bed of leaving milk and a loaf of bread on the table, as well as bedding for any visitor arriving late from the station. The door was never locked.[20] She and Lenin often awoke in the morning to find newly arrived comrades camping out in the dining room. The villa was always full of people: couriers came and went daily to deliver mail and the newspapers and receive Lenin's latest instructions. Often they were asked to stand and wait as Lenin rattled off an article to go back to St Petersburg by return without pause for thought or making any changes.[21]

A colourful visitor to Lenin's hideaway at this time was an agent code-named Kamo, one of the most notorious and successful expro-priators from Georgia. An Armenian by birth, his real name was Semen Ter-Petrosiyan and during 1905–7, together with Stalin, he graduated from local acts of banditry and extortion to masterminding a string of spectacularly violent bank, stagecoach and train robberies in Baku, Kutaisi and Tiflis, raising thousands of rubles, the bulk of which were sent to Lenin in Finland.[22] In the autumn of 1906 Stalin even turned his hand to piracy, with a team of bandits wresting 16,000 rubles or more from a steamship off the coast of the Black Sea.[23] Bogdanov too had contacts with a Bolshevik fighting unit in the Urals that pulled off more than a hundred robberies, confiscating arms and weapons from govern-ment depots, soldiers and local police and even expropriating printing presses and equipment from publishers to produce their own illegal liter-ature. They also robbed post offices and wine stores, but their exploits paled in comparison with the flamboyant gangsterism of the Georgians. Such banditry attracted the scorn of the Mensheviks who dubbed Lenin and his cohorts little more than common criminals and 'swindlers'.[24] How the Bolsheviks used this money was even more of a contentious issue; it seemed to Martov and his colleagues that its primary function was to buy Leninist supremacy over the party at their expense, partic-ularly in the run-up to party congresses. Certainly the Bolshevik St Petersburg Committee of the RSDLP was now being financed to the tune of 1,000 rubles a month. This dirty money also funded the dissem-ination of Bolshevik literature and the sending out of party activists into the provinces to galvanise support and set up bomb-making schools.[25]

The revolutionary trade in contraband arms greatly exercised the Okhrana abroad as it attempted to monitor Russian gun-smuggling through the European ports, assisted by local detectives. Their agents reported daily on meetings in Paris, Berlin and other German cities where revolutionaries were openly dealing with armaments firms, the supplies being stored all over Europe before being smuggled mainly by sea to the Russian ports of the Baltic and Black Sea or, on a smaller scale, by land across the borders with Finland and Latvia into Russia.[26] Greatly unnerved by the *John Grafton* affair, the Okhrana resorted to bribing foreign shipping agents, consulates and customs houses to pass on information on Russian arms smuggling.

Maxim Litvinov, a Polish-born Jew whose real name was Meyer Wallach and who went under the code names Felix, Maksimovich and Papasha, became one of the party's most successful gun-runners, managing to successfully fool the Okhrana for some time as to his true identity. From his base in Paris on rue Port Royal he posed as a respectable army officer from the South American state of Ecuador (riven by internecine warfare at the time) under which persona he travelled Europe, inspecting and buying up arms. Mausers were obtained in Brussels and bullets for them at a munitions factory in Karlsruhe. In Vienna he purchased the ammunition for rifles acquired in Trieste – and on to Hamburg, Berlin, The Hague and Liège, where he pulled off a succession of arms deals without arousing the least suspicion.[27] In Karlsruhe, with extraordinary sang froid, he even attended a demonstration of live ammunition alongside officers from the Russian army. He shared a beer with them afterwards and handed them his visiting card as he left. That autumn Litvinov conspired with Kamo in shipping a consignment of arms to Russia. He took great care beforehand to recce the possible exit ports, visiting Holland, Belgium, France and Austria-Hungary before finally deciding on the Bulgarian port of Varna on the Black Sea. From there the arms, accompanied by Kamo, would be shipped across to the Georgian port of Batumi. But the Okhrana were by now hot on Litvinov's trail and frenziedly sending telegrams across Europe in an attempt to apprehend their elusive quarry, who was now travelling on a false German passport as 'Gustav Graf'.[28] Two Okhrana spooks picked up Litvinov's trail by train from Warsaw to Vilna, but when the train arrived at its destination, Litvinov had disappeared. Coded telegrams flew back and forth between the Okhrana offices in

Vilna and St Petersburg: Litvinov must be apprehended at all costs. Two agents managed to pick up his trail when he arrived in St Petersburg, but once again the clever Litvinov disappeared into thin air. The Okhrana men were beside themselves; as they searched for him, Litvinov made his way to Terijoki in Finland and from there to Varna, where he saw his shipment of arms on its way. But, just like the *John Grafton*, the yacht bought for the purpose proved unreliable and it too was wrecked three days later during a storm off the coast of Romania. Kamo, who had rigged up an explosive device to destroy the boat in such an eventuality, managed to get away but his device failed to go off. Litvinov rushed to Romania to try and save the cargo but the 2,000 rifles and 650,000 rounds of ammunition were seized by the Romanian authorities. This debacle did not stop the indefatigable Litvinov, who soon after was back in Finland, organising the shipment of arms via the old *Iskra* routes, with the help of Latvian activists. Shortly after he was in Berlin, having eluded the Okhrana yet again. Early in January 1908 he found a new safe haven – Camden Town in north London.[29]

As the gun-runners and expropriators went about their dangerous work and Lenin privately encouraged their ongoing experiment in guerrilla warfare, he and Bogdanov remained holed up at the Villa Wasa writing lengthy theoretical pieces. Lenin, now with an eye to the future and to securing his role in it, made enquiries about having his written works legally published. From Kuokkala he did what came best to him: unable to return to Russia, he listened, watched, convinced and commanded, keeping the flame of Bolshevism alive as he fought back his own doubts about whether his socialist revolution would ever be achievable. With the government now engaged in a systematic programme of repression, he sensed that a period of strategic retreat was looming for the revolutionary movement. The best tactical response would be to do an about face over his opposition to the Duma and support elections to the 2nd Duma early the following year. Better for the RSDLP to have some kind of political forum in Russia than none at all; the Mensheviks had certainly recognised the wisdom of cooperating with progressive elements in the Duma rather than turning their back on it altogether.

And so he concentrated on his political journalism and party conferences in Tammerfors, St Petersburg and Terijoki (Finland), while remaining unrelenting in his frequent published attacks on the Mensheviks. Eventually his vitriolic assaults brought him into conflict with the

RSDLP as a whole and in April 1907 he was arraigned before a party tribunal. His defence was full of bile, an arrogant reassertion of his unshakeable belief that anything was justifiable in the cause of the party and the revolution. The Mensheviks were his political enemies; the party had been wilfully split by them and Lenin had no scruples in admitting that he was intent on 'a war of extermination' with them. The nihilistic fervour of his words were the 'poisoned weapons' that he justifiably employed to this end.[30] In a few days' time he would once more be on the move – this time to the 5th Party Congress, to be convened in the more politically enlightened climate of Copenhagen. It would be the biggest gathering yet of the RSDLP and he had every intention of imposing his will on it.

CHAPTER TEN

'The Congress of Undesirables'

London: May–June 1907

The Brotherhood Church, Southgate Road, Islington

They only knew each other by their underground code names – Bukva, Nikolay, Zakhar and Skorokhodov – but the four young delegates from the industrial city of Ivanovo-Voznesensk in central Russia were filled with excitement at the prospect of leaving Russia for the first time to attend an important congress of the party – destination unknown. When they arrived at their Moscow safe house all they had with them, as instructed, were the clothes they stood up in. They had been specifically told to wear their smartest clothes – buy new suits if necessary – as well as hats, coats and ties, in order to look like ordinary, respectable travellers, businessmen or civil servants. The trouble was, as the four travelling companions soon noticed, there was one thing that gave many of the revolutionaries boarding the train that day away: their shabby, worn out boots, which they had been too poor to replace. It would be a matter of luck if they all managed to get out of Russia undetected. They were to leave at night, travelling by train out to Finland, from where they would receive instructions on the location of the congress.

The train was in fact full of delegates from all over the Russian Empire – the Urals, Siberia, Ukraine, Odessa and as far south as the Caucasus – all trying hard to look innocent and not draw attention to themselves. As the four colleagues sweated in their suits in the stuffy third-class carriage, the train passed through the town of Beloostrov; they held their breath as customs officials boarded. Although passports were not asked for as they were still within the Russian Empire, the men were convinced that the gendarmes and customs inspectors who walked up and down the train scrutinising the passengers would spot them as being illegals on their way out. As the train rattled on into the night through the forests of southern Finland, the men sat shoulder-to-shoulder on the hard wooden seats, unable to lie down and sleep, trying hard to observe the rules of *konspiratsiya* by not acknowledging each other and not engaging in conversation. They recognised some of the others on the train but they only knew them by their underground aliases. Finally, down the line at Hangö (Hanko), where they disembarked and were given false passports by Finnish Social Democrats, they were told their destination was to be Copenhagen.[1]

After suffering a night of violent sea-sickness on the steamship from Finland, the delegates had already settled into their cheap hotels when the Social Democrats in the Danish parliament, under pressure from the Ministry of Justice, suddenly withdrew their offer of hosting the congress. The government was in an embarrassing situation: the Danish king, Frederick VIII, was Nicholas II's uncle and maintained close links with his sister, the dowager empress Maria Fedorovna and the Russian court. Royal blood ties, it would seem, were thicker than solidarity among socialists. The delegates must leave Denmark within twelve hours or face being being deported to Russia, which would mean certain arrest. So where else was there to go? Sweden seemed the next best choice. And so, undaunted, 180 delegates boarded a chartered steamer for Malmo. The Swedish authorities, however, gave them equally short shrift, not wishing for a repetition of the 'secret' RSDLP congress held under their noses in Stockholm the previous year. The hungry and exhausted delegates were therefore dispersed in small groups across Malmo's cheap hotels, though some did not receive any accommodation and spent the night huddled on their pathetic bundles of possessions by the statue of

King Charles X on Sturtoret Square. The following morning, 6 May, they all traipsed back to Copenhagen, where they were again allowed a brief respite while the organisers made last-ditch attempts to find an alternative venue. Lenin sent a telegram to the leader of the Norwegian Labour Party, Oskar Nissen, enlisting his help.[2] But the Norwegian government banned the congress, in deference to its Danish and Swedish neighbours.

London now seemed the only option left to the RSDLP. A telegram was sent to John Burns, MP, a trade union radical who had taken the post of President of the Local Government Board in Henry Campbell-Bannerman's Liberal government. After an agonising wait, word came back that the British government gave refuge to all political emigrants and was not concerned with what the congress members engaged in, provided they did nothing illegal.[3] However, the additional costs already incurred by many of the impoverished delegates and the party itself in having to move on from two abortive locations was already creating serious problems; a small delegation was despatched to Berlin to beg funding from the German Social Democrats, who donated 10,000 marks, though not without their leader August Bebel complaining that 'these Russians spend too much time talking at their Congresses; ours last five days flat, but they go on jabbering for a whole month'. It was no wonder that the Russians' money ran out.[4]

At noon on 8 May the first group of delegates left the port of Esberg for Harwich docks, after being given a rousing send-off from the quayside by Danish socialists singing revolutionary songs and waving red flags. During their journey this motley crew of Russians who appeared to be travelling abroad without baggage – many of them for the first time – received disparaging looks from other, better-dressed passengers and were treated with disdain by the ship's crew.[5] At Harwich the gaggle of travellers boarded the train to London's Liverpool Street Station. Much to their surprise, unlike the Russian police, the British 'bobbies' on duty took no notice of them. They arrived in London at 9.25 that night, cold and tired after their twelve-hour journey. The culture shock of London after the relative tranquillity of Copenhagen and Stockholm was enormous. At Liverpool Street their senses were assaulted by all the noise – the smoke, steam and hubbub of London. Outside, the trams and buses, the crowds of people and the bright lights illuminating shop windows were even more arresting. Some delegates reeled in horror at the prospect of being taken down to the Underground for their onward journey. Outside the station, others stood in a state of bewilderment at the 'grandiose fantasmagoria' that was London, waiting patiently at the corner of Aldgate High Street for the eastward-bound omnibus to Whitechapel.[6]

If the delegates from Eastern Europe, the remainder of whom arrived on the 9th and 10th, were bewildered – if not alarmed – by the sights of the great modern metropolis of London, then the inhabitants of London were equally alarmed to find themselves unexpected hosts to what was to be the biggest gathering of the 'alien menace' ever seen in any European city. The *Daily Mail* was quick to label it a 'congress of undesirables'. London might have been oblivious to the presence of Lenin and his associates in 1902–3 but it now found itself the venue for a most extraordinary coming together of Russian, Polish, Latvian, Caucasian and Jewish revolutionaries from all over the tsarist empire – who between them had served six hundred years in various terms of imprisonment and exile.[7] For the next three weeks Londoners were stopped in their tracks at the sight of groups of foreign-looking men – this 'nameless army from Russia', that had 'forced their unwelcome attentions' on the city.[8] Although many of them wore conventional starched collar and tie and homburgs, others, from the Russian provinces and far-flung republics, provoked consternation with their 'picturesque' style of dress and their wild appearance in Caucasian sheepskin hats, dark cloaks, black, flowing cravats and wideawake hats or Russian-style working men's tunics and high boots. They seemed the very epitome of conspiracy and intrigue, speaking strange languages and with even stranger manners, as they made their way round the streets of Islington and Whitechapel.[9]

The intellectuals might still be in the majority in the RSDLP but the ranks of the party were now swelled by more than one hundred representatives from Russia's burgeoning urban working classes. The four delegates from the textile town of Ivanovo-Voznesensk were typical. They had all been vetted by a Credentials Commission, in which Nadezhda Krupskaya played a leading role, before they left St Petersburg for Finland, ensuring they were aware of the elaborate precautionary measures necessary for getting out of Russia undetected. A group of seventeen had found their way to Villa Wasa in hopes of meeting their hero, but Lenin had already left. Nadya offered all of them food, warmth and somewhere to sleep for the night before seeing them on their journey. But she would be staying in Finland to continue her essential work for the party.[10]

Lenin had been far too wary of Okhrana surveillance to travel with the main body of delegates from Copenhagen. Instead, he had taken a train south to Berlin where he met up with his new-found friend Gorky, and spent time at the theatre and relaxing in the Tiergarten with him and Mariya Andreeva before their departure for England.

He enjoyed being back in London but he remained deeply ambivalent towards what was to him the most advanced land of bourgeois capitalism. He had, however, to concede that Britain was also a country where its citizens enjoyed full political liberty, which was why the congress was being tolerated here and nowhere else. On arrival, with his usual frugality he had found himself a cheap room in Bloomsbury – 'just a bit larger than a compartment in a railway carriage', as a colleague observed, where his landlady gave him fish and chips and a cup of coffee for breakfast throughout the congress.[11] Gorky and Mariya Andreeva, as special guests of the congress, were found a room at the Hotel Imperial on Russell Square, near to Lenin's lodgings. Concerned for their welfare, he went over to vet the couple's room, which was small, cold and not very comfortable. The weather in London that May was dreadful: unseasonly cold and rainy and day after day the springtime sky was obscured by fog. Lenin was worried that their sheets were damp – not good for the tubercular Gorky, now living on Capri for the sake of his health – and he suggested they air them in front of the gas fire.[12]

Meanwhile, the delegates, whose final complement was about 336, were having difficulty finding places to stay. After registering for the congress at the Polish Socialist Club on the corner of Fulbourne Street in Whitechapel, where they were given maps and issued with secret passwords to be used in order to maintain a veil of secrecy over the proceedings, they were sent out to a range of billets. Some were lucky enough to be housed with sympathetic British socialist families; others were taken in by Russo-Polish Jewish immigrants, but the majority were dispersed across cheap boarding houses, socialist clubs and overnight shelters in the East End with only two shillings and sixpence a day allocated to each of them for their board and lodging. This meant that the majority ended up queueing with London's down and outs at the local dosshouse for their first few nights till better lodgings could be found for them. The most conveniently placed of these was the great 'monster doss house', as writer Jack London described it, of Rowton House, a temple of Victorian philanthropy built in 1902.[13] Here, for sixpence a day, up to 816 men could have the use of various communal facilities and, after 7.00 p.m., the privilege of squeezing themselves into a tiny cubicle with a horsehair mattress on an iron bedstead. Here the bewildered Russians were obliged to run the gauntlet of London's most feral low life – drunks, criminals and the socially desperate. It was, for delegate Konstantin Gandurin, an extremely unnerving experience seeing people reduced by poverty and unemployment to such a brutal existence; he was extremely relieved to be found accommodation with a Jewish tailor in Whitechapel, where, hearing Russian spoken all around him, he immediately felt more at home. But even here, the abyss of human suffering was all too evident.[14]

Much to their disgust and dismay, two of the four non-official delegates, Joseph Stalin and Maxim Litvinov, were forced to endure the dubious comforts of Rowton House for a couple of nights before their voluble protests got them a rented back room at no. 77 Jubilee Road, costing three shillings and sixpence a week. From here they enlisted the services of a local boy, Arthur Bacon, to run errands from house to house for 'Mr Ivanovich' (one of Stalin's many pseudonyms), delivering letters to delegates and raking the ash from his fireplace. In return, the boy brought Stalin toffees, for which he had developed a great liking. The generous Mr Ivanovich paid young Arthur well – sometimes half a crown – not realising its equivalent value in rubles, but then he had ways and means of raising the money to fund his own appearance at the congress, as the delegates would later hotly debate.[15]

The arrival of so many perceived troublemakers in London did not go unnoted. Detectives from the Special Political Branch were well primed this time, watching at a discreet distance from the first day, as too were a couple of agents sent over by the Okhrana from its Paris agency. The 'Russian problem' had increasingly become an issue in London since the revolution of 1905 had provoked an influx of immigrants. With so many Russians now in evidence, it seemed to the thinly stretched Special Branch as though the city that May had become the 'world's storm-centre of anarchism'.[16] Their manpower, however, was very limited – some fifteen to twenty officers who could hardly have kept tabs on more than three hundred foreign delegates scattered around the East End for the duration of the congress, particularly as in 1907 much of the detectives' time was also taken up with monitoring a much more vocal and sometimes violent protest movement – that of the militant suffragettes.

Most of the men recruited into Special Branch were fluent Russian, Yiddish, German and French speakers, notably Herbert Fitch who, going on his 1905 surveillance of the secret RSDLP congress in London, was quickly singled out as an expert on Russian extremists. He was one of several detectives sent to monitor various meetings of 'anarchists' (as the Branch then labelled all Russian and Jewish revolutionaries, be they anarchist, nihilist or Social Democrat) in parks, pubs, and clubs across London in the run-up to the congress. The most important was the inaugural meeting, held 'secretly' on Friday 10 May, at the Workers' Friend Club in Whitechapel.[17]

Popularly known as the Anarchist Club, this large, two-storey building at 165 Jubilee Street had been a Salvation Army depot before it was rented in 1906 by German émigré Rudolf Rocker as a meeting house, with classrooms and a reading room for Jewish immigrant workers. It could house up to eight hundred people in its gaslit meeting hall on the ground floor and by 1907 had become a focal point for East End Jewish radicals, with its socialist newspaper *Arbeter Fraint* being printed next door.[18] But it had also long been under police surveillance. Special Branch detectives were hovering incognito (or so they thought) outside the day of the meeting, when the legendary émigré anarchist, Prince Peter Kropotkin, arrived as a guest of honour. He immediately recognised Detective Edwin Woodhall outside, with whom he was on cordial terms, and motioned to him to approach. 'This is my friend Lenin', he said, turning to 'a short man with a very intellectual face'. 'He it is whom they have all gathered to meet', but the detective and his colleagues were wasting their time, asserted Kropotkin – there would be no trouble.[19]

Although Woodhall remained posted outside, Herbert Fitch managed to get past the pickets on the door and into the meeting itself. He had made himself up to look suitably Eastern European, and after giving the requisite secret handshake at the door he was allowed to enter the hall. He immediately recognised Maxim Gorky on the podium – an unmistakable figure, tall and gangly, with his pale face, high cheekbones, darting green-grey eyes and thick, bushy moustache. Fitch heard him deliver a passionate speech on the sufferings of political exiles in Siberia and the exploitation of the peasantry, calling not for bloody revolution but for the peaceful deposition of Nicholas II. At the end of the speech there was a burst of shouting of revolutionary exhortations followed by the deep and, even to Fitch's ears, 'thrilling' singing of the funeral anthem for executed revolutionaries and Siberian exiles. The intensity of the collective hatred for tsardom and an overwhelming determination in that draughty hall to effect revolutionary change in Russia made Fitch shiver. Gorky was followed by a dynamic young Leon Trotsky who snarled and shook and clenched his fists. He had just made his way to London from Finland, having spent four long, arduous weeks on the run from his second exile in Siberia. Trotsky was followed by young 'fresh-faced girls with long plaits' who proved more bloodthirsty than all the others put together in their passionate demands for armed insurrection in Russia. As the meeting echoed to the singing of the 'Red Flag', the tone was clearly set for an inspiring and turbulent congress to come.[20]

A venue for the congress, however, had only been found at the very last minute. British sympathisers in the Social Democratic Federation, including George Lansbury and journalist Henry Brailsford, had settled on the Brotherhood Church, located on Southgate Road at the junction of the run-down, working-class boroughs of Islington, Dalston and Hackney. This formerly derelict Congregational Church had been taken over in 1892 by a Christian Socialist group founded by British mystic and Tolstoyan, J. Bruce Wallace.[21] More an intellectual forum than a place of worship, its brief Sunday morning services were characterised by Bible readings and political discussion, to the accompaniment of socialist songs rather than the traditional hymns. This was followed by an improvised vegetarian meal and ongoing discussion until late into the afternoon.[22] Many of the church's congregation of around two hundred, including Labour MP Ramsay MacDonald, were active in the British Socialist movement and openly sympathetic to the Russian revolutionary cause. One of the Russians could not, however, fail to see the irony of a church being the refuge for a group of the godless and enemies of organised religion.[23] Nevertheless, its pastor, Arthur Baker, happily made over the use of the building outside Sunday mornings and Wednesday evening prayers for the duration of the congress.[24]

When the delegates arrived on the first day, 13 May, a police officer was already on duty outside (with half a dozen more plain-clothes detectives in the vicinity) as they entered by a side door on Balmes Road. Only those with the appropriate signed and counter-signed blue admission tickets were allowed in through the zealously guarded door. Inside they crammed into the stuffy little church with its narrow lancet windows and its plain, wooden walls and benches ranged on either side, with the pulpit serving as the speaker's rostrum.[25] The Mensheviks, considering themselves to be 'the real left-wing of the party', had contrived to arrive first and took the pews on the left, forcing the Bolsheviks to the right. The Poles, Jewish Bund and Latvians very rightly held the middle ground in the central pews, while guests and observers took their seats in the overhead galleries to right and left, which were reached by an iron ladder. Guest of honour, Maxim Gorky, however, sat downstairs among the Bolshevik contingent for days on end, holed up with them like pupils in the classroom of a charity school, as the debate heated up, their bellies rumbled and the German money started to run out.

Once installed, the major question on members' lips as they greeted each other was 'To which faction do you belong?'[26] It was a sign of things to come. Not long after they had arrived in London, Lenin had jokingly told Gorky how glad he was to have him there. 'I believe you're fond of a scrap', he had remarked. Well, 'there's going to be a fine old free-for-all here'. He was right: the days that followed were 'protracted, crowded, stormy and chaotic', as Trotsky later recalled; the Russian émigrée Angelica Balabanoff, now a leader of the Italian Socialist Party, remembered them being marked by an 'all-absorbing, almost fanatical, spirit of factionalism'.[27] Although the windows were kept tightly shut to prevent outsiders over-hearing the proceedings, the sound of raised voices and the singing of revolutionary songs frequently echoed around the neighbouring streets. Released temporarily from the oppressive political conditions of their home-land and constant surveillance by the secret police, the 336 delegates grasped the opportunity for free and open political discussion without fear of arrest and imprisonment like hungry prisoners released from jail.

They did not anticipate, however, the reaction of the British press who were only too quick to exploit – in traditional cloak-and-dagger style – the presence of so many alien agitators in their midst. Journalists and photographers staked out the Brotherhood Church from the outset, and it was Winston Churchill's 'pothouse press', namely the *Daily Mirror*, that seized on the congress with all the intrusive persistence of today's tabloids. As early as 10 May it had alerted readers to the presence in London of dangerous revolutionists plotting against the Russian throne and proved relentless in its pursuit of the secretive and deliberately pseudonymous delegates as they came and went at the Brotherhood Church each day, screening their faces with umbrellas, hats and raised newspapers. Despite their unwieldy camera equipment, these 1900s-style paparazzi tenaciously pursued their prey, until it was pointed out to them that by photographing the delegates they were playing into the hands of the tsarist secret police. In Russia, belonging to a socialist organisation was enough to get you sent to Siberia. Nor would the delegates give the press their names: 'The Russian police have long ears, and, you see, we shall be going back to Russia', as one of them explained.[28] They also objected to being char-acterised as anarchists with bombs under their coats. Nevertheless, sensa-tionalist stories were made of the most innocuous of delegates, particularly the few women, who were, so the *Daily Mirror* told its readers, practised at handling revolvers and 'drill themselves constantly in front of mirrors by which they become adept in aiming and pulling the trigger'.[29] One young female trade union delegate, a cotton weaver from Ivanovo-Voznesensk, was exposed by the press as in fact being 'Princess so-and-so', the daughter of a Russian Governor-General, who 'carried bombs in her muff' and had personally assassinated several high-profile tsarist officials. Even *The Times* thundered that the covert purpose of these Social Democratic visitors was to 'make extensive purchase of arms', an allegation vociferously denied by the socialist *Daily News* as 'arrant nonsense'.[30] But it was more than enough to alarm the local residents, one of whom complained across her fence to a *Daily Mirror* reporter that she hadn't been able to sleep since 'them foreigners' arrived. Every day they came out into the yard at the back of the church during breaks 'and gabble[d] away something dreadful'. 'They aren't here for no good, I'm sure', she declared, 'and I don't like it.'[31]

The press weren't the only ones harassing the delegates; at the end of each day's proceedings, a group of 'idlers and loafers' – the 'hooligan element of the neighbourhood' – gathered outside the Brotherhood Church in order to hurl derisive remarks at delegates as they left; one night Stalin only just avoided being set upon by a group of dockers in a pub. From now until the end of the congress uniformed bobbies were also in evidence.[32] Meanwhile, inside, tension was rising. Lenin had arrived intent on edging the Mensheviks out of their precarious majority on the Central Committee of the party, gained in Stockholm the previous year. Thanks to a concerted recruitment campaign beforehand in Russia, his Bolshevik delegation at the congress had gained the edge over Martov's Mensheviks with 105 to 97 and although the intention of the congress was, as before, to patch up differences, it rapidly became apparent that in the battle for control of the party the Congress was heading for a showdown. Many of the delegates, particularly the non-intellectual workers whose first congress experience it was, were unused to the long hours of debate indulged in by political exiles for whom this had become second nature. No sooner had they arrived than they found themselves subjected to three days of mainly incomprehensible, protracted and stormy argument between Bolsheviks and Mensheviks over the congress's agenda. As Lenin stonewalled, the Mensheviks raised endless objections and attempted to get him excluded from the presidium (he was eventually voted chairman), the proceedings went on late into the evening, degenerating into endlessly laboured points of order and matters of principle, with Trotsky attempting and failing to mediate between the two factions. At times the proceedings became so heated that they had to be interrupted in order to prevent a fist fight breaking out.[33] By the time the agenda was agreed many of the delegates had already had enough; Gorky noted that the 'festive' mood in which he had arrived and the proceedings had started had rapidly evaporated during those first protracted wrangles over procedures: 'the fury of the disputes', he later wrote, 'chilled my enthusiasm'.[34] Zelda Kahan, who had befriended Lenin in 1902 and had helped find accommodation for the delegates, attended as an observer. She too was horrified by the virulence with which the Bolsheviks and Mensheviks tore into each other during debates; they had no shame, she recalled, in using, she thought, the most unparliamentary and insulting language – Russian politics were quite another country in comparison with the confrontations between Liberals and Tories at Westminster. But that, Lenin assured her, was because here they were fighting for vital principles which would affect the future happiness 'of our people, indeed of all mankind' and there was no way he or anybody else could be conciliatory when so much was at stake.[35]

From the outset Lenin took centre stage in his inimitable, charismatic way, dominating the podium for hours on end, talking without notes, fighting, arguing and hectoring through every point on the agenda. He was in his element: tireless if not effervescent, he enjoyed a good quarrel, standing there stocky and pugnacious, his fingers poked up under his armpits, with a challenging, sardonic look in his eye, his voice unmistakable with its thick guttural r's that he couldn't quite roll properly. The transformative power of Lenin's arguments and his persuasiveness carried all before him during the fifteen sessions of the congress that he energetically chaired. Gorky was captivated by him, seduced by Lenin's bullish physicality as a speaker and his passionate exhortations to his 'comrades'. Lenin's greatness for him, as for so many others during those three weeks in May, lay in his direct manner. He had the ability to breathe life and logic into the most complex of political questions, treating them 'so simply, no striving after eloquent phrases . . . but every word uttered distinctly, and its meaning marvellously plain'. In comparison, Gorky remained unmoved by the fey pince-nez of Plekhanov, all 'closely buttoned up like a Protestant pastor' in his elegant frock coat and cravat and speaking with the portentousness of a preacher.[36]

The major theoretical bone of contention at the congress was the ongoing disagreement between the Bolsheviks and Mensheviks over the true nature of the Russian bourgeoisie. Lenin was by now convinced that Marx's concept of an initial, bourgeois-led revolution leading to a republic, followed by a workers' revolution instituting a proletarian state would not be effective. Russian revolutionaries should not take Marx's predictions literally but should work towards an immediate proletarian revolution. The Russian liberal bourgeoisie was in his view treacherous and anti-revolutionary; it had sold out to compromise in the Duma by dropping demands for a properly elected Constitutent Assembly. With the Mensheviks still clinging to the ideal of a bourgeoisie-led revolution like that in France in 1789, Lenin continued to argue that the only way a revolution in Russia could be brought to victory was through the united leadership of the urban proletariat and the peasantry.[37] After the events of 1905 a resurgence of armed struggle against the tsarist government was now inevitable, as well as the exposure of its pseudo-democratic promises. The collaboration of the party with the trade unions, which had been on the rise since 1905 in the drive to recruit more workers, had given a political lift to activism. But Lenin, seeking to adopt more violent tactics to achieve his ends in the face of tsarist repression, wanted the party to revert to small underground groups of professional revolution-aries; he put forward a militant agenda for armed insurrection but the Mensheviks, led by Martov, succeeded in defeating it.

At the end of each day's proceedings, most of the impoverished dele-gates had little intellectual or cultural curiosity, let alone the money, to explore the huge and oppressive city they found themselves in. Fearful of surveillance, they could do little but tramp the streets back to their lodgings in full view of the dark and corrupt underbelly of the East End, before wearily grabbing a night's rest. London was a stark lesson in the contradictions of the British class system. What struck the Russians most forcefully were the numbers of prostitutes on the streets – thin, sickly, dressed in torn and dirty clothes, many old and withered before their time. Their desperate brazenness seemed a pitiful manifestation of the torment of the human spirit, standing on the edge of the grave.[38]

During breaks between sessions Lenin was irrepressible. He enjoyed the company of Gorky as often as he was able, on one occasion accom-panying him to the music hall, where he had laughed loudly at the prat-falls of the clowns.[39] Otherwise, he and his inner circle liked to eat together and review the day's proceedings. 'You don't want to risk your weak digestion and waste your money on diplomatic restaurants,' he warned one of the Latvian Bolsheviks. He knew just the place – a good wholesome workers' restaurant near his lodgings in King's Cross where their limited money could buy them eggs and bacon, or a ham sandwich and a mug of stout or porter. But in the main, he spent as much time as he could talking to worker delegates in pubs and cheap eating houses. As far as these young, impressionable Russians were concerned, Plekhanov might be 'the teacher', the figurehead of the movement, but Lenin was undoubtedly 'the comrade and leader'. If he had one gift it was being a man of the people at the times when it most counted.[40] On Sundays, eager to educate the young delegates, Lenin took them to witness the debates at Speakers' Corner in Hyde Park. Coming as they did from such a politically repressive regime, the Russians marvelled at how ordinary Londoners enjoyed so much freedom of speech. How long might it be, Lenin asked his companions, before they would be allowed to meet freely like this in Russia? During a tour of the British Museum he was sure to point out, when admiring the Elgin Marbles and other treasures, that the museum was, of course, a 'hoard of colossal wealth' plundered by Britain from its colonies. Like everything else about this magnificent modern city the museum was a wonderful example of the corrupting power of the capitalist world.

Inevitably, wherever the congress delegates went the British detectives followed; the two camps got to know each other and in the end, with the Russians sanguine about being followed, they invited their tails to share a pint with them so that they could find out which side they were working for – the British or the tsarist secret police. In the Russian scheme of things *agents provocateurs* and double agents were par for the course. It turned out that the men from Special Branch weren't just watching the congress but were also watching the Russian agents who were watching the delegates.[41] The Okhrana, however, had been left on the back foot by the sudden diversion of the congress to London, having spent weeks carefully positioning its agents in Copenhagen for the job. Herbert Fitch of Special Branch had a very poor opinion of them; it seemed to him that every Okhrana officer was expected to spy on his fellows and the 'biggest bribe was always the final factor'. Even here, at the 5th Congress, they had two of their own key agents at work – not just that, but one of them had infiltrated the very heart of Lenin's Bolshevik group. It would be several more years before Lenin would find out that Dr Yakov Zhitomirsky, head of the Bolshevik émigré organisation in Europe, was a traitor.

Although the congress was dominated by intense discussion of the role of the peasantry in the revolutionary movement and the future of legal parliamentary campaigning in elections for the 2nd Duma, the Mensheviks were greatly preoccupied by the thorny subject of financial resources, which they still technically controlled. They were bitter and vocal about the unfair advantage the Bolsheviks had over them, made possible by a massive injection of expropriated funds, as well as private donation (such as the 60,000 rubles bequeathed to the party by the industrialist millionaire Savva Morozov).[42] Money from expropriations had been used to fortify Bolshevik ranks in advance of the congress and had also funded widespread activism in Russia in favour of Lenin's faction – enabling the party to send out legions of agents to found journals and distribute pamphlets – all with the objective of obtaining additional mandates for Bolshevik delegates to the congress. Large sums of illegally obtained funds had allowed the Bolsheviks to buy power over the party with very little of it going into general funds – hence the present financial shortages.

Expropriations had already been outlawed by a vote of the presidium at the congress in Stockholm and Lenin tried hard to deflect discussion of the subject. For the fact was he had ignored the decision and the 'exes' had persisted in the Caucasus and in Moscow, monitored by Lenin's inner circle. Their notoriety had spread, despite repeated Menshevik protests that they were bad publicity for the party. Money – or the lack of it – dominated behind the scenes, too. Ten days into the congress, Leo Deutsch, head of the economic committee, announced that funds were almost exhausted and many of the delegates clearly were not getting enough to eat. Concerned that 'the comrades' were hungry, Lenin had, at the outset, asked Mariya Andreeva and Bogdanov's wife to organise supplies of sandwiches, oranges, milk and a large barrel of beer during the breaks between sittings. The delegates, in any event, had no desire to run the gauntlet of the press gathered outside and go in search of food. Most were stoical – they had all been hungrier in Russia; they could endure a few more days hunger in London if it meant seeing the congress through to its end. Meanwhile, as the Mensheviks talked of closing the congress down early for this reason, Leo Deutsch made appeals – using celebrity guest Maxim Gorky as the lure – for donations from wealthy British socialists and sympathisers to bale the congress out. In the end the Society of Friends of Russian Freedom suggested that a fundraising dinner be staged at which the leading lights of the congress could make personal appeals for support.

Thus, much to his extreme annoyance, Lenin found himself obliged to endure the social discomforts of a dinner party with rich industrialists and philanthropists held on the evening of Sunday 26 May by the artist Felix Moscheles at his studio in Chelsea. Neither Lenin nor Gorky had evening dress in their modest luggage but they did their best to make themselves presentable. Lenin found the whole experience absolutely excruciating, 'a stupid affair', he later grumbled.[43] Although he spoke English it was obvious that his peculiarly strangled accent was impenetrable to the guests. When he was called upon to give a short speech, he did not mince his words – even though speaking in Russian – asserting that 'as bourgeois and capitalists' those gathered there, despite being his class enemies, should be supportive of the victory of 'our revolution' over tsarism. It would give them a chance to export more goods to a more cultured and free Russia. Although the speech was interpreted by a Russian émigré, the solemn, emaciated looking Russians in their shapeless black suits clearly left the gathering cold. The glitterati stood around in their evening attire staring at the Russians as though they were 'wild beasts in a zoological garden'.[44] Despite the elaborate dinner, and some damage limitation from the elegant Plekhanov with a charming speech in fluent French, the Russians were sent home empty-handed. Lenin, angry and humiliated, vowed he would never beg from capitalists again. But he had impressed at least one of those present: the Russianist Constance Garnett (who had pioneered the first English translations of Chekhov and Turgenev) was, despite Lenin's bad temper and gruffness, deeply impressed by him as a 'man of tremendously strong character', while being of the opinion that the other Bolsheviks at the congress were 'a set of self-righteous crooks'.[45]

It was Lenin's good friend, the Russian émigré Theodore Rothstein, who had settled in England in 1890 and become a member of the RSDLP in exile, who finally came up with a solution to the very pressing financial needs of the 5th Congress.[46] As a journalist for the *Daily News* he worked alongside the left-wing radical and revolutionary sympathiser Henry Brailsford. Brailsford had suggested they appeal to the Russian-born American magnate and philanthropist Joseph Fels, who had made his fortune from naphtha laundry soap and was now living in north Kent. Rothstein originally suggested a figure of £500, but on discussion it rapidly became clear that a much larger sum was needed. Fels was immediately sympathetic when approached but asked if he could see the congress in session before agreeing to stump up the £1,700 being asked for. He took a taxi to Southgate Road with Brailsford and Rothstein. An afternoon at the Brotherhood Church and the sight of the animated, young and often inspired faces of the delegates soon persuaded him. As too did the charismatic figure of Lenin engaged in a blistering attack on the Mensheviks; he had begun his speech the previous evening, broken off only at midnight and had resumed that morning. It was now 1.00 p.m. and he was still on his feet.[47] Fels could not fail to be impressed, even though he was not a socialist, but an eccentric proponent of the single tax on land values. He agreed to a loan bond, provided all the delegates signed their names to it, guaranteeing its repayment by the following January. Most of the congress members dutifully did so, but took the precaution of using their party pseudonyms. Lenin managed a few brusque words of thanks to Fels in German. In response, as he left, Fels pressed one of the single-tax leaflets he always carried into a bemused Lenin's hand.[48]

By the time the congress ended on 1 June, the congregation of the Brotherhood Church were feeling decidedly less than brotherly about the taking over of their church by so many argumentative revolutionaries for so long. With typical British *politesse* and naivety they had assumed that Russians did things the way they did and that the congress would last a mere two or three days at the most. Three weeks after first seeing their church invaded they were glad to wrest it back again as the delegates, each clasping a gold sovereign generously donated by Fels in addition to the loan, trailed their various ways back to Liverpool Street and then Harwich.

Lenin left London with a sense of satisfaction; he had as always extracted the maximum political advantage from the situation in his relentless drive to secure his hegemony over the Bolshevik faction. Angelica Balabanoff observed that throughout the congress he had been 'the most sedulous delegate, and certainly the most punctual one'. Not a single word had escaped him, 'not one gesture' as he meticulously made notes in his tight little handwriting.[49] No one had been able to match his vigour and assurance, nor his cool and merciless argument. Meanwhile, in a secret meeting held immediately after the congress, his faction had elected their own 'Central Bureau' of Bolsheviks to press home their dominion over the Mensheviks.

Martov was profoundly affected by the congress and the now irreconcilable divisions within the party. It effectively marked the end of his political life; bitterly disillusioned, he was as Gorky observed, a 'lost soul' and settled back in Paris where he would be seen to haunt his favourite café La Rotonde – sitting, talking and writing about revolution to the end.[50] But he never forgot the 'accursed month' in London that had marked the dismal end of his political hopes.[51]

As a non-aligned delegate (he had not been able to raise the five hundred Bolshevik supporters in Georgia to obtain a mandate to vote at the congress), Stalin had remained enigmatically silent throughout – as yet uncertain of his political position – so much so that Gorky did not even note his presence in his memoir of the congress. But for Stalin at least the congress had ended in a victory for Bolshevism and he had seen his hero Lenin triumph in forcing through the adoption of the tactics of 'irreconcilable proletarian class struggle'. The 'intellectualist vacillation' of the Mensheviks had been dealt a 'mortal blow', except in one area; they had secured a vote condemning bank robberies and 'gangsterism' – at which Stalin was now a master along with his alter ego Kamo – on pain of expulsion from the party.[52] But he wasn't going to take any notice of that. Nor was Lenin, who was only too aware of Stalin's talent for raising much-needed, illicit funds. A month later, back in Tiflis, Stalin and Kamo staged a spectacular bank heist netting 250,000 rubles, a large proportion of which (about £1.7 million in today's money) found its way to Lenin and Bolshevik funds in Finland.[53]

At the end of the congress, which proved to be the last great gathering of Russian socialists before the Revolution of 1917, Georgy Plekhanov publicly expressed his thanks to the British people for the freedom they had accorded its delegates. In response, His Majesty's Government was proud to state that throughout the duration it had not interfered with the political freedom of the delegates, who had, like other political refugees enjoyed the protection of the British flag.[54] Behind the scenes, however, the presidium of the congress had complained about the way certain newspapers had harassed delegates for their photographs, as too did the socialist journal *Free Russia*, which described the paparazzi at the Brotherhood Church as a 'swarm of wasps'. Henry Brailsford, reporting the congress for the *Daily News*, had written to Ramsay MacDonald complaining about the number of Special Branch men staking it out. One of the detectives had complained to a Reuter's reporter outside the Brotherhood Church that he was 'very fagged', having spent the last three or four days traipsing all over the East End in order, as instructed, to 'locate the residences of every delegate in London', and they had only just completed their onerous task. He pitied the delegates, however, for 'they would have a warm time on their return in Russia'.[55] The complaint was passed on to Home Secretary Herbert Gladstone who raised questions in parliament about harassment, but not before the congress was almost at an end.

As the delegates prepared to leave, a specially selected 'conspiratorial commission' was given responsibility for seeing them on their way back covertly to Russia via Finland. Lenin stayed on in London for a few days, working at his lodgings with the congress's one and only stenographer, ensuring that an accurate written record of the sessions – and particularly of his own numerous speeches – was produced.[56] He also found time to do some reading at the British Library, in between attending a second congress held by the Latvian Social Democrat contingent in the East End. Then he headed back to Nadya in Finland and the safe house at Kuokkala. Much to her amusement, he arrived sporting a large white straw hat, having clipped his moustache and shaved off his beard in order to evade identification and arrest.[57]

During his time in London, the British press had paid no particular attention to Lenin, all reports of the congress emphasising the presence of Gorky, as well as that of Plekhanov, Trotsky and Kropotkin. Gorky was the person whom the Western press had wanted to know more about, viewing him as the hero of the Russian working classes and 'the prophet of revolution'. 'What Gorki [sic] thinks to-day Russia will do tomorrow', declared the Daily Mirror, adding, 'History is now being made in London'.[58] That much indeed was true, only back in Russia they saw things somewhat differently. Lenin may have successfully maintained a low profile in Britain, but in Russia, where his police file stretched back to the 1880s, he was now public enemy no. 1. A warrant had been issued for the arrest of 'Vladimir Ulyanov, alias Lenin', a 'writer on economic subjects', now regarded as 'the most dangerous and most capable of all the Revolutionary leaders'.[59] And also the most elusive; for while the story was being syndicated across the world's newspapers Lenin once more disappeared from sight. The Russian Secret Police were now searching for him all over southern Finland.

CHAPTER ELEVEN

On Thin Ice

Finland–Geneva–Capri–London:
December 1907–December 1908

The Fredrikksen Farm, Nörgarden

Lenin arrived back at the Villa Wasa exhausted, overwrought and unable to eat or sleep. A month of sustained, frenetic political debate in London had sucked the energy from him. Nadya, with her usual calm efficiency, sorted out his things and packed him off to rest and recuperate at the dacha of a comrade, Lidiya Knippovich, at Styrs Udde (Stirsudden), a remote village on the Gulf of Finland. Here he briefly let go: he rode round on a rickety old bicycle, swam, walked alone in the pine forest and sat by the lighthouse contemplating the sea.[1] But within weeks, having put on weight and recovered his strength, he was on the road again. Two more contentious socialist conferences – at Terijoki and Kotka in Finland – were followed by yet another interminable incognito train ride across Europe to the International Socialist Congress in Stuttgart, Germany, and then back to Helsingfors for another conference. In June 1907, the 2nd Duma had been dissolved; with the savage clampdown on opposition groups that followed, the arrest of many prominent party workers and deportation to Siberia without trial for others, active support for the party in Russia was haemorrhaging away.

Finland was no longer the haven it had once been for politicals on the run. Since 1905 the tsarist authorities had been debating whether or not to infringe the supposedly autonomous status of the Duchy of Finland and make arrests of politicals hiding out there. By the beginning of December 1907 they had begun to close in. At Villa Wasa, with rumours of a police raid to come, Lenin left Nadya and her mother with the Bogdanovs and went into hiding in a small village called Åggleby (Oulunkylä) set in woodland on the edge of a hillside near Helsingfors. As he left, Nadya and Natalya Bogdanova began days of sorting the party archives, burning great heaps of documents, which scattered ash out in the snow all round the house. It was now clear to the Bolshevik Centre that it was no longer safe to continue publishing *Proletarii* in Finland, where it had been produced since the summer of 1906; it would have to be transferred either to London or Geneva, but London was more expensive so the decision was made to go back to Switzerland. The important work of transferring the operation there devolved to Nadya. She and Lenin would have to sit things out in Geneva again; for it was clear, as Nadya admitted, that in Russia 'the reaction was going to drag on for years'.[2] His flight out of Finland, however, was to prove one of the most dramatic journeys of Lenin's years in exile.

He was now living under a new false identity – that of 'Professor Müller', a German geologist who was studying the limestone deposits of south-western Finland. His accommodation, not far from the railway station at Åggleby (so he could keep an eye on comings and goings and be able to leave in a hurry if necessary) was arranged by Vladimir Smirnov (his old colleague in Helsingfors from *Iskra* smuggling days) at the Pension Gärdobacka owned by the Winsten sisters. The two ladies had very little chance to get to know their lodger; he kept to his room on the first floor where, behind the net curtains, he worked incessantly and rarely ventured out, except for meals, when he spoke a few words of German to them. His room was clean, orderly – and formidably cold, as Nadya recalled after visiting him there once.[3] The Winsten sisters were out at work during the day but during the evenings, as they chatted and played the piano in the sitting room next door, Lenin scribbled away at his latest work, 'The Agrarian Programme of Social Democracy', and walked up and down on tiptoes as he composed, so as not to disturb his train of thought with his own footsteps. Then one day three weeks later Professor Müller was gone. The sisters knew their guest was a political émigré but it was only in the autumn of 1917, when they saw his photograph in the newspaper, that the two women learned Lenin's true identity.[4]

Lenin's original intention had been to take the train from Åggleby to Åbo (the former capital of Finland) and from there to board a steamship to Sweden by the usual route across the Baltic Sea, the sea lanes being kept open by ice-breakers during the winter. The underground railroad for Russian politicals was run by Smirnov in Helsingfors, in collaboration with Finnish activists at various staging posts, the key one being Åbo, which was run by local businessman and lawyer Walter Borg, assisted by Santeri Nuorteva – editor of the local party newspaper *Socialist* – and a teacher, Ludwig Lindström. Borg represented several foreign firms in Åbo and had valuable connections with the captains and crews of the steamships that plied the sea route to Sweden.[5]

At the beginning of December Smirnov had contacted the Åbo cell, telling them a very important party worker would soon need their help in getting out of Finland. They weren't given his name but they guessed that it was Lenin. A coded message finally came announcing the time Lenin's train would arrive at Åbo; meanwhile, Borg arranged a berth for him on the *Bore I*, one of two ships of the Bore Steamship Company that regularly plied the Finland–Sweden route. That night, Walter Borg's two young sons, who were also active in the underground, were sent off to the station, charged with looking out for a man in a heavy coat with astrakhan collar and hat clutching a copy of the *Hufvudstadsbladet*. They were to bring this 'Dr Muller' to Borg's apartment, where he and others gathered to wait for their famous guest. The frost was severe that night; the ship was due to sail at eleven o'clock and would only be able to leave port by a very narrow channel, close on the heels of an ice-breaker. But at ten o'clock the Borg brothers returned. There was no one on the train. Perhaps they had failed to recognise Lenin, thought Borg, who telephoned to check with an anxious Smirnov in Helsingfors that Lenin had indeed left. The brothers were sent back to have another good look round the station. Borg, knowing that Lenin had been given his address, hoped he would find his way to his apartment if he had indeed missed the others and set a candle in the window as a sign. Meanwhile, he went down to the quayside to ask the captain of the *Bore I* to delay his sailing.[6]

The waiting dragged on into the freezing night as Borg watched the clock tick towards midnight, the latest the captain was prepared to wait. If the passenger missed the boat at Åbo, the captain had advised that he should try to get across by sledge to Dragsfjärd, where he might just pick the boat up when it stopped to take on supplies and coal. But still Lenin did not arrive. By 2.00 a.m. there was only one logical conclusion that could regretfully be reached: the gendarmes had picked him up en route. And then, suddenly, came a soft thud at the window. Down below, standing in the soft white glow of the snow, stood a lonely figure, clutching a small suitcase. Lenin, fearful of knocking at the front door at this time of night, had thrown a snowball up at Borg's window to attract his attention.[7]

He had indeed almost fallen into the hands of the Okhrana. Leaving Helsingfors by train he soon spotted that he was being tailed by two agents. When he got off the train at Karis to have some supper in the station buffet the men followed and watched him closely. He had to get away from them; they would arrest him the minute he got off the train at Åbo, the end of the line. So, as the train gathered speed out of the tiny station of Littois (Littoinen), the last before Åbo, he slipped out on to the running board, threw his suitcase ahead of him and leaped from the train. Luckily, a deep snowdrift broke his fall. The two agents decided it was not worth risking their necks to follow, and as he watched the red of the train's tail lights disappear into the night, Lenin heaved a sigh of relief. He picked himself up and trudged off in the crackling frost the seven miles of country road into Åbo, his only point of reference the dark, looming pine forest on all sides.

At Borg's apartment, seeing that he was frozen, hungry and exhausted, the Finns removed Lenin's coat and boots. As he lay on the divan to recover, Borg's wife Ida fed him hot milk with cognac and rubbed spirit on his hands and feet to get the circulation going. By now extremely agitated at the thought of being captured, as soon as Lenin heard there was still a chance of catching the *Bore I*, he insisted on being found a sledge so that he could leave straight away. Ludwig Lindström, who was to be his guide, told him that it would be very hard finding the way in the snow and the dark and they would have to wait till morning. Lenin was hysterical that the spooks would catch up with him before then. 'I've already been in Siberia and I don't want to end up there again!' he exclaimed. If Lindström wasn't prepared to take him, he would set off on foot, alone and head north for the Gulf of Bothnia. He'd walk all the way to the northern border with Sweden at Torneo if he had to: 'I've walked further distances in Siberia.'[8] His only option now was to try to pick up the *Bore* at Dragsfjärd, and, failing that, to continue west across the south-west archipelago – a chain of thousands of granite, tree-covered skerries and small islands that stretch out beyond Åbo into the Baltic Sea – and pick up the boat at a more isolated spot. There was no going back to Åbo; the police would be watching the port very closely.

So, at four o'clock that morning Lenin left by sledge with Lindström as his driver. But after crossing the frozen Kustosund to the island of Kirjala, the horse stumbled on the icy road and lamed itself; it could go no further. There was only one place to find another horse at that time of night – the local policeman on Pargas (now Parainen). But beyond Kirjala there were no more bridges across the skerries. On the shore they had to ring a bell summoning someone from the other side to come and lead them across the ice. Two men arrived – Karl and Wilhelm, the sons of a local man, Gustav Fredriksson, who had a farm at Norrgården. The young men were active in smuggling politicals out of Finland and would guide Lenin on the next stage, over the ice to the island of Pargas. But when they went down to make an inspection at the water's edge they discovered the ice was not strong enough; a thaw and heavy rain a few days earlier had weakened it. Lenin wouldn't make it to Dragsfjärd now. He could do nothing but remain at the Fredriksson house. 'Don't worry, you can sleep easy', Gustav reassured him, 'no one will take you from here by force.' And with that he opened a large cupboard full of rifles and revolvers.[9] Food and hot grog were offered, but Lenin refused the alcohol. The following morning, after an uncomfortable night in a tiny truckle bed, he woke late to a beautiful flurry of snow crystals, but he was in no mood to admire the scenery. He was anxious to be on the move again. Gustav Fredriksson could see that Lenin was highly stressed and exhausted and needed to rest. He tried to reassure him: his guest would be safe there until the next fall of snow, when they could head off on skis. Reluctantly, Lenin agreed to hang on at the Fredriksson house for a couple more days. But he was incapable of letting go; the major topic of conversation round the stove with Lindström, even in the winter-bound farmhouse in the wilds of Finland, was politics, and yet more politics.

On the third day, as dusk fell, Lenin and Lindström left Norrgården for Pargas, where they headed off to the cooperative store to meet up with local activist Carl Jeansen. For all its remoteness, Pargas, a small huddle of clapboard houses not far from the water's edge, was a hotbed of Finnish resistance, and home to a Russian bomb-making school whose instructor went by the code name name Dingo.[10] By the time he arrived, the network at Helsingfors and Åbo had become anxious about Lenin's whereabouts and a series of phone calls had been made to and from Pargas. As the three men sat chatting, the local policeman, Walter Rohde, walked in. In charge also of the village telephone exchange, he was curious to know why so many calls had been flying back and forth between Pargas, Helsingfors and Åbo. Lindström could do only one thing – openly enlist the policeman's sympathy and help in getting his 'very important' companion to the next island, Lillmälö. The policeman seemed only too happy to help – he invited Lindström and Lenin back to his house just down the lane from the store, for tea and hot grog – it was nearly Christmas, after all, and he had stocked up for the festivities on confiscated alcohol (prohibition being in effect in Finland at that time).[11] But Lenin once again refused to take a drink. Much against Lenin's anxious protestations about the risk, in no small part due to Rohde's inebriated state, Rohde said he would drive them in his own horse and sledge to the crossing point to Lillmälö – it would be the best possible cover. As the two men walked back to the store to wait for their transport, Lenin suddenly stopped and grasped Lindström by the arm: now he understood, he said, why the Finns would never be cowed by tsarism. Here was a nation where even the police, unlike in Russia, were fighting against oppression. They would never surrender.[12]

At Pargas, Lindström said goodbye as Lenin, Jeansen and Rohde continued on to Lenin's next refuge. A pleasant, wooden two-storey farmhouse at Västergården, on the island of Lillmälö, it overlooked the vast, frozen expanse of the Örfjärden Sound – the final stage in Lenin's escape route across the ice. The owner was a local farmer, Gideon Söderholm. But the next day brought bad news: a strong wind and fierce currents had broken up the ice and it was impossible to cross. Lenin was beside himself. He thought he had come, in more ways than one, to the end of the road. Here he was, a prisoner of the weather, and all he could do was sit in the company of Söderholm and a relative, Svante Bergman, with whom he could not communicate, and wait for the gendarmes to catch up with him. His hosts were kind enough, but it was Christmas and the two men were getting drunker by the day, laughing and joking in Swedish, and they kept slapping him disconcertingly on the shoulder. Lenin's stress levels about the journey he was to make across the ice rose every time the glasses were refilled; quite apart from fears for his own safety, he was terrified that too much drink would lead to careless talk and his betrayal. And worse, he couldn't understand a word of what his hosts were saying.

Early on Christmas Day 1907, Söderholm and Bergman went down to the sound to check the strength of the ice with poles and agreed that it was now safe for Lenin to make the two-mile journey across to Prostvik on the island of Nagu (Nauvo). Prostvik was the final staging post on the Finnish underground network for smuggling arms, illegal literature and people out of the country.[13] As he prepared to cross the ice with Söderholm and their guide, Gustav Wallstens, a local seaman from Kimito (Kemiö), Lenin said goodbye at the water's edge to Svante and his four-teen-year-old brother Gunnar Bergman. One of them broke off a branch of a pine tree and gave it to Lenin to use as a walking stick. For many years afterwards, local rumour had it that, before stepping out on to the ice, Lenin made the sign of the cross and muttered a prayer.[14] The crossing in the faint light of early morning, with a piercing wind cutting into them across the open sound, was terrifying. Wallstens, who spoke a little English, constantly warned Lenin of the dangers, and at one point the men felt the ice beginning to move away from beneath their feet and they only just managed to extricate themselves in time. Lenin later confided to Nadya that he truly thought his time had come: 'Oh, what a silly way to have to die', he had thought, as Wallstens helped him to struggle to safety.[15]

At Prostvik Lenin was met by Johan Sjöholm, a tailor from Åbo and another local activist in the chain. He owned a summer cottage on the island and knew the terrain like the back of his hand. From there, after being warmed with a hearty bowl of *joulupuuro* – Finnish Christmas rice porridge – Lenin was taken by Sjöholm (either on skis or by sledge) to the remote skerry of Själö, where the steamship from Åbo could pick him up on its way to Stockholm.[16] Late in the afternoon of 25 December 1907 Lenin boarded the *Stella* steamship of the Bore Company for Sweden.[17] It had taken him the best part of six days to make his way the tortuous twenty miles to Nagu from Åbo. His luck stayed with him when he disembarked at Stockholm the next morning. The suspicions of the gendarmes were not aroused by the ordinary little man with the astrakhan collar and hat, who produced a German passport, this time in the name of 'Wilhelm Frei'.

While Lenin had been making his way out of Finland, Nadya had seen her mother safely back from Villa Wasa to St Petersburg. Elizaveta Vasil'evna was ailing and did not want a return to a life in transit, in emigration.[18] Eventually Nadya persuaded her to come and live with them in Geneva, but for now she set off for Stockholm to join Lenin at the Malmsten Hotel. On 3 January 1908 the couple took the train to Trelleborg on the south coast of Sweden where they picked up the steamer for Sassnitz on the Baltic coast.[19] From here they boarded the train again, breaking the rail journey to Geneva in Berlin to pay a call on the socialist leader Rosa Luxembourg.

Lenin's time in Russia and its neighbouring Finnish duchy had lasted barely a year, with numerous interruptions. His 'second emigration', that was about to commence, would be a long, hard one, lasting nine years, during which he would once again come to rely heavily on the protection of others.

★   ★   ★

The return to Geneva was as bleak and cold as the weather. To make matters worse, Lenin and Nadya arrived there on 7 January suffering from a serious bout of food poisoning, which they had picked up eating fish in a restaurant in Berlin. Their hotel chambermaid had had to call a doctor, and, with Nadya then travelling on a false American passport, had plumped for an American physician, who overcharged them when he realised that the couple were clearly not who they claimed to be.[20]

Lenin was more depressed than ever about being back in Switzerland: 'I feel just as if I'd come here to be buried', he told Nadya in despair.[21] For the first few weeks they rented a cheap room in the house of a Madame Kupfer at no. 17 rue des Deux Ponts. But it was cold and cheerless and they hated sitting there in the evenings after a long day in the library. So they spent what little money they had going to the cinema or the theatre, or simply walking round the lake in the dark.[22] Then, at the end of April, they moved to a larger apartment at 61 rue de Maraîchers where they were joined by Elizaveta Vasil'evna; Lenin's sister Mariya also arrived, having come to Geneva to continue her studies and rented an apartment above them in the same block.

Ironically, there were now more Russians in Geneva than ever before. Events of 1905–6 had sent political refugees flocking back to Switzerland, but few of Lenin and Nadya's old circle returned. As the year progressed, a new Geneva Bolshevik circle was established around Lenin, its mainstays being Grigory Zinoviev and his wife Zina, followed soon after by Lev Kamenev and his family. But in general the streets of Geneva this time seemed 'friendless' to Lenin and Nadya and they had no desire to mix with the émigré community. Lenin realised now, even more acutely than before, that émigré politics were a far remove from real activism in Russia: 'there is no *live* work or an environment for live work to speak of', he wrote to a colleague.[23] He and Nadya, he complained, now waited more for letters than they received them. To militate against his frustration he slipped back into his old, carefully ordered routine: theory once more supplanted live politics, as he spent his days writing and studying at the Société de Lecture, which he rejoined in February. Deciding they were in for the long haul and with more time on her hands now that party work was evaporating in Russia, Nadya set about learning French and enrolled in a course at Geneva University. Volodya, she recalled, would calm his overwrought nerves in the evenings by lying in bed and reading her French grammar primers for relaxation.[24]

Occasionally, he cycled off for secretive visits to Elizaveta de K, who was now herself an émigré in Geneva, taking the precaution of carrying with him a piece of rubber from some old galoshes that he had carried about him since St Petersburg days, in order to deal with any puncture. They would sit by the lake together and read; sometimes he tried to teach her chess but invariably gave up in disgust. By now he had clearly given up all hopes of indoctrinating the independently minded Elizaveta into his own authoritarian way of Marxist thinking: 'I have yet to meet a single woman who can do these three things,' he complained: 'understand Marx, play chess or make out a railroad timetable.' Elizaveta was content enough to be in his company and let him read, not asking any questions or ever mentioning Nadya as he covered the margins with scribbled notes.[25] But odd moments of relaxation such as this were rare and Lenin's romantic friendship with Elizaveta petered out once he left Geneva for Paris at the end of the year.[26]

The return to 'this damned Geneva' stretched Lenin's resilience to the extreme. The city was 'an awful hole', he complained and being stuck there was made worse as relentlessly bad news came of the arrest and imprisonment of party workers back in Russia. Political work there had become a 'spy infested shambles', the arrest of professional revolutionaries making it ever more easy for surviving cadres to be infiltrated by double agents and spies.[27] The arrests had spread to Europe as well: in Berlin, Munich, Paris, Copenhagen, Stockholm and even Geneva key activists involved in the laundering of the proceeds of the Tiflis bank robbery had been arrested when trying to use the 500 ruble banknotes, by local police acting on tipoffs from the Okhrana. The Russian government was demanding their extradition.[28] All of this bad news served to compound the already pervasive air of defeatism in the party. The intelligentsia were deserting in droves and in response, the masses, as Nadya observed, 'withdrew into their shell' to take stock of the situation, weary of strikes and insurrection. Membership of the party plummeted; in Moscow it was down to five hundred members in 1908, which dwindled to a third of that by the end of 1909, as Stolypin's government continued its policies of retrenchment and a new, 3rd Duma, its voting system rigged to shift the political make-up of delegates, moved further to the right.

Lenin was increasingly worried by how 'depression, demoralisation, splits, discord, defection and pornography' were all taking the place of politics both in Russia and the diaspora. The whole impetus of the revolutionary movement seemed to be going into reverse and the time for revolution in Russia had come and gone. Stolypin, by introducing agricultural reforms abolishing the peasant commune and giving land to individual peasants, was steering that class towards the solid, bourgeois middle ground; the peasantry – the honest shock troops in Lenin's revolutionary scenario – were being corrupted by the lure of Mammon and needed to be saved from themselves. His only recourse lay in a return to propaganda and the dissemination of a strong party organ to fight against further disintegration of the party.[29] And so he threw himself back into the editing and production of *Proletarii*, at its offices in the old émigré heartland of rue de Carouge. A new printshop and equipment had to be established, stretching already low party funds. The plan now was to have the newspaper smuggled into Russia, with help from Gorky and Andreeva on Capri, via Italian steamships crossing to ports such as Odessa.[30] But the copies only reached Russia initially in a pitiful trickle: thirteen copies of the first issue made their way through, and only sixty-two of the second, third and fourth.[31]

In the cold light of retreat theoretical differences and the fight against political heresy within the party once more loomed large. Reaction to events in Russia could be seen in the .worrying drift away from Lenin's own brand of hard-nosed Marxist materialism to the vaguer, and to some increasingly more consoling, disciplines of philosophy, religion and metaphysics. Revisionism was in the air and one of its increasingly high-profile exponents was Lenin's colleague Aleksandr Bogdanov, with whom he worked on *Proletarii*. Bogdanov and his colleagues had objected to Lenin's support for Bolshevik participation in the Duma elections, even as an outlet for propaganda. They wanted the Bolshevik deputies recalled and the whole tokenistic farce of Duma politics to be denounced, earning themselves the nickname of 'recallists' (*otzovists* in Russian). Lenin, however, was loath to let go of what little political influence the Duma allowed him.

Reading the kind of 'drivel' written by Bogdanov and others made Lenin swear 'like a fishwife', he admitted to Maxim Gorky.[32] Things came to a head when Bogdanov, Anatoly Lunacharsky and others published a collection, *Essays on the Philosophy of Marxism*.[33] It was like a red rag to a bull. Lenin loathed all forms of 'political decadence' and was incensed by what he saw as an attempt to fuse politics with philosophy and other such dubious nonsense.[34] Back in 1904 he had seen off his promising acolyte Nikolay Valentinov for expressing similar interests and now he savagely rounded on Bogdanov, demonstrating his poor understanding and lack of respect for the very real moral issues at the heart of socialist thinking that so preoccupied his opponents. As far as he was concerned, all this drivel by 'empirio-critics, empirio-monists and empiro-symbolists' who were 'floundering in a bog' attempting to replace scientific knowledge with philosophy and religion was 'ridiculous, harmful and philistine'.[35] In a frenzy Lenin locked himself away for hours in the library researching and writing his riposte to a new religion of the masses that had been given the name 'god-building' (*bogostroitel'stvo*). Its major proponents, Bogdanov, Lunacharsky and Gorky, were now attempting to give a moral and religious dimension to Marxism by elevating the masses to divine status and substituting faith and philosophy for scientific Marxist knowledge. But he had to tread carefully. He liked and respected Gorky and needed to maintain good relations with him as a valuable supporter of the Bolshevik faction and a key figure in raising much needed money for the party; he also wanted him to contribute articles to *Proletarii*. In mid-January, Lenin had received an invitation from the writer to visit him and Mariya Andreeva on Capri. Lenin admitted to Gorky that the idea of 'dropping in' on them was 'delightfully tempting, dash it!' In preparation, he started teaching himself Italian, reprimanding Mariya Andreeva like a naughty schoolgirl for spelling *espresso* incorrectly as *expresso* in a letter to him.[36]

Gorky had in fact invited Lenin to visit him on Capri the previous summer after the 5th Party Congress, but Lenin had been too busy. He had originally had every intention of taking Nadya with him but in the event, perhaps for financial reasons, she stayed behind in Geneva. The invitation, for all that the two men had established a warm friendship, was a poorly disguised attempt by Gorky to effect reconciliation between Lenin, Bogdanov and Lunacharsky – now staying with him on Capri – before the rumbling theoretical disagreement between them escalated any further. He had seen enough of fierce political wrangling at the congress to know its potential destructiveness to the party. Lenin, however, left for Capri with no such thoughts in mind, having forewarned Gorky that he would have nothing to do with 'people who have set out to prop-agate unity between scientific socialism and religion'.[37]

After taking the train from Geneva across to Milan, he headed south through Italy by rail via Parma and Florence. Having been engrossed by books on the Roman Empire as a child, he stopped off in Rome to look at the Forum and Capitoline Hill and take a walk up the majestic Via Nazionale, before boarding the overnight express to Naples. Gorky and Mariya Andreeva met him off the train and together they crossed the azure waters of the Mediterranean by steamship to the south side of Capri, from there taking the funicular up the steep hillside to Gorky's villa. Lenin could not have wished to be more comfortably accommo-dated than at the Villa Blaesus o Settanni. Capri, with its fine, dry climate and its aromatic mix of myrtle, vines, orange groves and pine woods was renowned for its curative powers and had been the refuge of many tuberculosis sufferers like Gorky with the means to settle there. In the 1890s it had become a fashionable watering hole for tourists from Britain, America, Germany and Scandinavia as well as affluent Russians such as the opera singer Chaliapin and the novelist Ivan Bunin. Its isolated loca-tion also attracted a more bohemian element and a degree of homo-sexual tourism.[38]

Large and with opulent interiors, the Villa Blaesus had been built in 1900 on the south side of the island by an old Caprese family, the Settannis. It perched high on a cliff dropping away to the sheltered cove of the Marina Piccola below, and overlooked the stupendous Gardens of Augustus, in the grounds of which nestled Capri's finest hotel and spa, the Quisisana.[39] The house had five bedrooms and Lenin was delighted not only to discover that Gorky had an excellent library, but also to be given the room next to his study, with a magnificent view over the sea.

But Villa Blaesus had, by 1908, become a magnet to every Russian exile on Capri and Lenin's stay was punctuated by endless comings and goings. Gorky's rising celebrity in the international literary world (his latest, acclaimed novel, *Mother*, had been published the previous year), coupled with his legendary generosity, meant that he now attracted a constant stream of Russian friends and visitors, some of them rich émigrés but the majority impoverished exiles and hangers-on, whom he entertained and accommodated at his own expense. He also often paid off their debts to the local hotels and taverns. The solitary police officer on the island, Cavaliere Tiseo, who had been enlisted with the task of supervising the itinerant Russians, took little interest, so long as they didn't cause any trouble.[40]

During Lenin's stay he played the occasional game of chess with Bogdanov out on the verandah overlooking the sea (but – predictably – was a bad loser when Bogdanov beat him), or went for a walk with Gorky over the rocky, volcanic cliff paths thick with spiky, golden broom to view the ruins of Emperor Tiberius' Villa Jovis.[41] There were impromptu musical entertainments with songs sung by the servants in the local Neapolitan dialect as well as the old Russian favourites. While he appreciated the beauty of the location, the translucency of the sea and enjoyed drinking the local wine, in general Lenin found the scenery rather too 'theatrical'. It seemed unreal somehow, and prompted nostalgia for the open expanses of his much-loved River Volga back home.

Theoretical clashes with Bogdanov and Lunacharsky were, of course, inevitable and often went on late into the night. Lenin later remarked to Gorky that it was only with his arrival that things 'got out of hand'; before, everyone had gone to bed at the right time.[42] Gorky was dismayed by what he saw: Lenin seemed 'even more firm and more inflexible' than at the London Congress the previous spring. Gorky disliked the cold, contemptuous manner in which his friend took constant swipes at Bogdanov, a man who, in Gorky's estimation, was 'an extremely attractive person, of a very mild character' undeserving of such verbal savagery.[43] But away from polemics, Lenin revealed another side when he relaxed among the local Caprese fishermen. He was light-hearted, with an engaging laugh and when he chose to showed a 'lively, inexhaustible interest in everything in the world'. He could, at such times, also be 'strikingly gentle'. Gorky sensed the peculiar magnetism Lenin possessed and which drew ordinary people, outside the political context, instinctively to him. For Lenin the Caprese were the 'simple in heart' and he wanted to know all about them: what they earned, their schools, their attitude to the Catholic clergy – and they in turn warmed to the almost childlike interest he took in them.[44] His happiest time on Capri was spent with fisherman Giovanni Spadaro and his brother Francesco, Mariya Andreeva joining them as interpreter. The two men taught him to fish without a rod, using only the line and his finger to sense for the vibration when a fish took the bait. 'Cosi, drin-drin,' they gesticulated. 'Capisce?'* When Lenin landed his first mullet by this method, he delightedly repeated the catch phrase 'drin-drin'; it stuck and for the rest of his time on Capri the Italian locals referred to him as 'Signor Drin Drin'.[45]

Lenin's visit lasted only about six days and when he left Gorky accompanied him across to Naples. They booked into a pension so that Gorky could take him on a whistle-stop tour of the local sights: a climb up Vesuvius, for which the robust Lenin had plenty of energy but worried about Gorky's stamina; a visit to the ruins of Pompeii and a tour of the National Museum. When Lenin headed back to Geneva Gorky was disconsolate. The local fishermen never forgot him, or his jovial laughter – 'Only a good man could laugh like that', remarked old Giovanni Spadaro. For years after he would often ask after Signor Drin Drin and how he was getting on. 'The Tsar hasn't caught him yet?' he would remark with a grin.[46]

★   ★   ★

From Capri, after a brief return to Geneva and lectures in Brussels and Paris on the 1905 revolution, Lenin, now fired up for his confrontation with Bogdanov and the 'god-builders', headed for London on 16 May. He was intent on gathering essential source material at the British Museum on physics, economics and philosophy that was not available in the libraries in Geneva. During this, his fourth visit, he stayed in a cheap room at 21 Tavistock Place, in his old King's Cross stamping ground, a short walk from the Reading Room of the British Museum. He knew the library's matchless facilities would not let him down. 'It's a wonderful institution', he declared; it was the best library in the world to work in. Paris, Berlin, Vienna, even Geneva were not a patch on it. He found it very comfortable working there and liked having his own separate seat rather than working at the same long table with others, as in other libraries. He particularly commended the library's help desk – which

* *'Like this, drin-drin. Understand?'*

always answered any enquiries very promptly and the speed with which books were produced when requested. The British Museum boasted a rich Russian section – with rare Russian-published books, now banned back home. Yes, the English bourgeoisie don't begrudge spending money on books, he conceded.[47]

Lenin's time in London in 1908 appears to have been particularly solitary; sometimes, after a day in the library, he went to the Anarchists Club in the East End, where they served cheap gefilte fish, chopped liver and herring. Volunteer Millie Sabel remembered him sitting alone in the corner, 'a small, intense man' drinking Russian tea.[48] Readers at the British Museum also noticed him; they were fascinated by the highly focused Russian who sat at his desk day in, day out with his nose in a pile of books. The poet John Masefield often saw Lenin there and wondered who that 'extraordinary man' was. He seemed like someone 'certain to make a mark in the world', Masefield later wrote, although he did not know the man's identity at the time.[49] Lenin was always unfailingly polite to the staff as well as fellow readers. Many years later, when Lenin had come to power, one of the old curators of the library recalled 'Mr Ulianov' to reader Miles Malleson as a 'very nicely-spoken gentleman'. 'Can you tell me, sir, what became of him?' he enquired.[50]

After a month's hard study, Lenin left London on 10 June, having powered his way through some two hundred books and articles in French, German and English during his stay. He returned to Nadya supremely confident that he had sorted out all the 'inexpressible vulgarities' of Bogdanov and his group; a split with them was now inevitable.[51] But an overload of so much work in such a short space of time had, as usual, eroded his health. Despite suffering from bouts of 'abdominal catarrh' he continued to push himself hard, turning out articles and working on a book to counter Bogdanov's arguments, entitled *Materialism and Empirio-criticism*, before taking a few days' break alone in July in the mountains near Diablerets, in the western part of the Bernese Alps. At the end of November with much trepidation he sent off his precious manuscript to his sister Anna in Moscow so that she could place it with a publisher. But even Anna, for all her loyalty to her brother, was alarmed by the book's vitriolic tone. She wrote to Lenin advising him to take out some of the hyperbole, vulgar expressions and abuse or at least tone the language down a little. Lenin agreed to a few changes but resolutely refused to allow Anna to modify any of the personal elements of his attack on Bogdanov.

Back in Geneva the political situation that year had changed. The Swiss police had been coming under increasing pressure from the Russian authorities to tighten up on the activities of political exiles, making it difficult for Russian émigrés to obtain residents' permits. Landlords were becoming worryingly reluctant to rent to the volatile and unpredictable Russians and signs appeared in windows: 'We rent only to people who have no dogs, no cats and no Russians'.[52] Lurid stories about the bank robberies and expropriations by Georgian revolutionaries in the Caucasus had filtered through to the Geneva papers; one day when a Caucasian colleague, Mikhail Tskhakaya, knocked at Lenin's door in full Georgian costume looking 'the picture of a brigand', his landlady had screamed and slammed the door in his face.[53] The Mensheviks in Switzerland were now also using the bad press over expropriations to discredit the Bolsheviks further, calling for the winding up of underground work in Russia and a concentration on legal party work via the trade unions. Even the rather restrained Swiss Social Democrats were discomfited by the presence of the Russians in their midst. Lenin was coming under intense pressure from Bogdanov and his colleagues on *Proletarii*, who were tired of the constraints of bourgeois Geneva, to move the editorial office to Paris, to where many Swiss-based Mensheviks and Socialist Revolutionaries were already decamping. He was reluctant about the expense of living in Paris and also of losing the research facilities of the Société de Lecture. But activists Martyn Lyadov and Yakov Zhitomirsky arrived from Paris and managed to persuade him to transfer there, the argument being that the operation would be less likely to be spied on in a bigger city. Paris was in any event now clearly becoming the new centre of Russian activism abroad. Unfortunately, it was also home to the headquarters of the Okhrana, and Zhitomirsky, unbeknown to Lenin, was one of its key double agents.[54]

On 14 December 1908 Lenin left Geneva with Nadya and her mother, having sent their possessions, including their bicycles, on ahead to Paris by slow train. He attempted to put a robust face on things: 'We hope that a big city will put some life into us all; we are tired of staying in this provincial backwater.'[55] After a few days at the Hôtel des Gobelins on the boulevard Saint-Marcel they rented a four-room flat on rue Beaunier in the 14th *arrondissement*, near the English-style Parc Montsouris, a favourite haunt of émigrés. Lenin's close colleagues Kamenev and Zinoviev both lived nearby and frequented the park with their wives and children; Lunacharsky pushed his son round the park in his pram

– under its innocent covers it contained a stash of illegal literature.[56] Rue Beaunier was, for impoverished socialists such as the Ulyanovs, inappropriately elegant – and expensive at 840 francs a year, plus sixty francs tax, plus another sixty for the services of the concièrge. The large, light and airy rooms had mirrors on the walls and marble fire-places, and the few pathetic sticks of furniture that Nadya and Lenin had brought from Geneva looked decidedly out of place there. What little they had was, nevertheless, arranged with the same obsessive neat-ness that Lenin demanded wherever he and Nadya lived, unlike the alarmingly untidy apartments of other Russian émigrés. But their French concièrge made no attempt to disguise her contempt for the cheap white deal table and 'common chairs and stools' that her tenants brought with them. And the apartment was cold – very cold; it took three weeks of endless toing and froing by Nadya to get the gas connected.[57] Despite their hopes for a better life in Paris, Lenin and Nadya were now embarking on what she would later describe as their 'most trying years of exile'.[58]

CHAPTER TWELVE

'Why the Hell Did We Go to Paris?'

Paris: January 1909–December 1910

The Eiffel Tower, Paris

The start of a new year in Paris marked a bleak and lonely time for Lenin and Nadya. The émigré Russian community lacked the unity and dynamic that had prevailed in Switzerland. With time, life in Geneva had become stultifying, but even though Paris had seen revolutions in 1789, 1848 and the Commune of 1871, 'There was none of that pulse-beat of Russian revolutionary life so clearly felt in Geneva', as activist Lidiya Fotieva observed. London, never a political centre of the party at the best of times, was now also 'locked in silence' with the Russian enclave there decimated and disconnected from the movement. Its virtually lone representative, Maxim Litvinov, did his best to hold together the bare bones of a Bolshevik group in a succession of damp and pokey rooms, but the gloom and the fog and British insularity had a deadening effect on the Russian spirit. Meanwhile, back in Russia itself, the whole of underground life was in a state of stasis, crippled by a lack of funds, personnel and morale. Early that year, Nadya, not normally one to give way to discouragement, wrote despairingly: 'We have no people at all. All are scattered in prison and places of exile.'[1] Lenin too was acutely dispirited by the falling away of morale and talent: 'There are few forces in Russia. Ah, if only we could send from here a good Party worker to the CC or for convening a conference! But here everyone is a "has-been".' He was reduced to corresponding with an ever shrinking network of activists; the grim reality by the beginning of 1909 was that the RSDLP had ceased to exist. The party *was*, effectively, Lenin and by sheer act of will he fought to keep the uncompromising flame of Bolshevism alive, as those around him left the party, conciliated with other groups and shifted political position.

Yet Paris in 1909 was a vibrant city embracing the modern age, with a rapidly expanding Metro, electric lighting, steam trams, the finest fashion houses in the world and glittering new department stores. By 1909 it had begun to attract a new Russian exile community – that of the cultural elite who had left after the 1905 revolution: poets and writers such as Zinaida Gippius, Andrey Bely, Dmitri Merezhkovsky; millionaire patrons of the arts the Shchukin brothers; the painters Aleksandr Benois and Marc Chagall; and Sergey Diaghilev, who had brought his *Ballets Russes* to Paris that year. The cream of Russian creative talent was heading for the French capital and taking its place at the centre of bohemian circles and the literary salons.[2] The Mensheviks were gathering in strength too – Plekhanov, Dan, Martov and others all now holding court in their favourite cafés, La Rotonde and the Café d'Harcourt. Plekhanov, despite suffering poor health (he later left for Italy) still very much occupied the émigré higher ground as elder statesman. The Socialist Revolutionaries had found their way to Paris too; even the legendary nihilist Vera Figner, finally released from her twenty-year incarceration in Shlisselburg Fortress, had arrived. But Lenin remained largely detached from the cultural life of the city, its people and the other Russian enclaves; nor could Nadya tolerate the bourgeois profligacy of the French. They survived well enough on Lenin's party salary (in the region of 350 Swiss francs a month, a rate fixed for the Bolshevik leaders[3]) topped up with a trickle of royalties. There were also occasional welcome injections of money from Lenin's mother who was preternaturally thrifty with the 'family fund' of annuities and helped all her children out financially.

As well as watching his own money, Lenin always kept careful, discreet control of party funds, be they legal or illicit. One of the most dubious recent sources of income, along with the bank robberies and expropriations, had been the clever purloining of the Shmit [sic] inheritance. Nikolay Shmit, nephew of Savva Morozov, the socialist sympathiser and millionaire, had committed suicide in prison in 1907 (to which he had been condemned after supporting the Moscow uprising of 1905). Two Bolsheviks were instructed, with Lenin's connivance, to ensure that Shmit's considerable fortune, devolving to his two sisters, should come to the party, for Shmit had previously intimated as much to Maxim Gorky. In order to ensure this, the two 'volunteers', Nikolay Andrikanis and Viktor Taratuta, each contrived their marriage to one of the sisters. The sisters proved surprisingly easy dupes in the affair, although Andrikanis later reneged on the deal and only handed over a small amount of his share. But in Paris in 1909 a substantial amount – 275,984 francs – from the second sister Elizaveta (who had married Taratuta) made its way into party funds and came under Lenin's direct control as chief controller of party finances.

After the Revolution, Soviet hagiographers tried hard to paint a portrait of Lenin living in abject poverty and self-denial during his years in exile, but although they were both naturally frugal Nadya was always quick to deny that they had ever gone without as other Russian exiles had done.[4] For all that they endured periods of hardship, they never suffered like some Russian émigrés who emerged penniless from the Gare du Nord after the long train journey from Russia to crowd out the draughty, damp garrets of the Gobelins district, three or four to a room. Many of these were never able to get proper paid work, nor did they receive financial help from relatives in Russia. They eked out their lives on borsch and kasha in the cheap Russian canteen on rue Pascal where the waiters were all former Siberian exiles, or sat aimlessly reading the papers all day in the Russian library on the avenue des Gobelins for want of something better to do.[5] Some of the comrades with skills managed to find employment, but French factory owners often refused to hire the Russians, fearful that they might breed discontent among their own workers. It was hardest of all for the intellectuals, many of whom were reduced to the most menial jobs, washing cars, cleaning, delivering milk, moving furniture, or getting up at 2.00 a.m. to wash the windows of restaurants and small shops. This latter work paid one franc a night – not even enough for a basic meal in the cheapest of eating places.[6]

In contrast, Lenin and Nadya always had money to buy bread, though the only meat they ever saw apart from some ham and sausage sent by Anna in Moscow was horsemeat. Occasional food parcels also arrived from Lenin's mother containing treats such as caviar and smoked sturgeon. Eating it reminded Lenin of home and provoked nostalgic thoughts of the Volga, but in general he took little interest in food and ate what he was given. He did, however, unfailingly show concern for the welfare of new arrivals, particularly those who were ailing, having contracted tuberculosis in prison or exile. One such colleague, Innokenty Dubrovinsky, had arrived in Paris with suppurating open wounds on his legs caused by the chafing of heavy chains in exile and Lenin quickly saw to it that he had medical attention. A hardship fund was set up jointly by the various Russian groups in Paris to help impoverished exiles but it was woefully inadequate; Lenin often added to the list the names of those he knew to be in the blackest of misery but who were too proud to ask for help. He also raised further monies by giving fee-paying lectures. When newcomers arrived, Nadya rooted around in her store of domestic items – lamps, cutlery and so on left behind by colleagues who had now left Paris – and handed them out.[7] But sometimes their best efforts came to nothing, particularly in several distressing cases of mental breakdown that they witnessed; one comrade, Shulyatikov, was an alcoholic who suffered attacks of the DTs during which he had nightmare visions of his sister who had been hanged in Russia for her revolutionary activities; Lenin sat up all night with him ensuring he did not harm himself. Another comrade, Prigara, who had fought on the barricades in Moscow in 1905, went mad from hunger and privation. Lenin had tried to talk him round after a suicide attempt but a couple of years later Prigara threw himself into the Seine.[8]

As Lenin surveyed his shrinking Bolshevik entourage of thirty or so who came and went over the next three years in Paris, he was forced to face up to the possible demise of his own faction. At such a low point, consolidation with the other Russian political émigrés would seem the most pressing logical option, yet, aside from nursing spasmodic hopes of a reunion with Plekhanov's followers, Lenin remained at war with his other detractors. His former colleagues Bogdanov, Lunacharsky – even Gorky – seemed to him now irredeemably wedded to finding non-Marxist ways of coming to terms with the disillusion and emptiness of the failure

of 1905. They might have little visible support back in Russia but intellectually they were his peers in the Bolshevist faction. Unfortunately,
Lenin could not and would not see this, adhering to his own interpretation of Marxism – as any religious fanatic might – as the one true
gospel. He could only ever look on political variance to his own dogmatic
view as a threat to his vision for the party and thus compulsively sought
to alienate detractors from the movement.

It was, as usual, only the women in his life – his wife, sisters, mother
and mother-in-law – who remained the devoted, unshakeable constants
in a life for ever disrupted by seething and frequently overblown political rivalries. In Lenin's surviving letters it is only ever his mother Mariya
Aleksandrovna, to whom he frequently and openly sent expressions of
love and 'many kisses' in brief moments of tenderness. Her failing health
was a constant worry and he was excessively solicitous about her wellbeing. He also showed considerable tolerance and respect towards Elizaveta Vasil'evna, for whom he often brought back spontaneous gifts of
fresh flowers picked on his many bicycle rides out of town. He would
often sit and play cards or chess with her and even tolerated her occasional cigarette. In return Elizaveta, while constantly complaining that
both he and Nadya worked far too hard, did what she could to be helpful,
cooking meals, tidying, and at regular intervals helping dispose of piles
of old letters and papers by sitting for hours meticulously tearing them
into minute pieces.[9]

Time weighed heavily on Lenin in Paris; factional quarrels filled the
empty days but made the atmosphere even heavier than it was already.
He looked worn and grey and wasn't eating properly. His sister Anna
when she visited from Russia noticed how shabby and shapeless his clothes
were and insisted on taking him out to buy a new overcoat, which he
did with the greatest reluctance.[10] He was plagued once more with
insomnia and headaches but nevertheless dragged himself off daily on
his bicycle to Paris's pre-eminent repository of knowledge, the Bibliothèque Nationale. Negotiating the cabs and horse trams all the way up
Paris's broad boulevards and across the Seine to the Rive Gauche was a
dangerous and exhausting exercise. In order to maximise his time at the
library he left at eight every morning to arrive for opening time at nine,
but he would have to cycle all the way back again when the library closed
for lunch at twelve till two and it was hardly worth returning afterwards,
as the library closed for the day at four.[11] The Bibliothèque itself was a
constant disappointment and frustration to Lenin: it was draughty, badly

organised and bureaucratic and he found the staff unhelpful. He missed the intimacy of the Société de Lecture in Geneva and the calm efficiency of the British Museum; in Paris the books he requested took an age to arrive and he was always in an impossible hurry to see them. He frequently cursed the Bibliothèque's inefficiencies to Nadya and was further frustrated when he found he could not borrow books from other libraries without a character witness from his landlord, who hesitated to do so, given the Ulyanovs' obvious poverty. He changed his mind when Lenin produced proof of his party bank account with the Crédit Lyonnais.

Lenin's great pride and joy at this time was his bicycle, which he had brought, along with Nadya's, from Geneva. During the cold winter months he carefully greased both machines and stored them away in the cellar, but when spring came they were brought out in anticipation of recreational rides into the countryside, such as out to Fontainebleau, Fontenay-aux-Roses, or Nadya's favourite, the Bois de Meudon.[12] Lenin would wheel both bikes out on to the pavement, take off his jacket and roll up his sleeves. There, surrounded by curious children from the nearby apartment block (for whom he always had a sweet in his pocket), he would happily strip, polish and oil every part of each bicycle and pump up the tyres. He thought nothing of cycling off on his own – for fifty miles out of Paris – simply to admire the view on a river bank, where he could swim and walk, or go to a particular wood to gather lilies of the valley.[13] His misery was therefore profound when his finely tuned vehicle was stolen from under the staircase at an apartment block on rue Richelieu near the Bibliothèque. He paid a daily charge of ten centimes to the concièrge and had expected her to keep an eye on it; her defence was that the money was merely for the privilege of parking the bicycle there. A replacement had to be obtained, but later Lenin gave up cycling across the city. The traffic, he said, was 'infernal', but with his usual restlessness he resented the half-hour tram ride in each direction to get there by other means.[14]

When he was not at the library, Lenin spent his time writing articles for the Russian political journals including a new weekly *Zvezda* (The Star) that he had founded in St Petersburg with the objective of keeping the underground movement alive (in direct response to the 'liquidators' in the party who wanted all illegal work to be abandoned). He invited a broad base of Social Democrats, including Plekhanov, to contribute, but dissent inevitably followed and by the autumn of 1911 *Zvezda*'s main contributors were himself and the men who were to be his two closest allies during the years up to the First World War, Zinoviev and Kamenev. Lenin also contributed regularly to *Proletarii* (until it was forcibly closed in January 1910) and its replacement émigré newspaper, *Sotsial-Demokrat*, sharing control of the editorial board of the latter with Zinoviev and two Mensheviks.

In the evenings he sometimes met up with members of his group at the Café du Lion, near the famous lion statue on Place-Denfert Rochereau, to play chess and read the free papers, but in general the Bolshevik group favoured two cafés on the avenue d'Orléans – the Aux Manilleurs at no. 11 and the Au Puits Rouge on the corner of avenue de Châtillon, opposite the church of Saint-Pierre de Montrouge.[15] Here, for the price of a beer or a cup of coffee, Lenin and his friends would sit and talk in an upstairs room. Some of them had taken to drinking sticky red grenadine and soda water – it was cheaper than alcohol – but not Lenin, who stuck to beer. Tempers sometimes ran high and meetings, particularly when gate-crashed by Mensheviks, occasionally degenerated into fisticuffs. It all served to depress the usually combative Lenin more than such conflicts had done in the past – on one occasion he walked the streets of Paris for hours in the dark, returning to Nadya pale and exhausted with stress. He was approaching forty, his political career was at its nadir and the battles were never-ending.

In May 1909, after weeks of typically obsessive worrying over the proofs and possible distortions of his meaning caused by misprints, Lenin finally saw publication in Moscow of his riposte to Bogdanov, *Materialism and Empirio-criticism*, under the pseudonym 'Vladimir Ilyin'. His letters in the run-up to publication had been full of endless exhortations to the beleaguered Anna about how 'hellishly important' it was to hurry things up.[16] Unfortunately, the print run of two thousand copies at the high price of two rubles and sixty kopeks did not bode well for sales. Nor did the withering, authoritarian tone of some of the writing. Lenin had forbidden Anna under any circumstances to mollify his attack on Bogdanov. The resulting three-hundred-page polemic stubbornly defended the objective truth of orthodox Marxism in the face of the new philosophical challenges posited by Bogdanov and his circle. In typically strident and often insulting language, Lenin made the most of this opportunity to condemn his various other detractors. He took swipes at the Mensheviks who were now working with trade unionists within the narrow legal limitations then allowed in Russia; such work, in Lenin's eyes, would emasculate the party – if not 'liquidate' it entirely – through decentralisation. The people would no longer have the stomach for underground work. He also continued his war on the 'recallists' in the party led by Bogdanov who demanded a withdrawal of Bolshevik deputies from the 3rd Duma and denigrated Lenin's support of cooperation with it, insisting that the party refocus its energies on an armed insurrection. Lenin expended great nervous energy throughout the book in attacking a range of political and philosophical thinking that failed to adhere to his own inflexible view of objective reality, demonising a host of now long-forgotten 'isms' – empiriomonism, recallism, idealism, machism, fideism, agnosticism, liquidationism, relativism, collectivism – all of them anathema to his own monomaniacal version of Marxism.[17] Citing the stalwarts of Marx and Engels, he accused Bogdanov and his associates of undermining materialist Marxist orthodoxy with their metaphysical and philosophical speculations. Their attempts, as 'god-builders', to create a new religion of the people would divert the masses from the real-life urgencies of the class struggle. Cynical, ironic, lambasting and dismissive by turn, *Materialism and Empirio-criticism* was a laboured polemic that not only attacked the Bogdanovites but also twenty or more distinguished European philosophers, including Hume and Kant, for failing to ground their ideas in what, in Lenin's terms, was material and knowable. The book found few listeners – 'a deployment of heavy artillery to a part of the battlefield that had largely been vacated'.[18] It had drained his energies, as did all his verbal and written battles, filling the long, futile months of exile with yet more thousands of words of frenetic theory.

Lenin had deliberately timed publication of *Materialism and Empirio-criticism* to precede a meeting of the editorial board of *Proletarii* in Paris that June. It was effectively a meeting of the Bolshevik Centre as it then stood – Lenin, Zinoviev, Kamenev, Bogdanov, plus an assortment of representatives from Russian regional centres. For nine days on end, at the rather appropriately named Café Caput, Lenin fought hard to win the majority over to his inflexible point of view: 'Bolshevism must now be strictly Marxist', he insisted,[19] and must distance itself from Bogdanov and his leftists, who were corrupting the party with their 'theoretical revisionism'.[20] When the meeting, dictated to throughout by Lenin's carefully prepared plans, condemned Bogdanov, he was expelled from the Bolshevik faction (and later reformed his own group around the journal *Vpered*).[21] Having rid himself of the 'vile scoundrels' and 'swindlers' in the party that he abhorred, Lenin also had at the same time ejected the best minds in the Bolshevik faction, unwittingly creating an imbalance within his own ranks. Many of his remaining followers, far from supporting his extremist and exclusive line, now favoured reconciliation with the Mensheviks.

The intensity of such political squabbles, on top of long hours in the library and at his desk, reduced Lenin once more to physical collapse. The ever vigilant Nadya was quick to suggest a holiday. Nice, the playground of the rich Russian émigré, was a surprising choice of venue, given Lenin's limited means, but nevertheless he joined his brother-in-law Mark Elizarov there, for an eleven-day holiday at the Hôtel l'Oasis on rue Gounod at the end of February. The surroundings were luxurious, as Lenin admitted with no hint of socialist shame, and the weather sunny, warm and dry.[22]

Despite this holiday, by summer Lenin was craving rest and recreation once more, scouring the papers for somewhere cheap to stay, fortunate that his own means could stretch to such self-indulgence when so many of the Parisian colleagues were totally destitute. But Lenin did not see things that way. As he observed to Gorky when reprimanding him for not taking sufficient care of his own health: 'to squander official property, i.e. to go on being ill and undermining your working capacity, is something quite intolerable in every respect'. Lenin considered his body a machine for revolution; it was only logical to keep it in tip-top condition.[23] He fixed on a modest boarding house at Bombon, thirty miles east of Paris in the *département* of Seine-et-Marne. The concièrge, Madame Lecreux, charged ten francs a day for him, Nadya, Elizaveta Vasil'evna and his sister Mariya, meals included. Mariya needed the rest as much as he did. She had suffered a bout of typhus before leaving Russia and then had succumbed to exhaustion, trying to hold down her work for the party with studies for a teaching diploma at the Sorbonne. She had then been taken seriously ill with appendicitis, upon which Lenin had had no hesitation in obtaining the best surgeon for an operation and a week's stay in a first-class surgical hospital. Lenin took good care of Mariya at Bombon, ensuring she had plenty of restorative food such as milk, curds and whey, though perhaps her recuperative reading – the protocols of the 5th Party Congress and her brother's *Materialism and Empirio-criticism* – left something to be desired. Despite this, the family tried not to talk politics during their stay and went out walking and cycling in the Clamart forest nine miles away. Madame Lecreux, who gathered her guests together for meals at 5 rue Grande each day from their various billets in the village, was accommodating enough but Nadya

Lenin's family in 1879.
Back row from left:
Olga, Aleksandr and Anna;
seated: Mariya Aleksandrovna
with Mariya on her knee,
Ilya Nikolaevich Ulyanov;
front: Dmitri, left,
and seated on the right,
Vladimir Ilyich, aged nine.

Lenin's elder brother, Aleksandr, was
hanged in 1887 for his involvement in an
assassination plot against Tsar Alexander III.

Lenin in 1897, aged 27, at the
time of his exile to Shushenskoe,
already bald and before he
adopted the shorter, neater beard.

Lenin's wife, Nadya, in 1903.

Nadya and her mother Elizaveta Vasil'evna in 1898, around the time they joined Lenin at Shushenskoe.

(*Above left*) Inessa Armand, the French-born activist who wore herself out in service to Lenin, the Party and the Revolution.

(*Above*) Inessa with her daughter Inna, born 1898; after Inessa's death in 1920 Nadya developed a particularly close relationship with Inna.

(*Above right*) Feodosiya Drabkina, the fearless bomb carrier from the St Petersburg Fighting Technical Group who carried weapons hidden under her coat.

(*Right*) Vera Zasulich shortly before her death in 1919. An iconic figure in the Russian revolutionary movement, she was bitterly disillusioned with Lenin's Bolshevik takeover.

Lenin's police mugshot from his first arrest in 1895.
Leo Trotsky's police mugshot of 1900 when he was 20; in 1902 he escaped from Siberian exile and joined Lenin in London but rapidly became disenchanted with his extremist views.

(*Left to right*) Georgy Plekhanov, the father of Russian Marxism whom Lenin initially revered but with whom he later bitterly quarrelled.
Karl Radek, the rising star of the Bolshevik Left at the Zimmerwald Conference of 1915 and a member of Lenin's party on the sealed train in April 1917.
Maxim Litvinov, code-named Papasha, the wily gun runner; in 1917 he became the Soviet Union's first diplomatic representative in Britain.
Roman Malinovsky, a trusted member of Lenin's inner sanctum, who turned out to be an Okhrana double agent and was shot on his return to Russia in 1918.

(*Left to right*) Yuli Martov, initially Lenin's closest revolutionary colleague. Alienated from Lenin after the 2nd Congress in 1903, he led the Mensheviks during the years in exile.
Grigory Zinoviev, a loyal yes-man in Lenin's Bolshevik faction. He later became a victim of the Stalinist purges and was shot in August 1936.
Nikolay Burenin, a key figure in the St Petersburg underground involved in the dissemination of illegal literature and bomb-making.
Konni Zilliacus, a Finnish lawyer and publisher responsible, in the early 1900s, for smuggling copies of *Iskra* and other illegal literature into Russia from Scandinavia.

Detective Herbert Fitch of London's Special Branch who doggedly tailed Lenin in London during the 1905 and 1907 party congresses.

The Crown & Woolpack pub on St John Street, Islington, where Lenin often held political meetings when in London. Detective Fitch hid in a cupboard in order to eavesdrop on a meeting here in 1905.

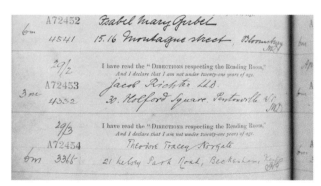

Lenin's application, in the name of Jacob Richter, for a reader's pass to the British Museum Reading Room, 29 April 1902.

Delegates arriving at the Brotherhood Church for the 5th party congress in 1907 try to cover their faces as they run the gauntlet of *Daily Mirror* photographers.

Lenin, right, during a game of chess with Aleksandr Bogdanov at the Villa Blaesus on Capri in 1908. An amused Maxim Gorky is seated between them.

Giovanni Spadaro, the boatman who took Lenin out sea fishing on Capri during his visits in 1908 and 1910.

Joseph Fels, the American-born soap magnate who came to the financial rescue of the 1907 party congress with a loan of £1,700. The Soviet Government finally repaid the loan in 1922.

Gaston Montéhus, star of the Parisian *café-chantants*, whose socialist songs such as 'Gloire au 17ème' were great favourites with Lenin. Montéhus sang at a party fund-raiser in Paris at Lenin's invitation.

Lenin out hiking in the Tatra Mountains of southern Poland, *c.*1913–14. Walking was always a solace and a pleasure for him.

Mendel Singer (seated right), the Jewish shopkeeper of Poronin who lent Lenin the money to get out of Galicia in 1914. Only three sons of the family, including Alojzy (second left back), who had sat on Lenin's knee as a child, survived the Holocaust.

Titus Kammerer, the shoemaker, outside his shop at no. 12 Speigelgasse, Zurich. Lenin and Nadya lodged with Kammerer and his family at no. 14 next door.

(*Above right*) A rather solemn Nadya, still plagued by her thyroid problem, photographed in Switzerland, *c.* 1915–16.

One of the few photographs taken of Lenin in exile – this one in Poronin in 1914 before his departure for Switzerland.

Lenin deep in conversation with Swedish socialist Ture Nerman, Nadya (behind in large hat), Inessa (in the fur-trimmed jacket), and other members of the Sealed Train, in Stockholm en route back to Petrograd, 13 April 1917.

WHY THE HELL DID WE GO TO PARIS?'   183

was bored and found the location dull, added to which she found the petit
bourgeois mentality of other guests at dinner somewhat grating. For all
this, their kindly hostess later remembered her Russian guests respectfully;
M. Oulianoff had been so affable and content with everything, she recalled,
and he had been kind enough to teach one of the little girls how to ride
his bicycle.[24]

Back in Paris on 14 September, Lenin and Nadya returned to the new
apartment they had moved to before going on holiday. Life at rue Beaunier had become difficult; the flat was too large and expensive and their
landlady had been making repeated complaints about the number of
scruffy 'anarchistes russes' who kept clumping up and down the stairs in
their dirty boots to visit them.[25] Lenin and Nadya had found a flat at no.
4 rue Marie Rose, a quiet side street four blocks further north near the
boulevard Montparnasse. As usual, Lenin left all the domestic arrangements and the logistics of the move to the women, Nadya conceding
that he 'had more important things to think about'.[26] By their standards
the flat was very comfortable. Located on the second floor, it had central
heating, its own lavatory and a kitchen with a proper range for cooking.
Lenin worked at a kitchen table covered with black oilcloth in the front
room overlooking the street, his books and papers carefully stacked
around him and neatly arranged on shelves; his only luxury a chess set.
Set into an alcove of this room and divided by a glass door stood his and
Nadya's two plain iron bedsteads with their pristine white bedspreads;
Elizaveta Vasil'evna had the best bedroom at their insistence and Nadya
did her own party work in there. As she was perpetually overloaded with
such work, they hired a domestic help, Louisa Faroche, to come in for
two to three hours in the morning to tidy the flat and wash dishes.[27] All
in all, as one visitor observed, rue Marie Rose presented a picture of
'extreme poverty and ideal cleanliness'.[28] Maxim Gorky thought it had
all the air of a student lodging but without the chaos. The kitchen, as
in Geneva, was the hub. You could barely get four people round the table
in there, but nevertheless it served as dining room and sitting room where
Lenin eagerly interrogated visitors from Russia, wanting to know
absolutely all that was going on there. 'There are no superfluous details
– everything has significance', he insisted and they all noticed how 'Ilych'
fell on news from Russia 'like a hungry man on food'.[29] Their concierge
at rue Marie Rose, the venerable Madame Roux, was struck by how
abstemious the couple's life was – there seemed to be no personal indul-
gences. 'Monsieur Oulianoff' was sober – neither drank or smoked, only

ever went out for meetings or the library and always kept to a very regular schedule. That in itself seemed dangerously abnormal behaviour to her. As, too, to his colleague Alexey Alin, did Lenin's daily insistence on going to the Gare du Nord personally to ensure that his articles for *Zvezda* got the mail train to Russia in time, refusing to delegate this task to one of the comrades.[30]

In the rich cultural heartland of Paris, Lenin had a range of art, music and theatre on his doorstep but his life, always so strictly regimented, allowed little or no time for anything other than bicycle rides into the country; these at least were sacrosanct. In general, he turned his back on most of the cultural life of this great European city and resisted the constant urging of colleagues to go out and enjoy himself more. He rarely ventured into the Louvre and made only one or two trips to the conventional theatre – such as to see Bourget's play about the class struggle, *La Barricade*. Paris was too ostentatious and bourgeois for his and Nadya's tastes and he remained unimpressed with the highbrow end of culture, preferring the music halls and café concerts of Montmartre, Port St Martin and Montparnasse, where, as in London, he could see and hear the music of the people. The year 1909 had been a turbulent one in France: an election year marked by a month-long postal strike during which Paris – and Lenin – had been cut off from the rest of France and the world and the proofs of his *Materialism and Empirio-criticism* had been held up in the backlog. The Parisian *café-chantant* artists had made much of reviling the double dealing of politicians that year, while extolling the militancy of the French proletariat. And none more so than Gaston Montéhus, of whom Lenin became a passionate admirer.

Montéhus, with his working-class message of rebellion, produced the kind of gritty 'poetry' that appealed to Lenin. He first heard Montéhus perform at an unglamorous suburban theatre on the outskirts of Paris. Thereafter, he scoured the papers for announcements of his concerts and he and Nadya often went off on their bicycles, map of Paris in hand, to seek out Montéhus's performances.[31] They saw him often at the workers' theatre-cum-music hall on the rue Gaieté in the 14th *arrondissement*.[32] Popularly known as 'Bobino', it had opened in 1812 and was located between Montparnasse station and the walls of the cemetery, not far from rue Marie Rose. For Parisian audiences, Montéhus, wearing his signature ragged workman's dungarees, red *foulard* around his neck and cloth cap, was a proven man of the people, singing as he did about the hardships of the worker's life and the virtues of solidarity.

For Lenin he came with the best possible revolutionary credentials: his father and grandfather had both taken part in the Paris Commune.[33] He wrote the lyrics and much of the music of his own songs which were a mix of sentiment, patriotism and revolutionary fervour, his most popular, 'Gloire au 17ème', being a tribute to French troops of the 17th regiment. On 21 June 1907 during a series of large demonstrations against government controls in the wine-growing Languedoc region, five hundred men of the 17th had refused to move against protesters in the town of Béziers and had taken their side. The song was a celebration of this effective mutiny against government oppression; for Lenin it had many obvious echoes of the situation in Russia. It was his great favourite and he would often burst into the words of the chorus: 'Salut, salut à vous, braves soldats du Dix-septième . . .' Not surprisingly, this song became the anthem for French anti-militarist rallies during this period, along with Montéhus's hugely popular 'La Grève des mères' and 'Le Chant de la jeune garde'.[34]

Eventually, Lenin invited Montéhus to sing at a fundraising Russian musical evening. It was staged, along with a buffet and lottery, to raise money for party printing costs, at the Sociétés Savants at rue Danton in the Latin Quarter. After the performance Lenin engaged Montéhus in an animated conversation about the future of world revolution, which went on till four in the morning. Nadya and his other colleagues had rarely seen him so animated and happy.[35] The two men became friendly; so much so that on one occasion Lenin visited Montéhus backstage at a time when he was desperately short of money, to ask him for a loan. He had never been immodest in making such requests of friends – Maxim Gorky had been another source of regular injections of cash. But that day he was out of luck. 'You should have come to the matinee, my friend', Montéhus told him, for others had already visited him that day with the same thought in mind and he hadn't a sou. All he could offer Lenin was his pocket watch to take and pawn. Lenin accepted his offer; years later Montéhus received a gift from the Soviet government of a magnificent gold watch to replace the one he had given Lenin.[36]

For all the fleeting pleasures of the café-chantants, visits to the sea and bicycle rides into the countryside, Nadya was weary that year; on top of all her party work she was still doggedly pursuing the French lessons she had started in Geneva. She found little to say about their lives in the dutiful letters she wrote to Lenin's mother and sisters. In a postscript to a letter to Anya she admitted that throughout the winter of 1909–10 she had been 'in a state of utter melancholy' and that all her time had been 'frittered away'. She hadn't been able to concentrate and work properly and, suffering from bouts of depression as she did, 'I was in no fit state to write'. Indeed, she added, there was nothing to write about. 'We are just jogging along.'[37] With Volodya so wrapped up in his work, their life, she said, differed only from the previous year at rue Beaunier in that the apartment at rue Marie Rose was, mercifully, 'very warm', and Volodya had become 'a stick-at-home'. He had, however, occasionally ventured forth on his bicycle in pursuit of a new and favourite pastime – watching air displays. In the summer of 1909 Frenchman Louis Blériot had been the first man to fly the English Channel and the whole of France had been captivated by this innovation. Lenin had taken to cycling out to the aerodromes at Issy-les-Moulineaux and Juvisy-sur-Orge outside Paris to watch the displays. One day in the summer, riding back from Issy, much to his annoyance another cyclist had run into the back of him, buckling his wheel and throwing him into a ditch. He fixed his bike the next day but in December, returning from another air show at Juvisy, a car hit Lenin on the way home and knocked him to the ground, leaving his bicycle a complete write-off. The driver of the vehicle turned out to be a French viscount, but Lenin, having trained as a lawyer, had no hesitation in taking him to court for compensation. He won his case and the following January was able to buy a replacement.[38]

The brief hibernation of winter at rue Marie Rose was interrupted early the following year by yet more frenetic political squabbles, when during January–February a plenary of the RSDLP was called in Paris. It lasted a long and bitter three weeks: 'three weeks of agony' as Lenin described it, where 'all nerves were on edge, the devil to pay!'.[39] The atmosphere was extraordinarily tense, as a last-ditch attempt was made by conciliators among Lenin's Bolsheviks to bring the various party factions to a degree of unity. Although Lenin was determined to remain at the head not of a faction but of a mainstream Bolshevik party, he now lost control of the party machinery and with it all-important control of Bolshevik funds (including the Shmid inheritance, which was transferred to the neutral control of German Social Democrats). Worse, demands were made to close down the factional newspaper *Proletarii* and with it the Bolshevik Centre in Paris and transfer operations back to the Central Committee in Russia. The plenary left him bitter and disenchanted and worse – feeling out of touch. 'Paris is a rotten hole in many respects,' he wrote to Mariya who had now returned to Russia. 'I am still unable to adapt myself *fully* to it (after living *here* for a year!).' Nevertheless, he admitted that 'only extraordinary circumstances could drive me back to Geneva!'[40]

During March and April 1910 an attempt by Lenin at rapprochement with Plekhanov and the Mensheviks failed and by April his disillusion was extreme: he wrote that 'Life in exile is now a hundred times harder than it was before the revolution' and with it came nothing but endless 'squabbling'.[41] Yet despite this he could not resist returning to the lion's den of theoretical conflict by accepting another invitation from Gorky to join him on Capri that summer. Perhaps the sunshine and sea air were overwhelmingly seductive at a time when he felt particularly weary and discouraged. He spent two weeks on Capri during June and July, travelling south by train to Marseilles where he picked up the steamer for Naples. The sea journey was cheap and very pleasant and evoked memories of home – it was, so he told his brother, 'like travelling on the Volga'.[42] By the time of this second visit Gorky had moved to a larger property – the Villa Spinola near the square on Via Lorgano. Lenin's visit inevitably provoked endless arguments with Bogdanov and Lunacharsky, who were already on Capri, and much talk of Russia on the terrace every evening after dinner. But there were nevertheless moments of relaxation, as before: games of chess, evenings listening to Russian songs played on Gorky's phonograph, fishing trips with the old Caprese boatmen and the diversion of the famous Sorrento tenor Giovannino who came to supper and sang for them, though he made the faux pas of singing the tsarist anthem 'Bozhe tsarya khrani' (God Save the Tsar).[43]

The main reason for the move to the Villa Spinola was that Gorky, Bogdanov and their colleagues wanted suitable premises from where they could run a party school to train new, young workers as activists. Capri seemed a particularly good location, relatively safe from police surveillance and official scrutiny. The facilities for undertaking such training now in Russia had evaporated; with so many arrests, new activists were desperately needed, to be trained in the underground skills of writing and disseminating propaganda and indoctrinating the workers. Discussions about the inauguration of party schools for this purpose had been going on since the 5th Party Congress in London in 1907. Gorky's 'First Higher Social-Democratic Propagandist-Agitator School for Workers' opened that August, funded by the income from Gorky's royalties as well as donations from admirers of his work and run by Gorky in close collaboration with Bogdanov, Lunacharsky and two additional colleagues, Gregory Aleksinsky and Nikifor Vilonov. In November a similar party school, funded by money from expropriations, opened in Bologna.

Gorky had hoped by inviting Lenin to Capri that he would agree to take a role in the party school, but Lenin would have none of it. If there were going to be any party schools, then he would control and run his own. Inevitably, he saw the Capri and later Bologna schools as a direct, factional threat to his own struggle to regain supremacy in the party. The Capri school only further underlined the split between himself and Bogdanov that had occurred during the June 1909 meeting of the board of *Proletarii*.[44] Lenin retaliated by inviting the students in Capri to come to Paris for additional lectures from him – most of them eventually did so at the end of the year before returning to Russia to take up active work.[45] He also tried hard to discredit the Bologna school and likewise lure its students to Paris. By now, physically revived, he was already plotting the calling of a new party congress at which he intended to bury his opponents.

While Lenin was away in Capri, Nadya and her mother had fled the scorching July heat of Paris and gone on holiday to the Vendée, in the Bay of Biscay. Initially they had stayed at a summer colony run by French socialists in hopes of getting to know them better. But the French kept their distance from the Russians and to Nadya seemed more petit bourgeois than socialist. Not enjoying themselves, she and Elizaveta decamped to the picturesque little seaside resort of Pornic nearby.[46] Here they rented two rooms on the first floor with a balcony, at the picturesque sounding Villa les Roses. Located on rue Mon Désir, it was a two-storey Breton-style house with shutters, its garden filled with the sweet smelling roses that gave it its name. Their hostess, a washerwoman, was very friendly towards Nadya and outspoken in her topics of conversation. She told her of her run-ins with the local Catholic priests when they had tried to pressure her son into studying for the priesthood and how she had seen them off, a fact that impressed Lenin when he joined them there from Paris on 22 July. Having already enjoyed two weeks of sun on Capri, he indulged in three more weeks of complete rest – days full of swimming and cycling, soaking up the sea air and sunshine and watching the waves roll in off the Atlantic. He seemed to have no other desire than to sit and chat with his landlord – the local coastguard – and eat the crabs he had caught. But work was not entirely forgotten; sometimes he could be seen sitting on the steps that led down from the balcony, hunched over a book or with a notebook in his lap.[47]

From Pornic, Lenin travelled straight on to an International Socialist Congress in Copenhagen, staying in a modest back room on Vesterbrogade arranged for him by a colleague. On 28 August the inaugural meeting was held at the Concert Palace, its walls adorned with socialist slogans and posters; 900 delegates and 100 press arrived to find themselves greeted by a huge rally of workers outside (it was a Sunday), who at the day's end marched with bands, red flags and banners through the streets of Copenhagen. Inside, the proceedings were inaugurated by a five hundred-strong Danish workers' choir. All the great leading socialists from the Second International were there: Karl Kautsky, Rosa Luxembourg and Clara Zetkin from Germany; Victor Adler from Austria; Jean Jaurès from France; Camille Huysmans, secretary of the International, from Belgium; and a strong British contingent featuring Keir Hardie, Ramsay MacDonald and Lenin's old friend Harry Quelch.[48]

Many at the congress were preoccupied with talk of an approaching war in Europe but this most serious issue was displaced by a great deal of discussion about unity in the trade union movement, particularly within the Austro-Hungarian Empire, and the work of the cooperative movement. Lenin, one of twenty Russian delegates at the congress representing the various Social Democrat groups, spoke on the importance of cooperatives in disseminating propaganda and spent much of the time working hard at winning new friends in the international movement. Ivan Maisky remembered seeing him 'sitting in a corner and gesticulating energetically, or with his thumbs stuck into the armholes of his waistcoat, eagerly trying to convince some European left-winger on some point'. He listened carefully to other speakers, even putting his hand to his ear to be sure to catch every word of a speech that particularly interested him and making rapid notes when he thought he had caught a political opponent out on a certain point.[49] By the end of the congress he had won over support from Polish Social Democrats, but others such as the Menshevik Fedor Dan resented his relentless assaults on anyone who would listen to him: 'There is no other man who thinks and dreams of nothing but revolution – twenty-four hours a day', he famously observed.[50] After the congress Lenin spent several days in the Royal Library at Copenhagen, registering under his real name Ulyanov in order to study statistical material on Danish agriculture and the cooperative movement before travelling to Stockholm on 13 September to meet up with his mother.

Throughout 1910 his nostalgia for home and his concerns for his mother, whom he had not seen since 1906, had seemed particularly acute. Mariya Aleksandrovna was now seventy-five and ailing. Sensing that time was running out, Lenin had at last been able to persuade her to travel from Russia with Mariya so that they could spend some precious time together. He had sent detailed instructions ahead of their meeting in Stockholm with strong warnings that his mother should not exert herself in any way. When she saw him, Mariya Aleksandrovna was shocked at how thin and changed her son looked but she took great pride in hearing him give a speech about the Copenhagen Congress to an audience of sixty while they were in Stockholm. During her stay they spent their time quietly, walking in the parks and sitting talking. When the time came to leave, Lenin was not allowed to board his sister and mother's Russian steamship to say goodbye, for he might have been arrested: 'I still remember the expression on his face as he stood there looking at mother', Mariya wrote later. 'How much pain there was on his face! He seemed to feel that this was the last time he would see her and treas-ured the plaid travelling rug she bought for him in Stockholm, solicitous to the last about his health.'[51]

It was a sad return to Paris for Lenin that September. He didn't enjoy the city and for years afterwards would repeatedly ask Nadya why the hell they had ever gone there.[52] And then, unexpectedly, his spirits were lifted just as his political fortunes also began to turn. Early that month, not long after the end of the Copenhagen Congress, a new activist had arrived in Paris. She would quickly come to take a leading role in organ-isational work for the party, with Lenin growing to rely on her for key assignments both in Europe and in Russia. 'She was a very ardent Bolshevik,' Nadya recalled, and with her natural charisma she 'soon gath-ered our Paris crowd around her.' Her presence and personality would, however, have their most profound effect on Lenin himself – not just in his official life but in the two most rigorously suppressed sides of his personality – his sexuality and his emotions.

Her name was Inessa Armand.

CHAPTER THIRTEEN

Inessa

Paris–Prague–Paris: January 1911–June 1912

The Café du Dôme, Montparnasse

Inessa Armand was a woman who came to embrace the Russian revolutionary movement with all the idealism and steadfastness of a true patriot. But she was born Elizabeth d'Herbenville in Paris in 1874, one of three daughters of a theatrical couple. Her French father, who went by the stage name Théodore Stéphane, had a reasonably successful career, touring in comic opera and operetta; her French mother, Natalie Wild, had Anglo-Scottish roots and was a sometime singing teacher and actress. Inessa's parents separated when Natalie was pregnant with her third child. Natalie's mother and her sister Sophie, who both worked as private tutors in Russia, came to Paris to persuade her to ease the burden by allowing them to take the eldest, five-year-old Inessa, back to live with them in Moscow. They taught her at home in all the social graces of a young lady of the day: Inès, as she was known in the family, became fluent in

Russian, German and English as well as her native French and played the piano beautifully. One of the families Sophie worked for were wealthy Russified French textile manufacturers, the Armands, who owned an estate at Pushkino about twenty miles from the city. Inessa often visited them; the liberally minded Armands, several of whom were actively involved in the revolutionary movement from the 1890s, welcomed her as part of their happy, extended family and provided additional tuition. It was not long before the eldest son, Aleksandr, succumbed to Inessa's undeniable charm and beauty and they fell in love. She was only eighteen when the Armand family accepted this fact with astonishingly good grace and allowed the couple to marry. Four children, two boys and two girls, followed in quick succession.[1]

During this time Inessa, troubled by a growing social conscience and eventually bored by domesticity, became interested in Tolstoyanism and joined the Moscow Society for the Improvement of the Lot of Women, its main work being the rescue and rehabilitation of prostitutes. But within a year or two, concluding that philanthropic work would never effect radical change, she moved away from religious-based social reform to more overtly political interests. In the early 1900s she became embroiled in an affair with her husband Aleksandr's younger brother Vladimir and in 1903 left Aleksandr to live with Vladimir in Switzerland, giving birth to a son later that year. Aleksandr accepted the situation with extraordinary dignity and continued to remain close to Inessa, supporting her financially and taking care of the children for considerable periods of time, particularly after 1905.

It was through Vladimir, who had been politicised as a student at Moscow University, that Inessa became involved in the revolutionary movement. She embraced Marxism and, after vacillating over which political faction to join, became a Social Democrat in 1903, though she would remain passionately interested in feminist politics and women's health issues throughout her life. In 1904 she returned to Russia by train from Switzerland, her trunk full of illegal literature, which she and Vladimir distributed from their Moscow apartment. In January 1905, during the political backlash to Bloody Sunday, Inessa came under police surveillance and was arrested. She was held in jail for four months until Aleksandr bailed her out with family money to the tune of 6,500 rubles. While she was imprisoned, Vladimir contracted tuberculosis and as soon as Inessa was released the couple left Russia so that he could take a rest cure in the South of France, leaving the children in the care of Aleksandr. Returning to Russia in 1906, and despite the risks, Inessa became heavily involved in the underground once more, taking charge of propaganda work in Lefortovo, a heavily industrialised district of Moscow. But in July 1907 she was arrested again. This time she was exiled, without trial, for two years at the town of Mezen in the northern province of Archangelsk, just outside the Arctic Circle. Vladimir followed her to this dreadful, inhospitable spot where the temperature could drop as low as minus 40 and the winters lasted six months. But the harsh climate aggravated his tuberculosis and he was forced to leave. Inessa managed to get away from Mezen two months before the end of her term and headed for the South of France where Vladimir was now gravely ill. He died two weeks after her arrival in January 1909.

Unable to return to Russia for fear of arrest and undecided about where to live, Inessa went to Paris where she met up with an émigré friend, Elena Vlasova. She encountered Lenin for the first time when she heard him speak at a political meeting in the Bolshevik café on the avenue d'Orléans in May.[2] She already knew the political Lenin from his written work, having been greatly impressed by his *Development of Capitalism in Russia* and 'What Is To Be Done?'. As a clever and highly politicised woman, she was attracted to his challenging manner, his dynamism and intellect but, on this first encounter, she was also deeply in awe of him if not a little afraid. One reason might have been Lenin's disconcerting habit, in conversation, of leaning towards his interlocutor and engaging with them eyeball-to-eyeball. In October, Inessa decided to move to Brussels to study at the Université Nouvelle for her baccalaureate in history and political economy, as well as to further her understanding of Marxist theory. Such was her diligence that she completed her two-year course in ten months. Lenin, already impressed by her, personally arranged tickets for her to attend the 8th Socialist International in Copenhagen in September, at which, as Inessa later recalled, her admiration for him was equalled only by her extreme self-consciousness in his presence.[3] The International may in part have been a catalyst in their developing relationship, for soon afterwards Inessa moved to Paris with her two youngest children, Varvara and Andrey. By now a convinced Leninist, she joined the Bolsheviks and was elected to their Paris section and made Bolshevik representative to the French Socialist Party.[4] With her fluent French and her obvious dedication to the cause, she became an integral part of the Lenin circle based at rue Marie Rose and a valuable party worker. At her own specific request she would now be known within the party simply as Inessa.

Inessa Armand was everything that Nadezhda Krupskaya was not. She was beautiful, sophisticated, multilingual, as well as being elegant and feminine in an instinctively French way. She was passionate and could be emotionally manipulative, where Nadya was straightforward, self-effacing and circumspect. Inessa had strong feminist instincts and placed great value on personal happiness; Nadya never spoke of her own needs and had long since learned to give in to Lenin's irascibility. Inessa enjoyed cooking for people, a skill which Nadya had never mastered, and was a wonderful pianist, music being Lenin's one vulnerable point and a way into his closely protected emotions. She was sexually unconventional where Nadya was physically and emotionally reticent. True, like Nadya she was sickly – imprisonment would bring with it tuberculosis – but Inessa had beautiful, large green eyes, fine features and a head of wavy chestnut hair, while the visible effects of Nadya's as yet undiagnosed thyroid condition were rapidly destroying her looks. Whereas she, by the autumn of 1910, was forty-one and had long succumbed to a self-inflicted dowdiness, Inessa was thirty-seven, slim and in her prime. Nadya had never taken good enough care of herself: her once tall, slim figure was becoming increasingly shapeless, not helped by the fact that she had no interest in fashion and wore the most functional, unfeminine clothes: 'always the same black frock in winter, a light one in summer; always the same simple hat without the least trimming'; the Okhrana spooks who tailed her described her appearance less generously as 'slovenly'.[5] Clara Zetkin in later years pitied Nadya's plain dress and worn out appearance as looking like that of 'a tired-out wife of a worker forever worrying whether she would manage to get everything done'.[6] Alexey Alin in Paris noted only one sartorial concession in her: at the beginning of each summer Nadya took her old straw hat out from its box and gave it a fresh coat of varnish – so that as time went on the accumulating layers of varnish acquired the contours of a geological cross-section.[7]

Lenin had spent the best part of the last eleven years in close proximity only with Nadya and his mother-in-law. He, of course, had had female colleagues within his Bolshevik circles in London, Geneva, Munich and even now in Paris, but none seem ever to have aroused a flicker of interest bar the enigmatic Elizaveta de K, whom he met in St Petersburg in 1905. While his marriage to Nadya had, according to her later claims, not been without love and a physical side, the couple had met and married as 'fully-formed Marxists', their union's fundamental purpose being to support *his* political life.[8] Yet Lenin was not incapable of demonstrating affection, as is clear from his letters to his mother and sisters and his concerns over their health and wellbeing. But in his public life he never showed any overt affection for his wife. His sexuality had long been subordinated – or so it seemed – along with his emotional needs, to the urgent and consuming life of politics. Sex, like music, exposed the revolutionary's emotional vulnerabilities. And that was a dangerous thing. But in Paris, with Inessa, and perhaps with others, Lenin's sexuality was finally unlocked.

While Nadya had presented Lenin with no emotional challenges, Inessa Armand was a different woman altogether. She fascinated Lenin from the first and he admired her political intuition. Official endorsement of her key role in his inner circle came when he invited her to organise a Bolshevik party school that ran in France from 11 May to 21 September 1911. It was rare indeed for Bolshevik women, aside perhaps from Nadya, or Elena Stasova in St Petersburg, to be given a leading role in any major party matters and, when they were, their contribution was largely mundane. Lenin's unequivocal favouritism of Inessa was reinforced when he asked her to take over the running of the Central Committee's Foreign Bureau that autumn. With her proven linguistic skills, Inessa would play a crucial role in liaising with emigrant groups, eventually across thirty-seven European cities, a function previously fulfilled in the main by Nadya.[9]

With his hostility towards Bogdanov undimmed, Lenin refused any association with his and Gorky's party schools on Capri and in Bologna. He was determined to create his own as the training ground for a new generation of Leninist party workers, who would work towards the rebuilding of his own, tight-knit Bolshevik group both inside and outside Russia. The party school, for the cost of which he released 10,000 francs from party funds, also signalled his final and irrevocable break with the Mensheviks.[10] He had already found what he thought to be the perfect location on one of his many bicycle rides out of Paris with Nadya – the village of Longjumeau, about nine miles south of the centre of Paris on the Toulouse road. Lenin was convinced that to hold the school outside Paris, in such a sleepy, undistinguished location, would free it from Okhrana surveillance. In a faint attempt at maintaining levels of *konspiratsiya*, the alarmed residents of Longjumeau were informed that the influx of Russian *anarchistes* who arrived that summer were in fact village schoolteachers on a refresher course.[11]

In the 1900s Longjumeau was little more than a long, narrow, cobbled street – the rue Grande – of old houses with red-tiled, gabled roofs, surrounded by gardens and orchards. It was a typically sleepy French town where time appeared to stand still, with a small central square and town hall and a café at either end. The village's major industry was tanning, which employed many of its men; its other inhabitants worked on the land or as gardeners, the women as laundresses. By day it might appear somnolent but at night the cobbled road through Longjumeau reverberated with the rattle of carts of milk, poultry and fresh vegetables being sent to the central market at Les Halles in Paris. Lenin and Nadya sublet their Paris apartment for the duration, as usual bringing her mother with them, and rented two rather dark and unappealing rooms on the first floor of a house owned by a mustard dealer, at 91 rue Grande; their fellow tenants on the ground floor were a tanner and his family. Zinoviev and his wife were rather better accommodated nearby and hired a maid to take care of their three-year old son.[12]

The town was linked to Paris by a local tramline but some of the tutors cycled out daily from the city, under strict instructions from Lenin to keep a lookout for any unwanted spooks on their tail. Lenin and Nadya's accommodation had a courtyard and well at the back from which they daily had to get their water, but they did not cook here, instead taking their meals the half-mile up the road where the school was based. These premises, at no. 17 rue Grande, had an attached, disused metalworker's shop at the back. Here the commune, who were farmed out to billets around the village, studied and had their meals – good, plain Russian food prepared by a former Siberian exile, Katya Mazonova, who slept in the kitchen with her two children. Inessa, who had gone on ahead to set up the school with a long table, lectern and wicker chairs for the students, had installed herself at no. 17 with her seven-year-old son Andrey. Three of the older students had come with her to help clean the place up, wash the large windows and scrub the floors.[13]

In May the students, all specially selected by Lenin's envoys in Russia, began arriving in Paris – eighteen industrial workers inexperienced in party work – among them tanners, textile workers and metalworkers, from St Petersburg, Moscow, Ekaterinoslav, Nikopol, Baku and Tiflis. They were predominantly Bolsheviks but included three Mensheviks.[14] Contrary to Lenin's hopes of maintaining secrecy, not only was the school and its activities closely watched from its opening in June, but among its pupils were two Okhrana spies who duly reported back to its Paris agency on all the participants when the school was over.

Inessa, Lenin, Kamenev and Zinoviev were the main tutors during the three-month-long course, backed up by a team of other lecturers and auditors. Lenin was in his element, adopting the mantle of head-master for the duration, intent on dinning ideological conformity into the heads of his students like the good pedagogue that he was. He opened the proceedings with an analysis of the Communist Manifesto and worked his pupils hard, from eight in the morning, insisting on absolute concen-tration on their part and meticulous preparation on that of his tutors. He himself gave the greatest number of lectures – fifty-six – on political economy, agrarian reform, materialism and the theory of socialism, often first thing in the morning, before cycling into Paris to take care of party matters. Zinoviev and Kamenev taught the history of the party, Lunacharsky lectured on literature and art and David Ryazanov presented the history of the workers' movement in Europe. Nadya took a low-key role in general, though she did give some classes in how to set up an underground newspaper, and Charles Rappoport came from Paris to speak on the French socialist movement. Lenin made a particular point of attending all four of Inessa's lectures on political economy and the history of the workers' movement in Belgium, though much to her disap-pointment vetoed her request to lecture on feminist issues such as the role of women workers. (Lenin might have been impressed with her performance, but one of the two Okhrana spies reported back that she was a 'weak' lecturer.[15]) Inessa later wrote to Lenin that it was only at Longjumeau that she finally began to get used to him and her affections grew. Sometimes the two slipped away to share a cup of coffee in one of the village cafés; on another occasion they went into Paris with Lunacharsky and Sergo Ordzhonikidze to see a proletarian play. That the two were drawing ever closer must have been noticed, but to most of those gathered at Longjumeau it seemed a mutually respectful comradeship. The fact that they talked animatedly at lunch was not, however, missed by Elizaveta Vasil'evna, who, unwell for most of that year and suffering from fits of depression, grumbled about the amount of attention Inessa was getting from her son-in-law.[16]

The weather that summer was infernally hot and Nadya found the small, airless pair of rooms they rented at Longjumeau oppressive, espe-cially with no garden to sit in. She found herself taking pity on their fellow tenant, a tanner, who worked extremely long hours and would sit outside in the evening air, exhausted, when he returned from work. His wife, who worked as a charwoman, seemed equally cowed; their daughter, left at home to look after the younger children all day, seemed to Nadya to live a life of drudgery. The family's only consolation was going to church on Sundays. What a difference, Nadya thought, between these exploited French workers, who unquestioningly accepted the social system, and men like one of their students, a tanner called Prisyagin, who was already a fully fledged 'class conscious fighter'.[17]

In the late afternoon when classes were over many of the commune members sought relief from the intense heat and walked barefoot out into the surrounding fields or took a swim in the nearby River Yvette. After this they would sit on the river bank or lounge on haystacks as the sun went down, singing Russian songs. Sometimes things got particularly uproarious and the Okhrana spies in their midst noted that rather too much of party money was spent on drinking wine.[18] Sundays were free for recreation. The commune had at its disposal four bicycles including those of Lenin and Nadya and on one or two occasions the students cycled into Paris under Lunacharsky's supervision, to visit the Louvre. Lenin enjoyed being away from the city and the 'commotion' of the Russian colony.[19] He and Nadya, so she wrote to his mother, 'cycled their heads off', going out for long excursions of forty or fifty miles at a time, leaving at six in the morning, cycling through forests which they loved, and returning late in the evening.[20] At other times Lenin cycled around the village with a student perched precariously on his crossbar due to the shortage of bicycles.

At the end of the course on 30 August the students were sent back into Russia with 200 francs each, as part of a 'Russian Organising Commission for calling an all-party-conference' under instructions to engineer their own election to it, with the help of three of the school auditors.[21] The loyal and impressionable Inessa was now given the important role of helping arrange this conference. If any indication were needed of the close relationship now established between her and Lenin, it came on their return to Paris in September 1911 when Inessa took an apartment next door to him and Nadya at no. 2 rue Marie Rose, bringing three of her children, Andrey, Inna and Varvara to live with her. Although their relationship had by no means been a *coup de foudre*, it began – and ultimately ended – as a close political one. By now Inessa was, by her own later admission, deeply in love with Lenin, having overcome her initial sense of awe.[22] He too had become attracted to her warm and ardent personality; she had two essential qualities that Nadya now lacked: youth and vitality. People liked being around her; even Nadya observed how their home 'grew brighter when Inessa entered it'.[23] Living in such close proximity over the next ten months would certainly have provided Lenin and Inessa with the opportunity for an affair, but it would have had to be conducted under Nadya's nose and probably with her full knowledge, for they clearly spent a great deal of time together. As Bolshevik colleagues this would have been perfectly natural. But how Nadya felt about her growing displacement as Lenin's right-hand woman, or how she dealt with her husband's obvious attraction to Inessa, remains unexplained. She certainly developed a deep affection for Inessa's three children, especially the two girls Inna and Varvara, that continued long after Inessa's death. In later life, in the few circumspect comments she made about Inessa, Nadya was always openly warm and generous towards her, writing that during their last year in Paris 'Inessa became a person close to us' and that she had also demonstrated great affection for Nadya's mother Elizaveta Vasil'evna.[24]

But in the end, Nadezhda Krupskaya, scrupulous as she was about her husband's reputation and memory, would say frustratingly little about the true nature of this triangular relationship, even after Inessa's death in 1920 and Lenin's in 1924. Criticism of Inessa would have reflected badly on her husband's obvious affection and respect for her. As a fellow feminist and collaborator on the first Soviet women's journal, *Rabotnitsa*, with Inessa, Nadya shared a sense of female solidarity and mutual respect in a highly chauvinistic party dominated by men. Like most of the *bolshevichki*, Nadya had never believed in the constraints of conventional marriage and it is said that, without any reproaches, she even offered to leave Lenin – either in 1911 or later in Galicia in 1913 – so that he could set up home with Inessa, but that he had refused to countenance it. He depended on her far too much; it was Nadya's support and unfailing loyalty that had kept him sane all these years and perhaps, for that, he loved her – in his own way.

Whatever the depths of his passion for Inessa may have been, Lenin's relationship with her appears to have been a turbulent one in contrast with that with the solid and dependable Nadya.[25] Charles Rappoport, who had become one of Lenin's closest French colleagues, often saw him and Inessa together in one of the Bolshevik cafés on the avenue d'Orléans. He had no doubts: Lenin, *'avec ses petits yeux mongols'*, was mesmerised by Inessa.[26] Perhaps the fundamental reason for Nadya's tolerance of the affair lay in recognition of her own diminished sex drive as a result of the worsening of her untreated thyroid condition. Known as Graves Disease, it caused her eyes to bulge, her neck and legs to swell, and brought on a general weakening of her energies. The hormonal imbalance precipitated by the condition also provoked mood swings, anxiety attacks, heart palpitations and rapid speech. It had also probably denied Nadya the one thing she most longed for, which Inessa had in abundance – children. Nadya's condition had possibly made her infertile; during their time in Shushenskoe, she had coyly remarked to Lenin's mother that as for the arrival of 'a little bird', somehow, none had 'yet wanted to come' – her first and only mention of the subject in her letters.[27] Evidence suggests that during their time in Paris Nadya ceased to have sexual relations with her husband – perhaps because of her loss of libido, or as a reaction to his growing closeness to Armand.[28] The only extant evidence of Lenin's own feelings remains in a few fragments of letters in which he addresses Inessa as *ty* – the Russian informal mode of address equivalent to the French *tu* – an attribution he reserved only for his mother, wife and sisters and one or two very close male associates, such as Martov.[29]

Nadya's apparently graceful acceptance of her husband's love for Inessa would, of course, have been the ultimate socialist gesture. It was reminiscent of the idealised, free-love relationships in Chernyshevsky's revolutionary commune in *What Is To Be Done?*, the socialist novel that all three of them so admired. If her husband's sexual needs could only be fulfilled elsewhere then the consolation to Nadya was that it was at least with a fellow Bolshevik and a woman she liked. To her way of thinking nothing should ever come before the health, wellbeing and needs of Ilyich in his predestined role as leader of the revolution. As a woman she must have felt deeply depressed but she never played the role of betrayed wife. She did not look on Inessa as a rival; in this, as in all things in her life with Lenin, Nadya managed to rise above her own personal feelings.

There remain, however, many unanswered questions about this, the longest and most urban period of Lenin's life in exile. Living in Paris for four years, with a sick wife who no longer wanted sex, if he were going to kick over the traces of his highly circumscribed sexual life (inhibited since 1900 by the almost constant presence in his various cramped living spaces of his mother-in-law) then Paris provided every possible temptation, including a thriving sex industry. It would be understandable for any normal heterosexual male such as Lenin appears to have been, once denied sexual relations in his married life, to have sought gratification elsewhere – not just with Inessa but maybe with other women. Where did Lenin go during those many long bicycle rides around Paris? Did he really spend his every waking moment in the library as the Soviet record and his loyal acolytes had everyone believe? And were his only ports of call the politically correct Bolshevik cafés of the avenue d'Orléans? The official hagiographers consistently denied that Lenin ever went near the more bohemian haunts of Paris, but this is not so. He lived in the heart of Montparnasse and it would have been difficult to avoid them. He was certainly seen at La Rotonde, the small café favoured by Russian artists, thick with the fug of Gauloises, where impoverished émigrés were allowed to sit talking with empty glasses well into the night and paid the owner, Père Libion, in kind, with their paintings. Modigliani, Léger, Chagall, Soutine and others from the Russian modernist school, as well as Picasso later, were all regulars. On one particular occasion, in a playful mood, Modigliani set fire to the Russian newspaper in which Lenin was engrossed. The English painter Christopher Nevinson remembered that many of the Russian artists at La Rotonde considered Lenin 'a cranky extremist'. Sometimes, for entertainment, they went to Russian meetings held just round the corner, where Lenin was listened to 'in a spirit of irreverence' and 'amused toleration'. There was no doubt he was in deadly earnest – he would froth at the mouth with excitement when speaking – but according to Nevinson 'that only made him the more amusing to the Russians'.[30]

Lenin was also seen at another famous venue, the Closerie de Lilas, on the corner of boulevards Montparnasse and Saint Michel, a café dominated by French writers and critics. He liked to go there to find chess partners and was often seen playing with the poet Apollinaire, always winning in spite of his best efforts to cede the occasional game to the French poet.[31] He even went occasionally across the road to the Café du Dôme, the preserve mainly of German painters and cartoonists of the Munich-based journal *Simplicissimus*, where he was remembered for his good humour and seen playing chess outside on its terrace. Needless to say, all of these watering holes were also frequented by Parisian prostitutes, and rumours later circulated in Paris that Lenin had a preference for a particular brothel, conveniently situated near the Bibliothèque Nationale.[32]

The French-born American writer Julien Green, who lived in this community during the war years, made a tantalising observation in his journal that overturns the sober, asexual image of the revolutionary leader. He noted meeting a Russian émigré painter, Evichev (or Ivichev), who had known Lenin in the Latin Quarter in 1912. Evichev recalled that they had never, ever talked about politics, but quite the opposite: 'We shared our women. Lenin was very gay and very good-natured, but, in matters of love, an absolute pig,'* he said, claiming still to have in his possession a letter from Lenin in which he talked, not of revolution – but of his interest in a certain pretty young Parisienne.[33] Clues to this other, unofficial side of Lenin's personality can be found in another French account published by the writer and Orientalist Franz Toussaint in 1952, in which he talked of making a trip to hear Lenin lecture at the party school at Longjumeau in the summer of 1911 through an introduction by the French socialist Jean Jaurès. He saw Lenin again in Paris shortly afterwards, this time through a mutual friend, Pierre Vabre, who met Lenin regularly in the Jardin de Luxembourg. Here the three men sat and chatted near the Medici Fountain one summer afternoon, but the subject of the conversation was an attractive young chair attendant in the gardens called Jeanette, in whom Lenin was interested.[34] And then there was Elisaveta de K, the young Russian activist Lenin had met in 1905–6 in St Petersburg and with whom he appears to have had a brief affair. They met again in Paris in May 1908 when he came to give a lecture. By this time the affair was over, but Elizaveta felt compelled to see him. There was something about Lenin this time, she remembered, that both attracted and repulsed her, something in his mobile, malicious little eyes, something ruthless and predatory that she did not like. They talked of the past, of 1905, Lenin's sardonic laugh punctuating the conversation as he expressed his regrets that he had failed to indoctrinate Elizaveta in his militant political beliefs. They separated as friends, on Elizaveta's condition that he would not send her any more letters full of Marxist lectures. She couldn't stand them: 'I'm a woman,' she told him, 'and I love life.'[35]

★   ★   ★

After Longjumeau, Lenin was called to an International Socialist Bureau meeting in Zurich in September and decided to take advantage of being

---

* 'Nous partagions nos poules. Lénine était très gai, très bon, et en amour, très cochon.'

back in Switzerland to give political lectures in Geneva and Berne as part of his drive to raise support for a party conference. His major topic was Stolypin and the Revolution – the reactionary Russian Prime Minister having recently been assassinated in the Kiev opera house by a Socialist Revolutionary. He gave the speech to socialist groups in Antwerp, Brussels and Liège before crossing to London for an appearance at the New King's Hall on 11 November. He was only in the city for three days but he could not leave without doing some work at the British Museum, where he bumped into émigré German Social Democrat Max Beer. They enjoyed a sixpenny lunch afterwards at a popular local restaurant. Not having seen Lenin since 1903, Beer noted that he had lost weight, his 'ascetic face' and 'burning eyes' giving him the look of 'a monk, a missionary and a crusader'. It was clear to him that Lenin had gained considerably in 'fervour, self-confidence and authority'. After their lunch the two men repaired to the nearby German Working Men's Club in Charlotte Street for a long talk about the future of the international socialist movement and the rumblings of war created by the growing naval rivalries of Germany and Britain. Lenin was convinced that a European war would be 'the prologue of a tremendous revolutionary drama'. And he was determined that the revolution when it came should be a socialist one and not 'as the Mensheviks desire, a liberal-democratic one'. It seemed to Beer that in the dispassionate and simple manner in which Lenin hammered home his beliefs that day, there was something so relentlessly logical, like that of 'an accountant explaining the various items on a balance sheet'.[37]

The same unshakeable, pedantic rationale was behind Lenin's drive to call a new party conference. He had no intention of running the risk of the three-week squabble that had prevailed in London in 1907. Having laid the groundwork at Longjumeau by indoctrinating his own key party workers, he was now bent on an effective coup by his Bolshevik faction at their own carefully stage-managed conference. It was no matter to him that his Bolshevik delegates would be second rate and inexperienced compared to the leading lights of the Mensheviks. As new blood and loyal Leninists they would serve to rubber stamp his seizing back of overall control of the party, and with it the creation of a Bolshevik Central Committee. Meanwhile, Lenin's major rivals Martov, Plekhanov, Axelrod and the non-aligned Trotsky, would be dismissed as being 'outside the party', even though Lenin had made the token gesture of inviting them, knowing full well they would decline to take part.[37]

Now was to come a prime example of Lenin's ruthlessness. The calling of the conference in Prague, in the heart of the Austro-Hungarian Empire, a location with no Russian colony, where more stringent passport controls prevailed and to which delegates from Russia might well have difficulty travelling (a couple were indeed arrested en route), was all part of his plan. On 19 January 1912 eighteen delegates – eight of them students from Longjumeau, and including the promising Sergo Ordzhonikidze, who had hand-picked most of the rest in Russia – gathered in strict secrecy in Prague; two Mensheviks were also admitted. The delegates were billeted with sympathetic Czech workers in the neighbourhood. There were no special concessions for Lenin, who arrived without Nadya and shared a room with delegate Stepan Onufriev – two beds, a commode, a table and chairs – in the home of a worker's family who gave up the better of their two rooms for them.[38] The conference – or rather cabal, for that is effectively what it was – took place in a second-floor room of the People's House, a rather grand, former palace on Hybernská Street, arranged by Czech Social Democrats. Contrary to Lenin's expectations, the proceedings were a 'stormy affair'. Some of the delegates protested that they were unrepresentational by excluding figures such as Plekhanov and Trotsky and representatives of the other émigré groups. Delegate Suren Spandaryan from Baku condemned the 'cavalier attitude' of Lenin and the émigrés for exposing workers groups back in Russia to risk and discovery: 'How many comrades are in prison because of that émigré squabbling?' He and Ordzhonikidze were not the only delegates to voice concerns that the émigrés were out of touch – Lenin included – and that the Social Democrats would do better to build their own, solid *Russian*-based organisation.[39] Lenin fought back with his usual bullying tactics and, thanks to the crucial support of his yes-men Zinoviev, Kamenev and others, got his way, his motions carried unanimously. The Prague meeting had, in Lenin's unconscionable words, 'constituted itself as the supreme and legitimate assembly of the entire RSDLP',[40] but there was no disguising his shameless usurpation of the protocols of a proper party conference. At Prague Lenin was elected as a representative to the International Socialist Bureau and member of a new Central Committee that included only one non-Bolshevik (and, despite all the warnings, which he stubbornly chose to ignore, a suspected double agent, Roman Malinovsky). In his usual underhand manner he also later managed to co-opt on to the CC his own, rising new protégé – Stalin, currently languishing in Siberian exile at Solvychegodsk. Approval was given for Bolshevik participation in elections to the 4th Duma and a legal party newspaper was established to replace *Zvezda*, by means of which the vacillating and disaffected membership in Russia could once more be galvanised. Lenin had no qualms about hijacking the title of a similarly named journal already established in Vienna by Trotsky. The first issue of *Pravda* (The Truth) appeared in a print run of 60,000 copies in St Petersburg that May, with Stalin contributing the first editorial. On the 9th, Lenin met with his Bolshevik colleagues in their café on the avenue d'Orléans brandishing a copy of the first issue: 'Here's our mighty agitator, our propagandist and organiser,' he announced with a flourish. 'It will rouse the nation, and call it to victory.'[42]

Lenin's effective *coup d'état* in Prague created much protest among Social Democrats back in Paris and the backbiting became worse than ever, with a rival conference eventually set up by those excluded from Prague. At Prague, Ordzhonikidze had very rightly pointed up the debilitating and destructive effect on party work, even in Russia, of this 'damned emigration' with its constant rivalries and 'polemical antics'. 'We know that the emigration has failed all along to give us anything of value,' he asserted. 'The emigration is nothing.'[43] Lenin knew only too well that this was true; and he was already planning to move on. Having finally achieved the party split that he had initiated in 1903, he saw no reason to remain in Paris; quite apart from the constant political infighting, it was too expensive and their rent had just gone up. His initial intention had been to move south to the countryside around Fontenay, which he had explored by bike with Nadya. But soon he realised a more decisive break was needed. It was time finally to detach himself from the political émigré centres of Western Europe. He felt an increasing need to be nearer to Russia, particularly worried as he was about his mother's frail health; his sisters had both been arrested in Saratov and could not take care of her. Perhaps this added to a growing sense of guilt that all these years he had never been able to be there for her.

In April, events in Russia played into his hands: a strike by miners in the Lena goldfields in south-east Siberia resulted in protesters being fired on indiscriminately by troops. Two hundred miners were killed and many more wounded. Echoes of Bloody Sunday reverberated across Russia in an ensuing wave of strikes and rallies that culminated on May Day in a mass protest and demands for an eight-hour working day. Russia was on

the move and becoming militant once more. Only the previous autumn
Lenin had been so discouraged that he had confided to his sister Anna
that he wondered whether they would live to see the rising of the tide
once more in Russia. In 1912 he was reinvigorated and began to believe
that he just might, in an article in memory of Herzen, writing of the
second wave of revolution that was developing 'before our very eyes'.
His fanatical belief in the eventual victory of the proletariat was as strong
as ever.[44] He wanted to ensure that his consolidated Bolshevik Party, as
it now effectively was, would be in the vanguard. Events at Prague had,
however, also been a clear indicator to Lenin that the Bolshevik movement in Russia was gaining strength – and credibility – without him.
Realising he might be in danger of losing control, he decided to move
his operation further east, nearer to Russia. He chose Galicia, once part
of Poland, at that time part of Austria-Hungary; his two primary collab-
orators, Zinoviev and Kamenev, would go with him.

On 17 June 1912, Lenin, Nadya and Elizaveta Vasil'evna left Paris quite
suddenly, without even forewarning their relatives in Russia, having sublet
their apartment to a Pole and leaving all their furniture behind. Lenin
travelled incognito as usual, wearing his bowler hat, with a bath towel
under his arm containing three shirts and two tooth brushes. Nadezhda
carried some parcels of books and Elizaveta brought their paltry possessions, cards and chess set. Many in their circle could not understand why
Lenin had not opted for Finland again – or even Sweden. Elizaveta de
K, who was now living in Paris, thought him mad to choose Galicia,
where the Russians were thought badly of. But at least the border with
Russia (or, rather, those Polish lands that were then part of the Russian
Empire) was only a couple of miles to the north and it was twenty-four
hours to St Petersburg on an express train. The local Galician police
would have no truck with the Okhrana, communications with Russia
were better and their letters would be safe from interception.[45]

Nadya was clear in her own mind that a change was a good thing:
'another year or two of life in this atmosphere of squabbling and emigrant
tragedy would have meant heading for a breakdown'; life abroad had
'frayed everyone's nerves considerably'.[46] Naturally enough, she made
no mention of Inessa, but her husband's affair must have added to her
desire to leave Paris. In any event, Lenin and Inessa appear to have broken
off their relationship at around this time, perhaps because Lenin insisted
that the revolution was once more demanding their overriding attention.
As dedicated revolutionists all three would have been reluctant to allow

passion, sexual jealousy or rivalry to undermine their far more important shared political goals. We shall never know the details, but that
summer they clearly resolved their problems by a combination of accommodation, dissimulation and discretion, sufficient to ensure that as
comrades they could continue working together.[46]

As his tenants M. and Mme Oulianoff departed from rue Marie-Rose,
their concièrge, like Mrs Yeo in London before her, was sad to see them
go. Never, in three years, had she had the slightest cause for complaint
– 'they always paid their 700 francs yearly rent most punctually'.[47]

CHAPTER FOURTEEN

'Almost Russia'

Kraków–Biały Dunajec–Poronin: June 1912–August 1914

The Sukiennice, Kraków's old cloth market

Having made a detour to Stuttgart so that Lenin could have a meeting with the German Social Democrat Clara Zetkin, the family continued their journey across Austria-Hungary to Kraków on train no. 13 from Vienna's Nordbahnhof. It was much slower than the express, which only took seven hours or so, and it didn't have sleeping cars. But they were extremely strapped for cash, so they had to travel overnight, leaving the previous evening. They did their best to get some rest on their uncomfortable, second-class seats as the train headed north, crossing the border with the province of Moravia at Lundenburg, and heading north-east into the Polish territory of Galicia, past the city of Oświęcim (later notorious for the nearby German concentration camp Auschwitz). After such slow and uncomfortable progress from Vienna they were glad to see the sunshine of Kraków when they emerged from the main station at 9.30 that Saturday morning, 22 June.[1] They could sense how near they were to their home-land. Galicia seemed familiar to Lenin; it was 'almost Russia!'. As far as they were all concerned, their life here would be a 'semi-exile', for the border with the Russian Empire was only a few miles away.[2]

Leaving their luggage at the station, they headed off to meet their contact, Sergiusz Bagocki, a Russian-born Pole and former exile who was now a medical student at the university. Bagocki was also secretary to the Kraków-based Committee of Aid to Political Prisoners and had plenty of contacts in the city. The rendezvous point was a short walk from the station outside the city's Jagiellonian University. It was a pleasant summer's day so they were not unduly worried as they sat and waited opposite the university on a bench in the Planty Gardens that circled the medieval perimeter, watching people promenade past and children playing on the grass. But after half an hour, with no one in sight, the ever watchful Lenin's nerves began to jangle. *They* had arrived on time but where was their escort? Bagocki, in fact, was sitting not far away from them wondering exactly the same thing. He had never met Lenin and did not realise that the rather inconsequential looking man sitting nearby with his dowdy wife was the political leader he revered above all others. It was only after he began pacing nervously up and down that Nadya plucked up the courage to ask him if he was Comrade Bagocki.

Kraków was a beautiful medieval city that till the end of the sixteenth century had been the capital of a great Polish–Lithuanian state, the seat of the Jagiellon dynasty of monarchs. For centuries it had been a centre of Polish and Jewish culture and was resplendent still with the architecture of that historical heyday, including its fourteenth-century university and medieval castle and one of the oldest Jewish quarters in Europe. In 1772 it had become a major city of the Kingdom of Galicia and Lodomeria, when Austria annexed territories there during the parti-tion of Poland; in 1815 the Congress of Vienna that ended the Napoleonic Wars gave it the status of an independent city state, but after a failed uprising in 1846 Kraków was formally annexed by Austria. Under the ageing Habsburg Emperor, Franz Joseph, Galicia had become that empire's most densely populated, northernmost province, bordering the Polish territories of the Russian Empire to the north and east, with a mix of Jews, Poles and Germans. It was also a hotbed of patriotic resistance to Habsburg domination.

The arrival of Mr and Mrs 'Włodimierz Ulianoff' from Paris at the Hotel Victoria was noted the next day in the local paper, *Czas*, but

they didn't stay long.[3] Lenin and Nadya had already rejected the centre
of Kraków, which at that time of year was hot, stuffy and overcrowded.
They were both keen to be nearer to woodland and open spaces and
Bagocki, by booking them into the Hotel Victoria west of the city,
suggested that the working-class suburb of Zwierzyniec, where it was
located, was a good option. In the end they chose the more salubrious,
newly developed end of Zwierzyniec, at Salvator, home to civil servants
and professionals. The streets might still be unpaved and muddy, but
at the end of the city tramline, at no. 218 Ulica Zwierzyniec, they
found a pleasant first-floor apartment in a large, unfurnished, detached
house which they shared with Zinoviev, his wife Zina and, much to
Lenin's considerable pleasure, their young son Stepa.[4] Permission for
Lenin to live and work in Kraków had been arranged with the Austrian
Minister of the Interior by Jakub Hanecki, a prominent Polish Social
Democrat, who lived just along the road.[5] Nadya enjoyed the company
of Zina on their daily trips into the vast central square of Kraków
with its busy market of Jewish traders inside the shopping arcade
known as the Sukiennice, once a medieval cloth hall. Outside, the
square was alive with the vibrant costumes of local, barefoot peasant
women in gaudy headscarves and picturesque national dress, offering
milk, cheese, vegetables and poultry for sale, as well as carved wooden
toys and long strings of wild, dried mushrooms. It all reminded Nadya
of Russia. Lenin felt the same; to his mind, even the Galician Jews
were like Russians.[6]

Compared to the smelly and populous heart of old Kraków, where
the impoverished Jews who laboured in its metalworks and cigarette
factories crowded out the dilapidated old tenements and cobbled courtyards, Zwierzyniec was a paradise. Located near to a lovely open stretch
of parkland known as the Błonie, it was an area free from the disease
and squalor of the working-class districts of Kraków and did not suffer
the intense heat of the city centre in summer. The mighty Wisła river
was a couple of miles away, where Lenin and Nadya could go swimming
in sight of the bell towers of the sixteenth-century Bielany Monastery
on a nearby hilltop. And they had the pleasures too, on their doorstep,
of the Las Wolski – a vestige of the vast primordial forest that had once
covered much of Central Europe and for centuries had been a royal
hunting forest. This last became a great favourite, where, after Lenin had
finished his daily quota of work, he and Nadya could indulge in bicycle
rides, as well as one of their favourite leisure pursuits – mushroom

picking.[7] In the winter, for the first time since leaving Munich, Lenin took up skating again – at the ice rink down the hill from the Botanical Gardens, often taking young Stepa Zinoviev with him. Back at the house in Zwierzyniec, he regularly enjoyed games of rough and tumble with Stepa. What a pity he and Nadya didn't have a boy like him, he told Zina; they were both so very fond of him.[8]

Although he openly used his real name, Ulyanov, Lenin's official cover for the benefit of his registration papers with the Austro-Hungarian police was that he was a correspondent of the newspapers *Pravda* (St Petersburg) and *Sotsial-Demokrat* (Paris). The political atmosphere for Lenin in Kraków was a deal more relaxed; the Austrian political system, unlike Russia, allowed freedom of the press and democractic election. The police, while having him under discreet surveillance, observed a Ruritanian laxity that did not trouble him and his circle. For all their shortage of money he and Nadya lived a fairly untrammelled, petit bourgeois existence that would have been the envy of many an exile elsewhere in Europe, or, for that matter, an underground activist back in Russia. Newspapers arrived from Russia within three days; their mail was not tampered with, although for safety's sake many letters to Lenin were sent care of a professor at the university.[9] Members of Bagocki's committee acted as couriers regularly taking letters, journals and parcels across the border into Russia, seven miles away; this avoided the use of foreign postage marks to which the Okhrana was always alert. They also made use of local workers and peasants as couriers in the border area, who were allowed by the Austro-Hungarian and Russian authorities to travel back and forth across the frontier on a *polupaska* (semi-passport) to their places of work or to sell goods at market. All activists visiting from Russia were nevertheless drilled in the arts of disguise and *konspiratsiya* by Lenin and Nadya. One such, named Shumkin, took it all rather too seriously, walking the streets of Kraków at several paces behind them with his cap pulled down over his eyes. Nadya recalled with amusement that he looked so patently conspiratorial that he immediately attracted the attention of the Kraków police. Bizarrely, an officer called on Lenin – of all people – soon after, asking whether he knew this man and could vouch for him.[10]

Unlike the other European cities in which, until now, Lenin and Nadya had lived out their exile, Kraków had no Russian political community, although it did have four thousand voluntary exiles – mainly Poles born in the territories controlled by the Russian Empire who had moved into the less repressive territories of Austria-Hungary. As Polish followers of Marx, Bagocki, Hanecki and their fellow activists were natural allies of the vehemently anti-tsarist Russians. But the Polish Social Democrats, like the Russians, had undergone their own split. The original Polish Socialist Party, founded in Paris in 1892 with Polish nationalism and independence as its primary objectives, had split in 1906 between a Marxist faction, the PPS-Left, which adopted an internationalist programme, and a right-wing group of non-Marxist nationalists under Józef Piłsudski, who dreamed first and foremost of violent insurrection and a once more unified and independent Poland.[11] With many Polish socialists therefore putting their patriotism before their socialism, Lenin dismissed them as being of little interest except in their anti-imperialist sentiments.

He clearly felt an intense sense of relief being here. He liked Kraków even though he regarded it as a backwater: 'No matter how provincial and barbarous this town of ours may be, by and large I am better off here than I was in Paris,' he told his family.[12] He made no effort, however, to learn Polish, resorting to German and sign language with the locals. He liked Polish food – especially the traditional hearty soup, *żurek*, and *kwaśne mleko* (sour milk) – but when it came to Polish culture he remained resolutely philistine. Nadya could not persuade him to go and look at Polish art – 'at any price'.[13] Lenin's only forays into the city extended to the occasional meeting with colleagues in the Noworolski Café at the Sukiennice, but he preferred the Jama Michalika Café on Floriańska, which, with its darkly Art Nouveau interior, reeked of Mitteleuropa, and where he and his colleagues could sit for hours in a corner and hardly be noticed.

Nadya, for her part, did at least have some rudimentary knowledge of Polish, sufficient to decipher the newspapers when needed. Her father, Konstantin Krupsky, had served in the Russian military in Poland and later returned as a government official to Warsaw, where she had lived from the ages of two to five. But she found Polish society very Catholic, if not feudal, and was sensitive to the marginalisation of the Jews and the wretched poverty she saw in Kraków. Otherwise, she went about her party and domestic duties as usual, without complaint.[14] Despite a steady stream of visitors from Russia, however, she felt very lonely and isolated; by January 1913 she was complaining in letters to Lenin's family that her life was very monotonous and she had 'scarcely any acquaintances here'.[15] After twelve years on the move, nothing could really mitigate the increasing sense of homesickness both she – and Lenin – were by now suffering. In their heart of hearts, they and Elizaveta Vasil'evna all longed to return, as did many of their long-term exiled friends. 'We avoided speaking of this subject,' wrote Nadya, 'but all of us secretly thought about it.'[16]

Part of the reason Nadya felt depressed was that she was far from well, suffering palpitations, dizzy spells and an increasing sense of exhaustion; continuing problems with her bulging eyes meant she found it more and more difficult to work on the coding and decoding of letters. To make matters worse, her elderly mother was now becoming senile and more of a burden than a help around the house. Nadya had long since trained herself to internalise her physical problems; she did not have time to be ill and did her best to hide how she felt. And Lenin, as usual, was too busy to notice. After settling into their new home, he reverted to the familiar routine of locking himself away for strictly regulated, uninterrupted periods of work – writing for the various Russian and émigré journals, corresponding with the editorial board of *Pravda*, which he was bombarding with articles on an almost daily basis, meeting with activists, firing off endless instructions to his Duma deputies and party workers in Russia. This was followed by periods of recreation – cycling, walking and swimming.

But for the most part Lenin stayed at home, churning out three hundred articles and other political tracts during his time in Galicia, peppering his letters with the usual complaints: the Kraków libraries weren't up to scratch and he wished he had the resources of Geneva or London; there weren't enough connections with and news of party workers in Russia; the editorial board of *Pravda* sent him 'stupid and impudent letters'; they were 'pitiful dish rags' who were ruining the cause and he wanted to 'kick them out'.[17] He became incensed when the newspapers were late arriving, and was obsessed about his favourite bogeymen – the 'liquidators' back in Russia – i.e. everyone and anyone who talked of conciliation and party reunification and, worse still, liberal reform. His daily life alternated between bouts of the all too familiar rage, stress and impatience. It was one thing to have fought in person for, and won domination over, the Bolshevik faction at close quarters in Prague. But after twelve years of exile, with his energies constantly diverted into often futile émigré squabbles, he was beginning to sense how tenuous his overall hold on the party was back home. Much to his dismay, Lenin's six Bolshevik delegates to the 4th Duma elections were working closely and peacefully with the seven Mensheviks, the final split initiated by Lenin in Prague still not having taken effect among them.[18] By far the most pressing preoccupation, however, was his lack of money. His regular articles for *Pravda* brought him 100 rubles a month contributor's fee, but this was now his primary source of income in the absence of literary work, which had all but dried up.

Inessa arrived in Kraków not long after Lenin and Nadya – and stayed with them only long enough to take instructions from him on a risky new mission. He needed her to go back into Russia undercover to pass on the resolutions of the Prague conference, keep an eye on the election of his Bolshevik candidates to the 4th Duma and find out what was going on at *Pravda*. Stalin and its other editors had been exhibiting a worryingly conciliatory line with the Mensheviks on its pages and had also turned down forty-seven of his articles and amended many others. He was fed up with writing for 'the waste-paper basket' without the courtesy of being told why.[19] It must have been clear to him the risks Inessa took as a former political prisoner and escapee wanted by the Okhrana; her return would invite almost immediate arrest, yet Lenin made light of it. Where party work was concerned he totally disengaged from any feelings he had for her – even as the mother of five children. She and her inexperienced travelling companion, Georgy Safarov (one of the newly trained Longjumeau party workers), were perfectly dispensable: 'If they are not arrested, this will be useful,' he wrote to Kamenev, as Inessa headed for the border, disguised as a Polish peasant under the improbable false passport of Frantsiska Kazimirovna Yankevich.[20] The mission was doomed: the Okhrana were watching Inessa from the moment she re-entered Russia. She was short of money and sickly, yet nevertheless tramped St Petersburg in her disguise of worn-out old boots and shawl, visiting underground cells. Soon word came back from her confirming that the party was in disarray. The police had greatly improved their techniques for infiltrating underground groups with spies and the cells had been decimated by a big wave of arrests that May. Those who survived were increasingly isolated from each other and from the party organisation abroad. Many of the secret addresses used by Nadya for correspondence had been uncovered by the Okhrana, or lost, and with them her network of contacts.[21]

Within a couple of months of settling in at Zwierzyniec, Lenin became impatient with its distance from Kraków's main station and post office. The house had no gas or electricity, which was also an inconvenience, and on 2 September the family moved into the city centre. Their new home was on the first floor of a two-storey apartment block on Ulica Lubomirskiego, a new development built in 1911 in the Wesoła district. Although it was in the city, it had an open view on the other side of the road across fields to the border with Russia to the north; much to her pleasure, Nadya could still hear the nightingales sing.[22] It was also conveniently located for Lenin's purposes just behind the railway station, with many of his Polish socialist contacts living in the nearby streets, whose addresses were used as safe houses for party correspondence and visiting comrades from Russia.

In November, Lenin decided it was time for a meeting with his Bolshevik 'six' from the new Central Committee he had established at Prague and he summoned his colleagues to his apartment in Kraków. Most of them, as Duma delegates, were able to leave Russia on legal passports, but Stalin, who only a few months before had absconded yet again from exile in Siberia, was obliged to make his way undercover from Russia, at considerable risk of re-arrest. He was smuggled out of St Petersburg in a covered cart, then crossed Finland by train on a fake Russian passport to Åbo, where, provided with a Finnish passport, he took the ferry across to Germany and a train to Kraków. Having gone straight to Lenin's flat, he was given a warm welcome. But the food, thanks to Nadya's poor culinary abilities – particularly when put under pressure to feed a roomful of party workers – left a lot to be desired. Stalin was dismayed at being fed Polish sausage and constantly craved his favourite Georgian shashlik.

During the meeting, he found Lenin's tactics too hard line and thought him out of touch with the mood of conciliation within the party in Russia. After ten days Stalin returned by a smuggler's route but was back yet again in December after Lenin demanded another visit – this time to discuss the nationalities question.[23] After another long journey, Stalin arrived ravenous but took the precaution this time of dining out at the Hawelka on Market Square. Lenin did his best to be solicitous for his comforts, even getting in bottles of beer for him, but the two men were nervous and watchful with each other. Nevertheless, Lenin saw in Stalin a loyal party worker and invited him to stay on in Kraków and write an important Leninist party paper on the nationalities question, aimed at garnering support for the Bolsheviks from minority groups in the Duma. Galicia, with its mix of nationalities, was good raw material. Stalin had little experience in writing political literature but under Lenin's watchful eye produced a document that suited his requirements. At Lenin's diktat it would underline the loyalty of all nationalities to a future federalist, socialist state, while offering token ideals of autonomy for national groups as smaller republics within it, with the right of secession.[24] Lenin was very pleased with the end result and his 'wonderful Georgian', who headed back to St Petersburg – where he was promptly arrested in February and sentenced to another four years in exile.[25]

By early 1913, Nadya's health was in serious decline; her sense of loneliness also continued to provoke bouts of depression. Despite seeing 'doctor-comrades' in the exile community who were trained physicians, no one had as yet correctly diagnosed her condition. After much persuasion by Lenin she took up Bagocki's recommendation to go to one of the best neurologists in Kraków, Dr Jan Landau, at the neurological clinic at the university where Bagocki was finishing his medical studies. Nadya was soon writing to inform her mother-in-law that 'on top of all that, it has been discovered that I have thyroid trouble'. The doctor had 'frightened' her by giving her three-hour sessions of 'electrical treatment' – electro-convulsive therapy to help counter her erratic behaviour and feeding her bromides, to bring down her rapid rate of speech, but all these did was to make her feel sick and dizzy, so that 'after it I wander about half the day like a lunatic'.[26] He also recommended she take several months' rest in the mountains. After much discussion, in early May Lenin and Nadya travelled to the Podhale region eighty-five miles south of Kraków where she could enjoy the clean air of the Tatra Mountains. The cost of living there was cheaper and it would also present a quiet location where Lenin could get on with his writing. But he refused to make a decision until Bagocki had checked and could assure him that the postal communications by rail from there were good and would not disrupt his contact with Petersburg.

They settled in a small hamlet called Biały Dunajec, due north of the larger village of Poronin – which itself was only a row of thatched cottages strung out along the road, with a couple of shops and a post office. They rented a large, chalet-style house with a verandah from a local Góral woman, Teresa Skupień, with Lenin, Nadya and her mother taking the downstairs rooms. The upstairs was kept free for visitors from Russia, and was constantly in use. Lenin rigorously made full use of the daylight, working hard until 7.00 p.m. There was no electricty in the area and after dark it was difficult reading by the light of a kerosene lamp.[27] The Zinovievs came with them, renting a house along the road in Poronin. It would have been preferable to live a little further south on the railway

line at the spa and health resort of Zakopane that nestled so picturesquely
in the foothills of the Tatra Mountains, but with its exclusive sanatoria
for TB patients it was far too crowded and expensive. Nadya loved the
Tatra Mountains, the tranquillity and the breathtaking views. The air
was wonderful, the surrounding scenery ravishing, with waterfalls, fast-
flowing mountain streams, lush meadows and a constant backdrop of
snow-capped mountains. When the weather was fine, Lenin rose early
for a daily swim in the nearby Dunajec mountain stream. But these lovely
sights were often obliterated by the persistent rain that descended almost
daily from the Tatras and swathed the entire area in a heavy mist. The
weather did not, of course, deter Lenin, who was at his happiest out in
the wilds on arduous hikes that were well off the tourist trail, always
ensuring he had with him both straw hat, hanging on a string from his
jacket, and umbrella-cum-walking stick, against either climatic contingency.[28] On clear days Nadya was able to walk the incline to a vantage
point at the back of their house to take in the view but her health
prevented her from undertaking the kind of arduous walks they had
done in Switzerland. Although it was hoped the mountain air would
help Nadya's condition, being 700 metres above sea level may well have
stressed her weak heart. Yet still she put Lenin first: his nerves were
'playing up' and the unmade roads and constant rain made the area
unsuitable for cycling, which frustrated him. Privately, Nadya was relieved.
It meant that Volodya couldn't 'overtire himself'. He certainly was always
one for a physical challenge. On one occasion he toiled for twenty-five
miles on his bicycle out of Biały Dunajec on the terrible Galician roads
in order to join Bagocki for a hike up Babia Góra, one of the highest
and most famous peaks in the western range of the Tatra Mountains.
The two men nearly got lost as night descended, but luckily found a
hikers' hut to shelter in. Much to Lenin's disappointment, heavy rain the
next morning prevented them from continuing to the top. Having got
back down the mountain, he and Bagocki then had to struggle all the
way back through thick mud on their bikes. Lenin remained bullish; the
mountain was not going to defeat him and the first free day he had he
vowed he would come back and do the job properly. Two weeks later
he was as good as his word – only this time wisely opting to travel to
Zakopane on the train and taking the precaution of bringing a lantern.
Leaving the hikers' hut at 4.00 a.m. on Lenin's insistence, he and Bagocki
clambered to the top of Babia Góra in heavy mist – and couldn't see a
thing. Lenin patiently sat down to wait in the early morning light until

suddenly the skies cleared, revealing a magnificent view of the Tatras. 'There you are', he laughed 'our efforts were not wasted.' Persistence in mountain climbing, as in politics, always paid off for him.[29]

The quiet life he led at Biały Dunajec certainly calmed Lenin's nerves but sometimes the remoteness reminded him of Shushenskoe – where life was reduced to counting the hours till the next mail. Every day if it was too muddy to cycle, Lenin would walk along the railway track from Biały Dunajec to the station at Poronin to collect his letters. The post office was located in a large house with wood carvings that also served as the local hotel. The postmaster, Tadeusz Radkiewicz, recalled that Lenin often used to stay for a while, talking to the locals and visitors. His wife was amazed at the great pile of letters and newspapers Lenin carried back each time. Nobody, she said, 'subscribed to so many newspapers in so many foreign languages'. Then he would be off again, down the track, reading his letters as he walked.[30]

To break the monotony of life at Biały Dunajec, Lenin often cycled down into Zakopane to use the library of the Society of the Tatras, which housed a collection of socialist writings. His main contact in town was Boris Vigilev, a Russian who had been expelled from Moscow University in 1902 for revolutionary activities. As a TB sufferer, he had gone to Zakopane for his health and now worked at the local meteorological station. Vigilev introduced Lenin to many of the local Polish intelligentsia and he sometimes stayed the night with him and his wife at their little house near Zakopane station. For some years now a thriving intellectual and artistic community had been growing at Zakopane. With their national awareness as Poles rather than Austro-Hungarian subjects, it was natural that they should gravitate to Galicia, which had increasingly been used as a propaganda base by Polish socialists campaigning against the Austrian government and where the Polish left had greeted revolutionary events in the Russian Empire in 1905 with great enthusiasm. Galicia was a region with strong nationalist sentiments – much the same as those that had created the state of Piedmont, which, during 1859–61, had been the springboard for Italy's unification. The vibrant Góral culture of the region's free peasants, who were not answerable to landlords, was an inspiration to politicians and writers alike. In the summer months Zakopane became the unofficial regional capital of Polish intellectual life. It was no accident either that the nationalist leader, Józef Piłsudski, who had been a member of the assassination plot against Alexander III for which Lenin's brother Aleksandr Ulyanov was hanged in 1887, had a house not far from where Lenin was staying in Biały Dunajec. The Podhale region provided him with the best political and intellectual network in Galicia and soon he would be very glad of it.[31]

On fine days in Zakopane – precious few as the rain was persistent – Lenin liked nothing better than to sit in front of the post office on the main street – Krupówki – reading the papers. Sometimes he and Vigilev met and played chess over coffee with the local intelligentsia at their popular haunts – the 'Morskie Oko' or the Café Trzaski.[32] Nobody in Zakopane took much notice of the Russian-looking intellectual – many sick ones came regularly for treatment at the sanatoria, so it was always a useful cover. In time Lenin met some of the leading Polish intellectuals of the day: the novelists Władysław Reymont and Stefan Żeromski; the poet and dean of the University of Lwów, Jan Kasprowicz and Władysław Orkan, one of the great descriptive novelists of peasant life in the Podhale.

Meanwhile, Nadya's condition, which she had suffered so stoically for so long, was becoming acute. Lenin's doctor brother Dmitri had advised against surgery but Lenin, meanwhile, had done his own research on the matter. Bagocki suggested he take Nadya to see the top expert on the condition who had a clinic in Berne, Switzerland. Professor Emil Theodor Kocher was no run-of-the-mill surgeon. He was a specialist in endocrinology and in 1909 had been awarded the Nobel prize specifically for his work on the thyroid gland; in 1912 he had donated a large sum to the founding of a Research Institute in Biology at the University of Berne. When it came to matters of personal health, Lenin always went to the very best doctors without hesitation, no matter the expense, and this applied to Nadya, too. But in order to raise the money for her treatment, he had to send urgent begging letters to the editors of Pravda to hurry up payment for articles that they had published.

Through Russian contacts in Berne, Professor Kocher was approached and agreed to undertake the operation. Nadya was now too ill to travel alone and so in early June 1913 Lenin, reluctant as ever to leave his work, accompanied her on the 700-mile train journey to Berne, where Nadya was to undergo the relatively new procedure of a thyroidectomy. Bagocki moved into their apartment for the duration to look after Elizaveta Vasil'evna who had become, in his estimation, increasingly 'helpless'.[33] Nadya was deeply apprehensive about undergoing the procedure but was in the best possible hands. By 1912 Kocher had performed two thousand

thyroidectomies, with a high success rate. The operation was nevertheless a traumatic experience but the only option at a time before drugs
had been developed to treat the condition. Arriving in Berne on the 25th,
Lenin was furious to discover that Professor Kocher was much in demand
and they would have to take their turn in line. The good doctor was
difficult: 'he's a celebrity and likes to be begged', Lenin remarked. But
worse, in such straitened circumstances, he found himself having to
haggle over the cost of the operation with the 'tight-fisted Frau
Professor'.[34]

As Nadya waited for her operation, Lenin filled the days reading medical
books on her condition, sitting with her for some of the time and then
disappearing off to the nearest library. His stress levels rose as two weeks
went by waiting while Nadya was subjected to tests. But on 10 June she
finally underwent a thyroidectomy; and she did so without a general
anaesthetic, her irregular heartbeat (due to a defect known as atrial fibril-
lation) making it too dangerous to administer one.[35] The following day
she was prostrated by a high temperature and delirium but began to
recover soon after. While Nadya remained in hospital recuperating, Lenin
made up for lost time, travelling to Lausanne, Berne, Geneva and Zurich
to give a series of lectures. Soon Nadya was anxious to get back to her
own party work and Lenin was not inclined to dissuade her. They left
Berne before she was fully recovered despite Dr Kocher, oblivious to the
couple's financial difficulties, ordering Nadya to take two weeks' rest and
recuperation in the Alps. The costs of the operation and travel to Switzerland had left them desperately short of money. Thereafter, Nadya fiercely
resisted all requests that she slow down with her party work and go to
the doctor's for regular checks. She made only one concession to her
impaired health: after their return to Biały Dunajec on 4 August there
would be no more long hikes for her in the mountains.[36]

No sooner were they back from Switzerland than Lenin called a
'Conference of Party Functionaries' that ran from 21 September to 1
October at their house, with Lenin enlisting the local inn owner in
Poronin to accommodate the twenty-two delegates. During the conference it was resolved to formally split the Social Democrat delegation in
the Duma into Bolsheviks and Mensheviks so that the Bolsheviks could
capitalise politically on a new wave of strikes and protests taking place
in Russia. Despite all the efforts to observe konspiratsiya, details of the
conference were later passed back to the Okhrana by two spies in their
midst.

Much to everyone's surprise, when the conference was in full swing Inessa arrived from Russia. In September the previous year the Okhrana, having gleaned what it wanted by tailing her across St Petersburg, swooped at a political meeting and arrested her. She had been held in solitary confinement for six months, where the freezing, damp conditions had brought on the first signs of tuberculosis. Once more, her husband Aleksandr gallantly bailed her out for 5,400 rubles. She managed to spend some time with her children at Pushkino and on holiday in the Caucasus before, with Aleksandr's blessing, fleeing Russia for Finland, leaving the children in his care.[37] From there she took the boat from Sweden to mainland Europe and headed straight for Galicia to join Lenin's Bolshevik circle.

Inessa was sick and exhausted yet, nevertheless, as Nadya noted with admiration, 'flung herself into party work with her usual ardour'.[38] After the conference, some of the delegates enjoyed mountain walks together, including a visit to the spectacular Czarny Staw – the 'Black Lake', so-called because its waters reflect the dark colours of the mountains that tower all around it. Located high in the Tatras, it leads on, in a magical double concentric circle, to another even larger lake, Morskie Oko – 'eye of the sea', set deep in a valley like the eyeball in a socket. As most of the group collapsed, exhausted, for lunch, rest and a cigarette, Lenin agitated to press on to the nearest peak. He did so with Bagocki in tow, but even at ten years younger, Bagocki found it hard to keep up with him as he scrambled up and down the steepest paths.[39]

The high point of Lenin and Inessa's emotional closeness may well have come here, in Galicia, during the last months of 1913, although it is unlikely, in such close proximity with their colleagues, that there was any sexual contact. Paris had been different; with Lenin so often out and about across the city providing plenty of opportunities. The happy mood continued when the group returned to Kraków in October. Inessa took a room at the Kamenevs' house. Her lively presence clearly lifted everyone's plummeting spirits, for life in Galicia was becoming very dull. Lenin and Nadya had run out of good Russian literature, having left the best of their books behind in Paris, and were yet again reading their dog-eared copy of *Anna Karenina*. Inessa played the piano for them and encouraged them to accompany her to a series of Beethoven concerts. Much as he loved hearing Inessa play the odd Beethoven Sonata, Lenin's patience that year did not stretch to a full-blown concert and he only stayed for part of one or two of them.[40] Nadya later recalled in her memoirs that

'that autumn all of us – our entire Kraków group, were drawn very close to Inessa . . . we lived together in a small, close and friendly circle'.[41] But in Kraków, what else was there to do but hang on each other's company, and go out walking, rejecting as they did the more philistine pursuits of the cinema enjoyed by some of their colleagues? And so, this strange, politically united yet emotionally disjointed trio took strolls together across the Błonie.

Nadya appears to have genuinely welcomed Inessa's companionship, taking an interest in her children and often talking about them with her. Lenin clearly worked well when Inessa was near; even mundane meetings with her brought light and happiness into his life.[42] But before long the emotional strain, for Inessa at least, precipitated some kind of crisis. Planning to stay in Kraków, she had written to Aleksandr asking him to prepare to send the children out to her in time for Christmas. Nadya even went out flat hunting with her; but on 18 December, without warning Inessa suddenly left for Paris.[43] Nadya tactfully suggested in her later memoirs that she had become bored with the cultural limitations of Kraków, but it is more likely that a resurgence of feeling between her and Lenin, or most certainly for her part, had led to difficulties in Lenin's marriage, at a time when Nadya was still barely recovered from her thyroid operation and feeling particularly vulnerable. Any demonstration of renewed affection between Lenin and Inessa at this time would have been very painful for her. It would also have aroused the demon of divided loyalties once more in Lenin – the pull of his personal feelings for Inessa versus its deleterious effect not just on his relationship with Nadya but also the overriding demands of the party, which always came first.

Nadya, of course, could afford to be magnanimous in her toleration, even though it hurt. She had devoted her life to Lenin and he valued her selflessness; Volodya would never leave her. But clearly Inessa had found the strain too much. A letter she wrote to Lenin in early January 1914 (but never posted) clearly conveys an end to the affair and her pain at having to part from him. For once the Parisienne in her did not enjoy being back in her native city; she now found Paris and all its bourgeois splendour 'repugnant'. It evoked too many memories of past feelings and no doubt their time together at rue Marie Rose after Longjumeau in the autumn of 1911. Being back in Paris was, for a clearly heartbroken Inessa, 'somehow so final': 'We have parted, you and I have parted my darling, and it is so painful. I know you won't come back here again! I feel it!' Never afraid of expressing her deepest-felt emotions, Inessa was candid as she had never been before: 'I know only too well, as I never did before, what a big place you occupied, here, in my life in Paris.' Yet even here, in a city from which she felt now alienated, she added, 'I could get by without your kisses if only just to see you.' But she accepted that her plaintive hopes even of just seeing Lenin sometimes were now dashed. There could be no idealised *ménage à trois*, Chernyshevsky-style, of herself, Lenin and Nadya, even though she might have been prepared to accept it on whatever modified terms he dictated. She clearly dreaded being deprived of his company but, as a good and loyal Bolshevik, accepted in the end that Lenin had 'carried through' their separation for reasons other than 'his own sake'. The fact that in her letter she then immediately went on to talk of her affection for Nadya, whom she had loved 'almost from the first meeting', makes the reason for their separation absolutely implicit – it was so as not to wound a vulnerable and sick woman further.[44]

For by early 1914, Nadya was suffering a recurrence of her physical problems. Her neck was swelling again and she was having bouts of heart palpitations. She wrote to Professor Kocher who asked to see her, but she resisted the thought of another traumatic operation – not to mention the expense.[45] The despair of her still physically weak state was compounded by her now growing sense of isolation, not helped by the fact that Lenin went to Paris in the second half of January – ostensibly to 'work in a library', as Nadya informed his mother, but almost certainly to try and patch things up with a wounded Inessa. The man who had previously despised Paris as 'a nasty hole' now headed straight for the boarding house where Inessa was living. He stayed there a week, but he was accompanied by one of his Bolshevik Duma deputies, Roman Malinovsky. Nevertheless, soon after, he was telling his mother that there was 'no better and more lively town to stay in for a short time' than Paris.[46] One can only conclude, in the absence of any documentary proof, that Inessa's gracious acceptance of their untenable situation had brought about this dramatic change of opinion and a readjustment in their relationship to that of a warm friendship, for soon after Lenin was sending his 'very, very, very best regards' to her. Inessa was back on side once more.

We have no way of knowing how deep the wounds of her thwarted love for Lenin went or how profoundly Inessa suffered the loneliness and despair of life back in Paris that year. In the end, throwing herself back into party work was the only abiding consolation. Lenin, having regained her affection, clearly adjusted much more quickly. Work was always a ready surrogate for the things missing in his life – those that give balance to most ordinary lives – and he had a ruthless ability to compartmentalise any emotional pain he might have felt. Soon after his return from Paris he was back in dictatorial, bureaucratic mode, writing more letters to Inessa than to anyone else in the party, relying as ever on her loyalty and good judgement. The usual admonitory and instructive missives on a wide range of party matters flowed from his businesslike pen, in which all too often he indulged his rage and bad language against his political adversaries, for which Inessa was an acquiescent sounding board. She was, after all, a good and unquestioning functionary; he trusted her and did not want to lose her. In Paris she could keep her ear to the ground on the underhand work of conciliators and liquidators within the émigré community and ensure that Lenin's Bolsheviks toed the line. In time, even the Okhrana would consider Inessa to be 'the right hand of Lenin' but it would become an increasingly onerous burden for her.[47] The peremptory commands came thick and fast that year in a torrent of letters, relieved only by the occasional placatory opening or closing allusion (where it has survived) to Inessa as his 'dear friend'. Enquire about this; get hold of that; who wrote this?; why had he not been sent the proofs of some article or other?; send me copies of this, that and the other. When Inessa failed to respond promptly, facetious comments followed about her tardiness. 'Is it the post again?' Lenin's histrionic demands for the 'strict execution' of his instructions were draining Inessa dry while he continued to enjoy the unchallenging 'narrow, quiet, sleepy' life of Kraków, equally unchallenged by the other loyal female lieutenant in his life – Nadya.[48]

Only occasionally has a passing observation of the pain he had caused Inessa survived in letters from Lenin that have clearly been tampered with and parts destroyed – either by him or perhaps even by Inessa herself. 'If possible do not be angry against me', he implored in June 1914. Nadya, no doubt perfectly aware of what Lenin's trip to Paris had entailed, was keeping her distance from Inessa, answering her letters in an uncharacteristically perfunctory manner, despite the fact that the two women were now collaborating on a new journal *Rabotnitsa* (The Woman Worker) launched that February.[49] In May 1914, as Lenin and Nadya returned to the house at Biały Dunajec for a second summer, Inessa quietly disappeared from Paris for a much needed reunion and holiday with her children at a resort near Trieste on the Adriatic coast. She had not seen them for a year; Lenin must have been aware of that, yet still she was not allowed to escape his demands for long. In July he called on her to take on a difficult, if not controversial leading role, representing his interests at a forthcoming 'unity' conference of Russian political groups called by the International Socialist Bureau in Brussels for 16–18 July. While it was clear that he trusted her – as a woman – where he distrusted most of the men in his orbit, and relied on her fluent French, it was the most self-serving of demands at a time when even a loyal party worker such as Inessa was entitled to some respite. He seems to have conveniently forgotten how he himself always ensured that he had holidays when he needed them.

Sending Inessa to Brussels was clearly an act of cowardice, a ploy to defuse a reprimand in front of the gathered members of the Socialist International on his aggressive and divisive behaviour that he knew was coming. The Belgian and German socialists were after his blood, but he could rely on Inessa to be his sacrificial lamb. Flattering, cajoling, bullying, he worked hard at persuading her, in letter after letter, to attend on his behalf: if she refused to go it would, he told her, 'place us in an *absolutely impossible* position'. 'You will manage splendidly!' he assured her. 'I am positive you will carry off your important role with flying colours.'[50] Inessa was exhausted, but Lenin insisted. All she had to do, after all, was 'fix up the children for 6–7 days'. Besides it was essential that she, with her impeccable French, should present his position at a conference where that would be the dominant language. He, of course, would ensure that her tactics were worked out down to the 'minutest detail', even to instructions on how to deflect the bullying and repartee of Plekhanov who enjoyed disconcerting women in the party. 'Consent, do!', he urged her. 'It will make a good change for you and you will help the cause!!'[51]

Ah, the cause – always the cause! A change of scene was the last thing Inessa needed. But how could she refuse, faced with the moral blackmail of her Duty to the Party – which in Lenin's eyes transcended that to children and family? Once again she capitulated to his demands. He wrote her speech for her, defending his Bolshevik Central Committee as representing the entire party, confident now that Bolshevik gains in the Duma had strengthened his position. Inessa was instructed to fight off any suggestions of 'idiotic conciliationism' and supplied with obsessively detailed notes. The International was shocked by Lenin's 'impudence' when a nervous Inessa read out his report in a low voice on 17 July. In it he enumerated fourteen conditions which he insisted be adopted if there was to be any unity on policy, such as agreeing the closure of all Menshevik newspapers opposed to the Bolsheviks. Lenin's demands were arrogant and monstrous; Inessa had struggled and not been able to read the whole report in the time allotted her, but Lenin was content. 'You handled things better than I could have done', he congratulated her, 'your task was heavy and . . . you have rendered a very great service to our Party.' She certainly had, for he knew full well that he would have lost his temper and only made matters worse. And then, as a palliative, having been told by another delegate that Inessa had seemed unwell, he asked if she was very tired – was she angry with him?[52] Inessa for once was unimpressed by Lenin's empty words and his flattery. She resisted his demand to traipse all the way to Biały Dunajec and report to him on the conference in person. All she wanted to do was go back to the Adriatic, to her children, and then hopefully return with them to Russia. In time this latest bout of disillusion with Lenin would fade, as party work once more took over; but for now Inessa went into emotional retreat from him.

CHAPTER FIFTEEN

A Russian Spy in Galicia

Biały Dunajec–Nowy Targ: August 1914

Poronin railway station, Galicia

On 1 August all Inessa's hopes of a reunion with her children, whom she had recently sent back to Russia from Italy, changed when Germany declared war on Russia. In Galicia, Lenin had not paid sufficient attention to the crisis in Europe that had been escalating since the assassination on 28 June in Sarajevo of Archduke Franz Ferdinand, heir to the Habsburg thrones. Although he had long argued that a European war would be a useful stepping stone to revolution and civil war in Russia, he had confided to Gorky that he doubted that 'Franz Jozef and Nicky will give us this pleasure'.[1] Not having believed the rumours of impending war when they began circulating in Galicia at the end of 1912, he was caught napping by the chain of events that occurred as rapidly in the summer of 1914 as they had in January 1905. On 28 July, the Austro-Hungarians, having not received satisfaction from the Serbs in response to their ultimatum demanding a full investigation into Franz Ferdinand's assassination, declared war on Serbia. The immediate response of Nicholas II's government was to declare war on Austria in Serbia's defence; Russian troops were rapidly mobilised on the border with Austro-Hungarian Galicia, in preparation for an invasion. Soon the Russians were joined by France and Britain, under the terms of their Triple Entente of 1907. Germany, already spoiling for a fight with Britain after a fierce naval race between the two nations over the last decade, and allied with Austria-Hungary since 1882 under the Triple Alliance with Italy, joined the fray.

An inevitable clash of interests – between socialist conscience and patriotic duty – now confronted the socialists of Europe. War precipitated the collapse of the Second International, as the various national groups within it turned their attention to their own national war effort. Soon after declaration of war in August, the German Social Democrats voted in the Reichstag to support the issuing of government war credits; British and French socialists, despite pockets of opposition in their ranks, similarly capitulated. Lenin was disgusted; his own Bolshevik deputies in the Duma had voted against such a move and refused to support the Tsar's war. But with the powerful German Social Democrats, who for so long had dominated international socialism, now on the side of government, the death knell of the International had sounded. It was the beginning of the end of a European-wide socialist movement established in London with the First International back in 1864 by Karl Marx and continued from 1889 with the Second, and in which Lenin had regularly participated since 1905. On 5 August, when he opened the papers and saw that the German Social Democrats had capitulated, Lenin declared to Bagocki: 'From today I cease to be a social democrat and have become a communist.'[2] It was a prophetic comment, marking Lenin's future emphasis on the militant, traditional origins of the Marxist movement. After the debacle of the 1913 meeting of the Socialist International in Brussels, to which Lenin had sent Inessa to do his dirty work, it was unlikely they would miss him. For fourteen years the International had tolerated the fierce factional quarrels of the Russians and their deleterious effect on the movement in Europe. They had become tired of Lenin's relentless invective and his doctrinaire pronouncements. At the International's headquarters in Brussels, its president, Emile Vandervelde – never one to like Lenin at the best of times – observed that no one had ever paid much attention to 'this little man with the narrow eyes, rusty beard and monotone voice, for ever explaining with exact and glacial politeness the traditional Marxist formulas'.[3]

When rumours of war had first begun circulating it had occurred to Lenin that a move to Vienna or Stockholm might be needed, but for now he preferred to stay in Galicia and 'take advantage of the desperate hatred of the Poles towards tsarism', for he realised that the conflict between Russia and Austria-Hungary could be useful to the cause and undermine the Russian government further, now that a new wave of strikes and discontent was hitting St Petersburg.[4] *Pravda,* which had been the victim of repeated closures, confiscations and the prosecution of its editorial board, had finally been closed down by the government in July for taking a stand against the war. Kamenev, who had been sent back to Petersburg early in 1914 by Lenin to edit it, had been arrested. Lenin's protégé, Stalin, had also recently been lost to him. The authorities had got wind of his plans to flee from exile in Turukhansk and had moved him up into the Arctic Circle to a remote settlement at Kureika from which there was no escape.[5]

As a resident alien in a country that was at war with Russia, Lenin could no longer afford to be complacent. When he had first arrived in Galicia he had been confident that the Austro-Hungarian authorities would not molest him; for their part the Austro-Hungarians had seen him as a useful anti-tsarist weapon in their running disputes with Russia. But war changed everything; the only trouble was, with no more money coming from *Pravda* and his party salary from Russia also interrupted by the war, Lenin didn't have the wherewithal to leave.[6] He hurriedly began making enquiries about retreating to neutral Switzerland or Sweden. If the local Austro-Hungarian police did not swoop soon and intern him as an enemy alien then once they entered Galicia, the Russian South-Western Army might do far worse.

Within days, the outbreak of xenophobia and spy mania spreading across Europe in the wake of war reached Poronin. The highly conservative local peasants nervously began eyeing Lenin's colony. The Roman Catholic priest at Poronin instructed his flock to keep an eye on the activities of the 'Muscovite' group, muttering darkly about Russians 'putting poison into the wells'.[7] The servant girl whom Nadya had hired, now that her mother was so incapacitated, to help around the house, had been spreading gossip about them and was promptly put on the train back to Kraków. But it was not long before a vigilant Góral peasant informed the local Austro-Hungarian gendarme that he had seen the mysterious Russian gentleman who often came to Poronin sitting on a hill, writing in a notebook. Perhaps he was making some kind of strategic observations to send back to his Russian paymasters?[8]

On 7 August the officer came and undertook a fairly inept search of Lenin's house at Biały Dunajec; he found an old, unloaded Browning pistol and several notebooks full of figures and statistics – Lenin's notes for a paper on agrarian reform. Thinking them to be some kind of secret code, the gendarme confiscated them, while overlooking the far more damning lists of addresses of revolutionary activists in Galicia kept by Nadya. He would have to escort Lenin to the local police station at the nearby town of Nowy Targ for questioning. Unfortunately, the last train that day had gone, so he ordered Lenin to be at Poronin station for the six o'clock train the following morning. The minute the policeman had left, Lenin hurtled into Poronin on his bicycle to consult with Bagocki. Bagocki immediately began enlisting the support of his network of Polish socialists and intellectuals in Zakopane. He and Lenin cycled the ten miles there to see Dr Kazimierz Długski who in 1902 had opened a pioneering TB sanatorium where Bagocki had been treated for the tuberculosis he had contracted in exile in Siberia. Długski, who was also lobbied by Zinoviev, offered to stand as a character witness for Lenin. Back at Poronin, Hanecki was primed to enlist his good local connections; if Lenin did not return from Nowy Targ the next day, having, it was hoped, convinced the police of his innocence, then Hanecki would lobby the *starosta* – the Galician provincial administrator in Nowy Targ – as well as government bureaucrats in Kraków. Later that afternoon Lenin went to the post office, where, using his real name, he wired the chief of the Kraków City Police:

> The local police suspect me of espionage. I lived in Kraków for two years, in Zwiezsynice [sic] and 51 Ul. Lubomirskiego [sic]. I personally gave information about myself to the commissary of police in Zwiezsyniec. I am an emigrant, a Social-Democrat. Please wire Poronin and mayor of Nowy Targ to avoid misunderstanding. *Ulyanov.*[9]

That night, Lenin and Nadya sat up, restless and unable to sleep. In time of war 'misunderstandings' such as this could be blown out of all proportion. Nothing could dispel the deep anxiety they both felt about the danger he was in.[10]

On his arrival the next day on the first train into Nowy Targ, nine miles to the north of Poronin, Lenin was escorted to the old jail in the south-west corner of the main market square. His new-found notoriety had preceded him. Word had reached the town from Poronin and spread like wildfire, from window to window and street to street, that the authorities had arrested 'a Russian spy' and were bringing him to the jail. Ten-year-old Leopold Trepper, who had friends in Poronin, was one of a gang of Jewish children who ran to the railway station to see the prisoner arrive. 'A short, stocky man got out, flanked by two policemen,' he later recalled. 'He had a little red beard and a big cap tilted over his forehead.' They followed the prisoner to the jail, which happened to be located opposite the synagogue. It was Saturday and observant members of the 2,500-strong Jewish community of Nowy Targ were at worship inside, but news of the 'spy's' arrival did not prevent them from leaving their prayers to come out and take a look at him.[11]

At the jail Lenin was incarcerated in a collective cell along with some local peasants, mainly noisy drunks who had not paid their taxes or had let their identity papers expire.[12] His formal interrogation was conducted by the county commissioner of police, Kazimierz Głowiński, who carefully noted the prisoner's personal effects: 91 kroner and 99 halers (about £4 in today's money), a black watch and a penknife.[13] They took him to the photographer's studio nearby to have his mugshot taken. It was his fourth time in prison but Lenin tried to keep his spirits up, convinced he would not be held for long and that this 'silly' accusation of spying would soon be rectified. The Kraków police, he knew, were 'well aware' of his anti-tsarist position and that there was no reason to hold him.

But while the authorities in Kraków might be sympathetic, the obtuse and bureaucratic *starosta*, when Hanecki visited him, played things stubbornly by the book. Austria and Russia were at war; this Russian had been caught with some kind of secret ciphers in his possession. It was clear he was a spy and must be tried by a military tribunal. There was nothing he could do.[14] The reality was deeply disturbing: held under suspicion of spying, his case, if the intercession of his influential patrons failed, would be handed over within a couple of days to the military court of the Kraków garrison. And there was only one possible end result: the firing squad.[15] Back in Russia the Okhrana had by now been informed by their agents of Lenin's arrest and had passed on secret instructions to General Mikhail Alekseev in command of the Russian forces on the south-western front with Galicia to arrest him at the first opportunity and send him back to Petrograd (as St Petersburg had recently been renamed).

Although they might not have known much about Lenin before his arrest, the local intelligentsia in Zakopane started to rally to his defence. Władysław Orkan wrote to the *starosta* at Nowy Targ saying he knew Lenin personally as a respected man of letters who had been 'compelled to live abroad because of his implacable opposition to the Russian authorities'. Stefan Żeromski drew up a petition to the Austro-Hungarian authorities for Lenin's release and circulated it in Zakopane (even as his son Adam was busy organising the local Polish Boy Scouts in setting up ammunition dumps in the mountains in anticipation of a Polish uprising under freedom fighter Piłsudski); the literary celebrity Jan Kasprowicz would have liked to do more, but, having a Russian wife, was under suspicion himself.[16] Now that war in Europe was facilitating their hoped-for armed struggle for an independent Poland, these patriots sympathised only too well with Lenin's revolutionary objectives in Russia, even though he may have cared little for their own Polish nationalist dreams.[17] Within days the jail at Nowy Targ was being bombarded with an endless stream of letters and telegrams demanding Lenin's release.

Having warned local officials that mistreatment of a distinguished international socialist could have serious repercussions, Hanecki widened his appeal to more influential contacts. He wrote to the noted Polish Social Democrat and lawyer Dr Zygmunt Marek, as well as Ignacy Daszyński, a Polish socialist and leader of the Austrian Social Democrat party at the Austrian parliament, both of whom had supported Lenin's move to Kraków. Marek in particular knew how to work the legal system. In his own communication to the Nowy Targ police, he insisted that Lenin was 'blameless and trustworthy'. The next step was to mobilise Social Democrats in the Austro-Hungarian government in Vienna itself to intercede on Lenin's behalf. On 11 August, Marek helped Nadya compose a letter to Victor Adler, a member of the International Socialist Bureau and leader of the Austrian Social Democrats, followed by another on the 14th to a prominent international socialist in Lwów, Herman Diamand. Adler, in fact, was one of the moderate socialists who had backed the Austrian government's decision to go to war. In normal circumstances, therefore, Lenin would have had no truck with him as a conciliator and 'opportunist'. Privately, he had no more respect for Adler than he did for many of the Polish socialists now helping him, but this was not the time for political scruples. Nor was it for Adler and Diamand, both of whom overlooked their own ideological differences with Lenin, feeling morally bound to defend a fellow socialist who had been wrongfully arrested and whose life was now at stake.[18]

Back in Nowy Targ, Hanecki had, by the 9th, wangled special privileges for Nadya so that she could visit Lenin daily by train from Poronin, bringing food parcels. In between visits she struggled to pack up their things in anticipation of his release. As she did so, she had to face the hostility of the locals who, despite the protestations of Lenin's innocence, were now gripped with war fever. Shades of the lynch mob loomed; Nadya heard the peasants coming out of church discuss what they would do to Russian spies if they got their hands on them. She and Hanecki feared that even if Lenin was released, the Góral peasants might come and finish him off.[19] To add to the strain, her mother was sick and had become increasingly bewildered and confused. 'What has happened to Volodya?' she asked repeatedly. Had he been drafted into the Russian army? She became so agitated every time Nadya left the house for Nowy Targ that one of the comrades had to come and watch over her.[20]

Practical support was to come from another and most unexpected quarter. During his twice-daily trips into Poronin, Lenin had befriended the local Jewish shopkeeper, as had the other Russians staying with him at Biały Dunajec. As Yiddish speakers the Galician Jews could converse with Lenin for he spoke excellent German, whereas Polish remained for him largely impenetrable – all he could manage with the local peasants was a kind of 'distorted Russian'.[21] They would have shared his political sympathies as a man of violently anti-tsarist sentiments, the Jews of the Russian Empire having suffered much over the last twenty years in a wave of savage pogroms. During his time in the mountains, Lenin had got into the habit of stopping off at the general store owned by Mendel (Emanuel) Singer – sometimes for supplies, more often than not simply for a chat. The shop, which had been established by Mendel's father Salomon, sold both retail and wholesale goods (to smaller stores in the region): everything from hardware to building material, to farming equipment, household goods and food – local favourites such as sheep's cheese, sour cherries and freshly baked rye bread. Lenin would often sit talking to Mendel, dandling the shopkeeper's young son Alojzy on his knee. Such was their cordial relationship and the Russians' state of unremitting penury that Singer had long been extending credit to Lenin and his colleagues down the road. The Jews in Poronin had advised Lenin to seek out the help of Dr Bernard Cohen, a noted Jewish lawyer in Nowy Targ, to undertake his defence should his case go to trial. Dr Cohen had added his voice to those lobbying his friend and fellow lawyer Dr Zygmunt Marek, who by then had also been approached by the Polish socialists. Even in Poronin, the Jews came to his defence, with Mendel Singer organising a committee of 'respectable citizens' to petition for his release and collect money towards his defence.[22]

While all this was going on, Herman Diamand had travelled to Vienna, where, with Adler, he petitioned for an interview with the Austro-Hungarian Minister of the Interior, Dr Karl Baron Heinold. Ulyanov, they assured him, was no threat but a fanatical enemy of tsardom – his imprisonment would only arouse the anger of Russian workers against Austria-Hungary, while Lenin's release would encourage them to take an anti-tsarist stand, which could only be to Austria's advantage. After Adler and Diamand had guaranteed that Lenin was no spy, Heinold wisely resolved that they were right and that Ulyanov 'may render great services under the present conditions'. On 17 August he telegraphed the police in Kraków ordering his release.[23]

Lenin left Nowy Targ on 19 August after twelve days in jail; Nadya was waiting for him at the gate. Not wishing to hang around for the train, they hired a horse and cart to return to Biały Dunajec to complete their packing. Lenin later made light of it all, claiming that the time he did in Nowy Targ was 'very easy' and he was well treated.[24] He had spent his days drawing on his old legal training, doing the proper socialist thing and advising fellow prisoners on how to conduct their defence. At night, sitting on his truckle bed, as Nadya later wrote, he pondered the 'further course of the Party' at length and dreamed of the current imperialist war being transformed into a heroic class war of proletariat versus bourgeoisie.[25] On his release he found that there was now an acute shortage of currency throughout Galicia. Once more out of funds, Lenin paid a visit to Mendel Singer in Poronin. The good shopkeeper needed no persuasion to lend him the money – several hundred kroners – to pay for his, Nadya's and Elizaveta Vasil'evna's fares out of Galicia.[26] On 27 August, having sent his thank yous to Adler and Diamand, as well as Kasprowicz and the community in Zakopane who had campaigned for him, Lenin left Biały Dunajec.

Even after the war was over, the Jews of Nowy Targ – to where, by this time, Mendel and his family had moved and opened a new store – still talked behind Mendel's back of his folly in lending money to the 'Russian spy' and his wife. But Lenin did not forget the favour, any more than he did the loan from Montéhus in 1909. In 1918, Mendel Singer received a letter from the Soviet leader: 'Please accept my apologies for leaving without paying you in 1914, owing to difficult circumstances. The money is enclosed. Vladimir Ilyich Lenin.' Two years later, a Soviet official came to the area to retrieve the many books and papers that Lenin and Nadya had been forced to leave behind – in safe keeping in the attic at Mendel's house.[27]

*   *   *

Shortly before Lenin's arrest in August 1914, an émigré Polish writer named Józef Korzienowski, who had been visiting Kraków with his family when war broke out, took the last civilian train out of the city, seeking refuge in Zakopane. As a British subject he was liable for arrest and joined many other refugees heading for the Tatras, where he remained trapped until October. By an uncanny coincidence, Joseph Conrad, the man who later immortalised the world of the Russian revolutionary in exile in his novels, passed by Lenin's door on the railway line south from Kraków on 2 August. It raises the tantalising possibility that during those five days preceding Lenin's arrest the two men may have encountered each other in one of the cafés in Zakopane, for they moved in the same intellectual circles. It was Conrad's first visit to his native Poland for forty years – and it would be his last. This necessary but painful pilgrimage into his Polish past had been a reminder of the tragic early deaths of his parents, imprisoned by the Russians for their part in the Polish Uprising of 1863; his native land held few happy memories for him and he was glad to return as soon as he could to his cosy, untrammelled exile in a farmhouse on the South Downs of Kent.[28] In contrast, Lenin, now longing to return to his homeland, had three more years of exile to endure. As their paths metaphorically crossed in Galicia, these two self-imposed exiles headed off along very different trajectories in history – as the Russian and Austro-Hungarian guns boomed across the Eastern Front one hundred miles away.

*   *   *

That summer of 1914, at a time when the Galician authorities were becoming increasingly paranoid about the presence of Russian spies in their midst, Lenin himself was finally forced to confront the presence of one particularly damaging spy – or, rather, *agent provocateur* – in his own. All those years of meticulous coding, ciphering and deciphering of letters, the adoption of disguises, false passports, dead-letter boxes and

endless complicated subterfuge – all the paraphernalia of Lenin's obsessive world of *konspiratsiya* – had failed to protect his closest, innermost
circle from penetration by a double agent. Worse, it was a man whom
Lenin had come to admire and trust.

Roman Malinovsky, a St Petersburg activist and secretary of the Metalworkers Union, had, by 1910, become a key party worker in Russia; this
despite his heavy drinking and convictions for theft and rape. That May,
when arrested by the Okhrana, he succumbed to bribery and blackmail,
agreeing to become their double agent in the Bolshevik faction, code-
named Portnoy (the Tailor). His starting salary of 100 rubles a month
rapidly rose to 5,000 and later to 7,000 rubles a year, with bonuses for
particularly valuable information.[29] Over the next four years, although
he was by no means the only spy in the Bolshevik ranks, Malinovsky
would reveal the party names and aliases of a string of key activists in
some fifty-seven reports to the Okhrana, as well as passing on details of
safe houses for meetings and hiding places for party propaganda. He was
soon reporting on a weekly basis, under the new but unoriginal code
name of 'Iks' (X) with his own personal telephone hotline to the Okhrana
installed in his apartment.[30]

Meanwhile, by 1912 he had so ingratiated himself with Lenin,
impressing him with his hard work, his oratory and his trade union
connections, that at the Prague Conference Malinovsky was elected to
the Central Committee, delegated to the International Socialist Bureau,
given a trusted position on the board of *Pravda* and leadership, that
autumn, of Lenin's six Bolshevik delegates to the 4th Duma. Once
inside the Duma, the Okhrana instructed Malinovsky to do his utmost
to accelerate a Bolshevik–Menshevik split in the RSDLP group. In
Galicia, Lenin was equally anxious to do so; for once the two sides
concurred though for very different reasons: the Okhrana wishing to
dilute the power of a united RSDLP front against the government and
Lenin wishing to establish the authority of his Bolshevik group over
all the others.

Despite Malinovsky's trusted position, not everyone in the party was
taken in by his handsome good looks and his swaggering, self-confident
manner.[31] He performed well on the podium and was a natural leader,
but several in the RSDLP had become suspicious of him, and in 1913 the
Menshevik Martov openly denounced him as a spy. Lenin refused to
listen to the growing chorus of doubt, even when several worryingly
suspicious arrests of activists occurred in Russia – notably that of

Ordzhonikidze in April 1912, and of two of Lenin's best lieutenants, Yakov Sverdlov in February and Stalin in March 1913 – all at times when Malinovsky had been one of the few people privy to the details of their movements in the underground.[32]

In early May 1914, Malinovsky's nerve finally broke; trying to juggle the two roles and fearing exposure, he was drinking heavily. The Okhrana in any event had become uneasy about the success of his militant speeches in the Duma, which began to run counter to his value as a double agent by 'pour[ing] water on the millwheel of revolution'; if Malinovsky was revealed as a government agent it would be deeply compromising to the Duma itself.[33] They ordered him to resign. Much to Lenin's consternation, Malinovsky left the Bolshevik Duma faction in disarray before heading for the frontier, the Okhrana having paid him off with 6,000 rubles, a passport, a revolver and a ticket out of Russia. (The remaining five Bolshevik deputies were later arrested for their opposition to the war.) In the meantime, Nikolay Bukharin, another upcoming Bolshevik theorist, based in Vienna, had added to the voices questioning Malinovsky's loyalty, convinced that his own arrest in Tula in 1911 had been engineered by him. He came to Biały Dunajec to try and persuade Lenin of the fact, and recalled how unsettled he was by it all. Matters were brought to a head when Malinovsky himself turned up soon after. As he hung around in Poronin lonely and alienated from the rest of Lenin's circle, Lenin pondered his options. Bukharin heard him pacing the floor in the room below his at night. The next morning Lenin greeted him as though there was nothing wrong, but he looked haggard. He had, as Bukharin concluded, 'simply put on the armour of his iron will' and refused to believe the allegations. 'Nothing,' as most in Lenin's entourage had long since discovered, 'could ever break through it.'[34] Lenin's continuing state of denial was deflected into one of his characteristically shrill newspaper pieces denouncing it all as a dirty, malicious slander and a Menshevik plot. He was backed up in his conclusions by Zinoviev and Hanecki, who likewise toed the line, vouching for Malinovsky's 'political honesty'.[35]

In the end Lenin was forced to hold a summary tribunal and made the token gesture of expelling Malinovsky from the Bolshevik Party – not on suspicion of being an *agent provocateur* but for abandoning his colleagues in the Duma. To admit that he had been such a bad judge of Malinovsky's character would have been too damning for the leader of the Bolsheviks. The ejection of Malinovsky, however, was not sufficient to dispel the bad atmosphere created by the affair. Malinovsky's suspected betrayal had been allowed to go on too long without inves-tigation; he had caused too much damage, poisoning the atmosphere surrounding Lenin and his entourage at a crucial time of political crisis in Europe. Preoccupied with this, the 'fetid back parlour of revolu-tionary politics', Lenin had allowed himself to be hoodwinked and his political acumen had let him down at one of the most important turning points in history.[36]

CHAPTER SIXTEEN

'This Damned Switzerland'

Berne: September 1914–February 1916

The Hotel Bon Séjour, location for the Zimmerwald Conference 1915

Lenin and Nadya stayed on in Kraków in temporary lodgings only long enough to witness with horror the arrival in the city of the first batches of wounded from the front. In late August, Victor Adler managed to arrange military papers for them and Elizaveta Vasil'evna to travel to Vienna where they could obtain the relevant documentation for a return to Switzerland. Before leaving Kraków, they hastily packed up those of Lenin's manuscripts, the Central Committee's archives and other party papers that they had been able to bring back with them from Biały Dunajec and left them for safekeeping with their Polish comrades.[1] On 29 August, with an overwhelming sense of weariness, they boarded yet another train, heading for yet another modest apartment, somewhere in yet another European city. Neutral Switzerland was the closest and only option. During their brief stopover in Vienna, Lenin went in person to thank Victor Adler for his intercession, during which Adler recounted his visit to the Minister of the Interior. 'Was he absolutely convinced,' Heinold had asked him, 'that this Ulyanov was an enemy of the tsarist government?' 'Oh yes, replied Adler, 'a more implacable enemy even than your excellency.'[2]

The rail journey to Switzerland was unbearably slow, with their train constantly shunted off into sidings to give way to military convoys, but on 5 September the family finally arrived in Zurich. This, however, was not their final destination; Zurich was too expensive and in any case was now filling up with Russian exiles from war-torn Europe. With their income from Russia cut off by the war as it became more difficult to sell articles or translations, the family faced serious financial problems. Lenin wasn't able either to get his hands on the Shmid monies in the protection of the German Social Democrats, which might have helped defray his party expenses. The only thing that saved them all from destitution was a 4,000-ruble legacy – the entire life savings of Elizaveta Vasil'evna's recently deceased and frugal sister, a teacher in Novocherkassk. A clever banker in Vienna managed to transfer the money out of Galicia for them – but not before retaining half of it for his services.[3]

The thought of being back in bourgeois Switzerland was a discouraging one. The couple decided to go to Berne, 'a dull little town', wrote a resigned Lenin to Inessa in late September, 'But . . . better than Galicia and the best there is.' At least he would have access to good libraries again. He had missed them.[4] On 16 October the family moved into two furnished rooms on the Distelweg, 'a tidy, quiet street' in the Längasse quarter near the Bremgarten forest; the Zinovievs found somewhere nearby. They rented their rooms from a woman who took in ironing, but they were so small that for a while they ate in a nearby subsidised student canteen, which charged only sixty-five centimes for dinner. In return for the discount they took turns washing dishes twice a month and performing other menial duties, from which Lenin, despite the comrades insisting otherwise, refused to be exempted.[5]

Inessa too was living in Switzerland – still on the run from the Russian police. Her tuberculosis had taken her to a mountain resort at Les Avants at the eastern end of Lake Geneva. Hearing of Lenin's departure from Galicia, she moved to Berne when he and Nadya arrived, taking an apartment about ten minutes' walk away on Drosselweg. Lenin ostensibly enlisted her to work on projects relating to socialist women as well as putting her linguistic skills to good use in the international socialist movement. Whatever her undoubted party skills, there was by now an inevitability about Inessa and Lenin's constantly fluctuating relationship and their enjoyment of each other's company that Nadya accepted and had been drawn into. That autumn, the trio, who had enjoyed walks on the Blonia together in Galicia, kicked the yellowing leaves across the forest roads of Berne in comradely fashion, so Nadya later wrote, while Lenin expounded on his plans for the international struggle ahead.[6]

With the long-standing female back-up team of Nadya, Inessa and, to a lesser extent, the now failing Elizaveta Vasil'evna, in place, and to temper his frustration at the lack of news from Russia, Lenin once more retreated to his research, taking little interest in the on-the-ground military campaigns of the war. Although impoverished, his life, now back in this 'damned Switzerland', actually became cosy, bourgeois and dull. 'Sleepy Berne' was highly conducive to work, particularly with the first-class facilities of the Swiss National Library on his doorstep.[7] The libraries were welcome surrogates now that the mail and newspapers from Russia were becoming increasingly intermittent. The past, as always, held far more interest for him than the present, as he threw himself into a renewed interest in the philosophy of Hegel and Aristotle, Shakespeare and the poetry of Goethe, Byron and Schiller. He even studied aesthetics – John Ruskin's writings on painters. To generate some income through journalism, in November he revived the émigré newspaper *Sotsial-Demokrat* (discontinued in 1913) and managed to get a major article on Karl Marx placed with the Russian *Granat* Encyclopaedia, urging his brother-in-law Mark Elizarov, to press for prompt payment on his behalf.[8]

Politically, Lenin now turned to a series of pamphlets and letters condemning the 'bourgeois chauvinism' of the war. September's 'The Tasks of Revolutionary Social Democracy in the European War' and November's 'The War and Russian Social Democracy' were the first of his many condemnations of the sell-out of the German Social Democrats, with calls for the tsarist monarchy to be defeated and the imperialist war turned into a European-wide civil war. These and other 'defeatist' propaganda tracts were smuggled into Russia via the Bolshevik underground that had had to be relocated under Aleksandr Shlyapnikov to Stockholm, but as the war continued the difficulties of maintaining this network in the face of the now more vigilant Swedish police increased.

The war raging in Europe was to Lenin a clear manifestation of the final, imperialist stage of capitalism long predicted by Karl Marx. The duty of all Russian socialists was in his view to propel this imperialist war from the trenches to the final stage in his longed-for scenario: nothing less than an all-out civil war across Europe between the proletariat and the bourgeoisie. The troops in the front lines must now turn their guns on their officers. From his base in Berne, Lenin took his message around the exile groups of Switzerland – Lausanne, Geneva, Zurich – arguing violently against the 'bourgeois reformism' in Russia that threatened to obstruct the path of revolution by settling for parliamentarianism and legality instead.[9] If he nursed any fears it was only that the war would not last long enough for it to develop into a European revolution. But as it continued to escalate, the Russian émigré camps began lining up against each other as so often before: the anti-war camp led by Lenin and his close circle of Bolsheviks in Switzerland, versus the social patriots, Plekhanov and Lenin's erstwhile colleague – that 'swine' Potresov – who were supporting the Russian monarchy's military campaign. Plekhanov would have been only too glad to join the army, he declared, if he were not 'too old and sick'; plenty of eager Russian exiles in Paris were even now signing up for the French army.[10] Knowing this, Lenin made sure he was in the audience at a crowded political meeting at the Maison du Peuple in Lausanne when Plekhanov gave a keynote speech in defence of the governments of France, Belgium and Britain having taken arms against German aggression. White with tension, his screwed-up eyes glittering with fury, Lenin took the floor in response. Clutching a glass of beer tight in his hand, he vehemently defended his belief that it was the duty of all Social Democrats to turn the war into a conflict between the proletariat and the ruling classes.[11]

Soon afterwards, he drafted a programme under which a future Bolshevik government would withdraw Russia from the war, nationalise the banks and the land and introduce an eight-hour working day. The Germans, by now *au fait* with the circumstances of Lenin's release at Nowy Targ, were already receiving intelligence from agents in Switzerland of his potential usefulness to them in sabotaging the Russian military campaign, and looking at ways of secretly funding the Bolshevik subversion of it. Russia, they knew, was the weakest link in the Triple Alliance. As for Lenin himself – capitulation to Germany was perfectly acceptable in his book if it precipitated the end of tsarism in Russia – which he believed was 'a hundred times worse than kaiserism'.[12]

With such thoughts increasingly preoccupying him, early in 1915 Lenin unexpectedly found himself drawn into a quite different debate with Inessa Armand. Prompted by a discussion of love and marriage with her daughters Inna and Varvara the previous autumn, in late 1914 Inessa had begun work on her own feminist-socialist discussion of the family, free love and women's rights in marriage. She had in fact long wanted to write a doctoral thesis on the subject and the first opinion she sought on the draft was, naturally enough, Lenin's. She anticipated a sympathetic response but the one she received was harsh and tactless in its demolition of what for her was an important discussion of sexual intimacy. Unfortunately, even in a socialist tract, such a subject would have had uncomfortable personal overtones for Lenin; sexuality was *not* a Marxist subject and he responded in the only way he could – with dry and dispassionate theory, dismissing Inessa's arguments out of hand in typical doctrinaire – not to say puritanical – fashion. She was politically incorrect in her interpretation of 'free love'; it was a bourgeois concept not a proletarian one. Such an immoral, self-interested pursuit all too often brought with it promiscuity and adultery in his opinion. Inessa angrily defended her position, exposing her own Achilles heel – a romantic psyche that would never sit happily with the self-denying rigours of party life. Surely even fleeting passion was 'more poetic and pure than the loveless kisses exchanged as a matter of habit between husband and wife' she had argued. Lenin's response was to nitpick over intent, pointing out that she made no real distinction between the 'loveless kisses' of marriage and the 'loveless kisses of a fleeting passion'. Weren't both equally reprehensible? But his main cavil was political – that Inessa had overlooked the class angle in her argument. The only logical and objective solution to the question of 'free love', based on strictly Marxist class principles, was civilian marriage – with love – entered into by true proletarians devoted to a shared cause.[13] In other words, the relationship that he had with Nadya.

Lenin's rejection of Inessa's fundamental belief in the honesty of love above all things must have cut to the quick; for this had been what had prompted her to leave her husband Aleksandr in 1905, driven by a consuming passion for his brother Vladimir. His response revealed a side of him she had not seen before and brought home to Inessa how little the need for love figured in Lenin's life. For an all too brief period he had succumbed sexually and emotionally to his attraction to her; from now on she would finally have to come to terms with inhabiting only a corner of his affections. He alluded to this in a rare admission that his 'experience of the *most complete* friendship and *absolute* trust was limited to only two or three women', she no doubt being one of them.[14] That was as far as it would ever go with him.

Meanwhile, there was, as always, work for Inessa to do. On 26–28 March she was to represent the Bolsheviks at an International Conference of Socialist Women held in the Volkshaus in Berne. Although as a man he was excluded, Lenin made sure he controlled what his female delegates – Nadya, Inessa and Zina Zinovieva – did by sitting the conference out in the café downstairs, firing off instructions at every juncture and ensuring that, though they lost the vote, his trusty delegates split the conference, overriding the largely pacifist sentiments of the women gathered there by propounding Lenin's highly inflammatory calls for revolution and civil war. At a Socialist Youth Conference held at the same venue only a week later, for which he was short of Bolshevik delegates, Lenin yet again commandeered Inessa to speak for him, although at forty-one she was hardly a 'youth'. Once again, Lenin hovered in the café below and sent Inessa in on the third day with a tough counter-resolution to the conference's calls for peace in Europe. The Bolsheviks again lost the vote but their opposition was published in the official record. As with the women's conference, the restatement publicly of Lenin's leftist position served to enhance his growing political profile.[15]

In the spring of 1915 Lenin, Nadya and Elizaveta Vasil'evna all went down with influenza, from which the latter never fully recovered. Nadya's mother was now chronically sick and shrunken and showing the unmistakable signs of senility. For some time she had longed to go back to Russia but Lenin and Nadya had refused to allow it as there was no one there to look after her. And so she had resolved to sit it out and go back with them when the time finally came. On the night of 20 March she died in her sleep at the age of seventy-five, having diligently served the cause coding and decoding letters, sewing special skirts and waistcoats for carrying illegal literature, scrupulously shredding mountains of party documents, cooking and dogsbodying as loyal helpmate and comrade.[16]

A rather different version of the story circulated in Russia for many years after the Revolution. During her mother's last illness Nadya had sat up with her night after night. She was exhausted and asked Lenin to relieve her so that she could go and get some rest, insisting, 'Don't fail to wake me up when mother needs me.' Lenin promised to do so, drew his chair alongside Elizaveta's bed and settled down with his books. During the night, as he sat there engrossed, Elizaveta quietly died. When Nadya emerged the following morning to take over once more, Lenin told her that her mother had died in the night. Nadya was heartbroken: 'Why didn't you wake me up?' 'But I acted strictly in accordance with your instructions,' he responded. 'You wanted to be awakened in case your mother needed you'. Elizaveta Vasil'evna had died and, quite simply and logically, 'did not need her any more'.[17]

For all that, Lenin's coldly pragmatic response hid a genuine sorrow he felt at his mother-in-law's death even though she had constantly complained that Lenin would kill both 'Nadyusha' and himself with the hard life they led. Elizaveta Vasil'evna had often quarrelled with Lenin over the subject of religious faith, but the long years in exile had changed all that. 'I was religious in my youth,' she told Nadya, 'but as I lived on and learned life, I saw it was all nonsense.' With this in mind, she requested that she be cremated after her death, a relatively recent practice only legalised at the turn of the century and still much frowned upon, particularly in bourgeois Switzerland. On 23 March, Nadya and Lenin sat and waited at the crematorium; two hours later they were handed a 'tin can' full of her mother's still-warm ashes. They buried them there, in the Bremgarten cemetery. Another tie with Mother Russia was lost to them.

Lenin and Nadya returned to their lodgings at Distelweg to discover they were now persona non grata with their landlady, who was horrified that Elizaveta Vasil'evna had not been given a decent Christian burial. She asked her tenants to leave; she wished only to rent the room out to 'believers'.[18] They found a small apartment not far away on Waldheimstrasse. It was sunny and pleasant and they got on well with their new landlady. But it didn't last long; Nadya was very sick again, experiencing a lot of heart pain, her condition no doubt aggravated by grief over her mother's death. She consulted another distinguished specialist – Professor Hermann Sahli in Berne – but, much to her relief, he did not favour surgery. He looked upon her condition as being partly psychosomatic, preferring to treat the condition as stress-related, requiring sedatives and a good rest in the mountains.[19] Lenin therefore sought out a suitably cheap retreat away from the tourist resorts, settling on the Hotel Marienthal at Sörenberg in sight of Mount Rothorn. It wasn't a particularly scenic location, just a few houses scattered along one long street, and the fifty-mile journey there at the beginning of June was tortuous to say the least – by post coach to Flühli and then by hired carriage, courtesy of the restaurant owner in Flühli, to their hotel. With money so short, the five francs a day full board had been the cheapest they could find. Inessa joined them soon after, loaded with special requests for Lenin – French novels, dozens of a particular kind of large envelope, citric acid crystals (*Zitronensaüre*) and details of the overnight huts in the mountains for hikers run by the Swiss Alpine Club.[20]

Inessa stayed on with them till the autumn. The residents did not know quite what to make of this strange Russian with his trio of women

(Inessa's colleague Lyudmila Stal' joined them from Paris for a visit) and the fact that he was spotted bathing nude in the nearby Emme river. But in essence the group kept to themselves, rising early and going to bed 'with the roosters'. They never in the end undertook any of Lenin's long overnight hikes but did walk together up on to the Rothorn on several occasions. Nadya must have been feeling better, for even this hike, modest by Lenin's standards, took eight hours. It was worth it for the views of the Bernese Oberland and Lake Lucerne. They also spent time leisurely picking berries and mushrooms in the forest. In the mornings Inessa played the piano, wrote many letters to her children and in the privacy of her room continued her work on love and the family. Lenin did not appear to do much party work; he read and enjoyed novels by Victor Hugo and often borrowed a bicycle and went off on his own.[21]

Six months of rest and pleasant recreation in the mountains – even if it were primarily for the sake of his wife's health – did not go down well later with Lenin's hagiographers. With a war on in Europe and Russia once more sliding into crisis, they had to work hard to convince the communist faithful that at Sörenberg Lenin did more than just pick mushrooms and enjoy the view.[22] The truth was that he was far more preoccupied with abstract theory than the terrible slaughter going on daily at the front; he never was able to identify with human suffering in all its brutal reality but only with the collective masses in an abstract way. There was only one thing about the war that interested him: what would follow in its aftermath. From Sörenberg he supposedly pursued party work, correspondence and political study – having books sent by post from libraries in Berne and Zurich – but he did not produce anything significant. The concrete proof of his intellectual efforts at this time was rather thin – only four published articles – although during the war he crammed twenty-three notebooks full of his political and economic musings.[23]

On around 2 September, Lenin and Inessa left Nadya at the hotel to travel to a major conference called by Swiss and Italian Social Democrats at Zimmerwald. As always, Lenin wanted to get there early to lobby delegates as they arrived. In particular he wanted to try and turn the German followers of Karl Kautsky, a Marxist intellectual whom Lenin had venerated in the *Iskra* years and for whose German publications he had written articles. Kautsky's group had now joined their leader in putting their patriotism before their socialism. To Lenin, these cowardly 'Kautskyite shitheads' were heading down the road of 'bourgeois pacifism'.[24] Thirty-eight delegates gathered on 5 September at the Volkshaus in Berne; British, American and French delegates had all been refused permission to travel by their governments. Those who did get to Switzerland were taken by horse-drawn carriage to the Calvinist village of Zimmerwald six miles away, which comprised a few farms and a hotel-pension, the Bon Séjour. Here they were booked in, unconvincingly, as members of an 'ornithological society' and would be cut off from letters from the outside for the duration.[25] The parochialness of it all prompted Trotsky, who was there as an independent, to observe that 'half a century after the founding of the First International, it was still possible to seat all of the internationalists in four coaches'.[26] Lenin arrived, suitably dressed with rucksack on his back, looking like 'a Swiss mountaineer'.[27] He was determined to use this, the first major wartime conference of the Socialist International, as a forum for his Marxist position on the war, irrespective of the pacifist voice rising within the movement. However, he and Zinoviev (Inessa was there only as interpreter) had to share the eight Russian votes with the Mensheviks Axelrod and Martov, two Socialist Revolutionaries, the unaligned Trotsky and a Latvian representative. The first couple of days followed the tired pattern of socialist conferences of yore with endless bickering over procedures, during which Karl Radek, the Polish representative now making his mark alongside Lenin on the left, fired the first volley in the opening address. Revolution not peace should be the objective of the present war, for only a socialist revolution could bring a genuine and lasting peace.[28]

Angelica Balabanoff was once more impressed with Lenin's verbal and polemical skills, demonstrated in his persistent interruptions and attempts to introduce his own counter-resolutions at every twist and turn of the agenda. But she found such political tactics primitive in their stubborn single-mindedness, and his use of his subordinate Zinoviev to perform 'unfair factional manoeuvres' distasteful. As the meeting moved towards the final vote, Balabanoff remembered how tense the atmosphere had become in that 'small, dark, enclosed, smoke-filled room, on a drear, cloudy autumn night'. The delegates were exhausted, she recalled, 'scraps of paper lay about on the tables – the work was completed, but the weariness was so great that almost no joy could be taken in its realization'.[29] Lenin failed to win a majority on his uncompromising resolution to turn the imperialist war to a civil war, with delegates unwilling to be seen as traitors back home by voting against their national war effort. But the resulting manifesto issued by the conference (Lenin's own far more militant draft having been rejected), while not satisfying his demands, did at least uphold the ongoing struggle: 'The war-makers lie when they assert that the war would liberate oppressed nations and serve democracy', it declared. 'The real struggle is the struggle for freedom, for the reconciliation among peoples, for socialism.'[30] As the delegates dispersed after this, the third conference that year during which Lenin's extreme left position had bulldozed its way into the agenda, it was now clear that he was the undisputed leader of a small but determined faction in the International, that would henceforth be referred to as the 'Zimmerwald Left'. The conference had been initiated with every good intention of creating unity among socialists in time of terrible war; instead, Lenin's faction of eight had furthered the growing schism between the moderates and the left, driving a controversial political wedge between them, underlining the failure of international socialism to find a common voice and setting the political tone in Europe for a century to come.[31] He left as he had arrived, stick in hand and rucksack on his back, to rejoin Nadya at Sörenberg. He was utterly exhausted, as he had been after the 1907 Congress in London. The next day they went for a walk up Mount Rothorn where, having reached the top, Lenin promptly lay down and fell fast asleep. Nadya sat there for an hour watching the clouds break over the Alps as her husband slept 'like the dead'.[32]

By September, Nadya's thyroid trouble was a great deal better. She and Lenin had intended to stay at Sörenberg until the autumn but bad weather closed in unexpectedly early in October. Back in Berne, they were forced to confront their old recurring demon: money. They were now so hard up that life had become 'devilishly difficult' and they were forced to move to even cheaper accommodation: a sparsely furnished single room with electricity and bath, on the third floor of a house at 4a Seidenweg.[33] While Lenin went off to give fee-paying lectures in Lausanne, Geneva and Zurich, Nadya tried to get work tutoring or writing. She produced a pamphlet on 'The Elementary School and Democracy' and asked her sister-in-law Mariya in Russia to try to get it published. Lenin also suggested they try and obtain a commission to jointly write a *Pedagogical Dictionary*. In January 1916 such were their straitened circumstances that they were allowed to apply for extension of their residence permit without having to pay the 200 francs fee.[34]

Early that year Inessa, once more under pressure from Lenin, returned to her party work in Paris, having already more than served the party at four contentious socialist conferences in 1915. Her task now was to liaise with anti-war French socialists on Lenin's behalf in hopes of building his Zimmerwald Left. As far as the French Sûreté agents who tailed Inessa were concerned, Inessa was *'la maîtresse de Lénine'*.[35] She had a difficult time in Paris trying to raise support for Lenin's anti-war stance. He, meanwhile, grew unreasonably impatient for results and was annoyed by her silences. Inessa resolutely ignored his letters demanding news, his expressions of faux 'surprise' that he had heard nothing from her and his half-hearted queries about whether he had 'offended' her or whether she was ill.[36] To put it bluntly, she was fed up with being constantly placed under enormous pressure to produce results. In the end she was able to report some limited success with socialist youth groups and a couple of trade unions. Lenin's response was highly dismissive. He had expected Inessa to achieve far more than that – nothing less than a split among French socialists for and against the war. For Inessa this must have been the final insult, particularly in view of all the risks she had taken in returning to Paris during wartime, a city not known for its pacifist sentiments.[37] An angry response by postcard to Lenin prompted nothing but a ticking off for her 'fit of temper' (as if he, a far worse hostage to rage, never succumbed to such things). Coming so soon after his profoundly wounding criticisms of her pamphlet on love and the family, it provoked in Inessa a deep depression which clearly transmitted itself to Lenin – if only by her silence. He continued to express genuine enough concern for her health in the letters that followed, but once her mission in Paris was over Inessa retreated from him, just as she had in December 1913.

CHAPTER SEVENTEEN

'One Fighting Campaign After Another'

Zurich: February 1916–April 1917

No. 14 Spiegelgasse, Zurich. Lenin and Nadya's room is marked with a cross

By early February 1916 life for Lenin and Nadya at Seidenweg was becoming difficult. They didn't get on with their landlady, who exasperated them with all kinds of demands, so they decided to spend a few weeks in Zurich where Lenin could use the libraries. Moisey Kharitonov, secretary of the Zurich Bolshevik section, met them off the train but Lenin and Nadya refused his offer of living with him and his wife – one of the reasons supposedly being Lenin's concern that the postman would have to cart their considerable quantities of mail up four flights of stairs several times a day.[1] Instead, they rented a room in a boarding house in the centre of the city, taking their meals nearby on Geigerstrasse at a small eating house on the second floor of a dilapidated old building near the Limmatquai run by a buxom blonde, Frau Prelog. The dining room was little more than a dimly lit corridor with bare walls and rough wooden tables and it smelled 'more like a mouldy cellar than a restaurant'. Lenin, however, seemed to like its plebeianness and the fact that his coffee was served in a cup with a broken handle. He and Nadya soon discovered that, aside from the unappetising thin soups and dried roasts on offer, they shared their dining room with a prostitute and other undesirables, what Nadya described as 'the lower depths of Zurich'.[2] Red Maria, so named for her long, golden, red hair, frequently regaled them both with her woes, of how she had turned to prostitution to support her old mother and younger siblings. The war, she complained, had taken her soldier lover from her; it was 'nothing but a robbery of men, a dirty trick invented by the rich', at which Frau Prelog would chime in, saying she couldn't understand why the soldiers didn't shoot their officers and go home. Such forthright comments were, of course, music to Lenin's ears, as the young Romanian socialist Valeriu Marcu noted on sharing a meal with him there. Lenin's face positively shone with pleasure; Frau Prelog was, in his opinion, quite 'magnificent'.[3]

An advertisement for a cheap room on the notice board at the Zur Eintracht – a workers' club set up by Swiss Social Democrats where they also went for cheap lunches – took Lenin and Nadya to new accommodation on Spiegelgasse shortly afterwards. Within a couple of weeks they had decided to stay in Zurich. They enjoyed the buzz of the city after the unchallenging peace and charm of Berne; the lakeside and nearby Zürichberg – a wooded hillside overlooking the city – were great favourites for walks. The city was even better served for libraries than Berne, with a fine public library, a Centre for Socialist Literature and the cantonal archives in the neo-gothic choir of the Predigerkirche, a seventeenth-century former church. There were also plenty of cheap eating places and lively political discussion clubs in the vicinity. In this, the last year of his exile, Lenin's peregrinations came fittingly full circle. Zurich, a great cultural centre that had been at the heart of the Protestant Reformation of the 1520s, was now a busy financial and commercial centre, as well as the *de facto* cultural capital of Europe during the war years. In the 1870s it had seen an influx of Russian student exiles with the arrival of two revolutionary heroes – the anarchist Mikhail Bakunin in 1872 and the revolutionary socialist Petr Lavrov soon after. It had been the first foreign university city to welcome young Russian women, many of whom came to study medicine at a time when university education in Russia was closed to them. The Russians congregated in a particular part of Zurich – the Oberstrasse, near the Polytechnic – living in the same extreme poverty as their fellow exiles in Geneva.

The outbreak of war in 1914 had seen a sudden rush of new Russian immigrants from other exile communities in Europe and such now was their impoverishment that a Committee of Social Salvation had been set up to rescue many of them from starvation.[4] Lenin and Nadya too were struggling; the cost of living 'makes one despair', Lenin wrote to his sister Mariya.[5] The inheritance money from Nadya's aunt had almost run out and war had brought rising prices and higher exchange rates. Shortage of money therefore brought them to a small, dark room overlooking an equally dark courtyard up a dingy staircase, at no. 14 Spiegelgasse.

The five-storey house, with its low ceilings and green wooden shutters, was sixteenth-century in origin and had a restaurant, the Jakobsbrunnen, on the ground floor. It was located on a narrow, cobbled alley lit by old cast-iron lanterns. They shared the building with an assortment of tenants, their room sublet by the tenants of a flat on the second floor – a shoemaker named Titus Kammerer, who ran his business from no. 12 next door. Barely six feet across the alley were a cabinetmaker's, a laundry and a second-hand bookshop. Here, in the heart of the old medieval city of Zurich, the winding alleys of closely packed, gabled houses whose top floors overhung the walkways, were perpetually dark and dank.[6] The winter was bitter when Lenin and Nadya moved in and they had no heating; their room was always dark, which meant they either had to go to the expense of burning kerosene lamps during the day or seek shelter in the nearby library. They only had a single table to eat and work on, a sofa and a couple of chairs, so when visitors arrived they had to sit on the beds. And they couldn't open their windows even if they wanted to, for on the other side of the courtyard at the back was a sausage maker's and the stink of boiling *Bratwurst* pervaded the whole street during the day.

The smell might have been terrible but Spiegelgasse had many compensations. Firstly, it was only a few minutes' walk from the libraries where Lenin now spent his days from nine till twelve – returning for lunch and promptly reclaiming his seat at two to make the most of the afternoon sessions. Secondly, their landlords, the Kammerers, were wonderful: good, kind-hearted and down to earth. They and their three sons happily watched out for the postman and took in the mail at their shop next door when Lenin and Nadya were out at the library. They also proved to be as vocal in their socialist and anti-imperialist sentiments as Frau Prelog and Red Maria. As soon as he had heard the good Frau Kammerer declare that 'the soldiers ought to turn their weapons against their governments', nothing would induce Lenin to leave. He had wanted all along to live with a 'Swiss working-class family' (ignoring the fact that the Kammerers, as shopkeepers, were decidedly petit bourgeois) and, even though they could have found somewhere better for the same twenty-eight francs a month (they'd managed to haggle the price down from thirty), they knew that they were among friends.[7]

Titus Kammerer, while concerned at how 'very plain' the Ulyanovs' mode of living was, considered Lenin 'a good fellow' – strong and stocky with 'a neck like a bull'. One of his sons remarked that if Lenin's thick neck was a sign of willpower then he 'must possess an iron will'.[8] He and his wife had been apprehensive when Nadya had first come to enquire about the room because she was 'of the Russian type' and rather unprepossessing. But they soon discovered she was 'a good soul' and felt sorry for her. She was sick a lot of the time and didn't take enough care of herself. 'Mrs Lenin would have been a good *Hausfrau*,' they concluded, 'but she had her mind always on her other work.' Because of this she still managed to burn even the simple pan of oatmeal they were reduced to eating for lunch. 'There!' remarked Lenin with a chuckle to his landlord. 'You see, we live in grand style. We have roasts every day.' Frau Kammerer took pity; all the 'Lenins' ever seemed to have at lunchtime was oatmeal or boiled potatoes; in the evening it was 'tea and buttered bread'. Meat was a special luxury on Sundays only. So she taught Nadya how to cook cheap and satisfying meals in her own kitchen – 'a narrow intestine of a room' where there was barely space for the two of them. Noticing how worn out Lenin's boots were, Titus made him a pair of 'very coarse, solid shoes', reinforced with thick nails for hiking. Lenin wore them all winter; whenever he went out in his boots and his worker's cap 'one would have taken him for a mechanic', observed Herr Kammerer.[9] That winter, such was their shortness of money that Nadya recalled the one and only minor indulgence they enjoyed – on Thursdays when the Predigerkirche was closed – which was the two bars of nut chocolate they bought before heading off for a walk on the Zurichberg. Such, now, was the 'doubly rigid economy in our personal life'.[10]

At the end of April 1915, Lenin attended a follow-up conference to Zimmerwald held at the Hotel Bären in Kienthal, a resort on the shores of Lake Thun in the Bernese Oberland. As usual he arrived early, at the head of a contingent of twelve that included Inessa and Zinoviev. He was well primed for his campaign to win delegates over – with sheaves of draft resolutions and notebooks 'full of calculations on the likely affiliation of each and every delegate on every conceivable issue'.[11] He worked extremely hard to win support but even though he was in a stronger position than at Zimmerwald he remained in the minority, again losing the vote on his call for all-out civil war in Europe. However, he came away feeling that in general his position had been strengthened since Zimmerwald. For although the majority remained firmly opposed to his position the conference did at least condemn pacifism and allude to the need for the eventual overthrow of the capitalist class. And there was no doubt that his increasingly commanding presence had been taken note of in the Second International.[12]

Returning to Spiegelgasse in early July, Lenin finished what was to become his best known theoretical work, *Imperialism the Highest Stage of Capitalism*, although it would not be published in Russia until after the Revolution. Like all his other work at this time, the incentive to write had been as much financial as political. But it served as a timely restatement of his militant Marxism, loaded with statistics and charts showing how Britain, Germany, France and the USA had carved up the exploitable world between them, now owning nearly 80 per cent of the world's finance capital. Western capitalism had reached an inevitable stage in its historical development: the point at which rival imperialist empires were now approaching cataclysm over their rival markets and colonies. Capitalism in its highest stage as it now was, by its very competitive nature bred war. An assiduous Marxist undermining of imperial rule would, in the end, prompt the proletariat to rebel in search of peace and self-determination, of that he was convinced.[13]

Political work was once again interrupted at the end of July when Nadya's health again collapsed. She refused to spend precious money on doctors and had struggled to keep up with a paid job she had taken as secretary of the Bureau for Political Emigrant Relief, but it was clear she had to take time off and recuperate. Lenin too was keen to get away somewhere quiet 'to think his ideas out to the end', away from the stifling and humid Spiegelgasse at the height of summer.[14] This time, they opted for a rest home, forty-six miles to the south-east of Zurich in the canton of St Gallen. Their hotel, the Pension Tschudiwiese, was situated on Mount Flums high in the Alps near the Austrian frontier – so inaccessible that they had to walk five miles up a steep narrow path to get to it, their bags following by donkey. Lenin considered the climb worth the effort – the pension was half the cost of Sörenberg all in, although it operated a strict regime involving copious doses of its 'milk cure' four times a day. Here they really were cut off from everything; even the postal service was dismal, amounting to a single decrepit donkey which toiled up and down the mountain once a day. With no Russian comrades to break the boredom all they could do was walk and gather mushrooms and berries, the wild raspberries and blackberries they picked being a guilty supplement to the tedious, sugarless milk diet. Lenin capitulated to the remoteness of Flums and did very little other than read the papers and clean his and Nadya's walking boots daily with military precision. Their only entertainment was the occasional accordion playing of their host's son in the evenings. Some of the guests would get up and dance but not Lenin. Nor could he abide the habit at the hotel of serenading departing guests at six in the morning with a rousing chorus of 'Goodbye Cuckoo'.[15]

Not long after the couple arrived at Flums came terrible news from home. On 25 July, Lenin's mother had died in Petrograd. She had been unwell when she had gone to Mariya's for a visit not long before and Mariya had insisted that she remain with the family in their flat on Shirokaya Street. But shortly after, on holiday at a village outside the city, the end came. Lenin had not seen his mother since Stockholm in 1910. His letters to his sisters in Russia expressing his grief at his mother's death have not survived and Nadya, careful always to avoid the personal in her later memoir, left no description of his response other than to note that Volodya went off for long walks alone in the mountains. He eventually received a small share out of what was left of his mother's estate but, quite aside from the personal loss, he and Nadya had both now lost the crucial financial support that they had intermittently received from both their mothers. With his mother gone, Lenin, never one for letter writing anyway, rarely wrote to his sisters thereafter; nor did Nadya, who had largely done so out of duty on her husband's behalf. Her relationship with Mariya and Anna had been an uneasy one at the best of times.

With their emotional links with Russia now broken, life became ever more cheerless and impoverished that winter in Zurich. Lenin did not enjoy hanging around in cafés full of 'revolutionary windbags' any more than he had elsewhere. He avoided the emigrants' clubs and stuck to his own small circle of a dozen or so people. But he felt fettered. His circle seemed to be growing smaller by the day; the political life around him less and less intense with the whole of his Bolshevik group scattered in small pockets across Europe. But did he sometimes venture forth from the library to take part in the discussions held at the Zur Eintracht, where he could read the free newspapers and hold meetings in its lecture room?

The Café Adler was another haunt where his group used a back room for meetings but perhaps the most famous venues favoured by the eclectic mix of bohemians, exiles and émigrés who haunted Zurich during the war years was the Café Odéon on Limmatquai. Here, at various times during the 1900s, James Joyce, Albert Einstein, the young Benito Mussolini and even the legendary spy Mata Hari had enjoyed coffee and cake. Lenin certainly went there to catch the latest of the six daily editions of the *Neue Zürcher Zeitung* and the international magazines. It is tempting to imagine him drinking coffee in sight of James Joyce, as the Irish writer wrestled with his new novel, *Ulysses*, at another table.[16]

On their return from the mountains in September, Lenin and Nadya changed rooms at no. 14 Spiegelgasse, moving to the front of the building overlooking the alleyway and the shops opposite.[17] From here they could not have failed to notice the presence of the Cabaret Voltaire at no. 1 on the corner, home since February to a new and anarchic form of art and entertainment, Dada. While he had no truck with the indiscipline of futurism and cubism and the other 'isms' in art currently considered to be 'the highest revelations of the artistic genius', the subversive nature of Dada as performance might well have aroused Lenin's curiosity enough to prompt him to cross the road and take a look, in the same way that the London music hall and the *cafés chantants* had done in Paris.[18] The avant-garde theatre director and founder of the Cabaret Voltaire, Hugo Ball, wrote that Lenin 'must have heard our music and tirades every evening' from across the street; another member, Richard Huelsenbeck, recalled that Lenin did pay a visit, as did the Romanian painter Marcel Janko.[19] Certainly the Dadaists associated with the Russian community in Zurich and held evenings at the Café Meierei for their 'Russian friends' – perhaps as fundraisers to bail them out of poverty. In later years the movement's leading light, Tristan Zara, claimed to have 'exchanged ideas' with Lenin and even played chess with him in Zurich, but it's more likely that Lenin would have had little interest in such artistic eccentricity at such a particularly difficult time. Hans Richter, another Dadaist, saw him often in the Central Library on Zähringerplatz and heard him speak at a political meeting in Berne and was impressed by Lenin's good German. The Swiss authorities, he noted, seemed 'much more suspicious of the Dadaists' than they were of 'these quiet, studious Russians'. For, after all, the Dadaists with their anarchic principles 'were capable of perpetrating some new enormity at any moment'; all the Russians were doing in their own unostentatious little way was 'planning a world revolution'.[20]

It was hard for the Swiss police to keep tabs on them all, for Switzerland in 1917 was swarming not just with artists, revolutionaries and bohemians but also with spies – from the professionals based at the various embassies of the belligerent nations to willing locals: waiters, serving maids, cleaners in all the hotels and cafés, who were bribed to watch, look and listen. Everything was reported, everything supervised as agents daily circulated their reports, telephones were tapped and 'wastepaper baskets and blotting pad correspondence was sedulously reconstructed'.[21] No one, however, was taking much notice of Lenin at the time; his deliberately inconspicuous lifestyle living near a sausage maker's on Spiegelgasse was all part of his tried and trusted conspiratorial method of blending into the background. The Austrian playwright Stefan Zweig, who had fled to Zurich because of his pacifist sympathies and also saw Lenin from time to time at the Café Odéon, recalled wondering afterwards how this obstinate little man could ever have become so important.

One young American on the bohemian circuit in Zurich certainly remembered Lenin – the sixteen-year old modernist composer Otto Leuning who had come to study at the Zurich Conservatory of Music. Short of money, he was taken by a fellow student, Otto Strauss, to eat at the cheap Tivoli restaurant near the university – it was where all the poor émigrés ate because you could get credit for up to three months. One day Strauss suddenly leaned over to him and hissed: 'Ssh, sshh. Revolutionaries . . . over there', pointing to three men making their way to a table at the rear. 'That's Ulyanov, a Russian revolutionary, also known as Lenin', he whispered. The men came almost every day at lunchtime, as unobtrusively as possible, sat in a corner and talked. Lenin, he said, was a well-known figure in the city libraries. Leuning took a long, hard look; Lenin's 'clean, sculpted features' were fascinating – there was something of a 'workingman's Cardinal Richelieu' about his pale face and marble-like forehead and his eyes transmitted 'a sense of great concentration and power'. All in all, Lenin 'gave out the vibrations of a completely coordinated human being, charged with electricity, in total command of the moment'.[22]

But in reality he was far from in command of events, living out his days in the libraries, churning out yet more articles, 'steeping himself in theoretical work' as Nadya loyally recalled, using work as a way of assuaging his grief over the loss of his mother, once more too engrossed intellectually to take note of what was going on in Russia.

There was, however, one other person to whom Lenin continued to pour out his general and growing sense of frustration, depression and utter weariness – Inessa Armand, who was now living at Clarens, near Montreux. He hadn't seen her since Kienthal the previous year and knew that she was now increasingly lonely and unwell. She had gone back to Les Avants in November, had drifted on to Sörenberg and from there to Clarens, perhaps in hopes of continuing her own work, for there was a good Russian library nearby. At the end of December, Lenin had told her that her latest letters had been 'so full of sadness' that they had 'evoked such gloomy thoughts in me and aroused such feelings of guilt, that I can't come to my senses'. With Inessa still punishing him with her silence, he finally had to admit, in a crushing understatement, that this indicated a 'certain changed mood' on her part.[23]

The fragments of evidence that remain in Lenin's letters to Inessa expressing his concern for her health all point to her suffering from depression or perhaps mental breakdown. She was tired of being a party factotum and Lenin's 'Girl Friday', and longed to find expression for her own socialist-feminist interests. But she also knew full well that the only way she could resist his bullying and the hurt she felt at his savage criticisms of her political thinking was to deny him news of herself. Lenin's endless letters, telephone calls and telegrams continued to follow her wherever she went, still complaining about her failure to respond. While simultaneously harassing her with endless instructions and queries, he urged her to take trips, go on a lecture tour, meet new people, move somewhere more conducive, get back into her stride with work that would 'engross her'. The solution for Inessa, as a woman, was, however, perfectly simple: what the romantic idealist in her craved was the one thing he couldn't and wouldn't give her – his unqualified love. Having wished he could 'press her cold hands and warm them' in November, by January 1917 he was telling her in no uncertain terms that when she did finally choose a place of residence she was '*not* to take into account whether I will come there. It would be quite absurd, reckless and ridiculous if I were to restrict you in your choice of a city by the notion that it "may" turn out in the *future* that I, too, will *come there*!!!'[24]

There may well have been a degree of that most *un*socialist thing in all this – emotional manipulation on Inessa's part, as well as a degree of dependency on Lenin's. He might be insensitive to many things but he had always been able to judge Inessa's mood swings, even from a distance, and he valued her company and approbation. It was clear now that Inessa wished to reconfigure the boundaries in her working relationship with him and assert her own political and intellectual equality and he found that unsettling. With this in mind she resisted his calls to return to Russia as an agent of the Central Committee or to work for it in Norway, instead merely taking on some translation of his political brochures – only for Lenin to nitpick over them. Such demands constantly deflected Inessa from her desire to write her own original material and improve her understanding of Marxist theory. Lenin as always refused to be drawn into any emotional response to her behaviour that might impinge on his political life. Her female irrationality was a trial; she was too mercurial, too erratic. Or perhaps it was hormonal – menopausal even? 'You must be in an excessively nervous state,' he wrote to her; it was, he said, the only explanation his infallible Marxist logic could find 'for the number of theoretical oddities in your letters'.[25] Even though she was, with Nadya, still an essential sounding board, there was a perceptible frostiness now in Lenin's letters to her. She had barely written to him at all that year and then only to challenge an inconsistency in his political writing. The predictable response from Lenin had been a theoretical lecture and accusations of being 'one-sided and formalistic'; the dispute between them rumbled on, with his responses becoming ever stiffer, as he retreated in his closing salutations from the 'friend' of earlier letters to simply 'Lenin', offering nothing but a 'firm handshake'. The kisses of the past might still be dear to Inessa but he had long suppressed all thought of them.[26] Nevertheless, the unfinished business between them lingered on.

That final winter in Switzerland Lenin felt increasingly out of touch with events in Russia as he battled against the 'socialist chauvinists' and pacifists in Europe intent on prematurely ending the war. Nor could he even rouse the socialist conscience of émigré Russian workers and other groups in Zurich, as he had hoped. Nadya had never seen her husband in a more 'irreconcilable mood'.[27] He was quarrelling with everyone, even his closest ally Zinoviev, and he dreaded giving lectures in case they aroused further political conflict. All his strength and energies were draining away. After sixteen homeless years of criss-crossing Europe, of which he had spent barely two in regular paid work, he was still living the peripatetic life of a 'café conspirator' whose name was little known in Russia beyond the political groups.[28] 'There it is, my fate' he shrugged in a letter to Inessa in late December 1916. 'One fighting campaign after another – against political stupidities, philistinism, opportunism and so forth.'[29]

But back in Russia, the tide was beginning to turn in his favour once more. Early Russian successes against the Austro-Hungarians in Galicia in 1914 had been followed by a succession of crushing defeats, as the ill-equipped and largely conscript army of peasants was pushed back from East Prussia by the well-oiled might of the German military machine. Defeat had brought disaffection and desertion in the army, made far worse when, in September 1915, Nicholas II sacked his uncle, Grand Duke Nikolay, as Commander-in-Chief, and himself assumed command of the troops. Voices of protest were raised in the Duma about the Tsar's incompetence as a military tactician as morale in the Russian army plummeted. The countryside was discontented too, crippled by a lack of labour with eighteen million men called up and many peasants abandoning the land to seek work in the munitions factories in the city. Taxation could no longer cover rocketing war debts as the cities ran short of food and fuel. The relentless spiral of hunger and demoralisation led to a resurgence of militancy among the peasantry and the urban working classes. Factories were brought to a standstill by a wave of strikes and the railway system descended into chaos. National unity was further undermined by the rapid hiring and firing of a succession of key ministers: four prime ministers, six ministers of the interior and four ministers of agriculture, as Tsaritsa Alexandra browbeat her husband into sacking any voices of moderation in his government. The reputation of the monarchy in the wake of Alexandra's favouritism of the religious charismatic and healer Rasputin, who seemed the only person able to control her haemophiliac son Alexey's life-threatening condition, was at an all-time low. Liberals in the government and even within the officer class and the aristocracy were now openly talking of Nicholas and Alexandra as a danger to the country. They should be removed from power, if not assassinated; otherwise, sooner or later a revolution would bring them down.[30]

From the confines of democratic, bourgeois Switzerland – a 'country of health resorts' with no perceptible revolutionary working class – Lenin and Nadya had some sense that 'a revolutionary struggle was mounting'. 'Life was astir,' she recalled later, 'but it was all so far away.'[31] On 22 January in a lecture on the 1905 revolution given to young socialists at the People's House in Zurich Lenin observed that the whole of Europe was 'pregnant with revolution'. Yet he had no idea whether his generation would live to see it. When pressed on the subject by Valeriu Marcu, he was unable to predict when exactly revolution in Russia might finally break – 'Perhaps in two, perhaps in five, at the latest in ten years', he offered. Despite the fact that this had been his constant, waking thought for the last twenty years or more he was totally unprepared when revolution was finally unleashed in Russia in March 1917.

Cut off from Russia, with few letters getting through, he was unable accurately to gauge the resurgence of popular antipathy towards the tsarist regime that broke on the anniversary of Bloody Sunday on 9 January, when 150,000 workers struck in Petrograd.[32] Lenin's response to this event was to conclude that the 'mood of the masses' was 'a good one'; shortly afterwards, revolution came rather sooner than he had expected. As the temperature in Petrograd plummeted to 35 degrees below, longer and longer queues of people stood waiting for bread deliveries. Cold and hunger brought acts of desperation and they began breaking into the bakeries. Bread rationing followed soon after as the queues grew for every basic commodity: meat, sugar, tea, potatoes. On International Women's Day on 23 February women left their factories to protest at food shortages; *khleb* – bread – was the one word on their lips as they marched the streets of the city. By the end of February much of industry in Petrograd was at a standstill and a large proportion of its population was on the streets protesting. Rioting was followed by looting and anarchy; crowds paraded through the streets carrying banners proclaiming 'Down with the German woman', 'Down with the Tsar'.

Force of history had finally carried discontent in Russia to the brink – against the mismanagement of the war, the collapse of the economy, the reckless squandering of Russian lives on the Eastern Front and the incompetence of a government dominated by a German-born Tsaritsa, whose political loyalties, for many, were in doubt. Socialist propaganda among the troops and the peasants had eroded confidence further. When the government called in the military, the Petrograd garrison refused to fire on strikers and mutinied. By 12 March the mob had broken into the Tauride Palace, the seat of the Duma. On 15 March 1917 Tsar Nicholas II abdicated and the Winter Palace was taken. Inside a week the empire of the Romanovs had fallen in an almost bloodless, people's revolution. Where the revolution went from here was fundamentally a matter of who was best placed to seize political power. For even as Russia ceased to be a monarchy it failed to become a republic, entering a period of chaos and uncertainty as the inexperienced, ad hoc Petrograd Soviet of Workers' and Soldiers' Deputies – an amalgam of these groups with unaligned socialists and Mensheviks – vied with Alexander Kerensky's Provisional Government for political control.[33] Lenin's hard core of seasoned Bolsheviks of around one thousand in Petrograd struggled to make their mark under the uncertain leadership of the thirty-three-year-old worker Aleksandr Shlyapnikov and an even younger Vyacheslav Molotov – playing a very secondary role compared to the greater numbers of Mensheviks and Socialist Revolutionaries. The Petrograd Bolsheviks now anxiously awaited only one thing – Lenin's return.[34]

CHAPTER EIGHTEEN

From the Spiegelgasse to the Finland Station

Zurich–Petrograd: March–April 1917

Locomotive no. 293 which brought Lenin back to Russia in April 1917

On the morning of 15 March the first news of the revolution reached Zurich. Lenin was just about to return to the library after lunch when a Polish colleague, Mieczysław Bronski, rushed through the door: 'Haven't you heard the news?' he said. 'There's a revolution in Russia!' Telegrams announcing the turmoil in Petrograd had been published in that day's paper. Lenin and Nadya hurried down to the windy lakeshore to read the *Neue Zürcher Zeitung* and other newspapers displayed on billboards along Bellevueplatz. They weren't sure what to believe, as Nadya told a friend, but all the Russians in Zurich were highly excited: 'Perhaps it is another hoax, but perhaps the truth.' They did not dare hope it was true.[1]

Titus Kammerer remembered that day very clearly: it was the only time he ever experienced rowdyism from his otherwise quiet tenants. Lenin and Nadya's tiny room was invaded by twenty or so Russians, who sat wherever they could 'on the bedside table, on the chest, on the washstand, on the beds', excitedly discussing events back home. Frau Kammerer was very anxious about Nadya when told they would be returning to 'this insecure land' Russia. But she had to go, Nadya assured her – that was where her work was. 'Here I have nothing to do.'[2]

Lenin's return to Russia was now imperative; all of his circle in Zurich and Berne were 'dreaming of leaving' and he had no intention of lingering in Switzerland for months, as he had done in 1905. History in Russia was moving too fast for him. Zinoviev arrived from Berne the following day to find Lenin sending out a stream of directives to his Bolshevik colleague Aleksandra Kollontai in Stockholm to increase revolutionary propaganda and further the struggle for an international proletarian revolution in advance of his return. For this the masses must be armed; proletarian organisation was the key. The Bolsheviks must engineer the wresting of power by the Petrograd Soviet from the hands not just of the bourgeoisie in the Provisional Government, but also all other political factions. Visions of the heroism of the Paris Commune, which had long been his revolutionary template, blended effortlessly in Lenin's mind with the future storming of the seat of government in Petrograd. The scenario might be heroic but the undemocratic means by which he intended to wrest power were entirely cynical. Bolshevik seizure of power, in his mind, should be followed by urgent pursuit of an armistice with Germany.[3] But in this Lenin, at a distance, was out of touch with popular feeling: in the current wave of patriotic, revolutionary fervour against an oppressive regime the last thing the people would countenance would be immediate capitulation to Germany and an end to the war. Nor was Lenin right in his misguided fears of a tsarist counter-revolution.[4]

He lived out his days in Switzerland in a state of consuming agitation, his nervous energy in overdrive. Knowing that the British and French would never allow him a transit visa to Russia through Allied territory in Europe, his first thought had been to return via England under a false passport, but that was far too risky – he would more than likely be arrested and interned for the duration of the war. His improvised plans for getting back became ever more crazy – in disguise wearing a wig via England to Holland and then on through Scandinavia; by plane perhaps; or even smuggled through Germany itself.[5]

On 19 March 1917 a meeting of Russian émigrés was held at the Zur

Eintracht club to discuss ways of getting home. The German socialist Willi Münzenberg was there; it was the first time he had ever seen Lenin 'so excited and so furious'. He paced up and down the room declaring, 'We must go at all costs, even if we go through hell'. It was actually the Menshevik Martov, equally eager to return to Russia (which he did a month after Lenin), who suggested that the best chance would be to send word to the Petrograd Soviet, asking them to offer the Germans repatriation of German and Austrian prisoners of war in exchange for the group's safe conduct home via Germany. For once Lenin deemed Martov's idea 'excellent' – 'we ought to get busy with it'.[6] But he was far too impatient to wait for agreement to the plan from Petrograd, knowing that such a trade off from the Russian side would be a protracted affair. Mindful of his own security and political reputation, he insisted that any negotiations with the Germans be conducted by an intermediary: 'I cannot personally make any move unless very "special" measures have been taken,' he wrote to Inessa.[7] The Swiss socialist Robert Grimm, a 'detestable centrist' in Lenin's eyes after the experience of Zimmerwald – but, like many who came and went according to political expediency, useful to him now – was recruited to negotiate.[8]

The Germans had, of course, been well aware, since Lenin's arrest in Galicia in 1914, of his usefulness to them in subverting the Russian war effort and bringing it towards a speedy conclusion. They had been pumping German marks into revolutionary anti-war propaganda in Russia since 1915, in hopes of engineering a defeatist peace in Russia so that their troops on the Eastern Front could be diverted to the deadlocked western campaign against Britain and France.[9] Grimm now approached Count Gisbert von Romberg, the German ambassador in Berne, who was coming under pressure even from the Kaiser himself to accede to the Russians' request for safe conduct through Germany. Lenin's Polish colleague Yakub Hanecki was already in Stockholm raising money for his return, and had been officially appointed as his foreign representative to the Bolshevik Central Committee, when another player and an associate of Hanecki's entered the game. Alexander Helphand, code-named Parvus, the enigmatic German Social Democrat who had provided Lenin with valuable assistance during *Iskra* days in Munich, arrived in Switzerland. Now grown fat, sexually corrupt and wealthy on business concerns in Turkey and with a penchant for expensive cigars, the opportunistic Helphand had gone over to the German government, operating as an arms contractor and recruiter for the war effort, with an import-export business based in Copenhagen as the front. He was profiteering on the illegal trade in medicines, drugs and smuggled goods to the Russians, as well as being heavily involved in the German propaganda drive among tsarist troops to destabilise the tsarist regime, thanks to millions of marks in seed money from the German government.[10] In order to effect Lenin's return to Russia, Helphand used his influence in high places, notably with First Quartermaster General, Erich Ludendorff, who soon became convinced that 'from a military point of view' Lenin's journey under German protection was justified, 'for it was imperative that Russia should fall'.[11] But it was ultimately the German Foreign Office that brokered the deal through its minister, Richard von Kühlmann, Ludendorff being responsible for the transportation side of things.[12]

Unlike Lenin, many of those in Zurich now so desperate to return to Russia were tormented by doubts; going back home with German help would be extremely compromising – both politically and morally. Lenin had no such qualms; in order to keep his hands clean he seconded Karl Radek to deal directly with Helphand, not caring where the money came from to get him back to Russia, no more than he had in the past had any scruples about using money from bank robberies and other expropriations to fund the cause.[13] What *did* keep him awake at night was the thought that events in Russia might leave him behind. He couldn't sleep; day after day he scoured the papers for scraps of news: the London *Times*, *Le Temps* from Paris, the *Berliner Tageblatt*, the *Frankfurter Zeitung*, as well as constantly checking the billboards for the latest editions of the *Zürcher Post* and *Neue Zürcher Zeitung*. He had to get back and make the Russian revolution his own revolution, the one he had envisaged all these long, hard years, before it became someone else's. 'What torture it is for all of us', he wrote to Hanecki, 'to be sitting here at such a time.' By the 23rd his rising hysteria was infecting all his letters: 'What if *no passage whatever* is allowed *either* by England *or* by Germany!!!,' he wailed to Inessa. 'And this is possible!'[14]

By 30 March Lenin was so desperate to get himself and Zinoviev to Petrograd that he asked Hanecki to find two deaf mutes in Sweden vaguely resembling them both so that they could have false passports made and impersonate them to get into Russia, an idea Nadya quickly scotched for its absurdity, by reminding Volodya that he often talked in his sleep and would soon give himself away.[15] His unease about what might await him in Russia rose when, soon after, Lenin read in the *Petit Parisien* that Pavel Milyukov, Minister of Foreign Affairs in the Provisional Government, had threatened to prosecute everybody who returned to Russia with German assistance.[16]

Meanwhile, Grimm's cautious enquiries were not moving fast enough for Lenin. On 3 April, Fritz Platten, the secretary of the Swiss Social Democrats, took over negotiations with Romberg in Berne on Lenin's behalf. By now the final move had been made in convincing the German High Command, which communicated its agreement to the transit of Russian revolutionaries to the Foreign Ministry in Berlin 'if effected in a special train with reliable escort'.[17] At a meeting at the Volkshaus in Berne, Platten, now as a neutral observer officially taking responsibility for the revolutionaries about to travel, outlined the procedure involved. He helped compose the statement they must all sign before leaving, acknowledging they were aware that the Provisional Government might put them on trial for high treason on their return and that they therefore took full responsibility for their own journey. It was one thing for moderates such as Plekhanov to return to the bosom of Russia (which he had done a week earlier), but quite another for radicals such as Lenin. Lenin accepted the terms in the full knowledge that he could not predict what would await him in Petrograd, demanding their train carriage be guaranteed extra-territorial immunity (it would thus be metaphorically 'sealed' from outside intrusion, hence the legend of the 'sealed train') and that there would be no passport inspection of those travelling.[18]

During Lenin and Nadya's final days in Zurich, the Kammerers moved to a bigger apartment on Culmannstrasse and offered them the rental of a large and airy room. But they had only been there a couple of days when word came from Platten on 5 April that the protocol for Lenin's travel had come through and he and his colleagues must gather at Berne for the arrangements for the journey to be finalised with Romberg. The couple had only two hours to 'liquidate' their household in Zurich, choose what few possessions they wanted to take and destroy many of their papers. They left for Berne on the next available train that afternoon. Much to her dismay, there was no time for Nadya to retrieve her mother's ashes from the crematorium and take them, as Elizaveta Vasil'evna would have wished, back to Russia.[19]

The war in Europe, meanwhile, had now entered a new and dramatic phase with the American declaration of war against Germany on 6 April; from now on, any new government in Russia would be closely scrutinised by the Americans, and with this in mind, only the day before his departure, Lenin put a call through to the American embassy in Berne.

It was Easter Sunday and the embassy was closed for business. Lenin's call was taken by a green young American diplomat newly arrived in the city, the twenty-four-year-old Allen Dulles. Passing through his office en route to a tennis match with a girlfriend, he was asked to take a telephone call from a disreputable sounding Russian émigré who was demanding to speak to someone in authority. At that particular moment, Dulles was less interested in the game of nations than in his game of tennis and he told the agitated caller to ring back on Monday as the office was closed. The voice insisted he had something important to negotiate with the embassy. Dulles equally insisted he should call back the following day. 'Pity,' said the voice, 'tomorrow will be too late.' It was a classic diplomatic blunder and one that Dulles would dine out on across America in later life as head of the CIA. He had missed his own personal historic moment; the moral of the tale was that a good diplomat should never refuse to listen to anyone, about anything, however improbable.[20]

As word of Lenin's return to Russia on a special train provided by the Germans seeped out to the news correspondents of Zurich, it also spread across the émigré cafés, where socialists, writers and reporters gathered to discuss this dramatic turn of events. Ernst Nobs, editor of the *Zürcher Volksrecht*, had broken the story to his colleagues on the French Journal *L'Humanité* and the Viennese *Arbeiterzeitung*; and they were all 'beside themselves with anger' at Lenin's treachery in accepting help from the Germans. 'Pandemonium broke out' at the Pfauen Café, which many of them haunted and where the German novelist Stefan Zweig and the 'habitually remote and dignified' Romain Rolland joined in the spontaneous discussions. Rolland, a high-profile international pacifist and socialist, showed Zweig a telegram he had received from Lenin, imploring him to join him on his journey to Russia. Rolland, however, would not be used to add moral authority to Lenin's cause.[21] Lunching with Austrian friends the next day, one of the journalists, J. Ley, was introduced to James Joyce, who remarked that Lenin's return on a 'sealed train' seemed 'just like the Trojan Horse' to him. Ludendorff must, he thought, be 'pretty desperate'. There was no avoiding the incongruity of the right-wing German militarist and the Bolshevik arch-revolutionary going in hand in hand. It seemed like some absurd practical joke.[22] But Lenin was in deadly earnest about the historic role now before him. The Spanish socialist Julio Alvarez del Vayo was one of many foreign observers and journalists who saw him address a gathering of the Russian colony of Berne on the Lengenstrasse the night before he left. 'We have before us a struggle of exceptional gravity and harshness,' he declaimed, as he paced up and down, clutching at his lapels. 'Let us go into that battle fully conscious of the responsibility we are taking. We know what we want to do. The law of history imposes our leadership, because it is through us that the proletariat speaks.'[23]

On 8 April those departing for Russia with Lenin gathered at the Volkshaus in Berne, the party including the Zinovievs and their son Stepa, aged nine, Radek, an upcoming activist Georgy Safarov and his wife Valentina, the Kharitonovs and another child – Robert, the four-year-old son of Jewish Bundists in the group, who kept everyone entertained with his ingenuous remarks en route. Inessa was there too at Lenin's specific request, but she kept a curiously low profile throughout the journey. The next day, Easter Monday, Lenin's party took an ordinary scheduled train back to Zurich. On arrival, he and Nadya stopped off at the Kammerers to say goodbye, pick up their belongings and leave some possessions in their safe-keeping, before joining the others for a farewell lunch at the Zahringerhof Hotel. Fritz Platten had arranged for as many as sixty people to travel but in the event there were thirty-two, including himself – nineteen of them Bolsheviks, including Lenin's inner circle of a dozen or so. During the lunch, Lenin read out a 'Farewell Address to the Swiss Workers', in which he expressed his reservations about events taking place in Russia. He was leaving in hopes that the revolution in a country as backward and unprepared as his homeland '*may*, to judge from the experience of 1905, give tremendous sweep to the bourgeois-democratic revolution in Russia and *may* make our revolution the *prologue* to the world socialist revolution'. It was, at the least, 'a *step* toward it'.[24]

The scene at Zurich's Hauptbahnhof that afternoon was chaotic, with a 'swarm of people around Lenin and Zinoviev, who were both being stormed with thousands of questions'. It looked, remembered Platten, 'more like a disturbed ant colony than anything else'.[25] They had all been given special numbered passes (no passports were used), Lenin entrusted with 3,000 Swiss francs for the tickets for their journey. This had been raised by a special Committee for the Return of Russian Political Exiles hastily set up by Grimm, to complement the 1,000 francs Lenin had already raised by other means in Zurich.[26] Being Russians, and insistent on accepting no other help from the Germans other than their transport, Lenin insisted they pay for their tickets and bring their own food – bread, sausage, cheese, chocolate and so on.

There were no newspaper reporters present nor even photographers to mark this historic event but word had spread like wildfire round the émigré student community that Lenin was leaving. The young American composer Otto Leuning and his friend Otto Strauss went to take a look, arriving at 10.30 a.m. that cold and drizzly Easter Monday. There was an air of great expectancy on the station as Lenin arrived, knapsack on back crammed full of books and papers. He was followed by a small and shabby group of Russians, carrying the few possessions they were able to take with them in a few battered suitcases plus an assortment of baskets and packages containing provisions for the journey as well as pillows and blankets.[27] Lenin and Nadya had little to show for their sixteen years in exile, their baggage amounting to 'a basket of household items, a basket with prized books, a box full of newspaper cuttings, and another of archival material, a basket of newspapers and a Swedish kerosene stove' (for making the all-essential tea en route).[28] Standing there on the platform, constantly checking his watch as the departure time approached, Lenin seemed anxious but also energised at the prospect of what lay ahead. Anatoly Lunacharsky couldn't help thinking as he observed him that, privately, Lenin knew that, 'At last, at last the thing for which I was created is happening.'[29]

A young medical student, Angelika Rohr, who lived up on the Zürich-berg, was also one of the students who had rushed to the station to see Lenin leave, slipping and falling as she hurried down the winding paths of the hillside to get to the Hauptbahnhof in time.[30] When she arrived, a crowd had gathered at the far end of the platform and was 'swarming around a man who stood in the open window of the car'. Lenin was leaning out, gesticulating to those outside, answering a deluge of questions in fluent German. One of the Swiss comrades seeing him off had said he hoped they would see him back among them all again soon; oh no, responded Lenin, 'That would be a bad political sign.'[31]

Lenin's send-off from Zurich was, however, not entirely warm. Some were there to protest at his journey home, supposedly in the pay of the Germans. International socialists had already voiced their disapproval, claiming that Lenin was betraying the Zimmerwald Left as 'a German child'. Scuffles broke out when a German socialist, Oscar Blum, tried to get on the train and was physically thrown from it by Lenin who feared he was a police spy. Right up to the last minute some of Lenin's friends stood there, begging him to abandon his mad journey through Germany.[32] Willi Münzenberg recalled how sanguine Lenin was about the risk they were all taking. As the train doors closed Lenin leaned from the carriage window, shook his hand and said, 'Either we'll be swinging from the gallows in three months or we shall be in power.'[33] When the bell sounded to signal the departure of the train a crush of people pressed forward trying to shake Lenin's hand: one hand after another stretched high to meet his up at the window. Angelica Rohr was one of those who ran alongside the train when, at 3.10 p.m. precisely, it slowly pulled out of the station; as it gathered speed, she desperately tried to grasp Lenin's hand. A loyal chorus of the Internationale, sung badly by Swiss socialists, echoed after the train. But it was equalled by shouts of 'German spies!' 'Traitors!' 'Pigs' and other catcalls, with some demonstrators running alongside the train and hitting it with sticks as it passed out of view into the smoke and fog. Excited but also disturbed by what they had witnessed, the two Ottos, Leuning and Strauss, repaired to the Café Odéon for an espresso and a long discussion of what they had witnessed.[34]

At Thengen on the Swiss border, much to their dismay the Russians had a large part of their food parcels confiscated by petty-minded Swiss customs officials, before heading on for the German frontier at the tiny station at Gottmadingen, where they were to transfer to their special 'sealed train'. Here they were herded into a customs shed in two groups – male and female – and made to wait. At this point, under the gaze of the German officers in uniform and high boots who were overseeing their transfer, they all feared that arrest was imminent. After an extremely nervous wait during which the group huddled protectively round Lenin, who had retreated as far out of sight as he could, they all expected the worst. But finally they were escorted to their own specially commandeered military train – a locomotive, plus a green-painted coach comprised of three second-class compartments (mainly for the couples and children) and five third-class compartments, where the single men and women would have to endure the hard wooden seats. The two German officers escorting them took a compartment at the rear, beyond which was a baggage wagon, but no sleeping cars were provided though there was a toilet at each end. A chalk mark drawn along the corridor indicated where the German section of the train began. Once the three of the carriage's four doors at the Russian end were closed shut, Platten marked them with chalk in German as 'sealed'.[35]

Lenin and Nadya were assigned their own second-class compartment at the end of the carriage where he could work, uninterrupted, on revising his 'theses' on revolution in Russia. For now, at the eleventh hour, Lenin, the archetypal pragmatist, was frantically reappraising and reconfiguring his take on the classic, Marxist two stages of revolution to which he had till now held so rigidly. Russia he had always felt was too backward to avoid the crucial first stage of a bourgeois revolution, which in its turn would be overthrown in the second stage by a triumphant proletariat after a period of politicisation and indoctrination by his elite Bolshevik shock troops. But such was the volatile situation now prevailing in Russia that he began to believe that an immediate and dramatic transition straight to the second stage could and ought to be achieved, led by an armed and militant Petrograd Soviet. The key to it all would be the massive Bolshevik propaganda campaign being funded by German money.

Soon after their departure from Gottmadingen, as Lenin wrestled with this major revision of his political thinking he became irritated by the laughter and joking coming from the compartment next door. Here, Inessa and others were being entertained by the irrepressible, impish Radek, with his Rabelaisian sense of humour. Lenin thought Radek, with his round-rimmed, pebble spectacles and yellow, tobacco-stained teeth, 'an insufferable fool'. Unfortunately, the raucous cackle of Olga Ravich, who found Radek's jokes, delivered in a thick Polish accent, hysterical, so irritated Lenin that he walked in and summarily marched her off to another compartment. Nor could he stand the thick fug of smoke that had rapidly enveloped the entire carriage. Radek's stinking pipe was the worst offender, for it was a permanent fixture in his mouth. Lenin therefore instituted a smoking ban on the train, only allowing it in the lavatory. Realising this would create a queue, he found a suitably socialist solution. Taking some paper he cut it up as tickets, issuing the group with one ticket for lavatory use and the other for smoking in order to prevent queues and uncomradely disgruntlement.[36]

Occasional sporadic bouts of singing nevertheless followed during the next few days of the journey, but as the deadeningly long train ride through Germany progressed most of those on board succumbed, in the absence of sleeping cars, to extreme exhaustion. Nor were they in the mood for the huge plates of pork and potato salad brought to them, when the train halted in an empty station on the third night, by pale, skinny girls, themselves visibly shaking from the hunger now gripping the whole of Germany. Having a little of their own food left, the Russians gave the food to the girls to eat.[37] As they traversed Germany the travellers soon remarked on how few adult German men they saw on the stations; the countryside too seemed empty, abandoned. Berlin, where their train was forced to wait an interminable twenty hours, struck them all as particularly silent and desolate. Indeed, people everywhere in

Germany had seemed to the Russians thin and cowed; they were all clearly tired of the war. During the long stopover in Berlin some German Social Democrats got on the train and tried to speak to them, but the Russians refused to communicate. Lenin stayed in his compartment writing and thinking, hardly noticing the grimness of Germany at war.[38]

The journey north to the Baltic took four days; thinking ahead against every possible contingency, the German High Command had also agreed that in the event of any difficulty getting the Russians across neutral Sweden the army itself would see them into Russia across its own front lines. Crossing Germany was not without hitches when troop movements caused missed connections in Frankfurt which meant that the party arrived at the German port of Sassnitz too late to take the boat that night. The Germans, with rather brusque efficiency, unceremoniously locked the group into a room overnight; the next morning they had to endure a rough, four-hour crossing to Trelleborg, providing the insistent Swedish authorities when they arrived with a list of false names when asked for a passenger list.[39] Old conspiratorial habits died hard. Many of the group had been violently ill during the crossing, but not Lenin: he had paced around on deck as though trying to hurry the boat across.[40] On the Swedish side Hanecki was waiting for them. They had only fifteen minutes to transfer to a train for Malmö where Swedish Social Democrats laid on a traditional smorgasbord for them – their first fresh food since Berlin – which the Russians duly 'annihilated . . . with incredible speed', the restaurant employees taking them 'for a band of barbarians'.[41] Then, after intense discussion of the latest news from Russia, the party travelled on to Stockholm with tickets provided by Hanecki. Meanwhile, Platten – the only one allowed to leave the train at stations en route – brought them their first newspapers and beer.

As the train headed off for the long haul to Stockholm the exhausted travellers tried to sleep. But Lenin would not rest and sat up half the night talking and planning with his colleagues. He refused to speak to the newspaper correspondents who boarded the train at nine o'clock the next morning, having seen Lenin's photograph in the Swedish daily *Politiken* – the first occasion on which his photograph had ever appeared in this way. An hour later the train reached the Swedish capital where Fredrik Ström and Ture Nerman, two of Lenin's Swedish supporters on the Zimmerwald Left, greeted them along with the mayor, Carl Lindhagen, and escorted them on foot to the Hotel Regina where they were given a grand reception.

Lenin would not hear of taking any rest in Stockholm – he crammed a lot into that one brief day in the city, his relentless energy like that of a 'locomotive', as Ström recalled.[42] First he composed a press release on the terms under which the group had travelled across Germany, followed by hurried consultations with the Swedish comrades and visits to bookshops. It was during the course of that day that the first flickering film images were captured of him. Lenin wisely refused a meeting with Helphand who had made his way to Stockholm, wishing to retain an alibi of supposed innocence in any of Helphand's nefarious dealings with the Germans. Finally, and much to his annoyance, he was prevailed upon to go shopping. The last two years of penury in Switzerland had reduced his few clothes to an extremely shabby state. His overcoat was threadbare around the hem; his trousers baggy at the knees from constant wear. As for the hobnail boots so kindly made for him by Herr Kammerer, they simply were not appropriate for a political leader returning in triumph to his homeland. Under pressure from Radek, Lenin ventured into Bergstrom's upmarket department store, courtesy of funds provided by the Vera Figner Society for Assistance to Emigrés and Returning Exiles, and 'after considerable strife', as Radek recalled, agreed to being bought a new pair of trousers and a decent pair of shoes. But he refused a new overcoat or extra underwear: he was 'not going back to Russia to open a gentleman's outfitters,' he grumbled, but he did agree also to a new bowler hat.[43] In a famous photograph taken of Lenin in Stockholm crossing the Wasagaten locked in conversation with Ture Nerman, he can be seen in a derby hat and carrying an umbrella – still an unlikely looking revolutionary figure. Fredrik Ström thought he looked 'like a workman on a Sunday excursion in unsettled weather'; another of his colleagues, that Lenin looked more like a provincial school teacher.[44] Behind him, her shapeless figure made even more so by a large, baggy coat and voluminous hat, walked Nadya, and behind her Inessa in a rather more svelte outfit and jaunty hat.

While in Stockholm, Lenin appealed to the Swedes for money to help with the costs of the journey. Money was found, including a donation from the Swedish foreign minister, who said he would gladly contribute 'so long as Lenin leaves today'. Lenin was equally glad to move on: 'every minute was precious' to him.[45] At 6.37 that evening one hundred people gathered to see Lenin's party off on the evening train to Finland, armed with bouquets of flowers. Lenin 'was the centre of attention', according to Swedish socialist Hugo Sillen, smiling and laughing from the window of his carriage. The mood was highly charged, as, the Internationale playing and red flags waving from the windows, the train headed off for the Finnish border. It was a long haul, the party not taking the usual and quicker route by boat across from Stockholm to Åbo, for fear of arrest the minute they set foot in Finland. So they took the circuitous route by train, a very slow way of getting on with the job for Lenin.[46] But at least they had bunks to sleep in. That first night Lenin and Nadya crammed into a sleeping compartment with Inessa and a Georgian Bolshevik, David Suliashvili. Lenin sat up late reading the first Russian newspapers he'd been able to get hold of, muttering curses at what he read in them and ignoring Nadya's entreaties not to catch cold and to get some sleep. A slow and frustrating three days round the Gulf of Bothnia followed, during which Lenin had plenty of time to ponder the next possible hurdle – a British refusal to allow them all entry into Finland. The British might well view them as subversives intent on undermining the Russian war effort on the Allied side.[47]

Early on a very frosty 15 April the train pulled into the Swedish border station of Haparanda. From there the party had to go by horse-drawn sledge, two at a time, downhill and across the frozen river to the railway depot at Torneo, a bleak and swampy area on the Finnish side, where they could pick up the main rail line to Helsingfors. They could see red flags flying from buildings in the town beyond and many shed tears knowing they were at last effectively on Russian soil. But Lenin's apprehensions about arrest grew. Torneo had till the war been a sleepy garrison town but since then it had became an important border crossing for supplies and people, and crucially, the only rail link by which the Russians could reach their Western Allies without crossing German and Austro-Hungarian territory. Such a strategic crossing point was haunted by spies; and Lenin was alarmed to see that the soldiers on the Russian side of the border were backed up by British officers, who had taken over control since the revolution. A telegram was immediately despatched by the British to Kerensky's Provisional Government in Petrograd asking whether 'a mistake had not been made in permitting Lenin to return'. The reply had come back that 'the new Russian government rested on a democratic foundation'; Lenin's group should be allowed to enter.[48] Nevertheless, the British were not inclined to let the Russians through without subjecting them to considerable humiliation. One by one the travellers were taken off to be strip searched – even the women and children – and interrogated; their luggage was opened and they were made to fill out questionnaires. In his, Lenin stated he was 'Russian Orthodox' by religion and that he was a political refugee who had gone abroad illegally. He had no intention of remaining in Finland, and gave his sister Mariya's address in Petrograd.[49] British Military Control Officer Harold Gruner was one of the MI5 officers on duty that night. Affectionately known as 'The Spy' among his friends, he spent many years later trying to live down his role in strip-searching the 'arch-revolutionary' Lenin and allowing him into Russian territory, even though the British ambassador in Stockholm had by now conceded that 'it appeared wiser to let things take their course' in Russia and allow the revolutionaries in. Gruner was teased unmercifully by his colleagues for 'locking the stable door when the horse was out, or rather, in'. It had felt as though he alone held responsibility for having brought about the Soviet revolution, remarked his colleague William Gerhardie. 'Were he a Japanese, he would have committed hari-kari.'[50]

Once the travellers had got past the British, the townspeople of Torneo were waiting with a much warmer welcome. Lenin stopped to give a short speech and take a look at the Russian papers – especially *Pravda* – but he didn't like what he read. Stalin and Molotov, who were running it, were taking too soft a line with the Provisional Government; worse, it contained confirmation of Malinovsky's betrayal as a double agent. Lenin was appalled: shooting was too good for him. At Torneo he had been forced to say goodbye to Fritz Platten who was refused permission to enter Finland, as too Karl Radek, his disguise as a Russian not fooling anyone. It was with enormous relief that Lenin finally sent a historic telegram ahead to Mariya in Petrograd:

Telegram No. 148, Form No. 71,
Received April 2, 1917 at 20 hrs 8 m.
Ulyanova, Shirokaya, 48/9, Apt. 24,
Petrograd,
From Torneo, 2. 18 hrs 12 m.

Arriving Monday 11 p.m. inform *Pravda*. *Ulyanov*

The stress of the long journey now turned to visible excitement; Lenin's face lit up with laughter as the group crammed into the 'wretched' third class compartments so familiar to them. Even Nadya found their rickety carriage strangely comforting: 'We are on home territory now,' Lenin said, brandishing his fist, 'and we'll show them we are the worthy masters of the future!'[51]

All the way to Petrograd, the train of the Finland State Railways was crammed full of Russian soldiers. Lenin spent his time talking with them about the war, the land, about the new Russia to come, as the train headed south along the coast, before turning inland to complete the six hundred miles to the border through great expanses of dense forest deep in snow, past dramatic outcrops of the pink granite so characteristic of Finland.[52] Eventually, the train emerged at the network of lakes surrounding Tammerfors, then headed across to the major rail junction at Riihimäki, north of Helsingfors, where they changed trains for the final leg on the Riihimäki–St Petersburg railroad. The travellers crowded at the windows for their first glimpses of familiar Russian territory as the train rumbled on through the birch trees, passing the little railway halts at Åggleby, Lahti, Terijoki, Kuokkala – so many places familiar to Lenin, Nadya and their associates from their days in hiding in Finland. At last the locomotive steamed into the Karelian Isthmus and arrived at Beloostrov, the border post between Finland and Russia. Lenin's sister Mariya was waiting in the dark and drizzle along with a large crowd of local workers and other comrades, including Kamenev, Aleksandr Shlyapnikov and Alexandra Kollontai. Kollontai was supposed to give a speech but so overwhelmed was she that she lost her nerve and simply planted a kiss on Lenin's cheek and thrust a bouquet into his hands.[53] While a half-hour customs check ensued, Lenin, growing increasingly apprehensive that he and the others might be arrested by the Provisional Government on their arrival, spent much of the time preparing their legal defence in such an eventuality.

Locomotive no. 293 of the Finnish State Railways, now decorated with red revolutionary bunting was hours late, never getting above forty miles an hour before, its bell clanging, it finally came in sight of Petrograd's Finland Station. The crowd, subjected to a long wait, was growing volatile and restive as the train finally pulled in at eleven o'clock that evening, its three front lights blinding everyone as it ground to a halt with a great hiss of steam. The impending arrest Lenin had dreaded turned out to be quite the contrary: a triumphant hero's return – a surprise welcome that had been planned ahead by the comrades in Petrograd and deliberately kept from him, Ilyich, as they knew, 'so hating every kind of ceremony'.[54] The Finland Station was far from majestic – small and very provincial in look and size – but Shlyapnikov had ensured the choreographing of a proliferation of banners emblazoned with socialist slogans and greetings and a sequence of triumphal arches of red and gold which filled the station, as worker and soldier bands played a rousing chorus of the Marseillaise (not yet having been taught the more appropriate melody of the socialist Internationale).

As the steam subsided, a small, stocky man in a shabby overcoat and a bowler hat descended from the train, still clutching the now forlorn bouquet given him by Kollontai. At forty-seven, Lenin epitomised the 'old man' image so long attached to him in the party. Feodosiya Drabkina, the intrepid bomb carrier from 1905 days, noted how bewildered and awkward he seemed to feel at this most unexpected of welcomes, particularly when he was escorted past a guard of honour made up of sailors from the 2nd Baltic Fleet based at Krondstadt, who promptly saluted him in their familiar navy blue uniforms, striped shirts and caps with red pompoms. Nadya followed at two paces, as always completely overlooked. Holding back the crowds, the official greeting party ushered Lenin, bouquet still awkwardly in hand, into what had until recently been the Imperial Waiting Room. He looked strained as he was forced to stand and listen to a pedestrian speech of welcome delivered by a gloomy looking Nikolay Chkheidze, the Menshevik president of the Petrograd Soviet and a man he disdained. Lenin looked round distractedly, gazing at the ceiling, his expression that of a man who was 'watching events which do not concern him in the least', as one observer noted, clearly thinking of other things. He cannot, however, have failed to notice the pointedness of Chkheidze's remark that the principal task ahead for the 'revolutionary democracy' was to 'defend our revolution both from within and from without'. Clearly there were already doubts in the Petrograd Soviet about Lenin's true intentions as returning political hero.[55]

After briefly acknowledging Chkheidze's welcome, Lenin reiterated with vigour the principles he had mouthed all along the way, promising that the present 'predatory imperialist war' was but the beginning of a civil war all over Europe and that the people should not trust the Provisional Government. The official delegation was alarmed by this uncompromisingly militant tone. There was no talk now of the textbook two-stage road to socialism Lenin had for so long propagated in all the illegal literature; Russia, to Lenin's mind, was ripe for immediate and dramatic transition to a socialist state.

The crowd outside the station shivering in the cold wind from off the nearby River Neva was, by now, increasingly vocal in its demand to see Lenin, and a group of soldiers and sailors entered the waiting room and carried him out on their shoulders. It was Easter weekend and there had been no newspapers, so word of Lenin's arrival had been hastily spread across the workers' tenements of Vyborg and the military barracks of the city by leaflet and billboard. 'Lenin arrives today. Meet him', they exhorted and the people had turned out in their thousands, holding aloft their banners, their faces lit by flaming torches, waiting patiently to see a man about whom they had heard so much but who was, to all intents and purposes, a stranger to them – and they to him. For now, on that cold night in April 1917, on the huge square outside the Finland Station, Lenin finally saw the Russian masses as they really were and witnessed what Nadya called 'the grand and solemn beauty of the Revolution' in all its visceral power and immediacy – an experience he had missed in 1905.[56] 'Yes,' he whispered under his breath, as he emerged out on to the square packed with thousands of eager faces: 'Yes, *this* is the revolution.'[57]

Izvestiya, the official organ of the Soviets, later described how, when Lenin appeared on the square outside the station, the sea of faces had surged and swayed in its efforts to see him as it greeted him with deafening cheers. Searchlights from the Peter and Paul Fortress nearby had been trained along the front of the station, eerily penetrating the late night fog descending on the city and illuminating the waving banners with their words of welcome.

By now, having exchanged his bowler hat for the worker's peaked cap that would become his hallmark, his coat open to the cold of the spring night, and with his shiny new shoes reflecting the light, Lenin was lifted on to one of the armoured cars specially provided for the occasion. The atmosphere was electric; the sense of euphoria palpable. 'Just think,' recalled an exhilarated Feodosiya Drabkina of that memorable night, 'in the course of only a few days Russia had made the transition from the most brutal and cruel arbitrary rule to the freest country in the world.' The same armoured car on which Lenin, leader of the new socialist order, now stood had only a week earlier been sent in against protesters on the Nevsky Prospekt.[58]

Exhausted though he was, Lenin launched into a short speech full of his implacable rage against the old order and illuminated by his breathtaking revolutionary certainty.[59] Nikolay Sukhanov from the Petrograd Soviet captured the mood when he later noted that Lenin's voice that night had seemed like 'a voice from the outside' – a voice that had not witnessed the events in Russia through which so many of those gathered there had suffered. Lenin's words seemed '*new* and brusque and rather deafening'. The man who had for the most part led the revolution from exile was clearly someone to be reckoned with, but they didn't yet know what to make of him.[60]

As the noise of the crowd rumbled ever louder, with sailors and soldiers hurling their caps in the air in joy, only a few fractured words of Lenin's speech penetrated the crowd. The people needed three things – peace, bread and land. They must 'fight for the social revolution, fight to the end, till the complete victory of the proletariat'. And then, amidst the clamour, one distinctive Leninist phrase was hurled at the crowd – a phrase that would echo down through the dislocations of a century moulded and ultimately haunted by the ruthless enshrinement of Lenin's communist dream – 'Long live the worldwide socialist revolution!'[61]

After sixteen years of exile and seven long days on this, the last of so many interminable train rides across Europe, Lenin was finally home.

EPILOGUE

Goodbye Lenin

Lenin's bust – consigned with other communist statuary to the dustbin of history

Lenin's worldwide socialist revolution never, of course, happened. Soon after his arrival in Petrograd he outlined his blueprint for Russia in his 'April Theses', but even his magnetism, his desperate oratory and petulant authority could not overnight abolish the forces of opposition. Nor was the proletariat ready to do things his way, any more than the masses in Germany were ready to rise up in the socialist revolution he had predicted there. Throughout the summer Lenin relentlessly hammered his argument home at rallies and conferences, but unrest continued as the Provisional Government entered a period of experimental democracy, in increasing conflict with the Petrograd Soviet. Chaos in the cities led to a resurgence of violence. When the Provisional Government released details of Lenin's secret deal with the Germans over his return to Russia, the public mood turned against the Bolsheviks. In July he was forced back into hiding in Finland until able to return once more, a slightly less high profile conquering hero, in October. He came back on the very same train to the Finland Station after the Bolsheviks, with the support of the Petrograd Soviet, had staged a final, decisive *coup d'état* against the Provisional Government. But there was no quick-fix transition to the new socialist state Lenin had theorised about for so long. By 1918, with his attitude hardening as he and the Bolsheviks struggled to hold on to power against counter-revolutionary groups, civil war loomed. It would rage across Russia for the next four years, leaving eleven million people dead.

As for the major players in Lenin's life in exile, one by one they were all destroyed or worn out by the revolution they had worked so hard to create. Plekhanov was the first casualty: now very sick, and unable to come to terms with Lenin's takeover in October, he expected to be arrested or assassinated at any time. Terminally ill, he once more went into exile – to a sanatorium in nearby Finland, where he died in May 1918 of tuberculosis. Martov continued to lead Menshevik opposition to Lenin's new government but in 1920 was also forced back into exile, this time in Germany. Here tuberculosis claimed him too, Martov having steadfastly refused to give up his chain smoking. A quiet, sad man, cruelly consigned by Trotsky in 1917 to the 'dustbin of history', his lonely life in exile went out, forgotten, like a guttering candle in 1923.[1] Trotsky himself survived as a political renegade in the Soviet Union until driven out by Stalin in 1928. A Spanish communist assassin caught up with him in Mexico City in 1940, by which time Stalin had systematically seen off most of the Old Bolsheviks of Lenin's émigré circle. Zinoviev and Kamenev were shot after a terrifying show trial in August 1936. Even Stepa Zinoviev perished in the round-up of sons, wives and daughters of those purged, shot in 1937.[2] The eternal optimist, Radek went to Germany in 1919, where he doggedly tried to incite Lenin's great socialist revolution. Returning to Russia in 1922, and feeling politically insecure after Lenin's death, he managed to ingratiate himself with Stalin for a while before falling out of favour. The knock eventually came on his door in 1937. He escaped execution, dying forgotten, somewhere in the Gulag, in 1939.

As for the women in Lenin's life – Vera Zasulich, his first comrade during the difficult early years in exile in London and Munich, and one he had at the time so greatly respected, returned to Russia after the 1905 revolution. Now aged fifty-seven and weary of underground life, she retired to a small cottage and her garden. Like Martov and Plekhanov she was appalled by Lenin's Bolshevik takeover and despaired at seeing the Russia she had loved so much disappear before her eyes. She lived out her days in increasing poverty and slovenliness in a Writers Home in Petrograd, dying at the age of seventy-one in 1919, having confided to her sister that 'Everything that was dear to me for my entire, long life has crumbled and died.'[3]

Lenin's sisters Anna and Mariya remained loyal Leninists and party workers till their dying days, in 1935 and 1937 respectively, their many arrests and periods of exile in service to the party marginalised in the history books, as were the roles of most other female Bolsheviks, bar Elena Stasova. She lived on into her nineties, the last of the old guard to die, in 1967. Inessa, despite her despair at the failure of her relationship with Lenin, remained under his spell to the end, rising to become one of the most outstanding Bolshevik women of her generation and using her elite position to fight tirelessly for women's equality in the Communist Party. But her exhausting duties to Lenin, the party and the state wore her out. She became increasingly lonely, reflecting morbidly on her past, never, ever coming to terms with her unfulfilled love for Lenin. By 1920 she was admitting in her diary to feeling 'dead inside'. All the joy had long gone out of her life; the only people she had warm feelings for still were her children – and Vladimir Ilyich. Sick and depressed, and disillusioned too, she took Lenin's advice and went away to the Caucasus to rest and wallow in her loneliness. But here she contracted cholera and, with no will left to go on living, succumbed and died on 24 September 1920.[4] Her body was brought back to Moscow for burial; Feodosiya Drabkina's daughter Liza saw the sad little funeral cortège of two bony black horses drawing Inessa's zinc coffin on a bier from the Kazan station, followed by a distraught Lenin, 'propped up' by Nadya, his face swathed in a thick scarf to hide his grief.[5]

Nadezhda Krupskaya outlived her husband by fifteen years. The devoted, childless wife whose only offspring during a long and arid intellectual partnership had been the shared abstraction of Revolution, became a respected educationist during the Stalin era and keeper of the official Leninist flame as propagated by Stalin's cult of the personality. She was, however, appalled by Lenin's embalming and enshrinement on Red Square, knowing he would have hated it and privately wishing he could have been cremated and laid to rest in the Kremlin Wall alongside Inessa's ashes. By the late 1930s she had become a thorn in Stalin's side as a constant reminder of the old guard of the party that he was now so systematically and brutally eliminating. She lived on, a powerless witness to the liquidation of her generation. In 1938 after being denounced by

Stalin's hatchet man, Nikolay Ezhov, head of the NKVD, she collapsed. Her health never recovered; she died the following year, supposedly of appendicitis. Some say she was poisoned.[6]

Inessa's death had a profound effect on Lenin; he seemed visibly destroyed by grief at her funeral, but of course never spoke publicly about her and the Soviet record remained stonily silent on the subject of their relationship. Her premature death no doubt contributed to his final decline. Effectively, he enjoyed only five years in power before, in December 1922, entering a terminal decline. He died on 21 January 1924, supposedly the victim of a series of seizures, but, as now seems likely, having succumbed to syphilis contracted some time in the 1900s. The diagnosis of syphilis has long been suggested as well as vigorously contested by historians and medical men both inside and outside Russia, with the Soviets adamant that Lenin died of a stroke, much like his father before him. Concealment of the truth about the private lives of Soviet political heroes, particularly every aspect of Lenin's private life, was raised to an art form under Stalin by legions of official historiographers. It could not really be otherwise: the puritanical Lenin, fountainhead of a cult of revolutionary sainthood, had no time for sex, or so the Soviet people were led to believe. But the clues are there about Lenin's natural sexuality and the sexual deprivation he probably suffered, as a result of Nadya's thyroidism and consequent loss of libido. The fact of Lenin's illness had long been known by his doctors in the Kremlin and the syphilis specialists in Germany and Switzerland, such as Professor Max Nonne, who had been treating him with arsenic since the war years; in his final months Lenin also received doses of Salvarsan, a pioneering treatment for syphilis first marketed in 1910. One of the reasons he had survived the assassination attempt on him by Fanny Kaplan in August 1918 was that the bullets coated in arsenic intended to finish him off if they did not hit the mark, had failed to work, so overdosed was he by then on arsenic that he had developed a high tolerance to it. In the end the brilliant brain that had turned out ten million words of political argument, to be published across fifty-five volumes of collected essays, pamphlets and letters, short-circuited and burned out, reducing Lenin in the final photographs taken of him to a confused and helpless cripple, deprived of the power of speech and with an insane, fixed stare.[7]

Between 1918 and 1968, 350 million copies of Lenin's works were published in sixty-three languages of the Soviet republics and thirty-five foreign ones. His collected works ran through five editions, the fifty-five-volume edition published during 1958–65, running to around fourteen million copies alone.[8] At the height of the Leninist cult and during the still friendly Allied relationship of the 1940s, the great leader's every step across Europe was memorialised. In London no one was ever certain of precisely which had been Lenin's favourite seat in the British Museum Reading Room in order to commemorate it, but the Marx Memorial Library, which took over the building at Clerkenwell Green where Lenin had edited *Iskra*, still to this day preserves his tiny editorial office as it was when he used it. The house he lived in at Percy Circus was redeveloped in 1970 but a blue plaque was erected on its surviving back wall, where it can still be seen today. The fate of the Lenin monument erected to commemorate Lenin's 1902–3 stay in Holford Square was rather more turbulent. The house itself, indeed much of Holford Square, was destroyed by bombing during the war, but in March 1942 the Soviet ambassador, Ivan Maisky, was invited, during 'Aid for Russia Week', to unveil a Lenin memorial featuring a bust designed by the Russian-born sculptor Berthold Lubetkin, erected near the site of no. 30.[9] It was at the time a mark of respect for a wartime ally but in the Cold War that followed the memorial suffered constant vandalism by right-wing Mosleyites. Eventually, the bust was removed and can be seen today in the Islington Museum at the Finsbury Library on St John Street, a short walk from Lenin's old London haunts.

Across the Channel in Paris, the apartment at no. 4 rue Marie Rose was acquired by the French Communist Party in 1945 and opened as the Musée Lénine, recreating the modest ambiance of the rooms occupied by Lenin though not with the original furniture. But with the falling away of interest in Lenin the museum finally closed its doors in November 2007 and the French Communist Party sublet the premises to a literary magazine. The plaque erected outside has recently been removed to discourage the curious.

Today, an experienced walker armed with a good map can still follow the route of Lenin and Nadya's long Swiss hike of 1904 – as has Professor R. Carter Elwood.[10] But there is little else left to record Lenin's presence in Switzerland, apart from the plaque that remains at no. 14 Spiegelgasse. When Lenin and Nadya left Zurich, as well as leaving a pile of letters and manuscripts to be destroyed they entrusted to Titus Kammerer a box of belongings. Lenin said he would reclaim them if he returned; otherwise Titus should do what he wanted with them. Titus had taken the furniture from their room on Spiegelgasse with him to Culmannstrasse where their beds were slept in by many subsequent lodgers who might well have been shocked to know that Lenin, the leader of the Russian Revolution, and his wife had once occupied them. After Lenin died in 1924 Titus opened the box to discover that moths had destroyed much of its contents, bar an old grey overcoat of Lenin's, which he gave to his son. The tea kettle, strainer, tea glasses and butter knives that had been such everyday essentials in Lenin and Nadya's life, he also gave to his son. When Kammerer died in 1951, Dr Johannes Itten, director of Zurich's Kunstgewerbemuseum, struck a bargain with Kammerer's son for this Lenin memorabilia to go into his museum. Soon after, however, he was pressured into handing these priceless communist relics over to the Soviets in East Berlin, as a trade-off for the return of valuable sculptures stolen from the Kunstgewerbemuseum by the Nazis.[11]

At two crucial points in his life in exile, Lenin was forced to rely on the help and on-the-ground knowledge of the locals: in Finland in 1907 and Galicia in 1914. Thanks to the intercession of the Finns and the Poles, Lenin evaded either being handed over to the Okhrana, being imprisoned or, worse, executed. After the revolution the Soviet hagiographers consistently and persistently played down the contribution of these national groups in the story, particularly that of the Poles; the role of the Jews in assisting Lenin's departure from Galicia was totally ignored. In the years of the post-war Soviet domination of Eastern Europe, plaques and museums commemorating Lenin's life and sometimes presence in their country appeared all over the Eastern Bloc. But with the rise of Gorbachev and *glasnost* in the 1980s and the destruction of the Berlin Wall at the end of 1989 they just as quickly began to disappear. The death knell of the Lenin memorabilia industry was finally sounded in 1991 with the collapse of the Soviet regime. A year later the major focus of the Lenin cult, the Lenin Museum in Moscow, was closed, its vast array of exhibits dismantled. In the years that followed, many Lenin statues and memorials disappeared from Russian cities, but two notable ones remain: his mausoleum on Red Square and the great statue of Lenin that dominates the still-named Lenin Square outside the Finland Station. However, on April Fool's Day 2009 someone planted 300g of TNT inside the statue and blew a gaping hole in Lenin's rear.

Today only one museum permanently dedicated to the story of Lenin in exile and during the revolution remains: that in Tampere, Finland. Despite their uneasy relationship with both the tsars and the Soviets, the Finns take a more pragmatic and tolerant view. Like him or loathe him,

Lenin, and to a lesser extent the Russian underground which made such good use of safe houses in Finland, are part of their history. Since opening their own Lenin Museum in 1946 the Finnish authorities have allowed the erection of a number of plaques, such as at the station at Littoinen where Lenin jumped from the train, a statue in Kotka and a commemorative bust in Turku (formerly Åbo). There is still a small Lenin museum at Parainen in the south-west archipelago, located in the Fredriksson house where he sought refuge during his escape from Finland during Christmas 1907; despite numerous calls for its name to be changed, there is also a Lenin Park in Helsinki. The Finns preserve this link with their past not out of a veneration for Lenin but out of respect for their own history and the part that socialism played in their struggle for independence from Russia.[12]

★   ★   ★

It is rather a different story with the Poles.[13] When Lenin arrived in Kraków as a political exile in the summer of 1912 he was welcomed by Polish socialists as a loyal Russian patriot and a man after their own heart. They gave him refuge and an introduction into Polish intellectual and political circles. They applauded his anti-tsarism and his vehement anti-imperialist stance, for Poland had suffered centuries of depredation at the hands of the Russian and other voracious empires, with vast tracts of territory at the time of war's outbreak in 1914 carved up between Austria-Hungary and Russia.

Eight years later, during the civil war that followed the 1917 Revolution, the Poles encountered the full horror of the new regime inaugurated by their former political ally and sympathiser when Lenin reneged on his promises of support for Polish independence and sent in the Red Army to push revolution west through Poland, and on into Germany. In 1920, against all the odds, the Poles, led, ironically, by Józef Piłsudski, repulsed the Russians from the gates of Warsaw in a humiliating defeat at the River Wisła. Polish resistance to Soviet domination during the ensuing century continued but it did not survive the juggernaut of Stalinism. Under the German–Soviet Non-Aggression Pact of 1939, the Soviets put paid to Poland's brief period of independence (of a kind) under Piłsudski. In 1944, as the German Wehrmacht retreated from Poland, one million Red Army troops replaced it, reducing Poland to a buffer state, as it had been so many times in the past.

The subsequent Sovietisation of Poland was one of Stalin's spoils of war. It was a territory over which he exercised the closest control and the most assertive campaign of indoctrination. Polish culture and autonomy were buried in the grey post-war years as its people descended into drabness, Stalinist drudgery and resignation. Soon after the end of the war the NKVD arrived to retrace Lenin's footsteps in Poland in order to create the official hagiography of his time there. As elsewhere in Eastern Europe, the Lenin plaques and statues, museums and memorabilia sprang up – at five major centres, even though the places concerned retained no visible trace of Lenin's sojourn there during 1912–14. The houses in Kraków at Zwierzyniec and Ulica Lubomirskiego were given commemorative plaques; the summer house at Biały Dunajec was made into a museum with a carefully reconstructed interior of suitably appropriate ethnic Polish furniture; the guest house along the road in Poronin where the Central Committee had stayed in 1913 became a Lenin museum in 1947. The prison at Nowy Targ was turned into the Lenin Scout House – an important local centre for the indoctrination of the young – and his cell there lovingly recreated for their edification. By the time Lenin museums had been set up in Kraków in 1954 and Warsaw in 1955, 617 people were employed in maintaining the Lenin industry in Poland. But the Soviet state did not pay the running costs: these were raised from 'voluntary' donations made by Polish workers.

It now became a civic duty for all good communist Poles to make at least one visit to Poronin. Every time they did so, their party card or trade union card was punched with a red stamp bearing Stalin's profile and a number. By May 1955 nine million Poles had visited Poronin.[14] The more such red stamps you had on your party card the better communist you were. By this time diligent party hacks were turning out paeans of praise to Lenin as an ardent champion of Poland's 'right to self-determination and national independence'. Lenin's views on the subject were 'consistently democratic and imbued with proletarian internationalism and a profound and sympathetic understanding of the Polish people's aspirations'.[15]

Stalin's more visible and enduring parting gift to the Polish people, however, was a great sprawling communist utopia – the model industrial suburb of Nowa Huta – completed after his death in 1953 in an area of green fields and marshes on the eastern outskirts of Kraków. This vast Socialist-Realist workers' paradise was built supposedly to 'counter the class imbalance' of old, bourgeois Kraków, by creating a working-class satellite town that would lead the way in the new Soviet era. The reality was a soulless and architecturally uniform travesty of the Polish architectural heritage – a carbuncle of steel and concrete in dramatic contrast to the colourful, meandering streets of medieval Kraków. Nowa Huta's primary purpose was to serve as a dormitory for the 40,000 or so workers who laboured in its vast new Lenin steelworks that covered an area of twenty square kilometres, its sulphurous air attacking the lungs of its 200,000 inhabitants and eating away at the fabric of Kraków's historic buildings. At the end of the long, straight Alley of Roses that intersected the town, its focal point was a hulking, seven-ton statue of Lenin, erected in 1973 in its central square. From here, nice, neat straight roads radiated out, cod-Renaissance style, from the Great Leader's looming presence, in a perfect and orderly grid, to Nova Huta's uniformly grey and dehumanising A, B, C and D districts and their ranks of concrete, utilitarian apartment blocks. The town had everything – theatres, parks, cultural and political centres, kindergartens, health centres and hospital facilities, schools and libraries and an efficient tram system. But it had no soul – nothing but the stink of heavy industry – and no spiritual heart either – the Soviet planners had forbidden the erection of a single church. Nor did the Lenin statue come free: workers from the Nowa Huta steelworks were induced to sacrifice their three-month bonuses to pay for it.

Nowa Huta's ominous communist ambiance may have cowed the ordinary working Poles who toiled in its leviathan steelworks, but the flame of Polish nationalism, and with it a violent hatred of Lenin and the Soviet legacy, never died down. It might have flickered and dimmed during the early years after the Soviet backlash to the Hungarian Uprising in the fifties, but with the rise to international prominence of Karol Wojtyła as Archbishop of Kraków (later Pope John Paul II) in the 1960s, it became a focal point for resistance to communist domination. Though the Soviets denied the devoutly Catholic Poles any churches, religious activism in Poland never ceased to have a vigorous underground life. In 1967, in a courageous assertion of nationhood and religious identity, the foundations were laid in Nowa Huta for a huge new Catholic church – The Ark of the Lord – consecrated by Wojtyła in 1977. It rose like a great defiant battleship in Nova Huta, its high stone walls and jutting presence creating a seemingly impregnable spiritual fortress for the Catholic faithful and dwarfing the statue of Lenin just along the road. Polish resistance to communism escalated rapidly thereafter, with the rise of the Solidarity movement in the 1980s here and in the shipyards in the northern port of Gdańsk. Nowa Huta's Lenin Avenue became Solidarity Avenue; it was the beginning of the end of communist dominion. Some time in the 1980s someone left a bicycle propped up against the statue in Nowa Huta with a message that Lenin should get on it and leave.

On the night of 24 November 1989, the eve of a state visit to Moscow by Polish Prime Minister Tadeusz Mazowiecki, the statue of Lenin at Nowa Huta was doused in paint and an attempt made to damage it by fire. It was the third time militant young members of the anti-communist Federation of Fighting Youth had tried to rid Nowa Huta of Lenin's unwanted presence, clashing with the militia in the process. A couple of weeks later, several thousand Nowa Hutans gathered in the heavy frost of early morning to watch the statue being dismantled by a massive crane. The local council had decided to remove it in order to avert further violence, assuring the invisible communist faithful that it was being taken away for 'necessary repairs'.

Down in the Podhale region of southern Poland, where Lenin and Nadya escaped the heat and claustrophobia of summers in overcrowded Kraków, the house where they lodged at no. 9 Piłsudska Ulica in Biały Dunajec still stands. A helpful local man will point it out to you for the price of a bottle of beer. But it isn't a Lenin museum any more. It was renovated nine years ago by its enterprising new owner and transformed into the Lenin Guesthouse. Gawping tourists are discouraged; the new owner does not want her lucrative business invaded by the Lenin sightseers – only paying guests, largely from Japan and Russia.

The people of Biały Dunajec and nearby Poronin, where Lenin walked daily to collect his mail from the post office and meet visitors off the train, have always been uncomfortable with the imposition of a cosmetic Leninist connection. They hated the phoney local history that told tales of him talking in the fields with indigenous Góral peasants – like Jesus preaching to the faithful (which overlooked the fact that Lenin had no knowledge whatsoever of their dialect). The Lenin Museum became the rallying point for enforced indoctrination under the Soviets, the Lenin statue erected outside in 1950 a gift from the workers of Leningrad. From Poronin, you could take the Lenin trail to the Tatras and Morskie Oko. But the Poles in Galicia only paid minimal lip service to the 'celebration' of Lenin's presence in their midst. During the communist years every train coming south from Kraków to Zakopane in the Tatras was obliged to stop at Poronin for worship by communist tourists at the Lenin Museum. Coachloads of children were brought on school trips. Everyone was obliged to attend the various Lenin ceremonials at the museum but felt ashamed at having to do so. As time went on it became increasingly difficult for the authorities to drum up enough crowds for such occasions and they had to resort to importing loyal communists from Leningrad to swell their numbers. In the end they were forced to manipulate events – ensuring that the big Lenin Day held in July in Poronin coincided with the public holiday and Saint's Day of St Mary Magdalene. Russian communists visiting Poronin on that day would be misled into thinking that the crowds pouring from the local churches in national costume were there to celebrate Lenin.[16]

Privately, Lenin's time in Poland became the butt of endless bad jokes and apocryphal stories. The local scouts took to singing rude songs around the campfire, including one which went: 'In Poronin, on the stove, hang the underpants of Lenin'. One of the most popular tales told was that by local Tatra guide, Stanisław Gąsienica-Byrcyn, who sometimes accompanied Lenin on hikes into the mountains. On one occasion in the autumn they were 2,200 metres up and coming back down the wet and slippery slope of a deep chasm. Lenin at that time was accompanied by three colleagues, including two women, when he slipped and fell into a gully between the snow and the rock face. They struggled in vain to get him out; in the end it was Stanisław who managed to haul Lenin clear on a rope. For years afterwards, whenever he had a drink too many, Stanisław would bore everyone with the story of how there had been a moment when he had held the fate of the entire world on a 'little piece of string'. Word eventually got back to the communist authorities and Stanisław suddenly stopped talking.[17]

Regular acts of protest against Lenin's posthumous presence in Poland continued, however, even up in the Tatra Mountains, where the Lenin memorials did not survive unscathed. Loyal communists on the Czechoslovakian side of the nearby border erected signs commemorating Lenin's hikes in the north-western peaks of Rysy and Babia Gora. Communist excursion groups toiled up there on pilgrimages on Lenin Day but that didn't stop the Poles on the other side from repeatedly vandalising the memorials. The Czech communists concreted the signs in place every summer; and every winter the Poles would come and hack them down again. In the heyday of Solidarity a local man, Piotr Bąk, carved the word *Solidarność* across the brow of Lenin's bronze plaque on its mountain shrine, and he remains proud to this day for having done so. When members of Ruch – an organisation dedicated to the overthrow of communism and the establishment of a truly free Polish state – tried to burn

down the Lenin Museum at Poronin on the occasion of the Lenin centenary in 1970, they were sentenced to seven years in jail. But such savage
sentences did not deter others from pouring red paint over the statue
every time a communist delegation from Russia was due, so much so that
the authorities had to mount a twenty-four-hour armed guard of plain-
clothes policemen and informers. After 1989, the vociferous demands to
'liquidate' the Poronin museum increased, with petitions being sent to
the Polish Minister of Culture.

The Poronin museum witnessed its last big propaganda exercise in
1988 on the occasion of the visit of Soviet President Mikhail Gorbachev.
The final decisive act of protest came on 30 January 1990, when, at six
a.m., one of the guards (by now less than vigilant in their duties) was
awoken by a tremendous crash. Outside they discovered Lenin's three-
ton bronze statue toppled over into the snow; the chains used to pull it
over were lying on the ground nearby and a steel wire still wrapped
round its neck. People in Poronin had a good idea who the culprit was,
but they were too unwilling to talk. The Soviets protested, but a wall of
silence greeted the official investigators from the Criminal Justice Department. Ten years later, a local Góral man and well known activist, Józef
Kaspruś, 'confessed' to the crime although he never named his accom-
plices.[18] Soon after the statue was pulled down, and despite the authorities' fear of Soviet reprisals, the museum was closed for 'renovation', its
artefacts carted off to the Museum of Communism in Kozłówka; it was
eventually turned into a library. The statue's concrete foundations are
still there, only they are now hidden by overgrown bushes; the orna-
mental lake that once graced the front of the museum is today a play
area for the local kindergarten.

If you venture to the small town of Nowy Targ today you can still find
the prison where Lenin was held in August 1914. But you would hardly
recognise it as such. Its unprepossessing, newly painted exterior announces
that it is now a youth centre. Although it ceased to be a jail in 1948, its life
as an obligatory place of pilgrimage for good Polish communists was not
a long one. All the plaques indicating Lenin's presence here were removed
in 1989. Inside, on the ground floor, Lenin's supposed cell, so carefully
preserved for sixty years or more, has been dismantled and its artefacts
destroyed or dispersed. The plaque outside, so frequently daubed with
paint by protesters, was taken down. But in the building's damp and dark
basement you can still see the cobwebbed iron bars of the original cell
windows of the old prison; and, randomly propped against a wall, the last

remaining scratched and dusty prison door with its rusty inspection hatch and lock. But Lenin's ghost no longer walks in Nowy Targ. If you ask locals to direct you to the old prison they are more likely nowadays to point you to the other one – where the Gestapo held and tortured members of the Polish resistance during World War II.

In the meantime, a new home has been found for the Lenin statue removed from Nowa Huta. After lying in storage at Wróblowice for three years it was bought in the 1990s by Swedish millionaire and businessman 'Big Bengt' Erlandsson for 100,000 Swedish crowns. It now graces his High Chaparral theme park outside Stockholm with a cigarette in its mouth and an earring in one ear. After only seventy-three years of Leninism, capitalism is rapidly debasing the last of the legacy of a communist icon. Meanwhile, in Nowa Huta plans were announced in 2008 for the establishment of a Museum of the History of Poland in the town's now decaying but architecturally important Kino Światowid, built in high Stalinist, Socialist-Realist style.

The final subversive act for Poles seeking to bury their Leninist past is the advent of the Crazy Guides communist tour of Nowa Huta in an old East German Trabant or a stay at one of the 'Goodbye Lenin' hostels. Cheap, cheerful and friendly, the latter offer a convivial environment where weary backpackers can lounge as scruffily and lazily as they like for as long as they wish, doing absolutely nothing. In the stairwell outside, Lenin and his fellow communist icons, Trotsky, Marx and Che are transmuted into punk rockers and hippies. They gaze down on visitors from psychedelic frescoes that, in the irreverent post-communist world, wave two Polish fingers at all the good old Leninist principles of tidiness, order and self-discipline.

Notes

Introduction: Shlisselburg Fortress, 1887

1. For a fascinating account of life as a prisoner in Shlisselburg see Vera Figner, *Memoirs of a Revolutionist*, Book Two: *When the Clock of Life Stopped*. Figner was held here for twenty years and released in 1904. Mikhail Novorussky, one of Aleksandr's co-conspirators who pleaded for mercy and was reprieved, wrote an account of his incarceration; see *Zapiski Shlisselburzhtsa*. For fuller details of the regime at Shlisselburg, including useful internal photographs and diagrams, see Gernet, *Istoriya Tsarskoi t'yurmi*, vol. 3, chapter 4, 'Shlisselburgskaya krepost'; for a compelling Western account of the prison, written by the émigré anarchist Prince Peter Kropotkin, see 'A Russian State Prison', *The Times*, 21 August 1903, p. 6.
2. Ivansky, *Comet in the Night*, p. 292. The story of Aleksandr Ulyanov's brief life and involvement in the plot to assassinate Alexander III is most easily accessible in English in Ivansky, which includes accounts of the trial and Aleksandr's testimony at it. For other accounts see Trotsky, *Young Lenin*, and Deutscher, *Lenin's Childhood*.
3. Krupskaya, *Memories of Lenin*, p. 18.
4. The rise of revolutionary Marxism has been discussed at length in many books, but see, for example, Leszek Kolawkowski, *Main Currents of Marxism: Its Rise, Growth and Dissolution* (3 vols, Oxford: Clarendon Press, 1978), and George Lichtheim, *Marxism: A Historical and Critical Study* (London: Routledge & Kegan Paul, 1964). For an eloquent résumé of Russian populism, see Isaiah Berlin, 'Introduction' to Venturi, *Roots of Revolution*. Berlin's essay on Plekhanov, 'The Father of Russian Marxism' in his *The Power of Ideas* (London: Chatto & Windus, 2000) encapsulates the man, his thinking and his legacy with clarity and brevity, as too does Lunacharsky's in *Revolutionary Silhouettes*.

Chapter 1: Leaving Shushenskoe

1. N. P. Silkova, *Ocherk istorii krasnoyarskoy kraevoy organizatsii KPSS 1895–1980*, (Krasnoyarsk: Knizhnoe Isdatel'stvo, 1982), p. 34. The saying went: '*Net mesta glushe Shushi, dal'she Shushi Sayany, za Sayanami krai svet.*'

2. *CW* 37: 111.

3. Deutscher, *Lenin's Childhood*, p. 60. For overviews of Lenin's childhood and education from which this chapter is drawn, see Deutscher, *Lenin's Childhood*; Trotsky *The Young Lenin*; Theen, *Lenin*; and Service, *Lenin: A Biography*, chapters 1–6.

4. Deutscher, *Lenin's Childhood*, pp. 66–7. By a strange irony of fate, Ulyanov's headmaster was the father of Aleksandr Kerensky, who in 1917 was briefly head of the Provisional Government after the Tsar's abdication in March. Kerensky would be ousted by Lenin after the October Revolution. Trotsky, *The Young Lenin*, pp. 112–13.

5. The memoirs of Lenin's sisters Anna and Mariya are the most valuable source; see *VoVIL*, vol. 1. These have been expanded on by Service from newly available archival sources in *Lenin: A Biography*, see especially chapters 1 and 2. Wolfe, *Three Who Made a Revolution*, chapters 2–5, remains a valuable source, as too Deutscher, *Lenin's Childhood*, Trotsky, *Young Lenin* and Valentinov, *The Early Years of Lenin*.

6. Deutscher, *Lenin's Childhood*, p. 30; Krupskaya, *Memories*, pp. 39–40.

7. Dmitri Ulyanov quoted in Beryl Williams, *Lenin*, p. 19.

8. Isaiah Berlin introduction to Franco Venturi, *The Roots of Revolution* (London: Phoenix Press), p. xx.

9. N. G. Chernyshevsky, *What Is To Be Done?* (New York: Vintage Books, 1961); see pp. 229–33.

10. Valentinov, *Encounters*, p. 67; Volkogonov, *Lenin*, pp. 20–21. For a discussion of Chernyshevsky's influence on Lenin, see Valentinov, *Early Years*, chapter VI, 'Chernyshevski's, *What is to be Done?* and the "Rebirth" of V. Ulyanov'.

11. Valentinov, *Early Years*, p. 136.

12. Krupskaya, *Memories*, pp. 15–18. Note that to Lenin she was and remained Nadya throughout their lives together. The later attribution of 'Krupskaya' is anachronistic to this story; it was an adoption of Nadya's after the Revolution.

13. Daly, *Autocracy*, pp. 77, 102.

14. Potresov, 'Lenin', p. 293.

15. A. I. Ivansky, *Petersburgskie gody*, pp. 88–90.

16. Weber, *Lenin*, p. 7.

17. Possony, *Lenin*, pp. 61–2.

18. Payne, *The Life and Death of Lenin*, p. 37.

19. Weber, *Lenin*, p. 9.

20. *Perepiska G. V. Plekhanova i P. B. Akselroda,* 2 vols (Moscow: Redaktsiya Berlina, 1925), pp. 269–70; Rice, *Lenin*, p. 45.

21. Clark, *Lenin*, p. 42; *CW* 37: 327; Krupskaya, *Memories*, p. 29.

22. Krzhizhanovsky in Tamara Deutscher, *Not by Politics Alone*, p. 50.

23. *CW* 37: 85.

24. Ibid.: 91–2.

25. See letter to sister Mariya, 10 March, *CW* 37: 94. In December 1906 the Yudin collection was acquired by the Library of Congress in Washington, DC.

26. *CW* 37: 98.

27. Ibid.: 95.

28. Ibid.: 107.

29. Ibid.: 160.

30. Fellow exile Gleb Krzhizhanovsky testified that Ulyanov would become incensed if anyone tried to read him news from papers out of the meticulous date sequence in which he had arranged them. See Tamara Deutscher, *Not By Politics Alone*, p. 53.

31. See letters 7 and 24 February in *CW* 37: 150–54, 160–62.

32. *CW* 37: 117.

33. Ibid.: 124.

34. Ibid.: 129.

35. Ibid.: 227.

36. Ibid.: 253.

37. Ibid.: 138.

38. Ibid.: 281.

Chapter 2: Igniting the Spark

1. Valentinov, *Early Years*, p. 158.

2. It is probable that she was suffering from a prolapsed womb, which might also explain her inability to conceive. Information from Professor Ronald Chaplain.

3. Lepeshinsky, *Na povorote*, p. 104.

4. For Ulyanov's surveillance in Pskov, organised by Colonel Piramidov of the St Petersburg Okhrana, see Erokhin, *Shushenskii arsenal*, p. 191.

5. Krupskaya, *Memories*, p. 55.

6. 'How the "Spark" Was Nearly Extinguished', *CW* 4: xx.

7. See Payne, *Life and Death*, pp. 144–7.

8. 'How the "Spark" Was Nearly Extinguished', *CW* 4: pp. 331–49; Wolfe, *Three Who Made a Revolution*, p. 174; Service, *Lenin: A Biography*, pp. 132–3.

9. 'How the "Spark" Was Nearly Extinguished', *CW* 4: xx.

10. Many Lenin sources labour Bernstein's theories at excessive length. For concise appraisals, see Read, *Lenin*, pp. 40–41; Payne, *Life and Death*, pp. 134–8; Wolfe, *Three Who Made a Revolution*, pp.164–9.

11. *CW* 37: 298.

12. See Johnson, 'Zagranichnaia Agentura', and Zuckerman, *The Tsarist Secret Police Abroad*, chapter 2.

13. Possony, *Lenin*, p. 74.

14. Williams, 'Russians in Germany', pp. 122–3.

15. Zuckerman, *The Tsarist Secret Police Abroad*, pp. 38–9.

16. See Robert Edward Norton, *Secret Germany: Stefan George and his Circle* (Ithaca: Cornell University Press, 2002), p. 165. See chapter 14, 'Schwabing'.

17. Payne, *Life and Death*, p. 140; Dann, *Lenin and Nadya*, pp. 72–4.

18. Bergman, *Vera Zasulich*, p. 164. For an interesting contemporary portrait of Zasulich see Stepniak, *Underground Russia*, 'Vera Zassulic' [sic], pp. 106–14; Payne, *Life and Death*, p. 144; Muraveva, *Lenin v Myunkhene*, p. 104.

19. For details see Brachmann, *Russische Sozialdemokraten* (Berlin: Akademie-Verlag, 1962), pp. 1–52.

20. *CW* 37: 307.

21. Ibid.: 310.

22. Ibid.: 37: 313–16.

23. Ibid.: 37: 323.

24. Krupskaya, *Memories*, p. 49.

25. Hitzer, *Lenin in München*, p. 206.

26. Krupskaya, *Memories*, p. 53.

27. For an amusing account of the Lenins' diet see Elwood, 'What Lenin Ate'.

28. Muraveva, *Lenin v Myunkhene*, pp. 48–9; Kaiser's original interview about the Ulyanovs as tenants appeared in *Süddeutsche Zeitung*, no. 97, 22 April 1960.

29. Krupskaya, 'Iz Otvetov na Ankety', *VoVIL*, vol. 1, p. 586.

30. Lunacharsky, *Revolutionary Silhouettes*, pp. 131–2.

31. Aline, *Lénine à Paris*, p. 21.

32. Krupskaya, *Memories*, p. 59; for a portrait of Martov see Lunacharsky, *Revolutionary Silhouettes*, pp. 131–40.

33. Haimson, *Making of Three Russian Revolutionaries*, p. 109.

34. Ibid., p. 125; Getzler, *Martov*, p. 64.

35. Ibid., pp. 34–6.

36. Quoted in McNeal, *Bride of the Revolution*, p. 91.

37. Krupskaya, *Memories*, p. 58.

38. See Struve, 'My Contacts and Conflicts with Lenin', particularly pp. 591–2.

39. Quoted in Pipes, *Struve*, p. 264.

40. *CW* 34: 63; see also Hill, *The Letters of Lenin*, footnotes on pp. 129, 137, 139, 141.

41. Ibid.: 59.

42. Ibid.34: 65–6.

43. McNeal, *Bride of the Revolution*, p. 98.

Chapter 3: Konspiratsiya

1.   Marcu, *Lenin*, p. 89; McNight, 'Lenin', p. 18.
2.   There are many published versions. See e.g.
     http://www.uoregon.edu/~kimball/Nqv.catechism.thm.htm
3.   Wildman, 'The *Iskra* Organization in Russia', p. 485.
4.   Lenin, quoted in Daly, *Autocracy under Siege*, p. 102; 'Nasushchnyi vopros',
     in *PSS* vol. 4, p. 194.
5.   See Possony, *A Lenin Reader*, p. 322; Lenin *Selected Works*, vol. 2, p. 151.
6.   Lyadov in *OVIL*, 1900–22, p. 45.
7.   Deich, *Rasskazy o Lenine*, pp. 155–6.
8.   Deich, *Rasskazy o Lenine*, p. 177; Bobrovskaya, *Twenty Years*, p. 59.
9.   Elwood, *Russian Social Democracy and the Underground*, p. 94; Krupskaya,
     Memories, pp. 70–1.
10. Stasova, *Vospominaniya*; for interesting insights into life in the underground,
     see pp. 39–45.
11. Written by Vladimir Makhnovets, it was published in 1900 by the League
     of Russian Social Democrats Abroad.
12. Shub, *Lenin*, pp. 62–5.
13. Ulam, *Lenin and the Bolsheviks*, pp. 214–15.
14. Clements, *Bolshevik Women*, pp. 10–13.
15. Krupskaya, *Memoirs*, p. 60.
16. See Turton, *Forgotten Lives*, pp. 34–5, and especially chapter 2, 'The Under-
     ground'. Turton illustrates the till now undervalued contribution of Anna
     and Mariya and the extent to which, rather than being 'worshipful devo-
     tees' of their brother's work, they lived full and independent lives within
     the movement.
17. Haimson, *Three Russian Revolutionaries*, p. 134.
18. Ibid., pp. 135–6.
19. Ibid., p. 137.
20. Clements, *Bolshevik Women*, pp. 79–81.
21. Ibid., p. 85.
22. Ibid., pp. 68–74.
23. Wolfe, *Three Who Made a Revolution*, p. 247.
24. Burenin, *Pamyatnye gody*, pp. 157–60.
25. See Muraveva, *Lenin v Myunkhene*, pp. 87–8; Wildman, 'The *Iskra* Organi-
     zation in Russia', p. 489.
26. See Futrell, *Northern Underground*, pp. 41–8.
27. Burenin, *Pamyatnye gody*, p. 28.
28. Dashkov, *Po leninskim mestam Skandinavii*, p. 21.
29. Burenin, *Pamyatnye gody*, p. 29.
30. Ibid., p. 38.
31. O'Connor, *Engineer of Revolution*, pp. 42–5.

32. Elwood, *Russian Social Democracy in the Underground*, p. 53.
33. See for example Daly, *Autocracy under Siege*, p. 42.
34. Deich, *Rasskazy o Lenine*, pp. 158–9.
35. Kahn, *Codebreakers*, p. 343; Williams, *The Other Bolsheviks*, pp. 8–14.
36. Lauchlan, *Russian Hide and Seek*, p. 120.
37. Krupskaya, *Memories*, p. 69.
38. Piatnitsky, *Memoirs*, p. 41.
39. Lyadov, *Iz zhizni partii*, p. 10.

Chapter 4: Becoming Lenin

1. Deich, *Rasskazy o Lenine*, p. 164.
2. Prokhorov in *OVIL*, pp. 22–3.
3. *CW* 34: 136.
4. Ibid.: 93, 100, 101.
5. Krupskaya, *Memories*, p. 60.
6. Payne, *Life and Death*, p. 151.
7. For discussions of 'What Is To Be Done?' see Ulam, *Lenin and the Bolsheviks*, pp. 228–36; Read, *Lenin*, pp. 52–9; Service, *Lenin: A Biography*, pp. 139–42.
8. Lenin, 'What Is To Be Done?', *Selected Works* vol. 1 (Moscow: Foreign Languages Publishing House, 1960), p. 212.
9 Meshcheryakov in *VoVIL*, vol. 1, 1956, p. 220.
10. *CW* 34: 103.
11. Read, *Lenin*, p. 44.
12. For an interesting discussion of the Lenin pseudonym see Shtein, *Ul'yanovy i Leniny*, chapter XI.
13. David Footman, *Red Prelude* (London: Barrie & Rockliff, 1968), p. 87; Williams, *Lenin*, p. 32; 'What Is To Be Done?' *CW* 5: 467.
14. Wildman, 'The *Iskra* Organization', p. 493.
15. Ibid., p. 497.
16. Krupskaya, *Memories*, p. 64.
17. Volner, *Psevdonimy V I Lenina*, p. 52.

Chapter 5: Dr and Mrs Richter

1. Thompson, *Guard from the Yard*, p. 34.
2. Henry Brailsford, 'When Lenin and Trotsky Were in London', p. 86.
3. Madame Olga Novikoff, *Russian Memories* (London: Herbert Jenkins, 1917), p. 201.
4. Woodhall, *Secrets of Scotland Yard*, p. 74; Slatter, *From the Other Shore*, pp. 13, 35.

5.   Brust, quoted in Aldred, *No Traitor's Gate*, vol. 1, no. 12, p. 278.

6.   Armfelt, 'Russia in East London', p. 25.

7.   Krupskaya, *Memories*, p. 69.

8.   Alekseev, 'V. I. Lenin v Londone', in *VoVIL*, vol. 2, p. 216.

9.   *CW* 43: 80.

10. 1901 Census, RG13, piece 145, folio 77, p. 13. The children were Louisa Mary, Leonard, Robert, Alfred and Harry. The Yeo family's side of the story was told by eldest son Leonard and his sister Louisa in 1939 at a press conference called by the Finsbury Communist Party after newspaper reports denied Lenin had ever lived at 30 Holford Square. See 'Lenin's Clerkenwell Home: Recollections of his Landlady', *Guardian*, 20 July 1939, p. 15.

11. Ibid.

12. Atkins, 'Lenin was their Lodger', p. 14. Muraveva, *Lenin in London*, p. 23.

13. 'Londoner's Diary', *Evening Standard*, 30 August 1941, p. 2.

14. See Maisky, *Journey into the Past*, pp. 83–7, for Rothstein's account of Lenin at Holford Square. Atkins, 'Lenin was their Lodger', p. 14.

15. Letters to the Editor, *Islington Gazette*, 15 October 1963, p. 4.

16. Atkins, 'Lenin was their Lodger', p. 14.

17. Maisky, *Journey into the Past*, p. 86.

18. Krupskaya, *Memories*, p. 74.

19. Karachan, *Lenin in London*, p. 15. The second commune address, at Percy Circus, was discovered by Bob Henderson in the British Museum's list of ticket holders – under Martov's name. See http://www.bobhenderson.co.uk/libhist.html/

20. The building now houses the Marx Memorial Library, an outstanding collection of socialist books and literature, established in 1933 in response to the book burning then taking place in Hitler's Germany.

21. Beer, *Fifty Years of International Socialism*, p. 14; Lenin, obituary for Harry Quelch, 1913, in *CW* 19: 369–71.

22. 'Londoner's Diary', *Evening Standard*, 30 August 1941, p. 2.

23. Pyatnitsky, *Memoirs*, p. 53.

24. Krupskaya, *Memories*, p. 65

25. Alekseev in *VoVIL*, vol. 1, p. 218.

26. Ibid., p. 216; Trotsky, *On Lenin*, pp. 40, 43.

27. *CW* 36: 123.

28. Maisky, *Journey into the Past*, p. 84.

29. Krupskaya, *Memories*, p. 65.

30. *Athenaeum* no. 3889, 10 May 1902, p. 577.

31. Henry Rayment, obituary, *The Times*, 11 October 1921, p. 13.

32. Semenov, *Po leninskim mestam*, pp. 18–20, whose 1960 account appears to have been based on a conversation with Zelda Kahan (1886–1969). In 1913, Kahan married the English communist William Peyton Coates, under which surname she was later known. Zelda Coates's short but valuable

'Memories of Lenin in London in 1902–3 and 1907' was published in *Labour Monthly*, November 1968, pp. 506–8.

33. Aldred, *No Traitor's Gate*, vol. I, no. 12, p. 278; Karachan, *Lenin in London*, p. 18; Semenov, *Po leninskim mestam*, p. 24; Coates, 'Memories of Lenin' p. 507.

34. Krupskaya, *Memories*, p. 65.

35. Semenov, *Po leninskim mestam*, p. 27.

36. Lenin, 'Interview with Arthur Ransome', 1922, in *CW* 33: 400.

37. Gorky quoted in Francis Sheppard, *London: A History* (Oxford: OUP, 2000), p. 301. The Pindar of Wakefield is still there. It is now a popular music venue known as The Water Rats – the music events are held in the old music hall at the back. The Crown and Woolpack on St John Street still has its original exterior but is now a smart hairdressing salon.

38. Krupskaya, *Memories*, p. 68.

39. *CW* 37: 358.

40. Maisky, *Journey into the Past*, p. 36.

41 See Pimlott, *Toynbee Hall*, pp. 151–3.

42. Bowman, 'Lenin in London', pp. 336–8.

43. Krupskaya, *Memories*, p. 66.

44. Coates, 'Memories of Lenin', p. 507.

45. *CW* 34: 105.

46. Ibid.: 111.

47. Trotsky, *My Life*, p. 126.

48. Trotsky, *On Lenin*, pp. 30, 45; Elizabeth Hill in her pseudonymous *For Readers Only* (London, Chapman & Hall, 1936) identifies one of Lenin's favourite venues for listening to socialist oratory as the 'Southwell Place Labour Church' but it has proved impossible to find any information on it.

49. Trotsky, *On Lenin*, p. 37.

50. Ibid., p. 35.

51. Alekseev, 'V. I. Lenin v Londone', in *VoVIL*, Vol. 1, p. 217.

52. The building was taken over in 1906 by the East End Jewish Anarchists Club founded by Rudolf Rocker, and thereafter was known as the Workers' Friend Club. In 1907 it would be a popular haunt of Russian delegates to the RSDLP Congress in London.

53. *CW* 37: 354.

54. Ibid.: 355. Possibly an allusion to a German language performance at the Communist Club in Charlotte Street. The club had a stage and was used at weekends for concerts and other theatrical performances.

55. Getzler, *Martov*, p. 65; Zasulich remained at Sidmouth Street till 1905, when she returned to Russia and dropped out of political life. She later opposed Lenin's Bolshevik takeover and died in 1919.

56. Weber, *Lenin*, p. 30.

57. Letters to the Editor, *Islington Gazette*, 15 October 1963, p. 4. The house at

30 Holford Square was badly damaged by bombing in 1940 and was demolished as part of the major redevelopment of Holford Square after the war. The flat occupied by Zasulich et al. at Sidmouth Street also disappeared during redevelopment.

58. 'Lenin's Clerkenwell Home', *Guardian*, 20 July 1939, p. 15; Atkins, 'Lenin was their Lodger', pp. 14–15; Krupskaya, *Memories*, p. 67.

Chapter 6: 'The Dirty Squabble Abroad'

1. Krupskaya, *Memories*, p. 79; Kudryavtsev, *Lenin's Geneva Addresses*, p. 38. For a possible alternative diagnosis of this 'rash' see n. 7 to the Epilogue, on p. 331.
2. Kulyabko in *VoVIL*, vol. 1, 1956, pp. 231–2.
3. Ibid., p. 230.
4. Kudryavtsev, *Lenin's Geneva Addresses*, p. 47.
5. See Bobrovskaya, *Twenty-Five Years* pp. 93–6; Stasova, *Stranitsy*, p. 49; Kudryavstsev, *Lenin's Geneva Addresses*, pp. 42–3; Krupskaya, *Memories*, pp. 80–1.
6. Trotsky, *My Life*, p. 138; Shotman, *Zapiski*, pp. 83–4.
7. Marcu, *Lenin*, p. 102; Shotman, *Zapiski*, pp. 83–4.
8. Shotman, *Zapiski*, pp. 83–4.
9. Lepeshinksy, *Protokoly*, part II, pp. 9–10.
10. Krupskaya, *Memories*, p. 83.
11. *CW* 34: 153.
12. Deutscher, *Prophet*, p. 63.
13. Wolfe, *Three Who Made a Revolution*, p. 274.
14. Shotman, *Zapiski*, p. 85.
15. Ibid., pp. 85–6.
16. Zemlyachka in *VoVIL*, vol. 1, p. 235.
17. 'Our London Correspondence', *Guardian*, 12 July 1939, p. 10, says Alekseev moved to Holford Square from 22 Ampton Street in October 1902; Muraveva, *Lenin in London*, p. 76.
18. Semenov, 'Lenin in London', *Soviet Weekly* 21 April 1960; Semenov, *Po Leninskim Mestam*, p. 48; Shotman, *Zapiski*, p. 87.
19. The Club was already regularly used as a venue by the British Social Democratic Federation, later becoming notorious as a venue for 'red agitation'. It came under increasing surveillance when war broke out in 1914 because of its German connections. Suspected of being a hotbed of anti-British sedition, it was closed down.
20. Rothstein, 'Lenin in Britain', p. 18. There has been some confusion that the Brotherhood Church on Southgate Road in Islington was a venue for the 1903 Congress but no evidence has been found to support this. It is

much more likely that the delegates, of whom there were far fewer than at the 1907 Congress, stuck to smaller venues in the area of the Communist Club off Tottenham Court Road.

21. Shotman, *Zapiski*, p. 87.

22. Weber, *Lenin*, p. 33.

23. Payne, *Lenin*, p. 172.

24. Trotsky, *On Lenin*, p. 61.

25. Shub, *Lenin*, p. 78.

26. Service, *Lenin: A Biography*, p. 155.

27. Kochan, 'Lenin in London', p. 232; Wolfe, *Three Who Made a Revolution*, p. 276.

24. Deutscher, *Prophet*, p. 67.

29. *CW* 34: 168–70.

30. Bergman, *Martov*, pp. 193–4; Krupskaya, *Memories*, p. 57.

31. Although the terms *bolshevik* (maximalist/majoritarian) and *menshevik* (minimalist/minoritarian) originate from the split at the 1903 Congress, it was some time before they became common currency for defining the two factions. For a while the two groups were known within the movement as the 'hards' and 'softs', with Lenin also favouring the disparaging term 'Martovites'. Much criticism has been made that Martov did not resist the attribution of 'menshevik'. Far from being in the minority, his group were for some time to come the majority. After the Bolshevik-only congress held in Finland in 1905, the usage of the two terms rapidly gained ground.

32. *CW* 34: 164.

33. Semenov, *Po Leninskim Mestam*, p. 49.

34. Deutscher, *Prophet*, p. 50.

35. Trotsky, *My Life*, p. 142; Trotsky, *On Lenin*, pp. 60–1.

36. Deutscher, *Prophet*, pp. 67–8.

37. Trotsky, *My Life*, p. 143.

38. Potresov, *Posmertnyi sbornik*, pp. 294, 299.

39. Krupskaya, *Memories*, p. 91.

40. Ulam, *Lenin*, p. 239.

41. Krupskaya, *Memories*, pp. 93–4.

42. Bonch-Bruevich, *Vospominaniya*, pp. 24–5.

43. Krupskaya, *Memories*, p. 94.

44. See ibid., pp. 92–3.

45. *CW* 36: 128.

46. Ibid. 34: 187.

47. Service, *Lenin: A Biography*, p. 157.

48. *CW* 36: 128.

49. Service, *Lenin: A Biography*, pp. 158–9; Kulyabko in *VOVIL*, vol. 1, p. 232.

50. Bonch-Bruevich, *Vospominaniya*, pp. 300–1.

51. 'Lenin's table', upon which curious visitors had a habit of carving their

own names and which was stained with the beer mugs of generations, was apparently still to be seen for many years afterwards at the Café Landolt, but some time in the 1970s it disappeared when the café was refurbished. An amusing account from the *Tribune de Geneve* 3 August 2006, p. 28, can be found at http://www.lescommunistes.org/lenine/table.html

52. Bonch-Bruevich, *Vospominaniya*, pp. 30–32; Kudryavtsev, *Lenin's Geneva Addresses*, pp. 51–3, 56.

53. Lunacharsky, *Revolutionary Silhouettes*, pp. 36–7.

Chapter 7: 'Strong Talk and Weak Tea'

1.   Valentinov, *Encounters*, pp. 9–10.

2.   Ibid., pp. 19–21.

3.   Fotieva, *Pages from Lenin's Life*, p. 5.

4.   Deborah Hardy, 'The Lonely Émigré: Petr Tkachev and the Russian Colony in Switzerland', *Russian Review*, 35 (1969), p. 401.

5.   Ulam, *Lenin and the Bolsheviks*, p. 239.

6.   Kudryavtsev, *Lenin's Geneva Addresses*, p. 7.

7.   Margherita Sarfatti, *The Life of Benito Mussolini* (London: Thornton Butterworth, 1925), pp. 104, 108, 112.

8.   Joseph Conrad, *Under Western Eyes* (London: Penguin, 2007), p. 91; Balabanoff, *My Life as a Rebel*, p. 83.

9.   For an interesting discussion of the Russian colony of *Karuzhka* as described in Joseph Conrad's *Under Western Eyes*, see Paul Kirshner, 'Topodialogic Narrative in *Under Western Eyes* and the Rasoumoffs of "La Petite Russie"', in Gene M. Moore, ed., *Conrad's Cities* (Amsterdam: Rodopi, 1992), pp. 223–54. See also Kudryavtsev, *Lenin's Geneva Addresses*, pp. 65–8.

10. Ibid., p. 244.

11. Ibid., p. 253.

12. Alexander Herzen, *My Past and Thoughts* (Berkeley: University of California Press, 1973), p. 358. For an interesting overview of Russian exiles in Geneva see also Balabanoff, *My Life as a Rebel*, pp. 81–4.

13. Valentinov, *Encounters*, p. 42.

14. Bobrovskaya, *Twenty Years*, chapter VI; Kudryavtsev, *Lenin's Geneva Addresses*, p. 51.

15. Essen in *VoVIL*, vol. 2, pp. 114–15.

16. Valentinov, *Encounters*, p. 43.

17. See Fotieva, *Pages from Lenin's Life*, pp. 15–16; Spiridovich, *Istoriya bol'shevizma v Rossii*, pp. 151–60; Getzler, *Martov*, pp. 90–95.

18. Lepeshinsky, *Na povorote*, p. 198.

19. Valentinov, *Encounters*, p. 113.

20. Ibid., pp. 121–5.

21. Ibid, pp. 127–9.

22. *CW* 37: 361–2.

23. Ibid.: 363.

24. Ibid., 37: 361–2; Krupskaya, *Memories*, p. 98.

25. For details of the route of this two and a half month walking tour, see Elwood 'Lenin on Holiday', pp. 121–3.

26. Essen in Golikov, *VoVIL*, vol. 2, p. 118.

27. Essen was sentenced to five years' exile in the far north at Archangel, but managed to escape and make her way back to St Petersburg in September 1905 to work once more for the revolution.

28. Elwood, 'Lenin on Holiday', p. 122.

29. The venue was arranged by Bonch-Bruevich; see his *Vospominaniya*, pp. 44–5.

30. Krupskaya, *Memories*, p. 98.

31. Fotieva, *Pages from Lenin's Life*, p. 11.

32. Bingley, *Lenin, Krupskaya and Libraries*, p. 61.

33. Krupskaya, *Memories*, p. 99.

34. Kudryavtsev, *Lenin's Geneva Addresses*, p. 77.

35. Fotieva, *Pages from Lenin's Life*, pp. 8–9.

36. Valentinov, *Encounters*, p. 142.

37. Tyrkova-Williams, *Na putyakh k svobode*, pp. 188–90.

38. Lepeshinsky, *Na povorote*, pp. 221–4; Lepeshinskaya, *Vstrechi s Ilichem*, pp. 40–48; Fotieva, *Pages from Lenin's* Life, pp. 11–12; Kudryavtsev, *Lenin's Geneva Addresses*, pp. 85–8.

39. *CW* 43: 132–3.

40. William, *The Other Bolsheviks*, p. 26.

41. Valentinov, *Encounters with Lenin*, pp. 211–15.

42. Kochan, 'Lenin in London', p. 232.

43. Andrei Maylunas and Sergei Mironenko, eds, *A Lifelong Passion: Nicholas and Alexandra in Their Own Words* (New York: Doubleday, 1997), p. 251.

Chapter 8: 'On the Eve of Barricades'

1. By the Gregorian, Russian Orthodox calendar the Old Style date was 9 January.

2. *The Times*, 23 January 1905, p. 5.

3. Gerald D. Surh, *1905 in St Petersburg* (Stanford: Stanford University Press, 1989), p. 165.

4. Payne, *Life and Death of Lenin*, p. 184.

5. For his eyewitness account of Bloody Sunday, see Father Gapon, *The Story of My Life* (London: Chapman & Hall, 1905), pp. 174–85; Salisbury, *Black Night*, pp. 116–28, contains a vivid account. See also Shukman, ed., *Ency-*

clopedia of the Russian Revolution, pp. 104–9; Figes, *People's Tragedy*, pp. 173–9; Pipes, *Russian Revolution* pp. 21–7.

6. *The Times*, 23 January 1905, p. 5.
7. Surh, *1905 in St Petersburg*, p. 165.
8. Pipes, *Russian Revolution*, p. 25; Gapon, *Story of My Life*, p. 185.
9. Khanin in *VoVIL, 1900–1922*, pp. 25–6.
10. As Lenin described events in February 1905, 'The First Lessons', *CW* 8: 140.
11. Read, *Lenin*, pp. 226-7; Wolfe, *Three Who Made a Revolution*, p. 360.
12. Salisbury, *Black Night*, pp. 118, 646.
13. Ibid., p. 117.
14. Valentinov, *Encounters*, p. 21.
15. Wolfe, *Three Who Made a Revolution*, p. 347.
16. Losev in *VoVIL*, vol. 1, p. 298.
17. Muraveva, *Lenin in London*, pp. 150–2.
18. Ibid., p. 151.
19. Fitch, *Traitors Within*, pp. 20–1.
20. Ibid., p. 23.
21. Ibid., p. 24. See also 'Memories of a Meeting with Lenin', *Islington Gazette*, 31 January 1964. Mr Harry Moring, who took over the Crown and Woolpack in 1941, said the cupboard was still there when he retired in 1955.
22. Salisbury, *Black Night*, p. 161.
23. Fitch, *Traitors Within*, pp. 25–6. Extensive checks by the archivist of the Metropolitan Police at the request of the author have confirmed that, sadly, none of the Special Branch reports by Fitch and his colleagues have survived for this or the 1907 Congress.
24. *CW* 34: 43.
25. Payne, *Lenin*, p. 189.
26. Wolfe, *Three Who Made a Revolution*, pp. 421–3.
27. Futrell, *Northern Underground*, p. 60.
28. Drabkina, *Chernye sukhari*, pp. 27–8. Drabkina was married to party man Sergey Gusev, Lenin's favourite singer from Geneva days, whose real name was Yakov Drabkin. In December 1904 Gusev had been sent back to St Petersburg undercover to work as secretary to the Petersburg Committee of the RSDLP and was instrumental in setting up the Fighting Technical Group with Burenin, to which his wife gave such dedicated support. See also Kalmykov, *Boevaya tekhnicheskaya gruppa*.
29. Kalmykov, *Boevaya tekhnicheskaya gruppa*, p. 101.
30. Burenin, *Pamyatnye gody*, pp. 59–60.
31. Ibid., pp. 57–8. For further invaluable and rare information on the many key activists in Burenin's group, see also Kalmykov, *Boevaya tekhnicheskaya gruppa pri PK i TsK RSDRP 1905–1908gg*.
32. Kalmykov, *Boevaya tekhnicheskaya*, p. 103.
33. *CW* 34: 158.

34. Salisbury, *Black Night*, pp. 152–5; Figes, *People's Tragedy*, p. 189; Wolfe, *Three Who Made a Revolution*, pp. 363–4.

35. Drabkina, *Chernye sukhari*, pp. 26–30.

36. Ibid., pp. 31–2. Soon after the suppression of the Moscow insurrection, Gorky and Andreeva were forced to flee to Finland, from where in 1906 they set off on a fundraising tour of the USA.

37. Figes, *People's Tragedy*, pp. 200–1; Salisbury, *Black Night*, pp. 171–3.

38. *CW* 34: 363–4.

39. Dashkov, *Po leninskim mestam Skandinavii*, pp. 54–5.

Chapter 9: Stolypin's Neckties

1. Krupskaya, *Memories*, pp. 122–3.

2. Ibid., p. 123.

3. Aline, *Lénine à Paris*, p. 20.

4. The claim was made by Lenin's close ally Zinoviev in his hagiography of Lenin. See Beucler, *Les amours secrètes*, p. 24.

5. Beucler, *Les amours secrètes*, p. 41.

6. Ibid., pp. 44–9.

7. Beucler and Alexinsky's 1937 book, *Les Amours secrètes de Lénine*, based on conversations with Elizaveta de K (referred to in French as Lise de K) in exile in Paris and letters she received from Lenin, claimed that the couple had an intermittent affair in 1905–6, with subsequent brief meetings in Geneva and Paris in 1908 and Galicia in 1914. Some of the letters were published simultaneously in France in 1936 in facsimile in the journals *L'Humanité* and the Russian émigré *Illyustrirovannaya Rossiya* but are now lost. *Les Amours* has inevitably been the subject of considerable debate among Lenin biographers, particularly David Shub and his detractors. See for example, Shub, 'Fact or Fiction on Lenin's Role', in *New International*, vol. 16, no. 2, 1958, pp. 86–91, section 6. While the Beucler book makes no overt claims of a sexual relationship, the title clearly has that intention. Although the affair cannot be substantiated (the anonymity of Elizaveta de K supposedly being maintained to protect the feelings of Nadezhda Krupskaya while she was still alive), there is much detailed observation of Lenin's personality in her account of their meetings that strikes one as first hand and which ring true in their detail; see Shub, *Lenin*, pp. 459–60, and Robert Payne, *Life and Death*, pp. 201–11. More recently, Volkogonov, *Lenin*, p. 31, supports the book's authenticity. It is plausibly suggested that one of the reasons Elizaveta de K's identity was never revealed and that her Lenin letters were later lost, is that her silence was effectively bought by the Soviets in return for a pension and the withdrawal of Soviet police intimidation. For both sides of the argument, see Robert H. McNeal, 'Lenin and "Lisa de K", a Fabrication', *Slavic Review*, vol. 28 no. 3,

pp. 471–4, and a refutation of this article by Folke Dovring in *Slavic Review*, vol. 29, no. 3, pp. 570–3.

8. Futrell, *Northern Underground*, pp. 68–9.

9. There is no popular history in English of the Finnish revolutionary movement at this time. But see Futrell, *Northern Underground* and the website of the Lenin Museum in Tampere, http://www.lenin.fi/uusi/uk/commun05.htm/ The Finns achieved independence from Russia on 18 December 1917.

10. Montefiore, *Young Stalin*, p. 97.

11 Ibid., p. 124; Rappaport, *Joseph Stalin*, pp. 163–4.

12. Krupskaya, *Memories*, p. 131.

13. Ibid., p. 134.

14. Ulam, *Lenin and the Bolsheviks*, pp. 303–4.

15. Shub, *Lenin*, p. 109.

16. Wolfe, *Three Who Made a Revolution*, p. 403.

17. Payne, *Life and Death*, p. 196.

18. 'Executions in Russia', *New York Times*, 20 March 1909, p. 3.

19. Montefiore, *Young Stalin*, p. 153; Figes, *People's Tragedy*, p. 221.

20. Krupskaya, *Memories*, p. 139.

21. Payne, *Life and Death*, p. 168.

22. For a detailed account of Stalin and Kamo's colourful bank-robbing career see Montefiore, *Young Stalin*, chapters 17, 18 and 20.

23. Ibid., pp. 138–9.

24. Geifman, *Thou Shalt Kill*, pp. 116–17.

25. Ibid., p. 118.

26. Zuckerman, *The Tsarist Secret Police Abroad*, pp. 170–1.

27. Sheinis, *Litvinov*, pp. 52–6.

28. Ibid., p. 61.

29. For Litvinov's underground career during the years 1906–8 see Sheinis, *Maxim Litvinov*, part I, *Papasha*. Litvinov lived in London for ten years from where he ran the UK wing of Bolshevik underground operations; after the Revolution he was appointed Russian ambassador to Britain.

30. Payne, *Life and Death*, pp. 198–9.

Chapter 10: 'The Congress of Undesirables'

1. Gandurin, *Epizody podpol'ya*, pp. 12–17; Dashkov, *Po leninskim mestam Skandinavii*, pp. 105–7.

2. Dashkov, *Po leninskim mestam Skandinavii*, pp. 108–10.

3. Lyadov, *Iz zhizni partii*, pp. 197–8.

4. Ibid., p. 198–9.

5. Gandurin, *Epizody podpol'ya*, p. 25.

6. 'Revolutionists in London', *Daily News*, 9 May, p. 7. Gandurin, *Epizody podpol'ya*, p. 26. See also Peter Higginbotham, 'Rowton Houses', at http://www.workhouses.org.uk/index.html?Rowton/Rowton.shtml

7. Elia Levin, 'The Social Democratic Party of Russia and Its Recent Congress', *Social Democrat*, vol. XI, no. 9, p. 540.

8. 'Nameless Army from Russia', *Daily Mail*, 10 May 1907, p. 5; 'A Congress of Undesirables', *Daily Mail*, 14 May 1907, p. 6.

9. Duden and Laue, 'The RSDLP and Joseph Fels', p. 23; Balabanoff, *My Life as a Rebel*, p. 86; *Daily News*, 10 May 1907, p. 7.

10. Krupskaya, *Memories*, p. 142; Kiselev in *OVIL, 1900–1922*, p. 85.

11. Bassalygo in *VoVIL*, vol. 3, 1960, p. 81. It is unclear exactly where Lenin stayed during the congress – but logic dictates that he would have returned to his old haunts in the King's Cross area, as he did in 1905. Simon Sebag Montefiore asserts in *Young Stalin*, p. 146, that Lenin and Krupskaya (who in fact did not attend the congress but stayed behind in Finland) were accommodated in relative comfort in a hotel in 'Kensington Square'. This would be quite out of character – for both of them, even had Nadya been with her husband. Lenin's frugality would never have allowed him to stay somewhere expensive in west London, let alone remove himself from the other delegates in the East End, over whom he was extremely anxious to maintain his influence. Congress delegate N. Nakoryakov mistakenly states in *OVIL, 1900–1922*, p. 70, that Lenin's lodgings were in 'Kingston Square', which might explain the confusion with Kensington Square – except that no such square existed. Lenin is much more likely to have stayed somewhere in the region of Holford Square or Percy Circus, which he knew from previous visits.

12. Andreeva, *Perepiski*, pp. 95–6.

13. Jack London, *People of the Abyss*, 1903, chapter 20, 'Coffee Houses and Doss Houses'; many editions, including online at http://london.sonoma.edu/Writings/PeopleOfTheAbyss/ Tower House, Whitechapel, was one of six Rowton Houses built in London by the philanthropist Montague William Lowry-Corry, 1st Lord Rowton. It was finally closed down in the late 1970s. For twenty years or more it lay derelict, the haunt of squatters, drunks and drug addicts, until sold to a developer in 2004. It has now been converted into expensive new apartments.

14. For a vivid description of the culture shock of this experience for the Russian delegates, see Gandurin, *Epizody podpol'ya*, pp. 26–8.

15. Many years later, Bacon told his story to the *Daily Express*. See 5 January 1950.

16. Fitch, *Traitors Within*, p. 33.

17. Ibid., p. 29; Thomas, 'History Was Made in London', p. 16.

18. Fishman, *East End Jewish Radicals*, pp. 262–4; Kendall, *Revolutionary Movement in Britain*, pp. 77, 81.

19. Woodhall, *Secrets of Scotland Yard*, pp. 94–5. Woodhall does not identify the year of this anecdote but the venue must make it 1907, as the Workers' Friend Club did not open till 1906 and Kropotkin's health failed shortly after and he moved to Brighton.

20. Fitch, *Traitors Within*, pp. 28–30.

21. *The Evangelical Alliance*, vol. XI, 1857, p. 183, lists the Southgate Road Congregational Chapel, in an area then known as De Beauvoir Town. Other evangelical publications allude to it having been newly built in 1852, as home for a Congregational community based at the eighteenth-century Pavement Chapel in the nearby New North Road. When Wallace's Brotherhood Church took it over in the 1890s the Southgate Road Chapel had been derelict for some time. For a description see Brailsford, 'When Lenin and Trotsky Were in London', p. 87; Willats, 'Lenin and London', p. 4, and Maisky, *Journey into the Past*, pp. 136–7. The church was used for Pacifist meetings during World War I, provoking a demonstration and riot outside in 1917. It was persistently targeted by vandals thereafter and remained derelict after the Brotherhood community left the premises. It was demolished in 1934.

22. The church was noted for its eccentric humanitarian pursuits, having been the venue for the 4th International Vegetarian Congress in 1897.

23. Gandurin, *Epizody podpol'ya*, p. 28.

24. Stanley Buder, *Visionaries and Planners: The Garden City Movement and the Modern Community* (Oxford: Oxford University Press, 1990), pp. 54–5. See also A. G. Higgins, *A History of the Brotherhood Church* (Stapleton, Yorks: Brotherhood Church, 1982). Descriptions of the 1907 Congress in previously published Lenin biographies refer erroneously to Frank Swann as being the resident incumbent. But Swann, a close friend of the British socialist and newspaperman George Lansbury, who was also a member, did not take over as pastor until 1912.

25. 'Revolutionaries' Surprise', *Daily Mail*, 13 May 1907, p. 5; 'In Fear of Spies', *Daily News*, 13 May 1907, p. 7; Gorky, *Days with Lenin*, p. 5.

26. Balabanoff, *My Life as a Rebel*, p. 87.

27. Trotsky, *My Life*, p. 175; Balabanoff, *My Life as a Rebel*, p. 87.

28. 'Nameless Army from Russia', *Daily Mail*, 10 May 1907, p. 5.

29. 'Revolutionists' Duma in London', *Daily Mail*, 11 May 1907.

30. Lyadov, *Iz zhizni*, p. 204; *The Times*, 13 May 1907, p. 5; *Daily News*, 16 May 1907, p. 7.

31. *Daily Mirror*, 16 May 1907, p. 4.

32. *Daily News*, 18 and 22 May 1907; Sebag Montefiore, *Young Stalin*, p. 150.

33. Balabanoff, *Impressions of Lenin*, p. 18.

34. Gorky, *Days with Lenin*, pp. 7, 11.

35. Coates, 'Memories of Lenin', p. 508.

36. Gorky, *Days with Lenin*, pp. 12, 15.

37. Stalin, 'Notes', pp. 21-3.

38. Nakoryakov in *OVIL*, 1900-22, p. 70; Gandurin, *Epizody podpol'ya*, p. 39.

39. Gorky in Golikov, *VoVIL*, vol. 2, 1969, p. 250.

40. Gorky, *Days with Lenin*, p. 17.

41. Lyadov, *Iz zhizni partii*, p. 205.

42. Service, *Lenin: A Political Life*, p. 166.

43. Dudden and Laue, 'The RSDLP and Joseph Fels', p. 34.

44. Lyadov, *Iz zhizni partii*, p. 203.

45. Ibid., 202–4; Garnett, *Constance Garnett*, pp. 233–4; Joseph Szigeti, *With Strings Attached*, London: Cassell, 1949, pp. 69–70.

46. Brailsford, 'When Lenin and Trotsky Were in London', p. 86.

47. Ibid., p. 87.

48. Dudden and Laue, 'The RSDLP and Joseph Fels', pp. 43–5. Fels asked for his money back after the Revolution in 1917 but the Bolsheviks rightly pleaded poverty and stalled. Fels died in 1914 and it was not until 1922 that the loan was eventually paid back to his widow by a Russian Trade Delegation when it came to London. See also Brailsford, 'When Lenin and Trotsky Were in London'. Angelica Balabanoff notes in *Impressions of Lenin*, p. 25, that Fels was also a dedicated collector of autographs, which is why he was so keen for the members of the congress to sign the loan agreement.

49. Balabanoff, *Impressions of Lenin*, pp. 17–18.

50. Andreeva, *Perepiski*, p. 96.

51. Getzler, *Martov*, p. 119.

52. Stalin, 'Notes of a Delegate', pp. 11, 13.

53. Sebag Montefiore, *Young Stalin*, pp. 154–5.

54. *The Times*, 28 May 1907, p. 6; *Daily News*, 3 June 1907, p. 7.

55. Letter from Reuter's correspondent T. Beaugard to Henry Brailsford at the *Daily News*, 3 June 1907. This and Brailsford's covering letter to MacDonald can be found in: PRO 30/69/151. See also *Daily News*, 23 May 1907, p. 7.

56. The obsessiveness with which Lenin exhaustively worked over every last detail is vividly captured in his memoir by the stenographer N. S. Karzhansky in 'V. I. Lenin na s'ezde RSDRP', *VoVIL*, vol. 1, 1956, pp. 356–63.

57. Krupskaya, *Memories*, p. 143.

58. 'Maxim Gorki at Secret Duma', *Daily Mirror*, 15 May 1907.

59. *New York Times*, 21 May 1907.

Chapter 11: On Thin Ice

1. Krupskaya, *Memories*, p. 143.

2. Ibid., p. 146.

3. Ibid., p. 145; Kudryavtsev, *Lenin's Geneva Addresses*, p. 113.

4. *Lenin v vospominaniyakh finnov*, p. 48.

5. Ibid., p. 49.

6. Ibid., p. 50.

7. Ibid., p. 51.

8. Ibid., p. 54.

9. Ibid., pp. 55–6.

10. Malmberg, 'What if Lenin had drowned here?' in English online at http://www.hs.fi/english/article/What+if+Lenin+had+drowned+here/ 1101977945887

11. *Lenin v vospominaniyakh finnov*, pp. 61–3.

12. Ibid., p. 62.

13. Dashkov, *Po leninskim mestam Skandinavii*, pp. 134, 138.

14. Malmberg, 'What if Lenin had drowned here?'

15. It is noticeable that Arkady Rylov's socialist-realist painting of this event, *Tyazhelyi put'* (The Hard Road) shows Lenin striding ahead of his two Finnish guides across the ice, when, in fact, coward that he was, he most certainly would have followed in the rear, letting them test the ice first.

16. Accounts of this final stage of Lenin's journey from Prostvik are very patchy and conflicting. See Dashkov, *Po leninskim mestam Skandinavii*, p. 138. In all, Lenin's journey out of Finland lasted five or six days, from about 19 to 25 December 1907. Ludwig Lindström was the only participant to publish a detailed account of his role in the escape, reprinted in *Lenin v vospominaniyakh Finnov*, pp. 53–64, some of which conflicts with other evidence and aggrandises his own role in events. The most accurate and well-researched account is in Dashkov, *Po leninskim mestam Skandinavii*, pp. 112–38, but it is still unclear as to whether Lenin boarded the steamship at Kaasluoto – which was about ten miles from the farm at Västergården – or nearer, from the tiny skerry of Själö. Local Finns favour the latter location.

17. There is some dispute as to which ship Lenin caught. In *Po leninskim mestam Skandinavii*, p. 130, Yuri Dashkov stated that Lenin took the *Bore I* from Åbo at 4.00 p.m. on 25 December that year. The Lenin Museum in Tampere is reliably informed that it was in fact the *Stella* of the same Bore Company. Lenin was already in Stockholm by 27 December, when he registered that day at the State Library.

18. Service, *Lenin: A Biography*, p. 185.

19. Hamilton-Dann, *Vladimir and Nadya*, p. 124.

20. Krupskaya, *Memories*, p. 147.

21. Ibid., p. 148.

22. Krupskaya, *Memories*, pp. 153–4.

23. *CW* 43: 134.

24. Krupskaya, *Memories*, p. 162.

25. Beucler, *Les amours secrètes*, pp. 105–6.

26. The couple continued to exchange desultory letters and postcards up until the outbreak of war in 1914; Elizaveta de K's to Lenin have been lost but some of the dozen or so he wrote to her, which are instructional rather than romantic, were reprinted in facsimile *L'Intransigéant* in 1936. See chapter 9, note 7. For résumés of their relationship see Payne, *Life and Death of Lenin*, pp. 201–11, and Shub, *Life and Death, passim*.

27. *CW* 37: 158; Beryl Williams, *Lenin*, p. 108.

28. Shub, *Lenin*, pp. 123–5.

29. Ulam, *Lenin and the Bolsheviks*, pp. 348–50.

30. Kudryavtsev, *Lenin's Geneva Addresses*, p. 114.

31. Wolfe, *Three Who Made a Revolution*, p. 538.

32. *CW* 34: 387.

33. Kudryavtsev, *Lenin's Geneva Addresses*, p. 115.

34. *CW* 34: 168.

35. Kudryavtsev, *Lenin's Geneva Addresses*, p. 116; see his letters to Gorky, February–April 1908, in which he expounds at length on his views on Bogdanov et al., *CW* 34: 379–90.

36. *CW* 34: 165.

37. Krupskaya, *Memories*, p. 160.

38. See Shirley Hazzard, *Green on Capri: A Memoir* (London: Virago, 2000), pp. 119–24.

39. The villa was not called Villa Krupp in 1908, as it is often mistakenly described in books about Gorky's time on Capri and Lenin's visit. Friedrich Krupp, the armaments millionaire, had visited the island regularly from 1898, staying at the Grand Hotel Quisisana in the grounds of the nearby Gardens of Augustus, from where he indulged in regular homosexual escapades. In gratitude to Capri for curing his asthma and depression, he gave his name to a road, the Via Krupp, for which he funded the construction to provide access from the hotel to the Marina Piccola below. Gorky lived at the Villa Blaesus from November 1906 to March 1909, moving to the larger Villa Behring, known as the 'Red House', to run his party school there, before moving one final time to the Villa Pierina on the south side of Capri. He left the island in 1913 to return to Russia. In later years the Villa Settanni was converted into a hotel and renamed the 'Villa Krupp'. A bust of Lenin on a stone plinth still can be seen in the Gardens of Augustus.

40. Cerio, *Masque of Capri*, p. 68.

41. During this visit the first photographs of Lenin to be taken since 1900 were captured by Mariya Andreeva's son, Yura Zhelyabuzhsky, Lenin till then having resisted, for obvious reasons, being photographed. Zhelyabuzhsky was a keen photographer and recorded a sequence of photographs of Lenin playing chess with Bogdanov on the terrace of Villa Blaesus, surrounded by various party activists and visitors. These photographs were

later the subject of considerable doctoring under Stalin. See David King, *The Commissar Vanishes* (Edinburgh: Canongate Books, 1997), pp. 18–21. See also Moskovsky, *Lenin v Italii*, p. 23.

42. *CW* 37: 83.
43. Gorky, *Days with Lenin*, p. 25.
44. Ibid., pp. 26–7; Cerio, *Masque of Capri*, pp. 95–6.
45. Gorky, *Days with Lenin*, p. 27; Cerio, *Masque of Capri*, p. 96; Vol'ner, *Psevdonimy*, p. 107. For an interesting fictionalisation of the visit based on research in Capri and interviews with Gorky's Italian servants, see Zinaida Guseva, *Svidanie na Kapri* (Moscow: Sovetskaya Rossiya, 1968), part 2.
46. Gorky, *Days with Lenin*, p. 28; Cerio, *Masque of Capri*, p. 96.
47. Simsova, *Lenin, Krupskaya and Libraries*, p. 61; Kudryavtsev, *Lenin's Geneva Addresses*, p. 116.
48. Bill Fishman, 'Millie Sabel, Yiddische Anarchist', *East London Arts Magazine*, Winter 1967, p. 3.
49. Masefield letter of 15 November 1964, quoted in Corliss Lamont, *Remembering John Masefield* (London: Kaye & Ward, 1972), pp. 83–4.
50. John Strachey, 'The Great Awakening', *Encounter*, pamphlet no. 5, 1961, p. 7.
51. *CW* 37: 166.
52. Kaganova, *Lenin vo Frantsii*, pp. 37–8.
53. Krupskaya, *Memories*, p. 152; Kaganova, *Lenin vo Frantsii*, pp. 35–8.
54. Ibid., p. 166; Kudryavtsev, *Lenin's Geneva Addresses*, p. 122.
55. *CW* 37: 172.
56. Aline, *Lénine à Paris*, pp. 38–9.
57. Grechnev in *OVIL*, 1900–22, p. 94; Krupskaya, *Memories*, p. 167.
58. Krupskaya, *Memories*, p. 166.

Chapter 12: 'Why the Hell Did We Go to Paris?'

1. Fotieva, *Pages from Lenin's Life*, p. 22; Wolfe, *Three Who Made the Revolution*, p. 543; *CW* 34: 415.
2. Salisbury, *Black Night*, pp. 216–17.
3. Volkogonov, *Lenin*, p. 57.
4. See Krupskaya, 'O Vladimire Il'iche' in Golikov, *VoVIL*, vol. 2, p. 581.
5. Ehrenburg, *People and Life*, pp. 75–7; Kaganova, *Lenin vo Frantsii*, p. 30.
6. Manuilsky in Petrov, *OVIL*, 1900–1922, pp. 107–8.
7. Kaganova, *Lenin vo Frantsii*, p. 42; Aline, *Lénine à Paris*, pp. 12–13, 29–30.
8. Krupskaya, *Memories of Lenin*, pp. 171, 185. 5 June 1914, *CW* 35: 144.
9. Aline, *Lénine à Paris*, p. 18.
10. Kaganova, *Lenin vo Frantsii*, pp. 41–2.
11. Ibid., p. 47; Krupskaya, *Memories*, p. 168.
12. Fréville, *Lénine à Paris*, p. 160.

13. Zinoviev, *Lenin*, pp. 68–9.

14. Krupskaya, *Memories*, pp. 168–9; Aline, *Lénine à Paris*, p. 16; *CW* 37: 456–7.

15. Fréville, *Lénine à Paris*, p. 137. Both the Au Puits Rouge and Aux Manilleurs cafés have long since disappeared. Avenue d'Orléans is now avenue du Général Leclerc.

16. *CW* 37: 426–7.

17. Williams, *The Other Bolsheviks*, pp. 138–9.

18. Payne, *Life and Death*, pp. 228–30.

19. Read, *Lenin*, p. 91

20. Wolfe, *Three Who Made a Revolution*, p. 569.

21. Weber, *Lenin*, pp. 65–6.

22. Elwood, 'Lenin on Holiday', p. 150.

23. *CW* 35: 112.

24. Krupskaya, *Memories*, p. 173; Fréville, *Lénine à Paris*, pp. 89–90.

25. Feld, *Quand Lénine vivait à Paris*, p. 38.

26. Krupskaya, *Memories of Lenin*, p. 167.

27. Mel'nichenko, *Ya tebya ochen' lyubila*, p. 88.

28. Lyudvinskaya in Golikov, *VoVIL*, vol. 2, pp. 281–2.

29. Gopner in Golikov, *VoVIL*, vol. 2, p. 289.

30. Kaganova, *Lenin vo Frantsii*, p. 342; Payne, *Life and Death of Lenin*, p. 232; Aline, *Lénine à Paris*, p. 44.

31. Krupskaya, 'O Vladimire Il'yche', p. 582; Beucler, *Les Amours secrètes*, p. 127.

32. Gaston Montéhus was a Jew, born Mardochée Brunswick in Paris in 1872. He rose to fame as a popular singer–songwriter, turning out more than three thousand songs. A socialist and ardent anti-militarist, he was hugely popular with the Parisian working classes after he moved to the capital in 1900, so much so that some of his performances were stopped for being politically subversive. At the height of his success when war broke out in 1914, his socialist sympathies were called into question. He was accused of being a police spy and fell into disfavour. He never recovered his popularity and died alone in 1952. See Boulouque, 'Mardochée Brunswick, 'Singer of Socialist Songs Sets Paris Aflame', *New York Times*, 30 June 1912; Kataev, *Malen'kaya zheleznaya dver'*, pp. 54–69, which, although a fictionalisation, includes Kataev's research on Montéhus in Paris and interviews with people who knew him. Montéhus became a Freemason in 1902 and it has been alleged that he introduced Lenin to his own lodge, the Union of Belleville, which Lenin joined. Cabaret Bobino still thrives today on the rue de la Gaieté.

33. Tat'yana Lyudvinskaya, who was in Lenin's Paris circle, remembered his enthusiasm for Montéhus in her memoir of Lenin, *Velikii, blizkii, prostoi*. Marcel Cachin, a French socialist and founder of the French Communist Party, also recalled (in conversation with Kataev) Lenin's visits to the *cafés concerts*, notably Bobino, to hear Montéhus perform.

For general background see Francois Caradec and Alain Weill, *Le café-concert* (Paris, Massin, 1980).

34. To hear an original recording of Montéhus singing 'Gloire au 17ème', go to http://www.chanson.udenap.org/fiches_bio/montehus.htm
35. Aline, *Lénine à Paris*, p. 46; Kaganova, *Lenin vo Frantsii*, pp. 320–21.
36. Leo Campion, *Les Anarchistes dans la F[ranc] M[aconnerie]* (Marseilles: Culture et Liberté, 1969) p. 52.
37. *CW* 37: 431.
38. Fréville, *Lénine à* Paris, pp. 161–2; Aline, *Lénine à Paris*, pp. 82 –3.
39. *CW* 34: 420.
40. Ibid., 37: 451.
41. Ibid., 34: 421.
42. Ibid., 37: 462.
43. Caruso, *Lenin à Capri*, pp. 101–2; see also Cerio, *That Capri Air*, p. 96.
44. For a study of the party schools, see Elwood, 'Lenin and the Social Democratic Schools'.
45. Elwood, ibid., pp. 374–6.
46. Fréville, *Lénine à Paris*, pp. 109–10.
47. Shaginyan, 'Retracing Lenin's Steps', p. 195.
48. For an account of the congress see Maisky, *Journey into the Past*, chapter 17.
49. Ibid., p. 16.
50. Shub, *Lenin*, p. 137.
51. Dann, *Lenin and Nadya*, p 137.
52. Krupskaya, *Memories*, p. 166, where the Russian '*I kakoi chert pones nas v Parizh!*' is more laboriously translated as 'what the devil made us go to Paris!'.

Chapter 13: Inessa

1. For details of Inessa's early life, see Pearson, *Inessa – Lenin's Mistress*, and Elwood, *Inessa Armand*.
2. This date is according to Inessa's colleague, Elena Vlasova; see Mel'nichenko, *Ya tebya ochen' lyubila*, p. 94. Elwood, *Inessa*, p. 69, concurs.
3. Pearson, *Inessa*, p. 90.
4. Elwood, *Inessa*, p. 77–8.
5. 'His Paris Concierge Pays Tribute to Lenin', *New York Times*, 25 April 1921, p. 2. McNeal, *Bride*, p. 138.
6. Zetkin, 'My Recollections of Lenin', in *They Knew Lenin*, p. 12.
7. Aline, *Lénine à Paris*, p. 27.
8. Vasilieva and Porter, *Kremlin Wives*, p. 10.
9. Elwood, 'Lenin and the Social Democratic School', pp. 86–9.

10. Ibid., p. 381.

11. Ibid., p. 383; Payne, *Life and Death of Lenin*, p. 239.

12. Fréville, *Lénine à Paris*, p. 195.

13. Elwood, 'Lenin and the Social Democratic School', p. 384; Fréville, *Lénine à Paris*, p. 195; Krupskaya, *Memories*, p. 191; Mel'nichenko, *Ya tebya ochen' lyubila*, pp. 124–5. The house in which Lenin and Nadya stayed is now no. 91 rue Président Mitterrand. For some evocative photographs of Longjumeau see Feld, *Quand Lénine vivait à Paris*, pp. 154–67.

14. See Elwood, 'Lenin and the Social Democratic Schools', pp. 384–5, for what little details are known of the students and their backgrounds.

15. Elwood, 'Lenin and the Social Democratic Schools', p. 386.

16. Mel'nichenko, *Ya tebya ochen' lyubila*, p. 128; Elwood, 'Lenin and the Social Democratic Schools, pp. 386–8.

17. Krupskaya, *Memories*, p. 192.

18. Elwood, 'Lenin and the Social Democratic Schools', p. 388.

19. Fréville, *Lénine à Paris*, p. 197; Elwood 'Lenin on Holiday', p. 124.

20. *CW* 37: 610.

21. Elwood, 'Lenin and the Social Democratic Schools', pp. 289–90.

22. Pearson, *Inessa*, p. 90.

23. Payne, *Life and Death*, p. 235.

24. McNeal, *Bride*, pp. 139–40.

25. Lidiya Dan, who worked on *Iskra* with Lenin in Munich, suggests that Lenin also had some kind of affair or flirtation with émigré Gregory Alexinsky's wife Alya in Paris, but, along with the alleged affair with Elizaveta de K, there is no hard, substantiating evidence for this, although Alexinsky certainly fell out with Lenin politically in Paris and formed an independent Left-Bolshevik group with Bogdanov and others. Dan claimed in an interview that another fellow activist, Ekaterina Kuskova, 'told me in great detail about his romance with Armand', confirming that it was 'a very stormy affair'. See Haimson, *Making of Three Russian Revolutionaries*, pp. 124–5. Similar, verbal rumours also filtered through from another leading *bolshevichka*, Aleksandra Kollontai, who supposedly fictionalised the Lenin–Inessa–Nadya triangle in her 1927 short story 'A Great Love'. Whether any of Lenin's contemporaries were more candid about his relationship with Armand in their letters or memoirs is not known; if they were, such material would have been ruthlessly expunged by Stalinist historiographers in the creation of the Leninist cult of personality, much as any personal comments in the surviving letters from Lenin to Armand were. Krupskaya, as loyal keeper of Lenin's flame, remained stonily silent on the subject. See also McNeal, *Bride*, pp. 140–1.

26. Valentinov, *Encounters with Lenin*, p. 60.

27. *CW* 37: 578.

28. According to Lidiya Fotieva, Nadya moved into her mother's bedroom at rue Marie Rose. *Fotieva iz zhizni Lenina*, p. 10.

29.   For Lenin's use of *ty* see Wolfe 'Lenin and Inessa', pp. 97–8, and Valentinov,
      Encounters with Lenin, pp. 60–1. Lenin wrote some 135 cards and letters to
      Inessa, the great majority between 1911 and 1917, but her daughter Inna,
      who was close to Nadya and wished to spare her feelings, did not hand
      them over to the Central Committee Archives until after Nadya's death in
      1939. The Soviet authorities, no doubt exercised by the possibly compro-
      mising nature of the letters, were reluctant to publish some or any of
      them for some time. But eventually, conscious that their largely political
      content was part of Lenin's historical legacy, a few were released in 1950.
      But it was not until 1964 that the first Lenin–Armand letters were published
      at any length – ninety-five of them in the fifth edition of his *Collected Works*
      and elsewhere. The first major collection of Armand's letters came in
      Russia in 1975, but these were mainly to her children. More of the missing
      Lenin letters to Armand did not appear in Russia until the 1990s. Of the
      Lenin letters published, many have clearly been tampered with; pages are
      missing and in others the no doubt affectionate opening and closing remarks
      to Inessa have been torn off. For a discussion of the Lenin–Armand letters,
      see Elwood, 'Lenin and Armand'.
30.   Alexey Aline, in *Lénine à Paris*, pp. 72–4, denied that Lenin ever set foot in
      a bohemian café in Montparnasse and that he did not like La Rotonde,
      but see C. R. W. Nevinson, *Paint and Prejudice* (London: Methuen, 1937),
      pp. 65–6; Jean-Paul Crespelle, *Chagall* (New York: Coward-McCann, 1970),
      pp. 19–23; Noel Riley Fitch and Andrew Midgely, *The Grand Literary Cafés
      of Europe* (New Holland Publishers, 2006), p. 36; Piers Letcher, *Eccentric
      France* (Bradt Travel Guides, 2003), p. 85.
31.   Cecily Mackworth, *Guillaume Apollinaire and the Cubist Life* (London: John
      Murray, 1961), p. 5.
32.   It is alleged that in a book or article published in 1960 French journalists
      tracked down some of the brothels in Paris that Lenin is said to have
      visited and interviewed some of the old prostitutes who had serviced him.
      The author has so far not been able to trace this source, alleged on p. 130
      of Juri Lina's *Under the Sign of the Scorpion: The Rise and Fall of the Soviet
      Empire* (Stockholm: Referent Publishing 2002). While Lina's book has a
      heavy anti-Russian bias and some of its politics are unsavoury, it is fully
      annotated in its detail and repeats allusions to Lenin's sexual activities in
      Paris that have filtered through from other French-based sources, including
      the suggestion that Paris is probably where he picked up the syphilis that
      killed him – possibly as early as 1902–3 when he made a couple of lecture
      trips over from London. Nicholas V. Feodoroff in his *Soviet Communists and
      Russian History* (New York: Nova Science Publishers, 1997), p. 27, suggests
      that Lenin's sexual encounters with prostitutes began during his student
      days in Kazan. See Epilogue, note 7.
33.   Julien Green, *Journal, 1928–1954* (Paris: Librairie Plon, 1938), vol. 4: entry for

5 February 1932, pp. 84–5. A rather coy English rendition of the original French is offered in the edited down version of the journal, in *Personal Record, 1928–1939* (New York: Harper Brothers, 1939), p. 76: 'We were sharing our ladies. Lenin was very gay and good-natured; he was a sensualist.' In his *Lénine Dada* (p. 26), Dominique Noguez says that the French critic Philippe Vanini telephoned Green on 16 February 1989 for confirmation of this story and was told by him that the painter's name was either '*Evitcheff ou Ivitcheff*' (Evichev or Ivichev). So far it has not been possible to identify him further.

34. Toussaint, *Lénine inconnu*, see the section 'La Chaisière de Luxembourg', pp. 9–57. Toussaint's totally unverified claims have, of course, been dismissed out of hand as pure fiction by the hagiographers, notably the French communist Jean Fréville, author of the official version, *Lénine à Paris* (see p. 179) and Alexey Aline in his book of the same title. But despite the perceived flippancy of this particular sequence, Toussaint's book contains a very detailed and serious recall by him of Lenin's extensive political arguments. Both Aline and Fréville had political reason to defend Lenin's spotless reputation as a moral puritan, yet one still gets the impression that there were times when he went off limits, away from his Russian political colleagues, to unwind. Detractors unwilling even to countenance another, sexual side to Lenin, the plaster saint, similarly refuse to entertain the memoirs of Elizaveta de K in *Les Amours secrètes de Lénine*. But the sheer fact that such rumour as there is about Lenin's sexual exploits has only tentatively emerged from his Paris period in itself suggests that there is some substance to them; either that or, as the Soviets would have it, there was a French conspiracy to discredit him. At this juncture there simply isn't enough concrete evidence to argue the case conclusively, but the clues are there in Lenin's relationship with Armand. See also the Epilogue to this book, p. 284.

35. Beucler and Alexinsky, *Les Amours secrètes*, pp. 95–101.

36. Beer, 'Interview with Lenin', pp. 148–9, 154, 158.

37. Elwood, 'Lenin and the Social Democratic Schools', p. 390.

38. Amort, 'Lenin in Prague', p. 20; Semashko in *OVIL*, *1900–1922*, pp. 229–301; Onufriev in *OVIL*, *1900–1922*, p. 304.

39. Swain, 'The Bolsheviks' Prague Conference Revisited', pp. 134–8.

40. Service, *Lenin: A Political Life*, vol. 2, p. 23.

41. Lyudvinskaya, *Veliki, blizki*, p. 21.

42. Service, *Lenin: A Political Life*, vol. 2, p. 21.

43. Krupskaya, *Memories*, p. 202; Mel'nichenko, *Ya tebya ochen' lyubila*, p. 144.

44. Krupskaya, *Memories*, p. 202; Alexinsky, *Les Amours secrètes*, pp. 200–1.

45. Krupskaya, *Memories*, p. 197.

46. Bob Gould, 'Lenin, Krupskaya and Inessa Armand', at http://members. optushome.com.au/spainter/Armand.html

47. 'His Paris Concierge Pays Tribute to Lenin', *New York Times*, 25 April 1921, p. 2.

Chapter 14: 'Almost Russia'

1. Adamczewski, *Lenin w Krakowie*, p. 56; I am grateful to Peter Northover for information on trains between Paris and Kraków.
2. *CW* 37: 479; Krupskaya, *Memories*, p. 204; Sobczak, 'Two Years in Poland', p. 16.
3. Adamczewksi, *Lenin w Krakowie*, p. 61; Najdus, '*Lenin i Krupska*, contains much useful information, especially chapter III: 'Lenin i Krupska pod Opieką Krakowskiego Związku'.
4. The house, now substantially renovated, is still there, although the street name and number has changed to no. 41 Królowej Jadwigi. The commemorative plaque to Lenin has long since been removed.
5. Hanecki is referred to as Yakov Ganetsky in Russian sources; as a financial expert responsible for laundering Bolshevik funding by Germany in 1917 he became better known by the pseudonym of Jakub Fürstenburg. In 1918 he became the first director of the Soviet Central Bank.
6. *CW* 37: 479.
7. Sergey Bagotsky's reminiscences of Lenin in Poland are the most extensive and useful: see Bagotsky [Bagocki], 'V. I. Lenin v Krakove i Poronine' in *VOVIL*, vol. 1, 1956, pp. 438–56. Sobczak, 'Two Years in Poland', while slavishly communist, contains valuable information. See also Krupskaya, *Memories*, p. 206; Adamczewski, *Lenin w Krakowie*, is a valuable source of contemporary photographs and other ephemera linked to the places where Lenin lived in Poland.
8. Shub, *Lenin*, pp. 145–6.
9. Sobczak, 'Two Years in Poland', p. 17; Krupskaya, *Memories*, p. 204.
10. Krupskaya, *Memories*, p. 205.
11. Józef Piłsudski's elder brother, Bronisław, had been a member of the conspiratorial group, along with Lenin's brother Aleksandr, that plotted the assassination of Alexander III. Józef was implicated and arrested in 1887 with his brother, serving five years' hard labour in Siberia. After mobilising his underground Polish forces during World War I, he became the first leader of an independent Poland in 1918.
12. *CW* 37: 519.
13. Ibid.: 508.
14. See Krupskaya, *Memories*, p. 207.
15. *CW* 37: 614; Najdus, *Lenin i Krupska*, pp. 102–3.
16. Krupskaya, *Memories*, p. 234.
17. Wolfe, *Three Who Made a Revolution*, pp. 605–6.

18. Ulam, *Lenin and the Bolsheviks*, pp. 386–7; Wolfe, *Three Who Made a Revolution*, pp. 604–5.

19. Krupskaya, *Memories*, p. 209; Salisbury, *Black Night*, pp. 243–4; *CW* 43: 293.

20. Pearson, *Inessa*, p. 97; Krupskaya, *Memories*, pp. 298–9.

21. Pearson, *Inessa*, pp. 99–100.

22. *CW* 37: 494.

23. Sebag Montefiore, *Young Stalin*, pp. 219–21.

24. Rappaport, *Joseph Stalin*, pp. 164, 189; Sebag Montefiore, *Young Stalin*, p. 227.

25. Krupskaya, *Memories*, p. 227.

26. Bagocki, 'V. I. Lenin', p. 447; *CW* 37: 617. Information from Professor Ronald Chaplain – see note 7 in Epilogue. For a discussion of Nadya's thyroidism see Leonhard Haas, 'Lenins Frau als Patientin bei Schweizer Arzten', in *Jahrbucher für Geschichte Osteuropas*, NF Band 17, 1969, pp. 420–36. Additional information from Professor Chaplain.

27. Bagotsky, 'V. I. Lenin', p. 449.

28. Ganetsky, 'S Leninym', p. 97.

29. Bagotsky, 'V. I. Lenin', pp. 441–2.

30. Sobczak, 'Two Years in Poland', pp. 17–18.

31. Information from Piotr Bąk, former mayor of Zakopane, who observed in conversation with the author that in their later memoirs, and for obvious reasons, some of these eminent Poles regretted helping Lenin in 1914. See also Bernov, *Lenin v Krakove*, p. 206; Adamczewski, *Lenin w Krakowie*, which contains a wonderful collection of contemporary photographs of the Podhale and the Góral peasants.

32. It was Vigilev who took a rare photograph of Lenin in Zakopane in 1914, one of only four taken of him prior to the Revolution. See Najdus, *Lenin i Krupska*, pp. 94–102. For a selection of photographs of Lenin's Polish associates in Zakopane, see Adamczewski, *Lenin w Krakowie*, pp 132–91. Another useful account of his time in the Tatras can be found in Bernov, *Lenin v Krakove*, chapter 10, 'Poronin i Tatry'.

33. Bagotsky, 'V. I. Lenin', p. 450.

34. *CW* 43: 58a.

35. Information from Professor Ronald Chaplain, op. cit.

36. Bagotsky, 'V. I. Lenin', p. 450.

37. Elwood, *Inessa Armand*, p. 95.

38. Pearson, *Inessa*, p. 104; Krupskaya, *Memories*, p. 231.

39. Bagotsky, 'V. I. Lenin', pp. 450–51.

40. Elwood, *Inessa Armand*, pp. 118, 99–100.

41. Krupskaya, *Memories*, p. 231.

42. Mel'nichenko, *Ya tebya ochen' lyubila*, pp. 180–81.

43. Ibid., p. 106.

44. 'Inessa Armand', *Svobodnaya mysl'*, no. 3, 1992, pp. 80–1. This crucial and

illuminating letter from Inessa is the only clear and unequivocal statement about their relationship from either party that has so far come to light. For obvious reasons, nothing remotely candid has survived in the many published editions of Lenin's letters, although there are passing hints of his affection for her. Drafted around January 1914 in Paris, it first came to light in the post-Soviet era, when it was published in 1992 in the Russian journal *Svobodnaya mysl'* (above). For a discussion of its implications, see Elwood, 'Lenin and Armand', and Pearson, *Inessa*, pp. 106–12 and Chapter 17, note 25, p. 327 of this book.

45. McNeal, *Bride*, p. 149.
46. *CW* 37: 514.
47. Elwood, *Inessa Armand*, p. 125.
48. Ibid., pp. 126–8; see Lenin's letters to Inessa in *CW* 43 for 1913 and 1914.
49. Pipes, *Unknown Lenin*, p. 26; Pearson, *Inessa*, pp. 119–20.
50. *CW* 43: pp. 406–7, 409–10, 417–20.
51. See *CW* 43: 409–10, 417–20, 423; Elwood, *Inessa Armand*, pp. 130–36; Pearson, *Inessa*, pp. 119–22.
52. *CW* 43: 425.

Chapter 15: A Russian Spy in Galicia

1.   *CW* 35: 76.
2.   Bagotsky [Bagocki], 'V. I. Lenin', p. 454.
3.   Barbara Tuchman, *The Proud Tower: A Portrait of the World Before the War, 1890–1914* (London: Papermac, 1980), p. 435.
4.   *CW* 35: 76.
5.   For once, his removal to Kureika defeated even the wily Stalin, who was forced to sit out the rest of his sentence in exile until the Revolution in 1917. See Rappaport, *Joseph Stalin*, pp. 262–3.
6.   Bernov, *Lenin v Krakove*, p. 223.
7.   Kupskaya, *Memories*, p. 240.
8.   Bagotsky, 'V. I. Lenin', pp. 45–6; Krupskaya, *Memories*, pp. 240–41.
9.   Bernov, *Lenin v Krakove*, p. 225; Krupskaya, *Memories*, p. 241; *CW* 43: 430–1.
10. Krupskaya, *Memories*, p. 241.
11. Trepper, *The Great Game*, p. 3. Trepper emphasises the fact that the devoutly Catholic and Jewish communities of Nowy Targ cohabited happily at that time. Economic hardship, not anti-semitism, drove out much of the Jewish population of Nowy Targ before World War I, with many Jews emigrating at this time to the USA and Canada. For a valuable first-hand portrait of the town and a vanished world see Trepper, pp. 5–11. The Jewish syngagoue is still there – but is now a cinema.
12. Trepper, *The Great Game*, p. 3, is very clear about this. Nowy Targ jail in

those days had only one collective cell for petty criminals. Yet according to all the subsequent Soviet books and, indeed, the sanctified 'prison cell no. 5' that was later lovingly recreated as part of the Leninist cult, the prison had several cells. It would appear therefore that the interior of the building that the author saw in September 2008 was a later modification.

13. Bernov, *Lenin v Krakove*, p. 225; information from Christina Zaba.
14. Ganetsky [Hanecki], 'S Leninym', p. 98.
15. See Wolfe, *Three Who Made a Revolution*, pp. 684–6.
16. Information from Christina Zaba and Piotr Bąk. Kasprowicz's assertion, as recorded by Bagotsky in 'V. I. Lenin', pp. 455–6, runs counter to the local story, which had it that Marisya Kasprowicz, a general's daughter from St Petersburg, asked her husband, who played cards with the local judge at Nowy Targ, to exert his influence in the campaign for Lenin's release. The Kasprowiczs' house in Zakopane, Villa Harenda, is now the Kasprowicz Museum.
17. Sobczak, 'Two Years in Poland', p. 17; Bagotsky, 'V. I. Lenin', pp. 455–6; Adamczewski, *Lenin w Krakowie*, pp. 248–53; information from Christina Zaba.
18. McNeal, *Bride*, pp. 153, 155. Sobczak, 'Two Years in Poland', p. 16; Bernov, *Lenin v Krakove*, pp. 226–7; Golikov, *Biokhronika*, vol. 3, p. 268.
19. Krupskaya, *Memories*, p. 242.
20. Ibid., p. 243.
21. *CW* 37: 496.
22. I am indebted to Stephanie Weiner in California for sharing information about her great-uncle Mendel Singer with me from Alojzy Singer's unpublished memoir. Passing allusions to this untold story can be found in Michael Walzer-Fass, *Remembrance Book of Nowy Targ and Vicinity* (Tel Aviv, 1979), p. 17, and in Trepper, *The Great Game*, pp. 3–4. As this is a very hard to find source, Fass is easiest accessed via the net at http://www.jewishgen.org/Yizkor/Nowy_targ/Nowy_Targ.html#TOC
23. Wolfe, *Three Who Made a Revolution*, p. 686; Bernov, *Lenin v Krakove*, pp. 230–1.
24. *CW* 37: 520.
25. Krupskaya, *Memories*, p. 242, a key part of Leninist folklore, perpetuated by the Soviets ever after, e.g. in Bernov, *Lenin v Krakove*, p. 228.
26. By the end of August, Inessa Armand in Switzerland had also raised money from 'unspecified sources' to help Lenin out and had organised its transfer, presumably to him in Kraków or more probably Vienna; Elwood, *Inessa Armand*, p. 143.
27. Information from Stephanie Weiner. Born in Nowy Targ in 1904, Trepper became a Zionist activist in Israel and later went to Moscow from where he organised and coordinated an intelligence network in Nazi-occupied Europe, known as the 'Red Orchestra'. Not long after Lenin left Galicia,

Mendel Singer's store was burned down by a disgruntled employee who had been dismissed for stealing. The family moved to Nowy Targ where Mendel built a new store. During World War II, in 1942 a ghetto was established by the Nazis at Nowy Targ and used as a holding centre for the Jewish population of Podhale. Many local Jews were forced to dig mass graves where they were shot and buried, others were gassed in mobile trucks or shipped in boxcars to the death camps, including Belzec and Auschwitz. Mendel Singer was taken away to Kraków and murdered. His wife Helena and three of his sons perished. But the other three, including Alojzy, who sat on Lenin's knee, survived the Holocaust.

28.   See Grazyna Branny, 'Conrad in Krakow', in *Conrad's Europe*, 3rd International Joseph Conrad Conference, Kamień Śląski, Kraków, September 2004, http://www.culture.pl/en/culture/artykuly/es_conrad_2004_branny Conrad wrote his own moving account of this visit, although it says very little about Zakopane, in the essay 'Poland Revisited', *Collected Works of Joseph Conrad*, vol. XIX (London: Routledge, 1995), pp. 141–73.

29.   Elwood, *Life Without a Cause*, p. 18.

30.   Ibid., pp. 33, 36.

31.   Wolfe, *Three Who Made a Revolution*, p. 600.

32.   Sebag Montefiore, *Young Stalin*, pp. 228–312; Shub, *Lenin*, p .148.

33.   Salisbury, *Black Night*, p. 246; Elwood, *Life Without Cause*, p. 42.

34.   Wolfe, *Three Who Made a Revolution*, pp. 614–15; Shub, *Lenin*, pp. 146, 152–3.

35.   Salisbury, *Black Night*, p. 245; Elwood, *Life Without Cause*, pp. 11, 57.

36.   Ibid., p. 247. After leaving Poronin, Malinovsky joined the Russian army, was wounded and captured by the Germans. From his prison camp he offered his services to Lenin again, disseminating anti-military propaganda among his fellow Russian prisoners. Lenin and Nadya responded by sending food parcels, clothes and books. In November 1918 he unwisely returned to Petrograd, where he was arrested and, after nine days of interrogation, tried by a revolutionary tribunal. When told he would be taken out and shot, Malinvosky agreed that the sentence was just. See Wolfe, *Three Who Made a Revolution*, chapter 31, 'The Case of Roman Malinovsky', and R. Carter Elwood, *Roman Malinovsky*.

Chapter 16: 'This Damned Switzerland'

1.   Bernov, *Lenin v Krakove*, p. 23, endorses this fact, though it makes no mention of the role of the local Poronin Jews, any more than do other Soviet sources. Their contribution, like that of the Poles during August 1914, was completely marginalised in the official record. It was 1924 before the first consignment of material held in Poland found its way back to the Central Committee in the Soviet Union; in 1933 another group of books and manuscripts turned

up and in 1953 a final collection of documents and letters was found in a Kraków archive, where it had been deposited for safekeeping by Bagotsky [Bagocki], and sent to the Soviet government. See 'Vladimir Lénine dans les bibliothèques polonaises' in *IFLA Annual*, 1970, p. 136.

2. Krupskaya, *Memories*, p. 244.
3. Ibid.
4. *CW* 43: 432.
5. Krupskaya, *Memories*, p. 252; Kudryavtsev, *Lenin v Berne*, p. 40.
6. Krupskaya, *Memories*, p. 252.
7. *CW* 37: 522; Kudryavtsev, *Lenin v Berne*, pp. 49–56.
8. See *CW* 35: 173–4
9. Read, *Lenin*, p. 113.
10. Ulam, *Lenin and the Bolsheviks*, pp. 395–6.
11. Krupskaya, *Memories*, p. 249; Read, *Lenin*, p. 131.
12. Clark, *Life and Death*, pp. 162–5; *CW* 35: 163.
13. For further discussion, see Elwood, *Inessa Armand*, pp. 145–9, and Service, *Lenin: A Biography*, pp. 231–2.
14. Volkogonov, *Lenin*, p. 46. This assertion was cut from the letter Lenin sent to Inessa in its original form when published in vol. 48 of Lenin's *Sobranie Sochinenii*. In the absence of names one can only surmise that the possible candidates were Nadya, Inessa and either his first, fleeting love in St Petersburg in the early 1890s, Apollinariya Yakubova, or the elusive Elizaveta de K. Inessa never finished writing her pamphlet on free love; perhaps she felt unable to continue without Lenin's approval. Her initial draft of it has not survived.
15. Elwood, *Inessa Armand*, pp. 157–60.
16. Krupskaya, *Memories*, pp. 261–2.
17. Levine, *The Man Lenin*, p.164; Wilson, *To the Finland Station*, p. 461.
18. Krupskaya, *Memories*, p. 262.
19. McNeal, *Bride*, p. 150. Information from Professor Ronald Chaplain. See also Haas, 'Lenins frau'.
20. *CW* 43: 347.
21. Krupskaya, *Memories*, p. 264; Elwood 'Lenin on Holiday', p. 125.
22. See for example Kudryavtsev, *Lenin v Berne I Tsyurikhe*, pp. 65–9.
23. Elwood, 'Lenin on Holiday', p. 126, and note 10; Krupskaya, *Memories*, p. 264; Service, *Lenin: A Political Biography*, vol. 2, pp. 95, 99.
24. Nation, *War on War*, pp. 78, 81; Wilson, *To the Finland Station*, p. 450.
25. Elwood, *Inessa Armand*, p. 164; Senn, *Russian Revolution in Switzerland*, p. 91.
26. Trotsky, *My Life*, p. 249.
27. Vasili Kolarov, 'At the Zimmerwald Conference', in *They Knew Lenin*, p. 70.
28. Nation, *War on War*, pp. 86–7.
29. Clark, *Lenin*, p. 173; Nation, *War on War*, p. 91.

30. Payne, *Life and Death*, p. 251.
31. See Nation, *War on War*, pp. 88–91. The Zimmerwald eight were: Lenin, Zinoviev, the Polish representative Radek, a Latvian J. Berzin, Julian Borkhat from Germany and two Swedes, Zeth Höglund and Ture Nerman. The final member, the Swiss socialist Fritz Platten, would play a key role in Lenin's return to Russia in 1917.
32. Krupskaya, *Memories*, p. 267.
33. *CW* 37: 530, 526–7.
34. Weber, *Lenin*, p. 115.
35. McNeal, *Bride*, p. 157; Elwood, *Inessa Armand*, p. 174.
36. *CW* 43: 504–6.
37. Elwood, *Inessa Armand*, pp. 167–71; Pearson, *Inessa*, pp. 133–4.

Chapter 17: 'One Fighting Campaign After Another'

1. Kudryavtsev, *Lenin v Berne*, p. 133.
2. Krupskaya. *Memories*, p. 271; Marcu, 'Lenin in Zurich', p. 550.
3. Marcu, 'Lenin in Zurich', pp. 550–1.
4. Meijer, *Knowledge and Revolution*, p. 60.
5. *CW* 37: 530.
6. Levine, *The Man Lenin*, p. 32; Kudryavtsev, *Lenin v Berne*, pp. 135–6. Kharitonova, 'V. I. Lenin v Tsyurikhskoy sektsii bol'shevikov', in *VoVIL*, p. 150. The lower end of Spiegelgasse opposite no. 14 was later widened when several houses were demolished.
7. Krupskaya, *Memories*, p. 272. Twenty-eight francs in 1917 was the American equivalent of $5 or £2.50 sterling.
8. Payne, *Life and Death*, p. 251; 'We Rented to the Lenins', pp. 26–7.
9. 'We Rented to the Lenins', pp. 26–8; Levine, *Lenin the Man*, pp. 32–3; Kharitonova, 'V. I. Lenin', in *VOVIL*, *1900–1922*, pp. 150–51; Ybarra, 'Lenin Lived Poorly', p. 5.
10. Krupskaya, *Memories*, p. 284.
11. Rice, *Lenin*, p. 32.
12. Ulam, *Lenin and the Bolsheviks*, pp. 400–1.
13. Ibid., pp. 406–7.
14. Krupskaya, *Memories*, pp. 277, 284.
15. Ibid., pp. 278–9; Elwood, 'Lenin on Holiday', pp. 126–7.
16. Leuning, *Odyssey*, pp. 122–3; Solzhenitsyn, *Lenin in Zurich*, p. 210.
17. Kudryavtsev, *Lenin v Berne*, p. 140.
18. Fischer, *Life of Lenin*, p. 489. The possibility of Lenin's path crossing with Tristan Zara, a founder of the Dadaist movement, and the writer Joyce was explored with considerable wit by Tom Stoppard in his 1974 play *Travesties*.

19. Ball, *Flight out of Time*, p. 117; Dominique Noguez, *Lénine Dada*, pp. 13–15, 147, 148. Noguez argues forcefully for a much closer association between Lenin and the Dadaists but sadly the evidence is too tenuous to hold water.

20. Richter, *Dada*, p. 16.

21. Zweig, 'The Sealed Train', pp. 241–2.

22. Leuning, *Odyssey*, p. 123.

23. Volkogonov, *Lenin*, pp. 42–3; this section was in the published edition of Lenin's letters.

24. Pipes, *Unknown Lenin*, p. 34.

25. Pearson, *Inessa*, p. 142. The issue of what exactly Inessa said in her letters to Lenin, bar the unposted letter of January 1914 published in Russia in 1992 (see Chapter 14, note 44), in which she poured out her heart to him (pp. 222–3 of this book), is profoundly frustrating. It leaves the Lenin–Inessa story fundamentally one-sided, with only passing clues in his surviving letters to her of the extent of the emotional content of her letters. Had there been any surviving letters from Inessa to Lenin in the archives in 1992, when the crucial letter was published, it is only logical they would have been republished as well. This suggests that Inessa's letters were probably destroyed by Lenin as and when he received them – he did so with much other correspondence from activists in the underground as a simple matter of security; Inessa's would have probably been far too candid and too private to keep. Lenin was mindful enough of his posthumous reputation to ask Inessa for the return of his own letters to her, which suggests that he most certainly would have ensured that hers to him did not fall into the wrong hands. The most likely scenario therefore is that either he destroyed them, or possibly Nadya did after his death, had he kept them out of sentiment. I am grateful to Professor R. Carter Elwood, Professor Robert Service and Michael Pearson for their comments in this regard.

26. See Lenin's letters to Inessa, 25 November to 13 December 1916, *CW* 35: 248–69. For a perceptive view of Inessa's behaviour at this time see Solzhenitsyn, *Lenin in Zurich*, pp. 69–73.

27. Ulam, *Lenin and the Bolsheviks*, p. 403; Krupskaya, *Memories*, p. 285.

28. Shub, *Lenin*, p. 181.

29. *CW* 35: 259.

30. For overviews of the rapidly degenerating situation in Russia, see Salisbury, *Black Night*; Pipes, *The Russian Revolution*; and Figes, *A People's Tragedy*.

31. Krupskaya, *Memories*, pp. 268, 275.

32. Because Lenin was living in Europe at the time events in Russia unfolded, and in order to avoid confusion between the Julian Calendar still operating in Russia at this time and the civil Gregorian one in use throughout Europe, all dates given here are as per the Gregorian calendar. The 'February

Revolution' as it is often referred to in Russia actually took place in March according to today's calendar.

33.   Ulam, *Lenin and the Bolsheviks*, pp. 409–11.
34.   Ibid., p. 420.

Chapter 18: From the Spiegelgasse to the Finland Station

1.   McNeal, *Bride of the Revolution*, p. 165.
2.   Krupskaya, *Memories*, pp. 286–7; 'We Rented to the Lenins', p. 28.
3.   *CW* 43: 616. For Lenin's directives see *CW* 35: 295–300. Krupskaya, *Memories*, p. 287.
4.   Volkogonov, *Lenin*, p. 106; Payne, *Life and Death*, pp. 274–5.
5.   Krupskaya, *Memories*, pp. 287–8; Zinoviev, *Lenin*, p. 290; *CW* 43: 616–18; *CW* 35: 300.
6.   Willi Münzenberg, 'Lenin and We', *They Knew Lenin*, pp. 84–6.
7.   *CW* 43: 617.
8.   Payne, *Life and Death*, p. 279.
9.   For further discussion of the German financial investment in Lenin's revolution, see Pearson, *The Sealed Train*, pp. 104, 114, 290–91, and Volkogonov, *Lenin*, p. 116.
10.   Clark, *Life and Death*, pp. 168–9.
11.   Shub, *Lenin*, p. 210.
12.   Ley, 'A Memorable Day', p. 497.
13.   Considerable debate continues on the precise extent of German financial support for Lenin's return to Russia and the October Bolshevik *coup d'état*. See Volkogonov, *Lenin*, pp. 109–28, for a discussion of the murky roles of Hanecki and Helphand. Volkogonov alleges that large amounts of money were transmitted from Berlin to Hanecki via the New Bank in Stockholm and laundered through a cover account at the Bank of Siberia in Petrograd. He also observes that much compromising documentary evidence relating to these monies was destroyed after the revolution, Lenin being 'very good at keeping secrets' (pp. 111, 121). In later years it would be alleged that the Bolsheviks received up to fifty million gold marks in subsidies from the Germans. For his pains the loyal Hanecki later suffered arrest and torture under Stalin and was shot, along with his wife and son, in November 1937 (Volgonov, *Lenin*, p. 128).
14.   Zinoviev, *Lenin*, p. 28; Payne, *Life and Death*, p. 276; Krupskaya *Memories*, p. 288; *CW* 35: 309; 43: 620.
15.   Radek, 'Lenin's Sealed Train', p. 92; Krupskaya, *Memories*, p. 288.
16.   *CW* 43: 625.
17.   Payne, *Life and Death*, p. 285.
18.   Münzenberg, *They Knew Lenin*, p. 86.

19. In 1969, in deference to Nadezhda Krupskaya's wishes, the Soviet Central Committee secured the return to Russia of Elizaveta Vasil'evna's ashes. See Service, *Lenin: A Biography*, pp. 509–10.

20. Peter Grose, *Allen Dulles, Spymaster* (London: André Deutsch, 1995), p. 26. Dulles' appointment in Berne did not officially commence until 23 April but he spent considerable amounts of time in the city prior to his transfer from Vienna. Lenin's motive for the call is not altogether clear: certainly to hedge his bets with America but perhaps also to secure tacit approval for a visa and a refuge should his usurpation of power in Russia not go to plan.

21. Stefan Zweig, *The World of Yesterday* (London: Cassell, 1987), pp. 203–4. Rolland soon after ran into trouble with the Swiss authorities and needed to get out of Zurich. Ironically, in view of his rejection of Lenin's invitation, it was thanks to Lenin's intervention that he was allowed to travel to Russia with Martov a month later on the second 'sealed train' laid on by the Germans for a large group of Mensheviks, pp. 207–8.

22. Ley, 'A Memorable Day', p. 496.

23. Vayo, *Last Optimist*, p. 124; see also Aline's account in *Lénine à Paris*, pp. 119–20.

24. *CW* 23: 367–74.

25. Heresch, *Blood on the Snow*, p. 86.

26. Clarke, *Life and Death*, p. 198.

27. Leuning, *Odyssey*, pp. 124–5.

28. Moskovsky, *Lenin v Shvetsii*, p. 100.

29. Salisbury, *Black Night*, p. 406.

30. Heresch, *Blood on the Snow*, p. 86.

31. Rozenthal, 'Lenin in Switzerland', p. 13.

32. Shub, *Lenin*, p. 21; Zinoviev, *Lenin*, p. 291.

33. Sean McMeekin, *The Red Millionaire: A Political Biography of Willi Münzenberg* (New Haven: Yale University Press, 2003), p. 45.

34. Heresch, *Blood on the Snow*, p. 87; Payne, *Life and Death*, p. 296; Pearson, *The Sealed Train*, p. 78; Leuning, *Odyssey*, p. 125.

35. Payne, *Life and Death*, p. 297; Pearson, *The Sealed Train*, p. 82; Clarke, *Life and Death*, p. 204.

36. Radek, 'V plombirovannom vagone', pp. 129–30; Krupskaya, *Memories*, p. 294; Haupt and Marie, *Makers of the Russian Revolution*, pp. 379–81.

37. Usevich, 'Iz vosmpominanii o V. I. Lenine', p. 149.

38. Lilina, Zina, 'Tov. Lenin edet v Rossiyu', p. 2.

39. Radek, 'V plombirovannom vagone', p. 313.

40. Pearson, *The Sealed Train*, pp. 100–101; Moskovsky, *Lenin v Shvetsii*, pp. 105–6.

41. Radek, 'Lenin's Sealed Train', p. 92, an American-published variant of Radek's 1924 *Pravda* article. The *New York Times* article is a translation of one published

around the same time by Radek in the French communist paper *L'Humanité* under the strapline 'How the Bolshevist Bacillus was Discovered by the Germans and Transported to Russia by General Ludendorff'.

42.   Moskovsky, *Lenin v Shvetsii*, p. 114.

43.   Radek, 'V plombirovannom vagone', p. 132; Moskovsky, *Lenin v Shvetsii*, p. 118; Elwood, *Inessa Armand*, p. 203. Radek noted that when he was finally allowed back into Russia in November 1917 he noticed that Lenin was still wearing the Stockholm trousers, already 'respectably tattered'.

44.   Futrell, *Northern Underground*, p. 155.

45.   Ibid., p. 156; Ganetsky, 'Priezd tov. Lenina', pp. 139–40; Moskovsky, *Lenin v Shvetsii*, p. 115.

46.   Dann, *Lenin and Nadya*, p. 192.

47.   Elwood, *Inessa Armand*, p. 204; Clarke, *Lenin*, p. 208.

48.   'Calls Soviet Foe of Trade Unionism', *New York Times*, 4 December 1911, p. 7, citing testimony of Lieutenant A. W. Kliefoth, Assistant Military attaché of the USA in Russia, who was passport officer at Torneo the day the Russians arrived.

49.   Zinoviev, *Lenin*, p. 291; Futrell *Northern Underground*, pp. 98 –9; Payne, *Life and Death*, pp. 305–6.

50.   Lord Howard of Penrith, *Theatre of Life*, vol. II (London: Hodder & Stoughton, 1936), p. 264; William Gerhardie, *Memoirs of a Polyglot* (London: MacDonald, 1973), p. 130; information from Phil Tomaselli to whom I am grateful for alerting me to this story.

51.   Moskovsky, *Lenin v Shvetsii*, p. 136.

52.   Krupskaya, *Memories*, p. 295; Wilson, *To the Finland Station*, pp. 469–70; Zinoviev, *Lenin*, p. 292.

53.   Kathy Porter, *Alexandra Kollontai* (London: Virago, 1980), p. 245.

54.   F. F. Raskolnikov, *Kronstadt and Petrograd in 1917* (London: New Park Publications, 1982), p. 68.

55.   Payne, *Life and Death*, pp. 310–11; Zinoviev, *Lenin*, p. 293; Krupskaya, *Memories*, p. 296; Wilson, *To the Finland Station*, pp. 472–3.

56.   Pearson, *The Sealed Train*, pp. 126–31; Krupskaya, *Memories*, pp. 295–6.

57.   Konstantin Eremeev, 'Vstrechi s Il'ichem', *Leningradskaya Pravda*, 30 January 1924, no. 23.

58.   Drabkina, 'Priezd tovarishch Lenina', p. 156.

59.   Ariadna Tyrkova-Williams, *From Liberty to Brest-Litovsk* (London: Macmillan, 1919), p. 62; Possony, *Lenin*, p. 240.

60.   Payne, *Life and Death*, pp. 311–12.

61.   The accounts of Lenin's return on the 'sealed train' are numerous; many were published in Soviet newspapers on the occasion of his death in 1924. For English accounts, see especially Pearson, *The Sealed Train*, and a vivid account that encapsulates some of the best eyewitnesses in Payne, *Lenin*, pp. 301–13. Nadezhda Krupskaya's memoir is disappointingly dull and unre-

vealing but see Krupskaya, *Memoirs*, pp. 293–6. Radek's brief account originally published in *Pravda* in 1924, and an English variant in the *New York Times* in 1922 is particularly interesting. See also accounts by Suliashvili in Moskovsky, *Lenin v Shvetsii*, pp. 85–141; Zinoviev in his *Lenin*, pp. 289–94; Hanecki and Drabkina in *Proletarskaya Revolyutsiya*; Lilina, in *Leningradskaya Pravda*. Locomotive 293 can still be seen today, enshrined in glass at St Petersburg's Finland Station.

Epilogue: Goodbye Lenin

1. Trotsky's remark came at a meeting of the Council of Soviets October 1917 when Martov registered his disgust at the Bolshevik seizure of power. 'You are pitiful isolated individuals; you are bankrupts; your role is played out. Go where you belong from now on – into the dustbin of history!' See Trotsky, *History of the Russian Revolution*, vol. 3, 1933, chapter 10; Volkogonov, *Lenin*, 102.
2. See Orlando Figes, *The Whisperers* (London: Allen Lane, 2007), p. 248.
3. Ana Siljak, *Angel of Vengeance* (New York: St Martin's Press, 2008), p. 311.
4. See 'Inessa Armand', *Svobodnaya mysl'*, p. 835; Pearson, *Inessa*, pp. 217–21.
5. Vasilieva and Porter, *Kremlin Wives*, pp. 23–4; Porter, *Alexandra Kollontai*, p. 345.
6. Rappaport, *Joseph Stalin* pp. 156–7. For an excellent summary of the Leninist legacy see Service, *Lenin: A Biography*, 'Lenin: the Afterlife', pp. 481–94.
7. Information from Professor Ronald Chaplain, formerly of Oxford University, who in his *bona fide* position as a Deputy Head of Professor Manfred von Ardenne's pioneering cancer hospital in Berlin in the 1970s was told by top medical advisers to the Soviet leadership that Lenin had died of syphilis. It is possible that the irritable red rash suffered by Lenin in April 1903, which he and Nadya self-diagnosed as 'Holy Fire', was in fact the classic maculo-papilar rash that is a second-stage symptom of syphilis. This rash usually appears between six weeks to six months after initial infection. If so, it substantiates rumours that Lenin had contracted syphilis on a trip to Paris, c. 1902, cited in Lina, *Under the Sign of the Scorpion*, p. 129 (see chapter 13, note 32; Lenin was in Paris in the summer of 1902 and again in early 1903).

In exile Lenin suffered ill temper, headaches, irritability and sleeplessness as well as periodic loss of appetite and excruciating headaches – all of which are characteristic of second-stage syphilis and which were often recorded in her memoirs by his wife. After his physical collapse in 1922 these symptoms became much more pronounced, and while they can also be symptomatic of arteriosclerosis of the brain, taking into account Lenin's cumulative medical history they can also be read as manifestations of the brain damage leading to dementia, progressive paralysis and aphasia, which is characteristic of neurosyphilis which develops after a ten- to twenty-year gestation period from initial infection. According to Professor Chaplain, the autopsy on Lenin's brain after his death showed up massive sclerosis of the blood vessels and areas of cystic change in both left and right hemispheres consistent with a diagnosis of neurosyphilis in its meningovascular form. Lenin's terminal neurosyphilis was an open secret – from the Soviet Minister for Health, Professor Boris Petrovsky, down through to the elite Kremlin doctors with whom Chaplain conversed. After the collapse of the Soviet Union, evidence emerged that the Chief Pathologist, Alexey Abrikosov, who had performed Lenin's postmortem, had been specifically instructed to falsify the record to cover up the diagnosis of syphilis. Eminent Swedish neuropathologists Salomon and Folke Henschen – both of them communist sympathisers – were also brought in, in March 1923, to examine Lenin and refute the diagnosis of syphilis. The results of the Wasserman test, used for the early diagnosis for syphilis, that were made on Lenin's blood in May 1922, have, according to Robert Service (*Lenin: A Biography*, p. 444), 'gone missing'. These, in any event, would have been irrelevant at this terminal stage of Lenin's disease.

See Linora Lawrence, 'Cold War Memories', an interview with Professor Chaplain published in *Oxfordshire, Limited Edition*, the magazine of the *Oxford Times*, June 2008, pp. 15–19; V. Lerner et al., 'The Enigma of Lenin's (1870–1924) malady', *European Journal of Neurology*, vol. 11, 2004, pp. 371–6, which features the photograph of Lenin mentioned on p. 284 of the Epilogue on its front cover; Juri Lina, *Under the Sign of the Scorpion: The Rise and Fall of the Soviet Empire* (Stockholm: Referent Publishing 2002). The only discussion of the possible diagnosis of syphilis in published Lenin biographies is to be found in Service: *Lenin: A Biography*, pp. 443–6. See also chapter 13, note 32.

8. See 'Leniniana', *World Marxist Review*, vol. 12, no. 4, April 1969, pp. 8–9.

9. See 'Lenin's London Home', *The Times*, 16 March 1942, p. 6, and 'The Shadow of Lenin on a "Budget" Hotel', *The Times*, 16 April 1970, p. 4.

10. See Elwood, 'Lenin on Holiday'.

11. 'We Rented to the Lenins', p. 28; *Time* magazine, 19 November 1951; *New York Times*, 15 June 1924, p. E5.

12. See Joni Krekola, 'Lenin Lives in Finland', in *The Cold War and the Politics of History* (Department of Social Science History, University of Helsinki and Edita Publishing, 2008).

13. Much of the information in this Polish section of the Epilogue comes from conversations with Poles in Kraków, Poronin, Biały Dunajec and Zakopane. I am particularly indebted to Piotr Bąk, former mayor of Zakopane, for a long and illuminating discussion.

14. 'Eyewitness Reports', *News from Behind the Iron Curtain*, p. 28. The news items in this regular section of the journal were based on information on

conditions behind the Iron Curtain from refugees interviewed by Radio Free Europe. See also Sobczak, 'Two Years in Poland', p. 18.

15. Sobczak, 'Two Years in Poland', p. 16.
16. Information from Piotr Bąk in Zakopane.
17. Ibid.
18. Marek Bartosik, 'Wódz obalony lebiodką', in *Gazeta Krakowska*, 5 September 2008, pp. 8–9.

Bibliography

1 Archives

Islington Local History Library, London. Box YJ853 09 BRO.
PRO Ramsay MacDonald papers, 30/69/1753.
PRO Lenin file KV2/585.
Hoover Institution, report of Y. A. Litkens on Lenin in Munich 1900–02, Boris Nicolaevsky collection.

2 Lenin: Family Background, Life and Works

Akhapin, *Lenin–Krupskaya–Ulyanovy: perepiska 1883–1900*, Moscow: Mysl', 1981.

Alexinsky, Gregory, 'Lenin v deistvitel'nosti: ego roman s Elizavetoi K***', in *Illyustrirovannaya Rossiya* 1936, issues for 31 Oct., 7, 14 and 21 Nov.

Ascher, A., *Pavel Axelrod and the Development of Menshevism*, Cambridge: Harvard University Press, 1972.

Balabanoff, Angelica, *Impressions of Lenin*, Ann Arbor: University of Michigan Press, 1964.

Beucler, André, and Grigory Alexinsky, *Les amours secrètes de Lénine*, Paris: Editions Baudinière, 1937.

Bonch-Bruevich, Vladimir, *Vospominaniya o Lenine*, Moscow: Izd. Nauka, 1969.

Clark, Ronald, *Lenin: The Man Behind the Mask*, London: Faber, 1988.

Deich, Lev, *Rasskazy o Lenine i Leninskoi Iskry*, Sverdlovsk: Sredne-ural'skoe knizhnoe izdatel'stvo, 1987.

Deutscher, Isaac, *Lenin's Childhood*, London: Oxford University Press, 1970.

Deutscher, Tamara, *Not by Politics Alone: The Other Lenin*, London: Allen & Unwin, 1973.

Donald, Moira, *Marxism and Revolution: Karl Kautsky and the Russian Marxists 1900–24*, New Haven: Yale University Press, 1993.

Dovring, Folke, *Leninism: Political Economy as Pseudoscience*, Westport: Praeger, 1996.

— 'To the Editor', *Slavic Review*, 29 (3), pp. 570–73 [a refutation of McNeal 1969].

Drabkina, Feodosiya, 'Priezd Tov. Lenina', *Proletarskaya revolyutsiya*, 1927, no. 4, pp. 150–63.

Elwood, R. Carter, 'Lenin and Armand: New Evidence of an Old Affair', *Canadian Slavonic Papers*, 43(1), March 2001, pp. 49–66.

— 'What Lenin Ate', *Revolutionary Russia*, 20(2), 2007, pp. 137–49.

— 'Lenin on Holiday', *Revolutionary Russia*, 21(2), 2008, pp. 115–134.

Erokhin, A. S., *Shushenskii Arsenal – O lichnoi biblioteke V. I. Lenina*, Moscow: Izd. Kniga, 1971.

Fedirko, P. S., *V. I. Lenin i Krasnoyarskii Krai*, Krasnoyarsk: Krasnoyarskoe knizhnoe izdatel'stvo, 1986.

Fischer, Louis, *The Life of Lenin*, London: Phoenix Press, 2002.

Fotieva, Lydia, *Pages from Lenin's Life*, Moscow: Foreign Languages Publishing House, 1960.

Fox, Ralph, *Lenin: A Biography*, London: Gollancz, 1933.

Ganetskii [Hanecki], Yakov, 'Priezd tovarishcha Lenina iz Shveitsarii v Rossiyu', in Platten, pp. 134–40.

Gernet, M. N. *Istoriya tsarskoi tyur'mi*, vol. 3, *1870–1900*, Moscow: Gos. izd. yuridicheskoi literaturoi, 1963.

Golikov, Georgy Nazarovich, *Vospominaniya o V. I. Lenine*, 5 vols, Moscow, Politizdat, 1968–70 [Golikov, *VoVIL*].

— *Vladimir Il'ich Lenin: Biograficheskaya Khronika, 1870-1924*, 12 vols, Moscow: Izd. politicheskoi literatury, 1970–82.

Gorky, Maxim, *Days with Lenin*, London: M. Lawrence, 1933.

Haimson, L., *Russian Marxists and the Origins of Bolshevism*, Cambridge, Mass.: Harvard University Press, 1955.

Hill, Elizabeth, ed., *The Letters of Lenin*, London: Chapman & Hall, 1937.

Institut Marksizma-Leninizma, *Vospominaniya oVladimire Il'iche Lenine*, 3 vols, Moscow: Izd. politicheskoi literatury 1956–60. [*VoVIL*]

'Inessa Armand: neizvestnoe pis'mo Leninu. Iz dnevnikov', *Svobodnaya Mysl'*, no. 3, 1992, pp. 80–88.

Ivanksy, A., ed., *Comet in the Night: The Story of Alexander Ulyanov's Heroic Life and Tragic Death*, Honolulu: University Press of the Pacific, 2004.

Ivansky, A. I., *Lenin v Sibirskoi ssylke*, Moscow: Izd. politicheskoi literatury, 1946.

Krasnovsky, A., *In the Footsteps of Lenin: Ul'yanovsk, Kazan, Krasnoyarsk, Shushenskoe*, Moscow: Progress, 1975.

Krupskaya, Nadezhda, *Memories of Lenin*, London: Panther, 1970.

Krupskaya, 'O Vladimire Il'iche', in Golikov, *VoVIL*, vol. 2, pp. 581–5.

Krzhizhanovsky, G., *O Vladimire Il'iche*, Moscow: Partiinoe izdatel'stvo, 1924.

Latyshev, Anatoly, *Rassekrechennyi Lenin*, Moscow: Izd. 'Mart', 1996.

Lenin, *Collected Works* (English edition), 45 vols, Moscow: Progress, 1963–70. [*CW*]

Lenin, *Perepiska V. I. Lenina s redaktsiei gazety Iskra*, 3 vols, Moscow: Mysl', 1969–70.

'Lenin and Libraries', *IFLA* Annual 1970, Moscow Centenary Conference, Copenhagen: Scandinavian Library Centre, 1970.

Lepeshinskaya, Ol'ga, *Vstrechi s Il'ichem* Moscow, Izd. politicheskoi literatury, 1966.

Levine, Isaac Don, *The Man Lenin*, New York: Thomas Seltzer, 1924.

Lied, Jonas, *Prospector in Siberia*, New York: Oxford University Press, 1945.

Lilina [Zinov'eva], Zina, 'Tov. Lenin edet v Rossiyu', *Leningradskaya Pravda*, 16 April 1924, no. 87.

Lyudvinskaya, T. F., *Velikii, blizkii, prostoi*, Moscow: Znanie, 1969.

McNeal, Professor Robert H., 'Lenin and Lise de K . . . A Fabrication', *Slavic Review*, XXVIII (3) Sept. 1969, pp. 471–4.

McNeal, Robert, *Bride of the Revolution: Krupskaya and Lenin*, London: Gollancz, 1973.

Marcu, Valeriu *Lenin*, London: Gollancz, 1928.

McNight, David, 'Lenin and the Reinvention of the Russian Conspiratorial Tradition', in McNight, *Espionage and the Roots of the Cold War*, London: Frank Cass, 2002.

Mel'nichenko, Vladimir, *Ya tebya ochen' lyubila: pravda o Lenine i Armand*, Moscow: Voskresen'e, 2002.

Meshalkin, Petr, *Sibirskaya ssylka V. I. Lenina*, Krasnoyarsk: Krasnoyarskoe knizhnoe izdatel'stvo, 1987.

Mirsky, D. S., *Lenin*, London: The Holme Press, 1931.

Mushtukov, V. E., *Zdes' zhil i rabotal Lenin*, Leningrad: Lenizdat, 1967.

Novikov, V., *Lenin i deyatel'nost' iskrovykh grupp v Rossii 1900–03*, Moscow: Mysl', 1978.

Novorussky, Mikhail, *Zapiski shlissel'burzhtsa 1887–1905*, Petrograd: Gosudarstvennoe izdatel'stvo, 1924.

Petrov, F. N, et al., *O Vladimire Il'iche Lenine: Vospominaniya 1900–1922 gody*, Moscow: Izd. politicheskoi literatury, 1963. [*OVIL, 1900–1922*]

Payne, R., *The Life and Death of Lenin*, London: Grafton Books, 1964.

Pearson, Michael, *Inessa, Lenin's Mistress*, London: Duckworth, 2001.

Perris, G. H. *Russia in Revolution*, London: Chapman & Hall, 1905, chapter VI, 'Annals of Schlüsselburg'.

Pipes, Richard, 'The Intellectual Evolution of Lenin', in Pipes, ed., *Revolutionary Russia*, London: Oxford University Press, 1968.

— *The Unknown Lenin*, New Haven: Yale University Press, 1998.

Possony, Stefan T., *Lenin: The Compulsive Revolutionary*, London: Allen & Unwin, 1966.

Potresov, Alexander N., 'Lenin', in *Posmertnyi sbornik proizvedenii*, Paris: Maison du Livre Etranger, 1927, pp. 293–304.

Radek, Karl, 'Lenin's "Sealed Train"', *New York Times*, 19 February 1922, p. 92.

—, 'V plombirovannom vagone'; in Platten, pp. 127–33.

Read, Christopher, *From Tsar to Soviets: The Russian People and their Revolution*, New York: Oxford University Press, 1996.

— *Lenin: A Revolutionary Life*, London: Routledge, 2005.

— 'Retrieving the Historical Lenin', in Ian D. Thatcher, ed., *Reinterpreting Revolutionary Russia: Essays in Honour of James D. White*, Basingstoke: Palgrave Macmillan, 2006.

Rice, C., *Lenin: Portrait of a Professional Revolutionary*, London: Cassell, 1990.

Schapiro, L., and P. Reddaway, *Lenin the Man, the Theorist, the Leader: A Reappraisal*, London: Pall Mall Press, 1967.

Service, Robert, *Lenin: A Political Life*, 3 vols, Basingstoke: Macmillan, 1985–1995

— *Lenin: A Biography*, London: Macmillan, 2000.

Shtein, Mikhail. *Ulyanovy i Leniny: semeinye tayny*, St Petersburg: Neva, 2004.

Shtein, M., and G. Sidorovnin, *Vozhd': Lenin, kotorogo my ne znali*, Saratov: 'Slovo', 1992.

Shub, David, *Lenin*, Harmondsworth: Penguin, 1966.

— 'Fact or fiction on Lenin's role', *New International*, 16(2), pp. 86–91.

Simsova, Sylva, *Lenin, Krupskaya and Libraries*, London: Bingley, 1968.

Solomon, G. A., *Lenin i ego sem'ya, Ul'yanovy*, Paris: Imprimerie des travailleurs intellectuels, 1931.

Struve, Petr, 'My Contacts and Conflicts with Lenin', *Slavonic and East European Review*, XII (36) April 1934, pp. 573–95, and 'My Meeting with Lenin', XIII, July 1934, pp. 66–84.

Suliashvili, D., 'Vstrechi s Leninym v emigratsii, *Neva* (2), 1957, pp. 135–44.

Theen, Rolf, and H. W. Theen, *Lenin*, London: Quartet Books, 1974.

They Knew Lenin: Reminiscences of Foreign Contemporaries, Honolulu: University of the Pacific, 2005.

Treadgold, Donald, *Lenin and His Rivals: The Struggle for Russia's Future 1898–1906*, London: Methuen, 1955.

Trotsky, Leon, *On Lenin: Notes Towards a Biography*, London: Harrap & Co., 1971.

— *The Young Lenin*, Harmondsworth: Penguin, 1972

Turton, Katy, *Forgotten Lives: The Role of Lenin's Sisters in the Russian Revolution, 1864–1937*, Basingstoke: Palgrave Macmillan, 2007.

Ulam, Adam B., *Lenin and the Bolsheviks*, London: Fontana, 1965.

Usievich, Elena, 'Iz vospominanii o V. I. Lenine', in Platten, pp. 141–55.

Valentinov, Nikolay, *The Early Years of Lenin*, Ann Arbor: University of Michigan, 1968.

— *Encounters with Lenin*, London: Oxford University Press, 1969.

Vasilieva, Larisa, and Kathy Porter, *Kremlin Wives*, London: Weidenfeld & Nicolson, 1994.

Volkogonov, Dmitri, *Lenn: Life and Legacy*, New York: The Free Press, 1994.

Vol'ner, I. N., 'Psevdonimy V. I. Lenina', Leningrad: Lenizdat, 1968.

Weber, G., and H., *Lenin: Life and Works*, New York: Facts on File, 1980.

White, James, *Lenin: The Practice and Theory of Revolution*, Basingstoke, Palgrave Macmillan, 2001.

Williams, Beryl, *Lenin*, London: Longman, 2000.

Williams. Robert C., *The Other Bolsheviks: Lenin and His Critics*, Bloomington: Indiana University Press, 1986.

Wolfe, Bertram D., *Three Who Made a Revolution*, Harmondsworth: Penguin, 1964.

— 'Lenin and Inessa Armand', *Slavic Review*, 22(1), March 1963, pp. 96–114.
Zinov'ev, Grigory, *Lenin*, Leningrad: Gosudarstvennoe izdatel'stvo, 1924.

3 The Revolutionary Movement and Its Surveillance

Allason, Rupert, *The Branch: A History of the Metropolitan Police Special Branch*, *1883–1983*, London: Secker & Warburg, 1983.

Ascher, Abraham, *The Revolution of 1905*, 2 vols, Stanford: Stanford University Press, 1988–92.

Baedeker's Russia, London: G. Allen & Unwin (1971 facsimile of 1914 edn).

Balabanoff, Angelica, *My Life as a Rebel*, London: Hamish Hamilton, 1938.

Baron, Samuel H., *Plekhanov the Father of Russian Marxism*, London: Routledge & Kegan Paul, 1963.

Bergman, Jay, *Vera Zasulich: A Biography*, Stanford: Stanford University Press, 1983.

Bobrovskaya, Cecilia, *Twenty Years in Underground Russia: Memoirs of a Rank and File Bolshevik*, San Francisco: Proletarian Publishers, 1934.

Brust, Harold, *In Plain Clothes*, London: Stanley Paul, 1937.

— *I Guarded Kings*, London, Stanley Paul, 1935.

Bunyan, Tony, *History and Practice of the Political Police in Britain*, London: J. Friedmann, 1976.

Burenin, N. E., *Pamyatnye gody: vospominaniya*, Leningrad: Lenizdat, 1961.

Chernyshevsky, Nikolay, *What Is To Be Done?*, New York: Vintage Books, 1961.

Clements, Barbara Evans, *Bolshevik Women*, Cambridge: Cambridge University Press, 1997.

Conrad, Joseph, *The Secret Agent*, Harmonsworth: Penguin, 1986.

— *Under Western Eyes*, London: Penguin, 2007.

Crisp, Olga, and Linda Edmondson, *Civil Rights in Imperial Russia*, Oxford: Clarendon Press, 1989.

Daly, J. W. *Autocracy under Siege: Security Police and Opposition in Russia 1860–1905*, De Kalb: Northern Illinois University Press, 1998.

Deutscher, *The Prophet Armed, Trotsky 1879–1992*, London: Verso, 2003.

Drabkina, Elizaveta, *Chernye sukhari*, Moscow: Khudozhestvennaya literatura, 1970.

Ehrenburg, Ilya, *People and Life*: *Memoirs of 1891–1917*, London: MacGibbon & Kee, 1961.

Elwood, R. Carter, *Russian Social-Democracy in the Underground (1907–14)*, Assen: Van Gorcum & Co., 1974.

— *Roman Malinovsky: A Life Without a Cause*, Newtonville, Mass.: Oriental Resource Partners, 1977.

— *Inessa Armand: Revolutionary and Feminist*, Cambridge: Cambridge University Press, 1992.

Figes, Orlando, *A People's Tragedy: The Russian Revolution 1891–1924*, London: Cape, 1996.

Figner, Vera, *Polnoe sobranie sochinenii*, vol. III, *Posle Shlissel'burga*, Moscow: Izd. vsesoyuznogo obshchestva politkatorzhani i ssylno-poslentsev, 1932.

— *Memoirs of a Revolutionist*, De Kalb: Northern Illinois University Press, 1991.

Fischer, Ben B., *Okhrana: The Paris Operations of the Russian Imperial Police*, Washington: Center for the Study of Intelligence, 1997.

Fitch, Herbert, *Traitors Within*, London: Hurst & Blackett, 1933.

Fomicheva, L. N., *N. K. Krupskaya: zhizn' i deyatelnost' v fotografiyakh i dokumentakh*, Moscow: Plakat, 1988.

Garnett, Richard, *Constance Garnett: A Heroic Life*, London: Sinclair-Stevenson, 1991.

Geifmann, Anna, *Thou Shalt Kill: Revolutionary Terrorism in Russia 1894–1917*, Princeton: Princeton University Press, 1993.

Getzler, Israel, *Martov: A Political Biography*, Cambridge: Cambridge University Press, 1967.

Goldman, Emma, 'The Tragedy of the Political Exiles', *The Nation*, 10 October 1934, pp. 401–2.

Gorelov, I. E., *Bol'sheviki: dokumenty po istorii bol'shevizma 1903–1916*, Moscow: Izd. Politicheskoi literatury, 1990.

Haupt, Georges, and Jean-Jacques Marie, *Makers of the Russian Revolution*, London: Allen & Unwin, 1974.

Hingley, Ronald, *The Russian Secret Police 1565–1970*, London: Hutchinson, 1970.

Holmes, Colin, 'Government Files and Privileged Access', *Social History* 6(3), 1981, pp. 335–50.

Hulse, J. W., *Revolutionists in London*, Oxford: Clarendon Press, 1970.

Kahn, David, *The Codebreakers: The Story of Secret Writing*, London: Sphere, 1977.

Kalmykov, A. G., ed., *Boevaya tekhnicheskaya gruppa pri PK i TsK RSDRP*, St Petersburg: Gosudarstvennyi muzei politcheskoi istorii Rossii, 1999.

Keep, J. H. L., *The Rise of Social Democracy in Russia*, Oxford: Clarendon Press, 1963.

Kimball, Alan, 'The Harassment of Russian Revolutionaries Abroad', *Oxford Slavonic Papers*, NS, 6 1973, pp. 48–65.

Kropotkin, Peter, *Memoirs of a Revolutionist*, London: Smith Elder, 1899.

Lauchlan, Iain, *Russian Hide and Seek: The Tsarist Secret Police in St Petersburg 1906–1914*, Helsinki: Vammalan Kirjapaino Oy, 2002.

Lepeshinskaya, Ol'ga, 'Vstrechi s Il'ichem', Moscow: Izd. politicheskoi literaturoi, 1971.

Lepeshinsky, Panteleimon, *Na povorote: ot kontsa 80-kh godov k 1905 g.*, Moscow: Nauka, 1922.

Lih, Lars T., 'The Organization Question: Lenin and the Underground', in Lih, *Lenin Rediscovered*, Boston: Brill, 2005, pp. 433–88.

Lyadov, Mikhail, *Iz zhizni partii: nakanune i v gody pervoi revolyutsii*. Moscow: Izd. kommunisticheskogo universiteta, 1926.

MacNaughton, Melville, *Days of My Years,* London: Arnold, 1914.

Meijer, Jan, *Knowledge and Revolution: The Russian Colony in Zurich, 1870–3,* Assen: Van Gorcum, 1955.

Montefiore, Simon Sebag, *Young Stalin,* London: Weidenfeld & Nicolson, 2007.

Naarden, Bruno, *Socialist Europe and Revolutionary Russia: Perception and Prejudice 1848–1923,* Cambridge: Cambridge University Press, 1992.

O'Connor, T. E., *The Engineer of the Revolution: L. B. Krasin and the Bolsheviks 1870–1926,* Boulder: Westview Press, 1992.

Piatnitsky, Osip, *Memoirs of a Bolshevik,* London: Martin Lawrence, 1925.

Pipes, Richard, *The Russian Revolution,* London: Fontana, 1992.

– *Social Democracy and the St Petersburg Labour Movement,* Cambridge, Mass.: Harvard University Press, 1963.

— *Struve, Liberal on the Left 1870–1905,* 2 vols, Cambridge, Mass.: Harvard University Press, 1970–80.

Pope, Arthur Upham, *Maxim Litvinoff,* London: Secker & Warburg, 1943.

Porter, Bernard, 'The British Government and Political Refugees 1880–1914', in Slatter.

— *The Origins of the Vigilant State: The London Metropolitan Police Special Branch before the First World War,* Woodbridge: Boydell, 1991.

Porter, Cathy, *Alexandra Kollontai,* London: Virago, 1980.

Pozner, S. M., *Pervaya boevaya organizatsiya bol'shevikov 1905–07 gg.,* Moscow: Staryi bol'shevik, 1934.

Rappaport, Helen, *Joseph Stalin: A Biographical Companion,* Santa Barbara: ABC-Clio, 1999.

Rudd, Charles A., *Fontanka 16: The Tsar's Secret Police,* Stroud: Sutton, 1999.

Salisbury, Harrison E., *Black Night, White Snow: Russia's Revolutions 1905–1917,* London: Cassell, 1977.

Sheinis, *Maxim Maksimovich Litvinov,* Moscow: Izd. politicheskoi literaturoi, 1989.

Shotman, Aleksandr, *Zapiski starogo bol'shevika,* Moscow: n.p., 1930.

Shukman, Harold, ed., *The Blackwell Encyclopedia of the Russian Revolution,* Oxford: Blackwell, 1988.

Shuranov, N. P., *Soratniki V. I. Lenina v Sibiri,* Kemerovo: Kemerovskoe knizhnoe izdatel'stvo, 1981.

Slatter, John, *From the Other Shore: Russian Political Emigrants in Britain 1880–1917,* London: Cass, 1984.

Stasova, Elena, *Vospominaniya,* Moscow: Izd. Mysl', 1969.

Stepniak, Sergey, *Underground Russia: Revolutionary Profiles and Sketches from Life,* New York: Scribner's, 1883.

Sukhanov, N. N., *Zapiski o revolyutsii,* vol. 2, Moscow: Izd. politicheskoi literaturoi, 1991.

Sweeney, John, *At Scotland Yard,* London: Grant Richards, 1904.

Thompson, W. H., *Guard from the Yard,* London: Jarrolds, 1938.

Trotsky, Leon, *My Life: An Attempt at Autobiography,* New York: Pathfinder, 1970.

Ulam, Adam B., *Prophets and Conspirators in Pre-Revolutionary Russia*, New Brunswick: Transaction Publications, 1998.

Venturi, Franco, *Roots of Revolution: A History of the Populist and Socialist Movements in 19th Century Russia*, London: Phoenix Press, 2001.

Wildman, A., 'Lenin's Battle with Kustarnichestvo: The *Iskra* Organization in Russia', *Slavic Review*, 23, 1964, pp. 479–503.

Woodall, Edwin T., *Secrets of Scotland Yard*, London: John Lane, 1936.

Zeman, Z. A. B., *The Merchant of Revolution: The Life of Alexander Israel Helphand (Parvus)*, London: Oxford University Press, 1965.

Zuckerman, Fredric S., *The Tsarist Secret Police in Russian Society 1880–1917*, London: Macmillan, 1996.

— *The Tsarist Secret Police Abroad*, Basingstoke: Palgrave Macmillan, 2003.

4 Lenin in Exile
Capri

Andreevna, Mariya, 'Vstrechi s Leninym', in *Perepiska, vospominaniya, stat'i, dokumenty*, Moscow: Iskusstvo, 1961.

Byalik, Boris, *V. I. Lenin i A. M. Gor'ky: Pis'ma, vospominaniya, dokumenty*, Moscow: Nauka, 1969.

Caruso, Bruno, *Lenin a Capri: intelletuali, marxismo, religione*, Bari: Dedalo Libri, 1978.

Cerio, Edwin, *That Capri Air*, London: Heineman 1929.

— *The Masque of Capri*, London: Thomas Nelson, 1957.

Desnitsky, Vasilii, *A. M. Gor'ky: ocherki zhizni i tvorchestva*, Moscow: Izd. khudozhestvennoi literatury, 1959.

Guseva, Zinaida, *Svidaniya na Kapri*, Moscow: Izd. Sovetskaya Rossiya, 1968.

Hazzard, Shirley, *Greene on Capri*, London: Virago, 2000.

Levin, Dan, *Stormy Petrel: Life and Work of Maxim Gorky*, New York: Appleton-Century, 1965.

Moskovskii, R. V., *Lenin v Italii, Chekhoslovakii, Pol'she*, Moscow: Izd. politicheskoi literatury, 1986.

Ross, Alan, *Reflections on Blue Water: Journeys in the Gulf of Naples*, London: Harvill Press, 1979.

Tamborra, Angelo, *Esuli Russi in Italia dal 1905 al 1917*, Rome: Tamborra, 1977.

Troyat, Henri, *Gorky*, London: Allison & Busby, 1989.

Wolfe, Bertram D., *The Bridge and the Abyss: The Troubled Friendship of Gorky and Lenin*, London: Pall Mall Press, 1968.

Yedlin, Tova, *Maxim Gorky: A Political Biography*, Westport: Praeger, 1999.

Finland, Sweden and Denmark

Dashkov, Yuri, *Po leninskim mestam Skandinavii: zhurnalistskii poisk*, Moscow: Sovetskaya Rossiya, 1971.

— *U istokov dobrososedstva: Iz istorii rossiisko-finlyandskikh revolyutsionnykh svyazei*, Moscow: Mysl', 1980.

Egede-Nissen, Adam, *Et Liv i Strid*, Oslo: J. W. Kappelen, 1945.

Futrell, Michael, *Northern Underground: Episodes of Russian Revolutionary Transport and Communications through Scandinavia and Finland 1863–1917*, London: Faber & Faber, 1963.

Koivisto, Mauno, *Itsenaiseki Imperiumin Kainalossa*, Helsinki: Kustanusosakehytiö Tammi, 2004.

Koronen, V. I. *Lenin i Finlyandiya*, Leningrad: Lenizdat, 1977.

[n.a.] *Lenin v vospominaniyakh finnov*, Moscow: Izd. Politicheskoi Literaturoi, 1979.

Lindström, Ludvig, 'På flykt Vladimir Uljanov mera bekant som Lenin', in *Allsvensk samling*, Gothenburg, December 1946, pp. 14–16, 44–8.

Malmberg, Ikka, 'What if Lenin had drowned here?', *Helsingin Sanomat*, 8 December 2004 (online English edition).

Moskovsky, Pavel, *Lenin v Shvetsii*, Moscow: Izd. politicheskoi literaturoi, 1972.

Nerman, Ture, *Allt Var Rott*, Stockholm: Kooperativa förbundets bökforlag, 1950.

Numminen, J., ed., *Lenin ja Suomi*, Helsinki: Opetusministeriö Valtion Painatuskeskus, 1987.

Semenov, V. G., *Lenin v Finlyandii*, M: Izd. politicheskoi literaturoi, 1977.

Ström, Fredrik, *I Stormig Tid: Memoarer*, Stockholm: P. A. Norstedt, 1942.

Thomsen, Carl, 'Lenin's Visits to Denmark', Copenhagen: Royal Library, 1970.

Willers, Uno, 'Lenin i Stockholm', Stockholm: Rabén & Sjögren, 1970.

France

Aline, A., *Lénine à Paris*, Paris: Les Revues, 1929.

Boulouque, Sylvain, 'Mardochée Brunswick, in *Archives Juives* 30(2) 1997, pp. 119–20.

Elwood, R. Carter, 'Lenin and the Social Democratic Schools for Underground Party Workers 1909–11', *Political Science Quarterly*, 81(3) September 1966, pp. 370–91.

'His Paris Concierge Pays Tribute to Lenin', *New York Times*, 25 April 1921.

Feld, Charles, *Quand Lénine vivait à Paris*, Paris: Editions Cercle d'Art et Club Messidor, 1967.

Fotieva, L. N., 'Vstrechi s Leninym v Zheneve i Parizhe, in Golikov, *VoVil*, vol. 2, pp. 140–57.

Fréville, Jean, *Lénine à Paris*, Paris: Editions socials, 1968.

Gabrilovich, Evgeny, and Sergei Yutkevich, 'Lenin in Paris', in *A Film Trilogy about Lenin*, Moscow: Progress, 1985.

Kaganova, R Yu., *Lenin vo Frantsii Dek. 1908– Iyun' 1912*, Moscow: Mysl', 1972.

Kataev, Valentin, *Malen'kaya zheleznaya dver' v stene*, in *Sobranie sochinenii*, Moscow: Khudozhestvennaya literatura, vol. 6, 1984, see esp. pp. 54–69.

[n.a.] 'Les refugiés révolutionnaires russes à Paris', *Cahiers du Monde russe et soviétique*, 6, July–Sept. 1965, pp. 419–36.

Lyudvinskaya, T. F., 'Parizh', in Lyudvinskaya, *Velikii, blizkii, prostoi*, Moscow: Izd. Znanie, 1969.

Moskovsky, P. V., and V. G. Semenov, *Lenin vo Frantsii, Bel'gii i Danii*, Moscow: Izd. Politicheskoĭ Literatury, 1982.

Rappoport, Charles, 'Lénine à Paris', in *Russie d'aujourd'hui*, no. 70, January 1938; reprinted in Rappoport, *Une vie révolutionnaire, 1883–1940*, Paris: Maison des sciences de l'homme.

Shaginyan, M., 'Retracing Lenin's Steps' [in France], in Mariya Prilezhaeva, *A Remarkable Year*, Moscow: Progress, 1980.

Toussaint, Franz, *Lénine inconnu*, Paris: Les Editions Universelles, 1952.

Galicia (now Poland)

Adamczewski, Jan, *Polskie Dni Lenina 1912–14*, Warsaw: Wydawnictwo Interpress, 1970.

— and Jozef Pociecha, *Lenin w Krakowie*, Kraków: Wydawnictwo Literackie, 1974.

Bagotsky [Bagocki], Sergiusz, 'V. I. Lenin v Krakove i Poronine', in *VOVIL*, vol. 1, pp. 438–56.

Bartosik, Marek, 'Wódz obalony lebiodka', in *Gazeta Krakowska*, 5 September 2008, pp. 8–9.

Bernov, Y., and A. Manusevich, *Lenin v Krakove*, Moscow: Izd. politicheskoi literaturoi, 1972.

— *V krakovskoi emigratsii. Zhizn' i deyatel'nost' V. I. Lenina. 1912–14*, Moscow: Izd. politicheskoi literaturoi, 1988.

Dubacki, Leonard et al., *Polacy o Leninie: wspomnienia*, Warsaw: Ksiazka i Wiedza, 1970.

'Eyewitness Reports' [on Lenin tourist industry in Poland], *News from Behind the Iron Curtain*, 1956, 5(2), p. 28.

Gabrilovich, Evgeny, and Sergei Yutkevich, 'Lenin in Poland', film script, in *A Film Trilogy about Lenin*, Progress, Moscow: Progess, 1985.

Ganetsky [Hanecki], Yakub, 'S Leninym', *Voprosy istorii KPSS*, 1970, no. 3, pp. 96–101.

Goncharova, S. M., 'Iz istorii krakovsko-poroninskogo arkhiva V. I. Lenina', in *Lenin i Pol'sha*, Moscow, 1970, pp. 392–401.

Hartig, Edward, *Krakow*, Warsaw: Wydawnictwo "Sport i Turystyka", 1980.

Little, Frances Delanoy, *Sketches in Poland*, London: Andrew Melrose, 1915.

Najdus, Walentyna, *Lenin i Krupska w Krakowskim Zwiazku Pomocy dla Wiezńiów Politycznych*, Kraków: Wydawnictwo Literackie, 1965.

Sieradzki, Jozef, *Pol'skie gody Lenina*, Moscow: Izd. politicheskoi literatury, 1966.

Sobczak, Jan, 'Two Years in Poland', in *World Marxist Review*, December 1969, 12(12), pp. 16–19.

Trepper, Leopold, *The Great Game: The Story of the Red Orchestra*, London: Michael Joseph, 1977.

'Upheaval in the East: Lenin Statue in Mothballs,' *New York Times*, 11 December 1989.

Watson, Peggy, 'Nowa Huta: The Politics of Postcommunism and the Past', in Edmunds, J., and B. S. Turner, eds, *Narrative, Generational Consciousness, and Politics*, Lanham, Md: Rowman & Littlefield.

Germany and Austria-Hungary

Amort, Cestir, 'Lenin in Prague', *World Marxist Review*, 13(6), 1970, pp. 19–21.

Baeumler, Ernst, *Verschwörung in Schwabing: Lenins Begegnung mit Deutschland*, Düsseldorf: Econ Verlag, 1972.

Baur, Johannes, *Die russische Kolonie in München 1900–1945*, Wiesbaden: Harrassowitz Verlag, 1998.

Brachmann, B., *Russische sozialdemokraten in Berlin, 1895–1914* Berlin: Akademie-Verlag, 1962.

Haimson, Leopold, *The Making of Three Russian Revolutionaries*, Cambridge: Cambridge University Press, 1987.

Hitzer, Friedrich, *Lenin in München*, Munich: Bayerischen Gesellschaft, 1977.

Huber, Gerdi, *Das klassische Schwabing*, Munich: Neue Schriftenreihe des Stadtarchivs, 1973.

Ivanov, Miroslav, *Lenin v Praze*, Prague: n.p., 1960.

Moskovsky, P. V., *Lenin v Italii, Chekhoslovakii, Pol'she*, Moscow: Izd. politicheskoi literatury, 1986.

Muraveva, L. L., et al., *Lenin v Myunkhene: pamyatnye mesta*, Moscow: Izd. politicheskoi literaturoi, 1976.

Onufriev, Evgeny, *Vstrechi s Leninym – vospominaniya delegata Prazhskoi konferentsii*, Moscow: Izd. politicheskoi literatury, 1966.

Ortmann, F., *Revolutionäre im Exil, 1888–1903*, Stuttgart: Steiner, 1994.

Sackett, Robert Eben, *Popular Entertainment, Class and Politics in Munich 1900–1923*, Cambridge, Mass.: Harvard University Press, 1982.

Schorske, Carl, *German Social Democracy 1905–1917*, New York: Harper & Row, 1972.

Swain, G., 'The Bolsheviks' Prague Conference Revisited', *Revolutionary Russia*, 2(1), June 1989, pp. 134–40.

Williams. Robert C., *Culture in Exile: Russian Emigrés in Germany 1881–1941*, Ithaca: Cornell University Press, 1972.

— 'Russians in Germany: 1900–1914', *Journal of Contemporary History* 1(4), 1966, pp. 121–49.

London

Aldred, Guy, *No Traitor's Gate*, 1(12) and 2(1), Glasgow: Strickland Press, 1957.

Alekseev, N. A., 'V. I. Lenin v Londone', in Golikov, *VoVIL*, pp. 86–91.

Armfelt, Count E., 'Russia in East London', in George Robert Sims, *Living London*, vol. 1, London, 1906.

Balabanoff, Angelica, 'Lenin and the London Congress of 1907', in *Impressions of Lenin*, pp. 17–25.

Bassalygo, D., in *VoVIL*, vol. 3, 1960.

Beer, Max, 'Interview with Lenin' in Beer, *Fifty Years of International Socialism*, 1935 pp. 144–59.

Bergman, Jay, *Vera Zasulich: A Biography*, Stanford: Stanford University Press, 1983.

Bowman, William J., 'Lenin in London', *Contemporary Review*, 151, Jan./June 1957, pp. 336–8.

Brailsford, Henry, 'The Russian Congress', *Daily News*, 4 June, 1907, p. 6.

— 'When Lenin and Trotsky Were in London', *Listener*, vol. XXXIX, 1 January 1948.

Briggs, Asa, and Anne Macartney, *Toynbee Hall: The First 100 Years*, London: Routledge & Kegan Paul, 1984.

Coates, Zelda Kahan, 'Memories of Lenin', *Labour Monthly*, 50, November 1968, pp. 506–8.

Daily Express, 5 January 1950.

Daily Mirror: isssues for 10, 11, 13, 14, 15, 16, 17, 18, 22 May 1907.

Deutsch, Leo, 'The Russian Social Democratic Congress', *Justice*, 8 June 1907.

Drabkina, F., *Vospominaniya o vtorom s"ezde RSDRP*, 1934.

Dudden, A. P., *Joseph Fels and the Single Tax Movement*, Philadelphia: Temple University Press, 1971.

Dudden, A. P., and T. H. von Laue, 'The RSDLP and Joseph Fels: A Study in Intercultural Contact, *American Historical Review*, vol. 61 (1955–6), pp. 21–47.

Fishman, William J., 'Lenin in London' *Anglia* 24(4) October 1967.

— 'Millie Sabel – Yiddish Anarchist' in *East London Arts Magazine* 4(1), winter 1967.

— *East End Jewish Radicals 1875–1914*, London: Duckworth, 1975.

Free Russia: the organ of the English Society of Friends of Russian Freedom, issues for May–June 1907.

Gandurin, K., *Epizody podpol'ya: vospominaniya starogo bol'shevika* Moscow: Molodaya gvardiya, 1934.

Henderson, Bob, 'Lenin and the British Museum Library', *Solanus*, NS 4, 1990, pp. 3–15.

— *Lenin at the British Library*, The British Library [Slavonic & East European Collections], 1990.

Higgins, A. G., 'A History of the Brotherhood Church', Stapleton, Yorks: Brotherhood Church, 1982.

Hollingsworth, Barry, 'The Society of Friends of Russian Freedom: English Liberals and Russian Socialists, 1890–1917', *Oxford Slavonic Papers* NS 3, 1970, pp. 45–64.

'Memoirs of a Meeting with Lenin', *Islington Gazette*, 31 January 1964.

Justice: The Organ of Social Democracy, 7 March, 2 May 1903; 15 July 1905; 30 March, 1 and 15 June 1907.

Karzhansky, N. S., in 'V. I. Lenin na s"ezde RSDRP', *VoVIL*, vol. 1 1956, pp. 356–63.

Kadish, Sharman, *Bolsheviks and British Jews*, London: Cass, 1992.

Karachan, N. V., *V. I. Lenin v Londone*, Leningrad: Izd. Prosveschchenie, 1969.

Kendall, Walter, 'Russian Emigration and British Marxist Socialism, *International Review of Social History*, 8, 1963, pp. 351–78.

Kendall, Walter, *The Revolutionary Movement in Britain, 1900–21*, London: Weidenfeld & Nicolson, 1969.

Kochan, Lionel, 'Lenin in London', *History Today* 20(4) 1970, April, pp. 229–35.

Lee, H. W., and E. Archbold, *Social-Democracy in Britain*, London: The Social-Democratic Federation, 1935.

Lenin, obituary for Harry Quelch 1913, in *CW* 19, pp. 369–71.

'Lenin and His Wife Were Good, Quiet Tenants', Letters to the Editor, *Islington Gazette*, 15 October 1963.

'Lenin's Clerkenwell Home: Recollections of his Landlady', *Guardian*, 20 July 1939, p. 15.

'Lenin Was Their Lodger', *Socialist Commentary*, May 1970, pp. 14–15.

Lepeshinsky, Panteleimon, *Protokoly vtorogo s"ezda RSDRP*, Leningrad: Priboi, 1924.

Leventhal, F. M., *The Last Dissenter: H. N. Brailsford and His World*, Oxford: Clarendon Press, 1985.

Levin, Elia, 'Conference of the Russian Socialists in London', *Justice*, 18 May 1907.

London Landmarks: Marx, Engels and Lenin, London: Communist Party, n.d.

Lyadov, *Iz zhizni partii nakanune i v gody pervoi revolyutsii*, Moscow: Izd. Kommunisticheskogo Universiteta, 1926.

Maisky, Ivan, *Journey into the Past*, London: Hutchinson, 1960.

Masefield, John, *Letters to Reyna*, London: Buchan & Enright, 1983.

Meacham, Standish, *Toynbee Hall and Social Reform 1880–1914*, New Haven: Yale University Press, 1987.

Mikhailov, I. K., 'Vospominaniya o V. I. Lenine', in *VoVIL*, vol. 3, 1960.

Morning Post, 11 and 18 May 1907.

Muraveva, Lyudmila, *Lenin in London: Memorial Places*, Moscow: Progress, 1983.

Murray-Browne, Caroline, 'Richter, alias Lenin, the forgotten exiles of Finsbury', *Islington Gazette*, 23 March 1978, p. 33.

Pimlott, J. A. R., *Toynbee Hall: Fifty Years of Social Progress*, London: J. M. Dent, 1935.

Quelch, Tom, interview re Lenin, *Evening Standard*, 30 August 1941, p. 2.

Rocker, Fermin, *The East End Years*, London: Freedom, 1998.

Rocker, Rudolf, *The London Years*, London: Robert Anscombe & Co., 1956.

Rothstein, Andrew, 'Lenin in Britain', London: Communist Party, 1970.

— 'A House on Clerkenwell Green', London: Lawrence & Wishart, 1966.

'Russian Labour Party: Their Congress in London', *Pall Mall Gazette*, May–June, 1907.

Scott, L., 'When the Lenins Lived in Holford Square', *Islington News*, 21 November, 1960.

Semenov, V. M., 'Po leninskim mestam v Londone', Moscow: Gospolitizdat, 1959.

— 'Lenin in London', *Soviet Weekly*, 21 April 1960.

Schapiro, Leonard, 'Lenin and the Russian Revolution', *History Today*, 20 May 1970, pp. 324–30.

Slatter, John, *From the Other Shore: Russian Political Emigrants in Britain 1880–1917*, London: Frank Cass, 1984.

— 'Our Friends from the East: Russian Revolutionaries and British Radicals', *History Today*, 53, October 2003, pp. 43–9.

Stalin, Joseph, 'Notes of a Delegate', London: Lawrence & Wishart, 1941.

Stracey, John, 'The Great Awakening', *Encounter*, pamphlet no. 5, London, 1961.

Surovtseva, N. N. et al., *Vospominaniya o II s"ezde RDSRP*, Moscow: Izd. politicheskoi literatury, 1983.

Thomas, Kay, 'History Was Made in London', *Soviet Weekly*, 18 April 1970, pp. 16–17.

Vernitsky , Anatoly, 'Russian Revolutionaries and English Sympathizers in 1890s London', *Journal of European Studies*, 35, 2005, pp. 299–314.

'The Visitor from Russia Who Wasn't Welcomed in Finsbury', *Islington Gazette*, 8 October 1963.

Willats, Eric A., 'Lenin and London', *Islington Gazette*, 18 and 25 June, 2 and 9 July 1968. [original T/S in Islington, Y J853.09 BRO]

Switzerland

Baedeker, Karl, *Switzerland and the Adjacent Portions of Switzerland, Savoy and Tyrol*, London: K. Baedeker, 1907.

Ball, Hugo, *Flight out of Time: A Dada Diary*, New York: Viking Press, 1974.

Essen, Mariya, 'Vstrechi s Leninym', in VoVIL, vol. 1, pp. 244–61.

Fotieva, L. N., 'Vstrechi s Leninym v Zheneve i Parizhe', in Golikov, VoVIL, vol. 2, pp. 140–57.

Feuer, Lewis S., Einstein and the Generations of Science, New Brunswick: Transaction Books, p. 198, 'Zurich: the Peaceful Cradle of European Revolution', pp. 4–14.

Gautschi, Willi, Lenin als Emigrant in der Schweiz, Zurich: Benziger Verlag, 1973.

Haas, Leonhard, 'Lenins Frau als Patientin bei Schweizer Ärtzen', Jahrbucher für Geschichte Osteuropas, NF Band17, 1969, pp. 420–36.

Hardy, Deborah, 'The Lonely Emigré: Peter Tkachev and the Russian Colony in Switzerland', Russian Review, 35(4), October 1976, pp. 400–16.

Kammerer, Titus, 'We Rented to the Lenins', Partisan Review 6(3) 1939, pp. 26–8.

Kudryavtsev, A. S. et al., Lenin v Berne i Tsyurikhe: pamyatnye mesta, Moscow: Izd. Politicheskoi literaturoi, 1972.

Kudryavtsev, A. et al., Lenin's Geneva Addresses, Moscow: Progess, 1969.

Leuning, Otto, Odyssey of an American Composer, New York: Charles Scribner's, 1980, chapter 6, 'Refugees and Dadaists in Zurich 1917–1920'.

Ley, J., 'A Memorable Day in April', New Statesman, LV (1414), 19 April 1958, pp. 496–8.

Marcu, Valeriu, 'Lenin in Zurich, a Memoir', in Foreign Affairs: An American Quarterly Review 21(1), 1942–3, pp. 548–59.

Meijer, J. M., Knowledge and Revolution: The Russian Colony in Zurich, 1870 –1873, Assen: Van Gorcum, 1955.

Münzenberg, Willi, 'Lenin and We', in They Knew Lenin, pp. 79–87.

Nation, Craig, War on War: Lenin, the Zimmerwald Left and the Origins of Communist Internationalism, Durham: Duke University Press, 1986.

Noguez, Dominique, Lenin Dada – Essay, Zurich: Le dilettante, 1990.

Novikov, Viktor, S imenem Lenina svyazano, Leningrad: Lenizdat, 1987.

'Ou est la table de Lénine?' Tribune de Genève, 3 August 2006, p. 28.

Pearson, Michael, The Sealed Train, Newton Abbot: Readers Union, 1975.

Pianzola, Maurice, Lenine en Suisse, Geneva: Librairie Rousseau, 1965.

Platten, Fritz, Lenin iz emigratsii v Rossiyu, Moscow: Moskovskii rabochii, 1990.

Richter, Hans, Dada: Art and Anti-Art, London: Thames & Hudson, 1965.

Rozental, E., 'Lenin in Switzerland', World Marxist Review, 12(6), June 1969, pp. 11–13.

Schazmann, Paul-Emile, 'Sur les traces en Suisse du chef de la revolution russe', Tribune de Genève, 21 April 1970.

Senn, Alfred, The Russian Revolution in Switzerland 1914–1917, Madison: University of Wisconsin Press, 1971.

Solzhenitsyn, Alexander, Lenin in Zurich, London: Bodley Head, 1975.

Tyrkova-Williams, Ariadna, Na putyakh k svobode, New York: Izd., im. Chekhova, 1952.

Ybarra, T. R., 'Lenin Lived Poorly in Days of Exile', *New York Times*, 15 June 1924.

Zweig, Stefan, 'The Sealed Train', in Zweig, *The Tide of Fortune: Twelve Historical Miniatures*, London: Cassell & Co., 1927.

Index